ALASTAIR SAWDAY'S
SPECIAL PLACES TO STAY

ALASTAIR SAWDAY'S
SPECIAL PLACES TO STAY

BRITISH
BED &
BREAKFAST

Contents

Alastair Sawday Publishing

We are the faceless toilers at the pit-face of publishing but, for us, the question of who we are and how we inter-react is important. For who we are shapes the books, the books shape your holidays, and thus are shaped the lives of people who own these 'special places'. So we are trying to be a little more than 'just a publishing company'.

New eco offices

By the end of 2005 we will have moved into our new eco-offices. By super-insulating, installing under-floor heating, a wood-pellet boiler, solar panels and a rainwater tank, we will have a working environment benign to ourselves and to the environment. Lighting will be low-energy, dark corners will be lit by sun-pipes and one building is of green oak. Carpet tiles are leased: some of recycled material, most of wool and some of natural fibres. We will sail through our environmental audit.

Environmental & ethical policies

We combine many other small gestures: company cars run on gas or recycled cooking oil; kitchen waste is composted and other waste recycled; cycling and car-sharing are encouraged; the company only buys organic or local food; we don't accept web links with companies we consider un-ethical; we use the ethical Triodos Bank, for our deposit account.

We have used recycled paper for some books but have settled on selecting paper and printer for their low energy use. Our printer is British and ISO14001-certified and together we will reduce our environmental impact.

Thanks partially to our Green Team, we recently won a Business Commitment to the Environment Award – which has boosted our resolve to stick to our own green policies. Our flagship gesture, however, is carbon offsetting; we calculate our carbon emissions and plant trees to compensate – however inadequately. In 2006 we will support projects overseas that plant trees or reduce carbon use; our money will work better by going direct to projects.

Ethics

But why, you may ask, take these things so seriously? You are just a little publishing company, for Heavens sake. Well, is there any good argument for not taking them seriously? The world, by the admission of the vast majority of scientists, is in terrible trouble. If we do not change our ways urgently we will doom the planet and all its creatures – whether innocent or not – to a variety of possible catastrophes. To maintain the status quo is unacceptable. Business does much of the damage and should undo it, and provide new models.

Who are we?

Pressure on companies to produce Corporate Social Responsibility policies is mounting. We are trying to keep ahead of it all, yet still to be as informal and human as possible. – the antithesis of 'corporate'. (We even have unofficial 'de-stress operatives' in the shape of several resident dogs.)

The books – and a dilemma

So, we have created fine books that do good work. They promote authenticity, individuality, high quality, local and organic food – far from the now-dominant corporate culture. Rural economies, pubs, small farms, villages and hamlets all benefit.

However, people use fossil fuel to get there. Should we aim to get our readers to offset their own carbon emissions, and the B&B and hotel owners too? That might have been a hopeless task a year or so ago, but less so now that the media has taken on board the enormity of the work ahead of us all.

We are slowly introducing green ideas into the books: the Fine Breakfast Scheme for local and organic food; celebrating owners who make an extra effort; gently encouraging the use of public transport. This year we are publishing a book focusing on responsible travel and eco-projects around the globe.

Our Fragile Earth series

The 'hard' side of our environmental publishing is the Fragile Earth series: *The Little Earth Book*, *The Little Food Book* and *The Little Money Book*. They have been a great success. They consist of bite-sized essays, polemical and hard-hitting but well researched and methodical. They are a 'must have' for people from all walks of life – anyone who is confused and needs clarity about some of the key issues of our time.

Lastly – what is special?

The notion of 'special' is at the heart of what we do, and highly subjective. We discuss this in the Introduction. We take huge pleasure from finding people and places that do their own thing – brilliantly, places that are unusual and follow no trends, places of peace and beauty, people who are kind and interesting – and genuine.

We seem to have touched a raw nerve with thousands of readers; they obviously want to stay in special places rather than the dull corporate monstrosities that have disfigured so many of our cities and towns. Life is too short to be wasted in the wrong places. A night in a special place can be a transforming experience.

Alastair Sawday

Acknowledgements

'Riding a tiger' should be part of the job description of the editor of this book. It is a powerful beast, with the efforts and achievements of nearly 700 house owners on display. It is very far from being a simple catalogue, even further from being a collection of advertisers. So the task of nurturing it and bringing new people into it is challenging. Laura Kinch has been both dogged and imaginative, and has been ably assisted by Jan Tomlinson who joined us this year.

This complex project has many contributors: researchers, accountants, writers, proof-readers, production assistants, PR and Sales people, inspectors – among others. There is not a soul among the names listed who has not contributed, some mightily and others occasionally. To single them out would be silly, though I do have to mention Jackie King's vital role as Managing Editor.

Alastair Sawday

Series Editor Alastair Sawday

Editor Laura Kinch

Assistant to Editor Jan Tomlinson

Editorial Director Annie Shillito

Managing Editor Jackie King

Production Manager Julia Richardson

Web & IT Russell Wilkinson, Chris Banks, Brian Kimberling

Production Paul Groom, Allys Williams, Philippa Rogers

Copy Editor Jo Boissevain

Editorial Roanne Finch, Maria Serrano, Rebecca Stevens, Danielle Williams

Sales & Marketing & PR Siobhán Flynn, Andreea Petre Goncalves, Sarah Bolton

Accounts Sheila Clifton, Bridget Bishop, Christine Buxton, Jenny Purdy, Sandra Hassell

Writing Jo Boissevain, Viv Cripps, Nicola Crosse, Laura Kinch, Sue Merriman, Helen Pickles

Inspections Jan Adam, David Ashby, Abigail Ballinger, Tom Bell, Elizabeth Carter, Annie Coates, Nicola Crosse, Trish Dugmore, Becca Harris, Andrea Leeman, Auriol Marson, Vickie McIver, Susie Mickleburgh, Brian Kinch, Laura Kinch, Aideen Reid, Penny Rogers, Jessica Williams
And many thanks to those people who did just a few inspections.

Previous Editor Jackie King

A word from Alastair Sawday

Future Shock was a cult book of the 1970s, an alarming exploration of the extent to which we were, even then, regularly exposed to change – much of it profound and far-reaching. Thank heavens the author couldn't see the first years of the new millennium – though the capacity of human beings to absorb the shock of change is impressive.

For the owners of these very special places, as for all of us, changes come thick and fast. They have had to grasp the nettle of the internet; it is now a major feature of their lives. They have had to adapt to the whims of young visitors, many of whom are far more affluent than their hosts were at the same age and who may care little about their hosts' personal culture. They have had to smarten up and install all manner of modern devices, such as power showers, loos and baths where there were none, web connections and – in some cases – central heating in remote corners of old buildings.

I much admire all those who have done this with enthusiasm and good humour. I also enjoy those who, owning wonderful old houses, have dug in their heels and refused faddishly to alter their structure. When I stay in a vast old bedroom lined with oak I revel in its authenticity, however far I may have to potter along a corridor to the loo.

I slept recently in the attic of an ancient house in Herefordshire, among oak beams upon which to thud my head and exposed joists upon which to dash my feet. The shower was squeezed between beams. I wouldn't have changed it for anything.

Use this book well and often, for it contains the possibility of more pleasure than you can dream of, more friendships, more good food, more comfortable nights and more reminders of the beauty of so much of this remarkable and surprising country. You will also be supporting local economies and – I include humans in this – striking a blow or two for bio-diversity.

Alastair Sawday

Introduction

Emerge from between crisp cotton sheets after a heavenly night's sleep. Throw open the windows and breathe in the birdsung air.
Pad downstairs to the aromas of oak-smoked, organic bacon, home-laid eggs with deep yellow yolks, vibrant vine tomatoes grown outside the kitchen window. Try homemade, warm nutty bread and sticky strawberry jam. Fresh organic apricots, velvety with Devon honey and thick organic yogurt.

These are no ordinary bed and breakfasts. We choose them for many reasons; a genuine welcome, fine breakfasts, good beds and dreamy views are among them. Staying in delightful, often historic, homes with lovely hosts takes B&B-ing to a new and special level.

Our Fine Breakfast Scheme celebrates seasonal, locally-sourced and organic food. This is something that we feel passionate about and we do appreciate the arguments and difficulties associated with food miles, fluctuating availability and the dominance of supermarkets. Launched in the last edition, the first year of the scheme (see page 396) has been a huge success. We have deepened our commitment to it this year making it a requirement that new owners to the guide are committed to the pledge, so a total of 513 entries are now taking part (look for the egg-cup symbol at the bottom of the page). And many owners are as careful with the sourcing of their ingredients for evening meals as for those used in their breakfasts.

Most of us care increasingly about the provenance of our food.
Do you choose the battery-farmed chicken or the locally-reared, f ree-range one? More and more of us choose 'happy meat'. Not only does it taste better, it has more nutritional value and is not pumped full of chemicals. It makes sense to support the local economy and seek out free-range or organic meat produced by nearby suppliers.
We are proud of our Fine Breakfast Scheme and feel it enriches the B&B experience.

What else makes our places special?
Our selection is made up predominantly of country-house B&Bs where just a couple of rooms are let to guests, so the experience is more like staying with friends.

Photo right Getty Images
Photo left The Orchard House, entry 338

Introduction

You'll also find a smattering of townhouses, modern bungalows with glorious sea views, moat houses, quirky castles and, new this year, an exceptional tree house.

You'll meet all sorts of interesting people: teachers, farmers, sculptors, painters, architects, ex-service folk, lawyers, chefs, writers and designers. Staying in someone's home as a B&B guest *is* a personal experience, yet these special owners seem to have a natural sense of when to chat and when to give you space, and they are generous, too. Welcomes may involve freshly-baked cake, tea or perhaps a glass of wine. Many of our owners have a passion for their surroundings and their community and are eager to share their knowledge with you. If something is amiss, please tell your hosts and they will sort it out.

The level of comfort, luxury even, in B&Bs is rising, to rival and even outstrip that of some hotels. But not all places in this book are luxurious – our descriptions and the prices will give you a good idea of what to expect. We include places that are good value at all price levels. Over 300 places have a double room for 2 for £60 or under. Many are in beautiful settings, with views to mountains, across fields and towards the ocean – sometimes from your bath! B&B boarding houses do not feature, neither do bog-standard breakfasts or places that are run purely on commercial lines. We don't like 'private' signs, laminated info, stacks of tourist brochures, strict timetables for breakfast or departures, and brash, exterior B&B signs.

Special green entries

There's something new to the book this year. We have chosen, very subjectively, half a dozen places which are making a particular effort to be eco-friendly and have given them a full page and an extra photo to illustrate what they're up to. This does not mean there are no other places in the guide taking green initiatives – there are many – but we have highlighted just a few examples. A growing number of our B&Bs recycle, use solar heating, tend their land and animals organically, plant woodlands to encourage wildlife, cycle to post letters rather than take the car, use natural cleaning products and renewable energy in their homes, eco-building methods and local building materials.

I hope that staying at these special places will be a special experience and that you will share our view that this selection takes B&B into a new league.

Laura Kinch

Inspections
We visit every place to get an accurate feel for how both house and owner tick. The sort of detail that cannot be gleaned during a phone call is important to us. We've visited many places now several times.

Writing
We write each entry avoiding, we hope, boring, repetitive, 'estate agent' speak. Words such as 'nestling', 'boasts' and 'spacious' are discouraged – along with a whole list of other words and clichés.

Finding the right place for you

Quick reference indices
At the back of the book we list those owners:

• with single rooms or those who charge no single supplement
• willing to collect you from local train or bus stations
• with houses suitable for wheelchair users
• with houses that have a ground-floor bedroom and bathroom, making them suitable for those of limited mobility
• who have pools
• who have tennis courts
• who can stable your horse
• who charge £60 or under for a room for two.

Photo The Dairy House, entry 397

A further listing refers to houses within two miles of a Sustrans National Cycle Network route (see page 401). Take your own or check if you can hire or borrow a bike from the owners before you travel, and factor in a cycle ride on your break.

Map
The best start to planning your trip is to look at the map at the front of the book. If you were seeking a house by the sea in Devon and you merely flicked through the Devon section, you would possibly miss a beachside gem just over the border. In cities, check individual entries for their position: www.multimap.com is a useful web site.

Introduction

the room with details of 'separate' baths/showers (outside the room but just for you) or 'shared' bathrooms (shared with the owner or other guests).

Bath/shower means a bath with shower over; bath and shower means there is a proper shower unit.

Prices

Each entry gives a price PER ROOM for two people. We try to include single room rates or the amount one person pays for a double room.

A few owners vary their prices during the year so do double-check if supplements or discounts apply. Many owners have special rates for stays of two or more nights, or reduced rates for children.

Rooms

We tell you if rooms are double, twin, suite (with a sitting area), family or single. Most owners are flexible and can juggle beds or bedrooms; talk to them about what you need before you book.

Under certain entries we mention that two rooms share a bathroom and are "let to same party". Please do not assume this means you must be a group of friends or a family to apply; it simply means you will not be sharing a bathroom with strangers.

Breakfasts

Unless we say otherwise, a full, cooked breakfast is included. Some owners – particularly in London – will give you a good continental breakfast instead. For organic or locally-sourced breakfasts, look out for the egg-cup symbol ♟ at the bottom of the page.

Bathrooms

If a bedroom is 'en suite' we say 'with' bath or shower. If it is not 'en suite', we follow the description of

If you want a particularly early or late breakfast, ask when booking. Note that breakfast may be shared with your hosts or other guests.

Photo above The Old Vicarage, entry 58
Photo right Gotten Manor, entry 245

Introduction

Symbols

At the very back of the book we explain our symbols. Use them as a guide, not as a statement of fact. Owners occasionally bend their own rules, so it's worth asking if you may take your dog or child even if they don't have the requisite symbol.

Types of houses

Some houses have rooms in annexes or stables, barns or garden 'wings', some of which feel part of the house, some of which don't. If you have a strong preference for being in the throng or for being apart, check those details carefully. Consider your surroundings when you are packing: large, ancient country houses may be cooler than you are used to; city

places and working farms may be noisy at times; and that peacock or cockerel we mention may disturb you. Light sleepers should pack ear plugs, and take a dressing gown if there's a separate bathroom (though these are sometimes provided). There is a large range of prices among our B&Bs and we hope that you'll find they are all good value – even the expensive ones. Price can be a guide to the level of luxury – though not always; do let us know if you find either prices or descriptions misleading.

City B&Bs

This is the second year of our 'city B&B' scheme in Bristol and Brighton (see entries 17 & 19). This was inspired by a shortage of special city places to stay. Through a central number you are linked to private homes that do not necessarily run as B&Bs full-time but have a spare room they are happy to use for occasional guests.

Practical matters

Meals

Apart from breakfast, no meals should be expected unless you have arranged them in advance. Although we don't say so on each entry – the repetition a few hundred times over would be tedious – all owners who provide packed lunch, lunch or dinner need ADVANCE NOTICE.

And they want to get things right for you so, when booking, discuss your diet and mealtimes. Prices are quoted per person, and dinner is often shared with your hosts and other guests.

Do eat in if you can – this book is awash with talented cooks. And how much more relaxing after a day out to have to move no further than the dining room for an excellent dinner, and to eat and drink knowing there's only a flight of stairs between you and your bed. Very few of our houses are licensed, but some entries state BYO (Bring Your Own). However, this 'offer' is not confined to these entries.

Seasons and public holidays

The price range for each B&B covers the cheapest room in low season to the most expensive in high season. Some owners charge supplements at certain times (during regattas or festivals, for example); others ask for a two-night minimum stay at weekends and we mention this where possible. Most of our houses could fill many times over on peak weekends and during the summer; book early, especially if you have specific needs.

Bookings

The most popular way of booking remains the phone. That way both sides can get the feel of people and place. Do be clear about the room

booked and the price for B&B and for meals. Say roughly what time you will arrive (normally after 4pm), as most hosts want to welcome you personally. Be on time if you have booked dinner; if, despite best efforts, you are delayed, phone to give warning.

Requests for deposits vary; some are non-refundable, especially in our London homes, and some owners may charge you for the whole of the booked stay in advance (see below).

Cancellations

Owners vary in their approach to cancelled bookings. Last-minute cancellations are the most irksome, even if the owners appreciate that everyone can be a victim of circumstance. Always let your host know as soon as possible and be prepared for wildly varying approaches to the money side of things. If an owner demands what may strike you as an unreasonable amount as compensation, it may be that you are the latest in a string of such cases. An owner with a more generous reaction may not often have experienced the problem. Some owners will charge you the total cost if you cancel at short notice. If an owner holds your credit card details he/she may deduct a cancellation fee from it and not contact you to discuss this. This is rare, but be aware of the legalities of this in the eyes of your credit or debit card company.

Photo above 22 Marville Road, entry 296
Photo right Getty Images

Payment
All our owners take cash and UK cheques with a cheque card.
Few take credit cards but if they do, we have given them the appropriate symbol 💳 .
Check that your credit card is acceptable.

Children
The 👶 symbol is given to owners who accept children of any age. They are unlikely to have cots, highchairs, safety equipment or all the paraphernalia you need, so do check.

If an owner welcomes children but only those above a certain age, we have put these details at the end of their write-up. These houses do not have the child symbol, but even these folk may accept your younger child if you are the only guests. Many who say no to children do so not because they don't like them but because they may have a steep stair, an unfenced pond or they find balancing the needs of mixed age groups too challenging.

Smoking
A ✗ symbol means no smoking anywhere – and that includes hanging out of the window! Smoking in bedrooms is generally a no-no.

Introduction

Pets

The  symbol is given to places where your pet can sleep in your bedroom but not on the bed.
Be realistic about your pet – if it is nervous or excitable or doesn't like the company of other dogs, people, chickens, children, then say so.

House keys

Some owners give you a front door key so you may come and go as you please; others are less flexible. If this matters to you, ask on booking.

Tipping

Owners do not expect tips. If you have been treated with extraordinary kindness, write to them, or leave a small gift. Please tell us, too – we note all feedback.

Subscriptions

Owners pay to appear in this guide. Their fee goes towards the high costs of a sophisticated inspection system and producing an all-colour book. We only include places and owners that we find positively special. It is not possible for anyone to buy his/her way into our guides.

Internet

www.specialplacestostay.com has online pages for all the special places featured here and from all our other books – around 4,500 in total. There's a searchable database, a taster of the write-ups and colour photos. And look out for our dedicated self-catering web site, www.specialescapes.co.uk. For more details see pages 406 & 432 at the back of the book.

Disclaimer

We make no claims to pure objectivity in choosing our Special Places. They are here because we like them. Our opinions and tastes are ours alone and this book is a statement of them; we hope that you will share them. We have done our utmost to get our facts right but apologise unreservedly for any mistakes that may have crept in. You should know that we do not check such things as fire alarms, swimming pool security or any other regulation with which owners of properties receiving paying guests should comply. This is the responsibility of the owners.

Photo right Plas Tan-yr-Allt, entry 654
Photo www.paulgroom.com

Introduction

Feedback

Feedback from you is invaluable and we follow up on comments. With your help and our own inspections we can maintain our reputation for accuracy.

The thriving relationship between ourselves, our owners and our readers makes this the most dependable B&B guide. With regular communication, things are kept relevant and fresh. We take people in and out of the book based upon what you and our inspectors tell us, so please stay in touch and tell us about your discoveries.

Our book celebrates human kindness, fine architecture, real food, history and landscape and we hope that it's your passport to uplifting and memorable experiences. Don't forget to let us know how you got on – write or email info@sawdays.co.uk – we care what you think.

Photo Tyr Chanter, entry 669

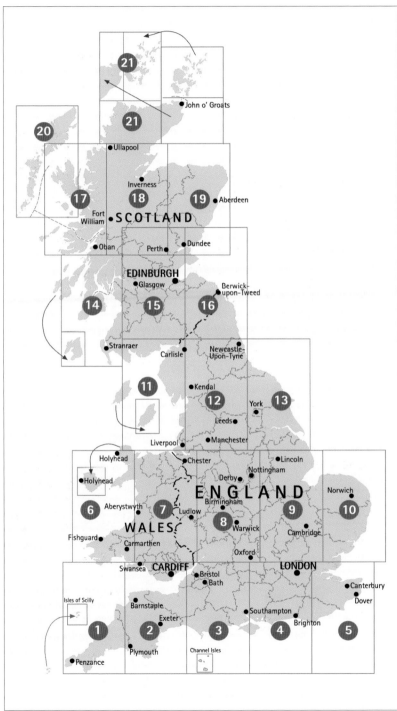

6

St. Govan's
Head

Lundy

Hartland Pt.
Hartland ○ Clovelly

A39

58

Bude ○ Stratton

Poundstock

60 **59**

Boscastle

Tintagel

Port **61**
Isaac **64**
62 **72** Bodmin **56**

65 Moor
74 **66** **68**
Padstow **63** **67**
73 Wadebridge **70** **69**
Bodmin A38 Liskeard A390
St. Columb **71**
Major CORNWALL
Newquay ○ Lostwithiel **54**
A392 **51** **53**
Looe
45 St. Austell **50** **52**
48 **47** Fowey Polperro
St. Agnes ○ **46** Mevagissey
Redruth **39** Truro **44** **49**
St. Ives **42**
36 Hayle **41**
34 **37** Camborne **43**
35 Penryn
33 **38** A394 **40** St. Mawes
St. Just ○ Marazion Falmouth
Penzance **30**
31 Helston
32
Land's End
29

28 ○ Lizard
Lizard Pt.

ISLES OF SCILLY

Isles of Scilly
Bryher St. Martin's
Tresco
Hugh Town
St. Mary's

Map 2

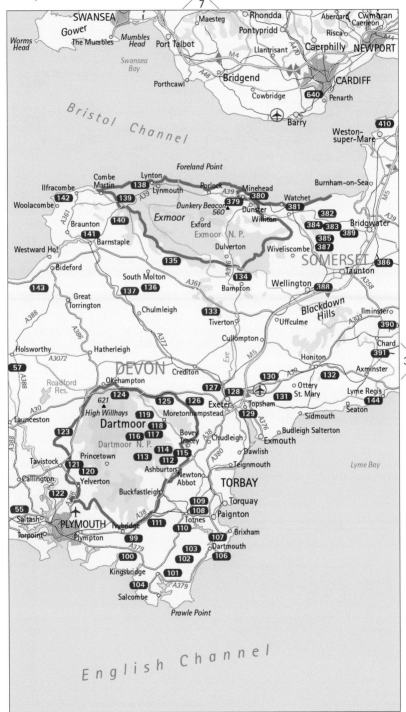

Map 3

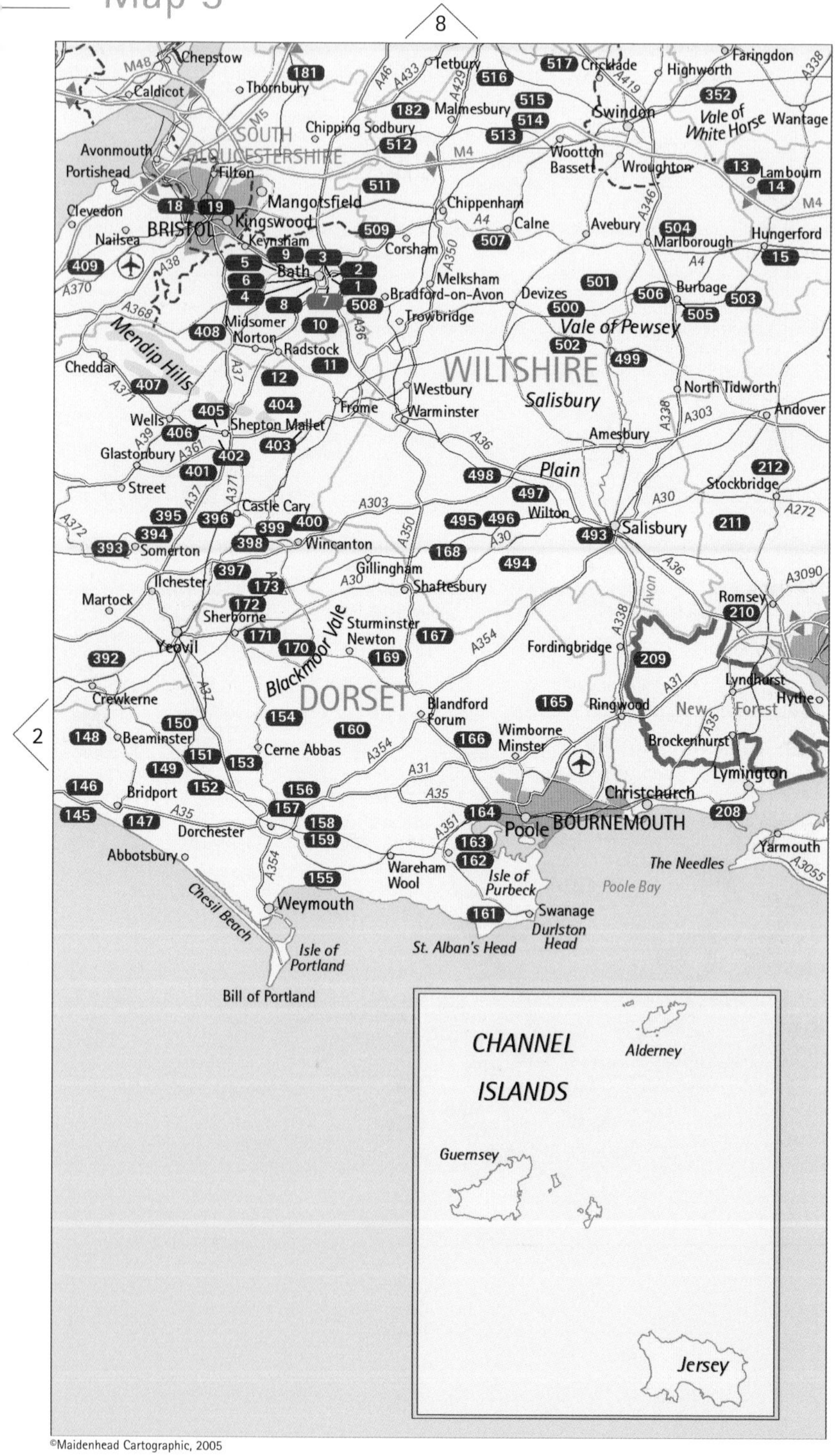

8

M48 Chepstow
181
Caldicot Thornbury
Avonmouth SOUTH GLOUCESTERSHIRE
Portishead Filton
Clevedon
Nailsea
BRISTOL Kingswood
Keynsham
Mangotsfield
Chipping Sodbury
512
182 Malmesbury
515
514
513
M4
516
517 Cricklade Highworth Faringdon
Swindon
Wootton Bassett Wroughton
352
Vale of White Horse Wantage
13
Lambourn
14
M4
511
Chippenham
A4 Calne Avebury
509
Corsham
507
504
Marlborough Hungerford
15
A4
9 3 2
5 Bath 1
6
4 8 7 508
Midsomer 10
Norton Radstock
12
Cheddar 407
Mendip Hills
Wells 406 405
Glastonbury 401 402 403
Street
A372 393 394 395 396
Somerton 398 399 400
397
Martock Ilchester 172 173
Sherborne 171
392 Yeovil 170
Blackmoor Vale
Crewkerne 150
2 148 Beaminster 151 153
149
146 152
Bridport
145 147 Dorchester
157
158
159
Abbotsbury 155
Chesil Beach Weymouth
Isle of Portland
Bill of Portland

Melksham
Bradford-on-Avon
Trowbridge
501
500 Devizes
502
Westbury
Frome Warminster
Shepton Mallet
Castle Cary
Wincanton
Gillingham
Shaftesbury
Sturminster Newton
169
154
160 Blandford Forum
Cerne Abbas
156
A35

WILTSHIRE
Salisbury
506 Burbage
505 503
Vale of Pewsey
499
North Tidworth
Andover
A303 Amesbury
498
497
495 496 Wilton
168 493 Salisbury
494
167 A354 Fordingbridge
165 Ringwood
166 Wimborne Minster
164
163
162
161
Wareham
Wool Isle of Purbeck
Swanage
Durlston
St. Alban's Head Head

Plain
Stockbridge
212
211
A272
A3090
Romsey
210
Lyndhurst Hythe
New Forest
Brockenhurst
Lymington
Christchurch
BOURNEMOUTH
Poole
208
The Needles Yarmouth
Poole Bay

DORSET

CHANNEL
ISLANDS
Alderney
Guernsey
Jersey

Map 4   27

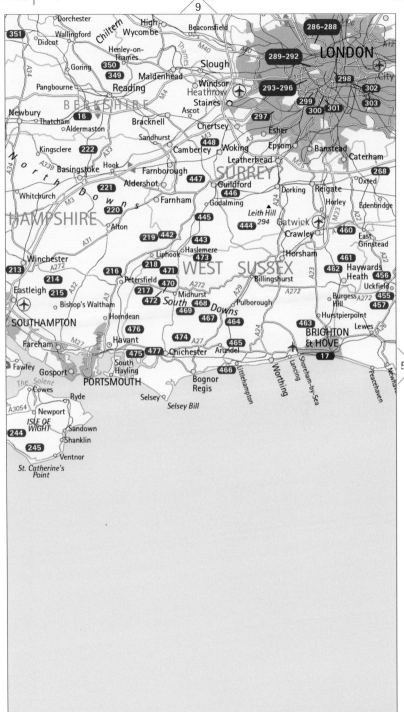

Map 5

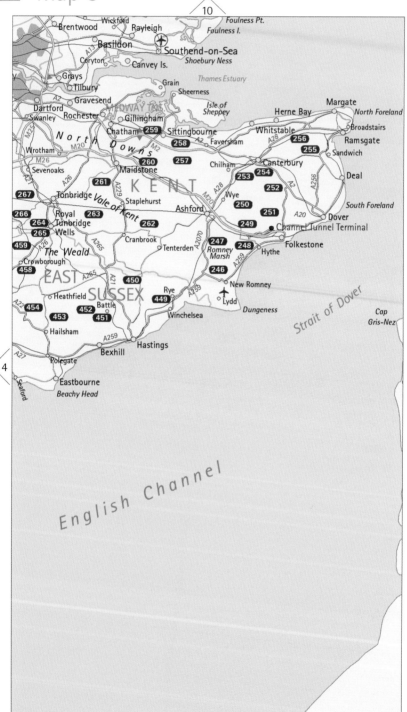

Map 6

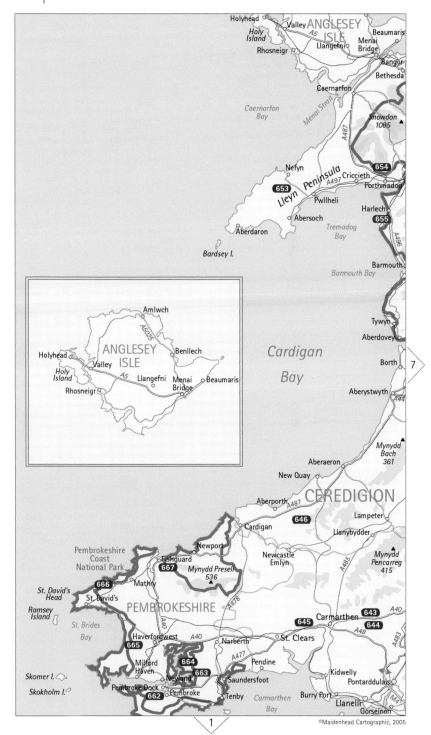

Holyhead
Valley **ANGLESEY**
ISLE
Holy
Island
Rhosneigr
Llangefni
Beaumaris
Menai
Bridge
Bangor
Bethesda
Caernarfon
Caernarfon
Bay
Menai Strait
A487
Snowdon
1085 ▲
Nefyn
Lleyn Peninsula
Criccieth
A497
654
653
Pwllheli
Porthmadog
Abersoch
Harlech
Aberdaron
Tremadog
Bay
655
A496
Aberdaron
Bardsey I.
Barmouth
Barmouth Bay
Tywyn
Aberdovey
Cardigan
Bay
Borth
7
Aberystwyth
A44
Mynydd
Bach
361 ▲
Aberaeron
New Quay
CEREDIGION
Aberporth
A487
Lampeter
Cardigan
646
Llanybydder
Newport
Mynydd
Pencarreg
415 ▲
Pembrokeshire
Coast
National Park
Fishguard
667
Mynydd Preseli
536 ▲
Newcastle
Emlyn
A485
Mathry
666
St. David's
Head
St. David's
PEMBROKESHIRE
A478
Mynydd
643 A40
Ramsey
Island
St. Brides
Bay
A40
A40
Carmarthen
645
644
A48
A483
Haverfordwest
A40
Narberth
St. Clears
665
A477
Pendine
Skomer I.
Milford
Haven
664
663
Neyland
Saundersfoot
Kidwelly
Pontarddulais
Skokholm I.
Pembroke Dock
662
Pembroke
Tenby
Burry Port
Carmarthen
Bay
Llanelli
Gorseinon
M4

ANGLESEY ISLE inset

Amlwch
A5025
ANGLESEY
ISLE
Benllech
Holyhead
Valley
A5
Llangefni
Menai
Bridge
Beaumaris
Holy
Island
Rhosneigr

©Maidenhead Cartographic, 2005

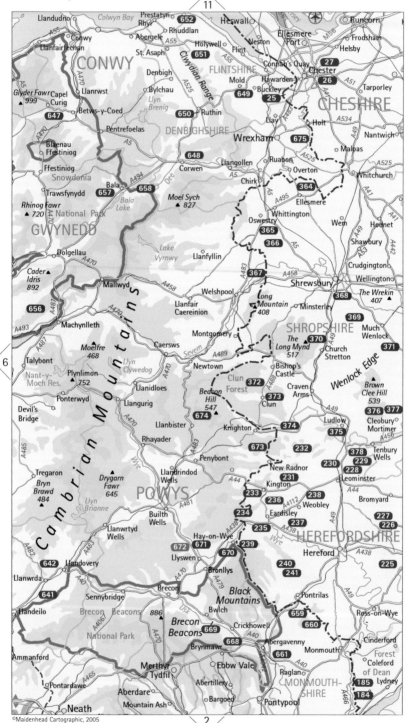

Map 8

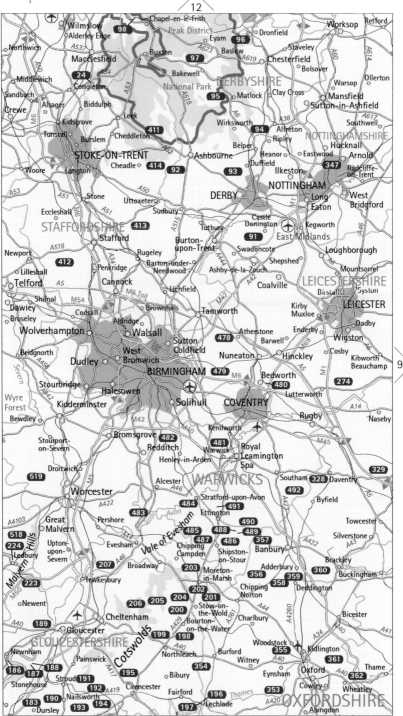

13

LINCOLNSHIRE Wolds

279 280 Wragby

Saxilby
A57
A156
Washingborough
Lincoln
A16 Alford
Bardney
A158
Horncastle
Ingoldmells
Sutton-on-Trent
A46
Woodhall Spa
Spilsby
Skegness
348
Coningsby
A617 Newark-on-Trent
A46 A15
Wainfleet All Saints
Cranwell
A17
Witham
A1
Sleaford
A17 Heckington
281 Boston
A52
Swineshead
A16
Brancaster
Bingham
A52 Grantham
A52
282
283 Folkingham
Donington
Hunstanton
The Wash
A607
A1
A15
A151
Long Sutton
A17
Heacham
Waltham-on-the-Wolds
Spalding
Holbeach
Terrington St. Clement
King's Lynn
A149
276 Colsterworth
285 284 Bourne
The Fens
A1101 A47
Sandringham
Melton Mowbray
RUTLAND
Market Deeping
Crowland
Wisbech
A606
A16
Oakham
Rutland Water
363 Stamford
A47 Thorney
A1122 Gt Ouse
Downham Market
A134
Uppingham
Duddington
Peterborough
March
Methwold
331
A605
Whittlesey
A15
275 Corby
Oundle
Stilton
Chatteris
Littleport
Lakenheath
Market Harborough
A427
Desborough
Rothwell
Thrapston
Sawtry
Ramsey
A141
CAMBRIDGESHIRE
Ely
A10
Mildenhall
A142
Kettering
Burton Latimer
A14
330
Raunds
Grafham Water
Huntingdon
St. Ives
Soham
Irthlingborough
Kimbolton
Godmanchester
A14
Cottenham
Histon
Burwell
415 Newmarket
Wellingborough
Rushden
A6
Gt Ouse
A428
Cambridge
A14
NORTHANTS
Northampton
A509
St. Neots
22
Great Shelford
A11
417 Haverhill
21 A130 Clare
Olney
Bedford
Sandy
Potton
Melbourn
A10
A505
Saffron Walden
A101
Newport Pagnell
Kempston
Biggleswade
23
Wolverton
BEDFORDSHIRE
Ampthill
Shefford
A505
Royston
M11
Milton Keynes
A421
Bletchley
Letchworth
Baldock
Buntingford
Thaxted 178
Winslow
Leighton Buzzard
Hitchin
Stevenage
A10
Stansted Mountfitchet
Great Dunmow
Braintree
Linslade
A6
Luton
A1(M)
Bishop's Stortford
Stansted
A120 A130
Dunstable
HERTS
Waddesdon
A418 A41 A146
Harpenden
243 Welwyn Garden City
242
Ware
Sawbridgeworth
ESS
Aylesbury
A41 Tring
Hemel Hempstead
St. Albans
A414
Hertford
Harlow
Chelmsford
Princes Risborough
20 Chesham
Hatfield
Hoddesdon
Chipping Ongar
A12
Amersham
Watford
Bushey
Potters Bar
Cheshunt
M25
Epping
Billericay
A130
Hills
WALTHAM FOREST
Chigwell

8

Map 10   33

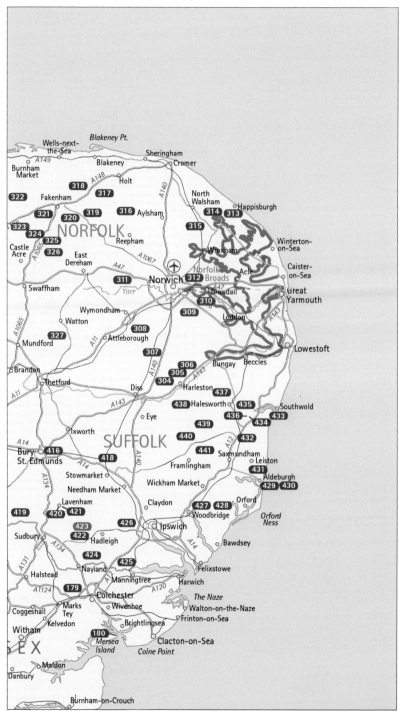

Blakeney Pt.
Wells-next-the-Sea
A149
Sheringham
Burnham Market
Blakeney
Cromer
318
Holt
A148
322
Fakenham
317
A140
North Walsham
Happisburgh
321
320
319
316 Aylsham
314 313
323
315
324
NORFOLK
Reepham
Wroxham
Winterton-on-Sea
Castle Acre
A1066
326
325
East Dereham
A1067
Norfolk Broads
Caister-on-Sea
A47
311
Norwich
312
Acle
Swaffham
Yare
Brundall
Great Yarmouth
Wymondham
310
Loddon
A143
Watton
309
327
A11
Attleborough
308
Mundford
307
Lowestoft
Brandon
A140
306
Bungay Beccles
Thetford
A11
305
A143
Diss
304
Harleston
437
A143
438 Halesworth
435
Southwold
Eye
436
433
434
A1065
Ixworth
439
440
432
A14
441
Bury St. Edmunds
416
Saxmundham
Leiston
SUFFOLK
418
431
Framlingham
Aldeburgh
Stowmarket
429 430
Needham Market
Wickham Market
Lavenham
Claydon
Orford
419
420 421
427 428
Woodbridge
Orford Ness
423
426
Ipswich
Sudbury
422
Hadleigh
A134
A131
424
Bawdsey
Halstead
425
Nayland
Felixstowe
A1124
179
Manningtree
Harwich
A120
Marks Tey
Coggeshall
Wivenhoe
The Naze
Kelvedon
Brightlingsea
Walton-on-the-Naze
Witham
Frinton-on-Sea
180
SEX
Mersea Island
Clacton-on-Sea
Maldon
Colne Point
Danbury
Burnham-on-Crouch

15

570

Gatehouse of
Fleet
Castle
Douglas
Dalbeattie

Longtown
75

Brampton

Kirkcudbright

Carlisle

Wigton

Aspatria

Wigtown Bay

Solway Firth

Maryport

CUMBRIA

Cockermouth
77
78
79

Penrith

Workington

Bassenthwaite
Lake

▲ Skiddaw
931
Keswick

A66
Saddleback
868
81

14

Whitehaven

Cleator
Moor

80

Helvellyn
949 ▲

Ullswater

Haweswater

St. Bees Head

Egremont

Great
Gable
▲ 899

Grasmere

Lake District
National Park

Lake

Scafell
Pike
978 ▲

District

Ambleside
86
85
Windermere
84

Cumbrian Mountains

Windermere

89
87

Kendal

Coniston
Water

88

90

Broughton-
in-Furness

Newby
Bridge

Point of Ayre

Millom

Ulverston

Milnthorpe

Ramsey

Dalton-in-Furness

Carnforth

Isle of Man

A3

A2

Laxey

Morecambe
Bay

Peel

A4

Barrow-
in-Furness

Bolton-le-Sands

A1

Isle of
Walney

Morecambe

A3

A5

Douglas

Heysham

Lancaster

Port Erin

Castletown

Fleetwood

Cleveleys
Thornton

Garstang

Poulton-le-Fylde

M55

BLACKPOOL

Kirkham
270

Kirkham

Lytham St. Anne's

A59

Leyland

Southport

Ormskirk

Formby

Skelmersdale

Liverpool
Bay

Crosby

Kirkby

Wallasey

Bootle

St. Helens

Hoylake

LIVERPOOL

Widnes

Great
Ormes
Head

Benllech

Birkenhead

8

Map 12 35

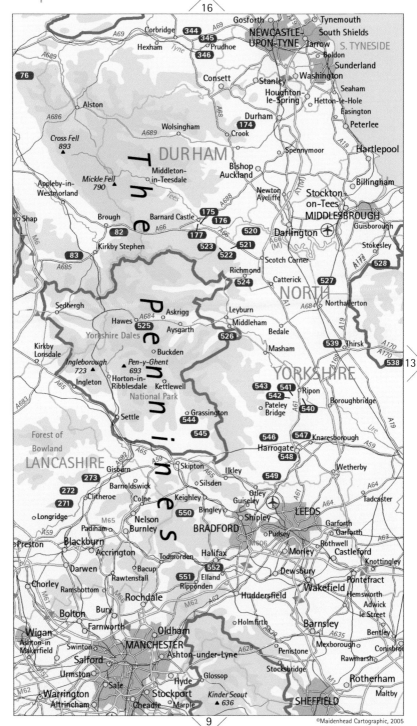

16

Gosforth
Corbridge 344 A69 Tynemouth
Hexham 345 Prudhoe NEWCASTLE South Shields
Tyne 346 UPON-TYNE Jarrow
Boldon S. TYNESIDE
A69
A689 Consett Stanley Washington Sunderland
76 Houghton- Seaham
Alston le-Spring Hetton-le-Hole
A686 Easington
Wolsingham Durham Peterlee
Cross Fell A689 174
893 Crook
Spennymoor Hartlepool
DURHAM
Appleby-in- Mickle Fell Middleton- Bishop Newton Billingham
Westmorland 790 in-Teesdale Auckland Aycliffe Stockton-
on-Tees A19 MIDDLESBROUGH
Shap Brough Barnard Castle 175 176 520 Guisborough
82 A66 177 521 Darlington
Kirkby Stephen 523 522 Stokesley
83 A66 Scotch Corner A173 528
A685 Richmond
524 Catterick 527
Sedbergh Leyburn Northallerton
Askrigg NORTH A684
Hawes 525 Middleham Bedale A19
Yorkshire Dales Aysgarth 526 Masham 539 Thirsk A170
A170
Kirkby Buckden 538 13
Lonsdale Ingleborough Pen-y-Ghent YORKSHIRE
723 693 543 541 Ripon
Ingleton Horton-in- Kettlewell 542
A65 Ribblesdale 544 Pateley 540 Boroughbridge
A683 National Park Settle Grassington Bridge A19
545 546 547 Knaresborough A59
Forest of 548 Ure
Bowland Harrogate
LANCASHIRE Gisburn Skipton Ilkley Wetherby
273 Barnoldswick 549
272 Clitheroe Colne Keighley Otley A64
271 Silsden Guiseley Tadcaster
Longridge Nelson 550 Bingley Shipley LEEDS A63
Preston Padiham Burnley BRADFORD Garforth
Blackburn M65 Pudsey Garforth
Accrington Halifax Morley Castleford
Darwen Todmorden 552 Dewsbury Knottingley
Chorley Bacup 551 Elland Pontefract
Ramsbottom Rawtenstall Ripponden Wakefield Hemsworth
Longridge Rochdale Huddersfield Adwick
Bury M62 le Street
Bolton Farnworth Holmfirth Barnsley Bentley
Wigan Oldham Mexborough Conisbro
Ashton-in- Swinton MANCHESTER Penistone Rawmarsh
Makerfield Salford Ashton-under-Lyne Stocksbridge
Urmston Hyde Glossop Rotherham
Sale Stockport Kinder Scout SHEFFIELD Maltby
Warrington Altrincham Cheadle Marple 636

9

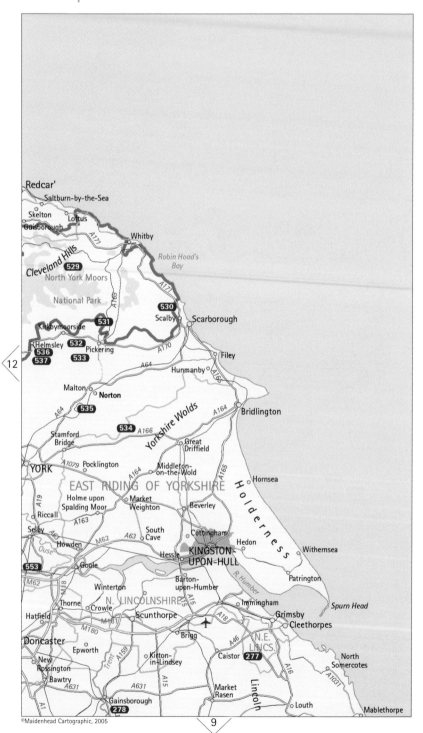

Redcar'
Saltburn-by-the-Sea
Skelton
Loftus
Guisborough
A171
Whitby
Robin Hood's Bay
Cleveland Hills
529
North York Moors
A169
National Park
530
Kirkbymoorside
531
Scalby
Scarborough
Helmsley
532
Pickering
A170
Filey
536
537
533
A64
Hunmanby
A165
Malton
Norton
535
A164
Bridlington
534 A166
Stamford Bridge
Yorkshire Wolds
Great Driffield
YORK
A1079 Pocklington
A164
Middleton-on-the-Wold
A165
Hornsea
EAST RIDING OF YORKSHIRE
A19
Holme upon Spalding Moor
Market Weighton
Beverley
Holderness
Riccall
A163
Selby
South Cave
A63
Cottingham
Hedon
Withernsea
Howden
M62
KINGSTON-UPON-HULL
553
Goole
Hessle
M62
Barton-upon-Humber
R. Humber
Patrington
M18
Winterton
A15
Spurn Head
Thorne
Crowle
N. LINCOLNSHIRE
Immingham
Hatfield
M181
Scunthorpe
A18
Grimsby
M180
Brigg
A46
Cleethorpes
Doncaster
Epworth
A159
N.E. LINCS.
New Rossington
Kirton-in-Lindsey
Caistor
277
North Somercotes
A16
Bawtry
A631
A631
A15
Lincoln
A1031
Gainsborough
Market Rasen
Louth
Mablethorpe
278

12

9

Map 14

37

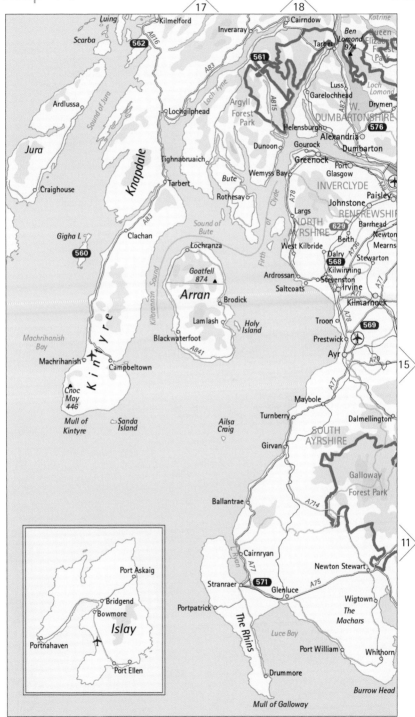

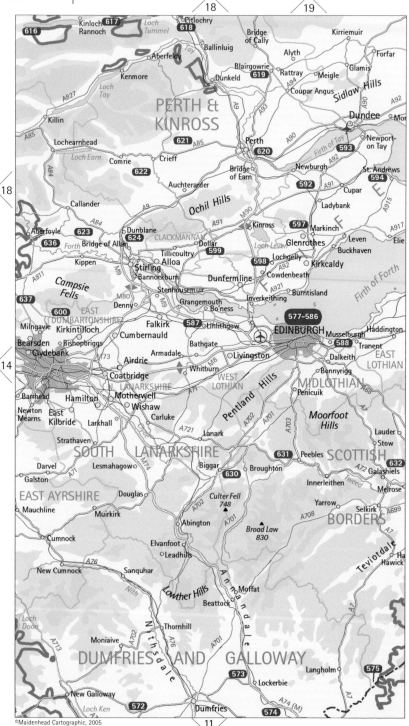

Map 16

39

19

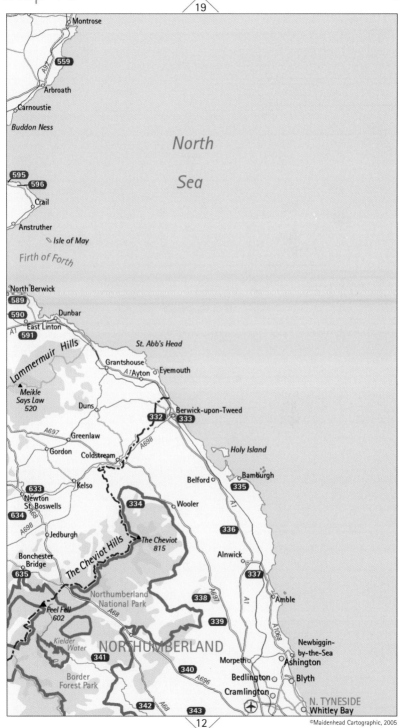

Montrose

559

Arbroath

Carnoustie

Buddon Ness

North

Sea

595

596

Crail

Anstruther

◇ *Isle of May*

Firth of Forth

North Berwick

589

590 Dunbar

East Linton

A1 591

Lammermuir Hills

St. Abb's Head

Grantshouse

A1 Ayton Eyemouth

▲ Meikle Says Law 520

Duns

332

333 Berwick-upon-Tweed

A697

Greenlaw

A698

Gordon Coldstream

Holy Island

Kelso

Belford ○ ○ Bamburgh

633

Newton St Boswells

334

335

Wooler

634

336

A698

Jedburgh

The Cheviot Hills

The Cheviot 815

Alnwick

Bonchester Bridge

635

The Cheviot Hills

337

▲ Peel Fell 602

Northumberland National Park

A68

338

A697

A1

Amble

Kielder Water

NORTHUMBERLAND

339

Newbiggin-by-the-Sea

341

Ashington

Border Forest Park

340 A696

Morpeth ○

Bedlington ○ ○ Blyth

Cramlington

342 A68

343

N. TYNESIDE
Whitley Bay

12

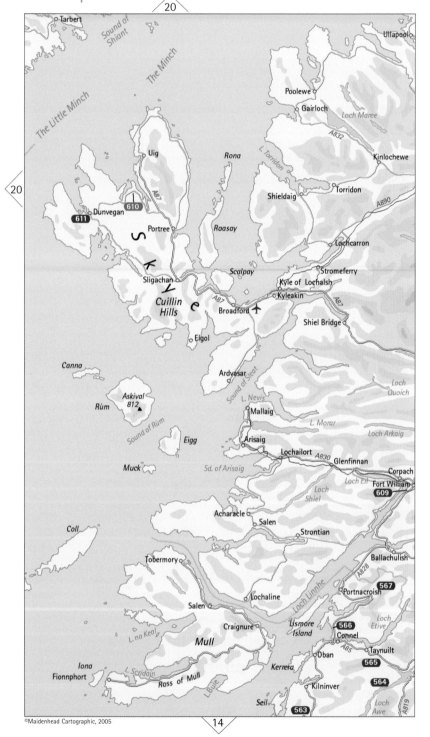

20

Tarbert
Sound of Shiant
The Minch
The Little Minch
Ullapool
Poolewe
Gairloch
Loch Maree
A832
Uig
Rona
Kinlochewe
L. Torridon
Torridon
A890
Shieldaig
Dunvegan
611
610
A87
Portree
Raasay
Lochcarron
S
k
Scalpay
Stromeferry
Sligachan
Kyle of Lochalsh
Cuillin Hills
e
Kyleakin
A87
Broadford
Shiel Bridge
A87
Elgol
Canna
Ardvasar
Sound of Sleat
Loch Quoich
Askival 812▲
L. Nevis
Mallaig
Rùm
Sound of Rùm
L. Morar
Loch Arkaig
Eigg
Arisaig
Muck
Sd. of Arisaig
Lochailort
A830
Glenfinnan
Corpach
Loch Eil
Fort William
609
Loch Shiel
Coll
Acharacle
Salen
Strontian
Ballachulish
Tobermory
A828
Loch Linnhe
Portnacroish
567
Lochaline
Loch Etive
Salen
Lismore Island
566
Connel
L. na Keal
Craignure
Kerrera
Oban
A85
Taynuilt
565
Mull
Iona
Fionnphort
L. Scridain
Ross of Mull
L. Buie
Kilninver
564
Seil
563
Loch Awe
A819

Map 18   41

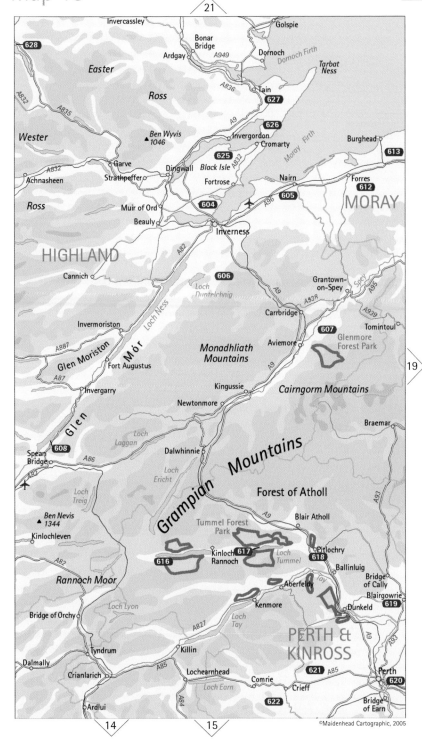

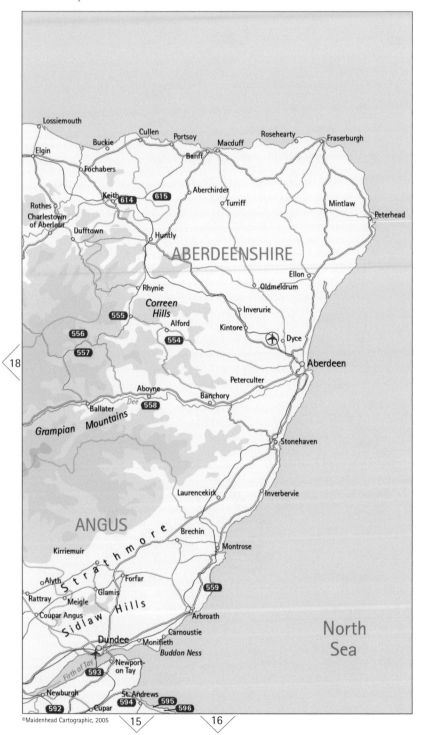

Map 20   43

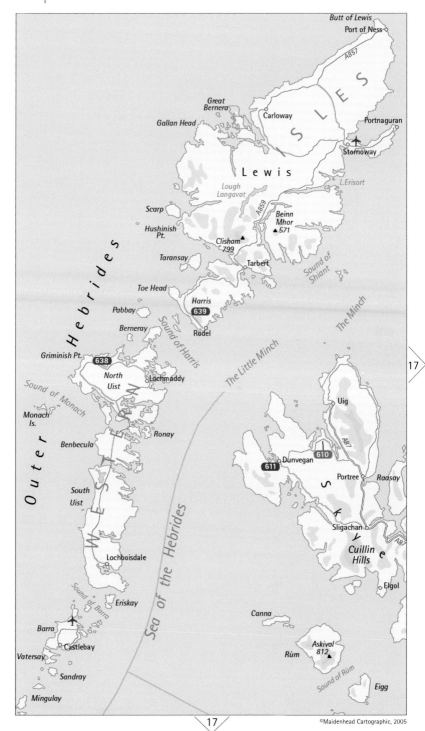

Butt of Lewis
Port of Ness
A857
ISLES
Great Bernera
Carloway
Gallan Head
Portnaguran
Stornoway
Lewis
Lough Langavat
L.Erisort
Scarp
A859
Beinn Mhor
▲ 571
Hushinish Pt.
Clisham 799 ▲
Taransay
Tarbert
Sound of Shiant
Toe Head
Harris
639
Pabbay
Rodel
Berneray
Sound of Harris
The Minch
Griminish Pt.
638
The Little Minch
North Uist
Lochmaddy
Hebrides
Sound of Monach
Monach Is.
Ronay
Uig
A87
Benbecula
Dunvegan
610
611
Portree
Raasay
Outer
South Uist
Skye
WESTERN
Sea of the Hebrides
Sligachan
A87
Cuillin Hills
Lochboisdale
Elgol
Sound of Barra
Eriskay
Canna
Barra
Castlebay
Askival 812 ▲
Vatersay
Rùm
Sandray
Sound of Rùm
Eigg
Mingulay

17 ▷

Map 21

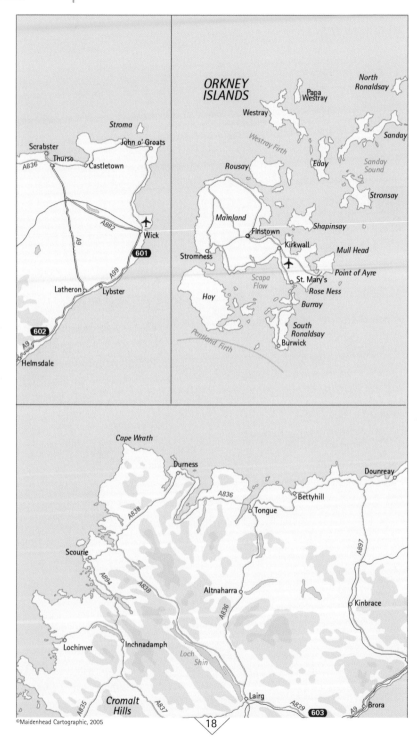

ORKNEY
ISLANDS

North
Ronaldsay

Papa
Westray

Westray

Westray Firth

Sanday

Rousay

Eday

Sanday
Sound

Stronsay

Mainland

Finstown

Shapinsay

Stroma

John o' Groats

Scrabster

Thurso

Castletown

A836

Kirkwall

Mull Head

Stromness

Point of Ayre

St. Mary's

Rose Ness

Hoy

Scapa
Flow

Burray

A882

Wick

601

A9

A99

Latheron

Lybster

South
Ronaldsay

Burwick

Pentland Firth

602

A9

Helmsdale

Cape Wrath

Durness

Dounreay

A836

Bettyhill

Tongue

A838

A897

Scourie

A894

A838

Altnaharra

A836

Kinbrace

Lochinver

Inchnadamph

Loch
Shin

Cromalt
Hills

A835

A837

Lairg

A839

603

A9

Brora

How to use this book

1 write up
Written by us after inspection.

2 rooms
We do not use the words 'en suite' but instead 'with' bath or 'with' shower. If a room is not 'en suite' we say 'with separate bathroom' or 'with shared bath': the former you will have to yourself, the latter may be shared with other guests or family members.

3 price
The price shown is the one-night price for two sharing a room with breakfast. A price range incorporates room/seasonal differences. We also give single occupancy rates.

4 meals
Prices are per person. Meals must be booked in advance. Usually you may bring your own wine.

5 closed
When given in months, this means for the whole of the named months and the time in between.

6 directions
Use as a guide; the owner can give more details.

7 symbols
See the last page for a fuller explanation:

    wheelchair facilities
    easily accessible bedrooms
   all children welcome
   no smoking
   credit cards accepted
   good vegetarian dinner options
   licensed premises
   guests' pets can sleep in room
   owners' pets live here
    farm
   pool
   bikes on premises
   tennis on the premises
   walking information provided
   fine breakfast scheme (See pages 396)

8 map & entry numbers

Cornwall

Polrode Mill Cottage

1 A lovely, solid, beamy, 17th-century cottage in a birdsung valley. Inside, flagged floors, chesterfields, a woodburner and a light open feel. Your friendly young hosts live next door; they are working hard on the informal flower and vegetable garden, much of the produce is used in David's delicious homemade dinners, and there's pumpkin marmalade and eggs from the hens. Bedrooms are cottage-cosy with stripped floors, comfy wrought-iron beds and silver cast-iron radiators; fresh bathrooms have double-ended roll-top baths. A slight hum of traffic outside but no matter, inside it is blissfully peaceful.

2	rooms	3: 2 doubles with bath/shower; 1 double with bath.
3	price	£72–£90. Singles £55.
4	meals	Dinner, 3 courses, £25.
5	closed	Rarely.
6	directions	From A395 take A39 towards Camelford. Through Camelford; continue on A39 to Knightsmill. From there, 1.8 miles up on left-hand side.

Deborah Hilborne & David Edwards
Polrode Mill Cottage,
Allen Valley, Nr. St Tudy, Bodmin,
Cornwall PL30 3NS
tel   01208 850203
e-mail   polrode@tesco.net
web   www.polrodemillcottage.co.uk

7   

8   Map 1   Entry 65

England

Bath & N.E. Somerset

47 Sydney Buildings

Simone has a natural sense of hospitality and spoils you with Franco-Caribbean colour: breakfasts of fruit, yogurt and cereals are served on beautiful Limoges china, as well as full English. Bedrooms have a touch of 18th-century boudoir with their embroidered sheets, antique brass beds, frou-frou easy chairs and sumptuous drapes; views sail over the charming garden – all box parterre, lavender and rambling roses in summer – to the floodlit Abbey. Close to Bath centre (10 minutes downhill), a luxurious place to lay your head.
Babies & children over 10 welcome.
Minimum stay two nights at weekends.

Tolley Cottage

Breakfast on the patio and watch the barges pass the bottom of the garden, raise your eyes to Bath Abbey on the skyline. This Victorian cottage is a 10-minute walk from the city and its heritage glories. Sunny and bright, rooms are a comfortable mix of contemporary and classical; books, art and interesting glass pieces catch the eye. Bedrooms are calming and charming with toile de jouy and elegant furniture and white bathrooms sparkle. Judy cooks special breakfasts – suppers, too; James, Master of Wine, can arrange tastings. Both are warm and relaxed, and love sharing their home.

rooms	2: 1 double with bath/shower; 1 twin/double with separate bath.
price	£70. Singles £50.
meals	Pubs/restaurants a 10-minute walk.
closed	Christmas Day.
directions	From Bath centre follow signs to American Museum. Pass Mercedes garage (300 yds up Bathwick Hill on right). 1st road on right after garage. On right, 300 yds down. All-day parking.

rooms	2: 1 double with bath/shower; 1 twin with shower & separate wc.
price	£75. Singles £60.
meals	Supper, 2 courses, from £15. Good pubs/restaurants a 10-minute walk.
closed	Christmas.
directions	Follow signs for American Museum & University up Bathwick Hill. Take first turn right to Sydney Buildings. House 200 yds on right.

Mrs S Johnson
47 Sydney Buildings,
Bathwick Hill,
Bath,
Bath & N.E. Somerset BA2 6DB

tel	01225 463033
fax	01225 461054
e-mail	sydneybuildings@bigfoot.com
web	www.sydneybuildings.co.uk

Judy John
Tolley Cottage,
23 Sydney Buildings,
Bath,
Bath & N.E. Somerset BA2 6BZ

tel	01225 463365
fax	01225 333275
e-mail	jj@judyj.plus.com
web	www.tolleycottage.co.uk

Map 3 Entry 1

Map 3 Entry 2

Bath & N.E. Somerset

Apartment One

Step inside and forget the city bustle – serenity pervades the Smiths' Grade I-listed Bath apartment. A Chinese lantern with hand-painted silk, a fascinating and exotic mix of furniture and pottery, and framed embroideries and art from all over the world hint at your hosts' life of travel; he was with the British Council, both are charming and multi-lingual. The calm bedroom – pale walls, Delft chandelier, cream counterpanes – has a collection of books on art/tea/opera; choose one to browse, then wander into the courtyard garden where the colourful pots are arranged as artfully as the treasures in the house.

Ravenscroft

An elegant Victorian house in a fine setting; thick pale carpets, ruched curtains, Regency stripes and pristine, light-filled bedrooms – each with space to sit, original fireplaces and cosy touches. Albert has views of Bath Abbey, magnificently illuminated at night; Palmerston has its own baby grand piano which the Bryans are happy for you to play. Stroll easily into Bath... or stay above the fray, with fine mature trees all around you, a croquet lawn and a delightful summer house. Breakfasts include fresh fruit and home-baked bread served on family china.

rooms	1 twin/double with bath.
price	£60. Singles £45-£50.
meals	Good restaurants nearby.
closed	Christmas & New Year.
directions	A46 to Bath, then A4 for city centre. Left onto A36 over Cleveland Bridge; follow signs to Holburne Museum. Gt Pulteney St opp. museum. Down steps to basement. Parking £1 per day.

rooms	4: 1 twin/double, 1 double, both with shower; 1 double, 1 single, sharing bath/shower.
price	£70-£80. Singles £55-£65.
meals	Excellent restaurants in Bath.
closed	Christmas.
directions	A36 (Warminster road) from Bath. At boundary Bath & Bathampton, right onto North Rd, pass Golf Club entrance on left, house 200 yds further on right.

Chan Loo Smith
Apartment One,
60 Great Pulteney Street,
Bath,
Bath & N.E. Somerset BA2 4DN

tel	01225 464134
fax	01225 483663
e-mail	aptone@chanloo.fsnet.co.uk

Patrick & Hilary Bryan
Ravenscroft,
North Road,
Bathwick, Bath,
Bath & N.E. Somerset BA2 6HZ

tel	01225 461919
fax	01225 461919
e-mail	patrick@ravenscroftbandb.co.uk
web	www.ravenscroftbandb.co.uk

Map 3 Entry 3

Map 3 Entry 4

Bath & N.E. Somerset

Corston Fields Farm

In rolling agricultural land, a short hop from Bath and Bristol, the Addicotts have given over a generous swathe of their farm to the creation of a natural habitat for indigenous wildlife – and have a Gold Award under the Duke of Cornwall's Habitat Award scheme to boot. The most generous of hosts, they are utterly committed to the environment, and flax from the vibrant blue linseed crops is used to heat their sturdy, stone-mullioned, listed house. The large rooms, one with far-reaching views towards Bath, have all the mod cons. Come for the setting and the wonderful hosts.

rooms	3: 1 double with bath; 1 double with shower; 1 twin with bath/shower.
price	£65–£75. Singles £45.
meals	Pub 300 yds.
closed	Christmas & New Year.
directions	From A4 west of Bath, A39 through Corston. 1 mile on, just before Wheatsheaf Pub (on right), right. Signed 200 yds along lane on right.

Gerald & Rosaline Addicott
Corston Fields Farm,
Corston,
Bath,
Bath & N.E. Somerset BA2 9EZ

tel	01225 873305
fax	01225 874421
e-mail	corston.fields@btinternet.com
web	www.corstonfields.com

Map 3   Entry 5

14 Raby Place

A listed Regency house within walking distance of the city centre, blessed with contemporary art and organic food: a treat. Muriel's is no run-of-the-mill chintzy B&B but part of a classic Bath stone three-storey terrace built in 1824 and filled with an eclectic selection of modern art – one of her passions. Her second is living by organic principles and everything tastes delicious: yoghurt, fruits, cereals, cooked breakfasts, coffee, tea. Some traffic hum is discernible but you are in one of England's finest cities and the beautifully proportioned bedrooms and spotless bathrooms hold all you need.

rooms	5: 2 doubles with bath; 1 double/twin with shower; 1 twin with separate shower; 1 single with separate bath.
price	£55–£60. Singles £35.
meals	Pub/restaurant nearby.
closed	Rarely.
directions	Bathwick Hill is a turning off the A36 towards Bristol; look for signs to university at top of hill. No. 14 on left hand side as you go uphill, before left turn into Raby Mews.

Muriel Guy
14 Raby Place,
Bath,
Bath & N.E. Somerset BA2 4EH

tel	01225 465120

Map 3   Entry 6

Grey Lodge
Summer Lane, Combe Down, Bath, Bath & N.E. Somerset BA2 7EU

You are in a conservation area, yet only a short drive from the centre of Bath – the views are breathtaking from wherever you stand. The steep valley rolls out ahead of you from most of the rooms, and from the garden comes a confusion and a profusion of scents and colours – a glory in its own right. The friendly and likeable Sticklands are conservationists as well as gardeners and have a Green Certificate to prove it. Breakfasts are a feast: bacon and eggs, cereals, home-grown jam, kedgeree and much more. Jane will tell you all about wonderful local gardens to visit.

A real effort is made here to source food and materials locally – normally within a 40-mile radius – and reduce carbon emissions. So, rather than using items that have had to travel across continents by plane, alternatives are found. As with many of our B&B owners, responsible waste control is important, thus recycling, reusing or composting waste as much as possible is also given serious thought. A solar heating system helps to ensure that energy loss is kept to a minimum.

rooms	3: 2 twins/doubles, 1 family, all with shower.
price	£70–£75. Singles £40–£45.
meals	Pub/restaurant 2 miles.
closed	Rarely.
directions	From A36, 3 miles out of Bath on Warminster road, take uphill road by lights & Viaduct Inn. 1st left, 100 yds, signed Monkton Combe. After village, house 1st on left; 0.5 miles on.

	Jane & Anthony Stickland
tel	01225 832069
fax	01225 830161
email	greylodge@freenet.co.uk
web	www.greylodge.co.uk

SPECIAL
GREEN ENTRY
see page 12

Map 3 Entry 7

Bath & N.E. Somerset

Manor Farm Barn

Duchy of Cornwall farmland stretches as far as the eye can see; the views from this recently-converted barn are magnificent by any standards, but remarkable considering you are so close to Bath. There's much wildlife, too: sparrowhawks nest in the gable end, buzzards circle above the valley, and deer may gaze at you eating your breakfast. Wood and stone dominate the open-plan spaces, and spruce guest rooms with built-in wardrobes, houseplants and excellent beds are painted in pale colours. For those in search of birdsong and country peace after a day on the hoof in Bath.

rooms	2: 1 twin/double with bath/shower; 1 double with separate shower.
price	£60–£65. Singles £40–£42.50.
meals	Excellent pubs/restaurants nearby.
closed	Christmas & New Year.
directions	From Bath, A367 (Wells Rd). At Red Lion r'bout right (Bristol A4). Straight on, pass Culverhay School on left. After 100 yds left to Englishcombe. There, right after postbox to church, fork right, follow road; last on right.

Sue & Giles Barber
Manor Farm Barn,
Englishcombe,
Bath,
Bath & N.E. Somerset BA2 9DU

tel	01225 424195
mobile	07966 501016
e-mail	info@manorfarmbarn.com
web	www.manorfarmbarn.com

Map 3 Entry 8

Park Farm

A gorgeous, mullion-windowed, rambler-rose-strewn home that basks in 450 acres with views to Bristol on a clear day. Graham runs the organic farm, makes the delicious Bath Soft Cheese, and helps sweet, sunny Gabrielle run the B&B. Uncomplicated bedrooms are in their own wing; they overlook the village gardens and are quiet, carpeted, decorated in soft colours and have mounds of towels on the bed. You can breakfast (as organically as possible) beside the inglenook fireplace, or in the garden on a warm summer's day. The guest book overflows with praise for Gabrielle's cooking – and her welcome.

rooms	2: 1 double with bath/shower; 1 double with shower.
price	£75. Singles by arrangement.
meals	Good pub in village.
closed	Rarely.
directions	From Bath A431 (Upper Bristol Rd), signed Bitton. Kelston 2.5 miles. 1st left into 1st turning in village by cul-de-sac sign. House 1st on right.

Gabrielle Padfield
Park Farm,
Kelston,
Bath,
Bath & N.E. Somerset BA1 9AG

tel	01225 424139
fax	01225 331906
e-mail	gabrielle.padfield@amserve.com
web	www.parkfarm.co.uk

Map 3 Entry 9

Honey Batch Cottage

A delicious place, combining elegance with cosiness and comfort. Logs smoulder in the fire, the colours are warm, the dresser is Welsh, the stones are flagged. And such a lovely kitchen, with Aga, terracotta tiles and inviting cherrywood table. There are winding stairs, an old bread oven, quirky touches everywhere – and the double bedroom is pure magic, with gorgeous furniture and a quilt made by Angharad. She is an aromatherapist (treatments can be booked) and has the same warmth and offbeat elegance as the house. Only a couple of doors away is an excellent village pub.

Hollytree Cottage

Meandering lanes lead to this 17th-century cottage, with roses round the door, a grandfather clock in the hall and an air of genteel tranquillity. The cottage charm has been updated with Regency mahogany and sumptuous sofas. There's even a four-poster bed for a single guest and the bedrooms have long views over farmland and undulating countryside. Behind is a newly enlarged conservatory – a lovely place for breakfast – and a sloping, south-facing garden with a pond and some rare trees and shrubs. Escorted children will enjoy visiting the farm opposite. Bath is 20 minutes away and Julia knows the city well.

rooms	2: 1 double with shower; 1 single with bath.
price	From £65. Singles £35.
meals	Light supper from £10.
closed	Rarely.
directions	A367 Bath-Exeter. After 3 miles, r'bout & Park & Ride; sharp left, signed 'Wellow 3 miles'. Park in square by Fox & Badger; house 2 doors down.

rooms	4: 2 doubles, 1 twin, 1 four-poster single, all with bath/shower.
price	£70-£80. Singles £40.
meals	Dinner from £18.
closed	Rarely.
directions	From Bath, A36 to Wolverton. Just past Red Lion, turn for Laverton. 1 mile to x-roads; towards Faukland; downhill for 80 yds. On left, just above farm entrance on right.

Angharad Rhys-Roberts
Honey Batch Cottage,
Railway Lane,
Wellow,
Bath,
Bath & N.E. Somerset BA2 8QG
tel   01225 833107
e-mail   angharad@waitrose.com

Mrs Julia Naismith
Hollytree Cottage,
Laverton,
Bath,
Bath & N.E. Somerset BA2 7QZ
tel   01373 830786
fax   01373 830786
e-mail   julia@naismith.fsbusiness.co.uk

Map 3 Entry 10

Map 3 Entry 11

Bath & N.E. Somerset

Melon Cottage Vineyard

Interesting, child-friendly hosts who are entirely natural and un-business-like make this place special; it's excellent value, too. The large Mendip-style 'long cottage' with mullioned windows and beams made of ships' timbers, fronted by a vineyard, is temptingly close to Babington House, the treasures of Bath and Wells, the gardens and concerts at Stourhead, and Gregorian chant in Downside Abbey. Rooms are very simple, the jams and marmalades are homemade, and the hosts the kindest you may meet. No sitting room, but tea in the walled garden is rich compensation. *Children over five welcome.*

rooms	3: 1 double, 1 single, sharing bath; 1 family (zip-link beds & divan) with shower.
price	£35–£45. Singles £17.50.
meals	Pubs 2 miles.
closed	Rarely.
directions	From Bath A367, Wells road, through Radstock. After 3 miles, at large r'bout, B3139 for Trowbridge. 1.1 miles on, right up drive. House at top, visible from road.

Virginia & Hugh Pountney
Melon Cottage Vineyard,
Charlton,
Radstock,
Bath,
Bath & N.E. Somerset BA3 5TN
tel   01761 435090
e-mail v.pountney@virgin.net

Map 3 Entry 12

Berkshire

Lodge Down

Tea and homemade cake or wine if it's that sort of time. John and Sally are convivial hosts who are easing out of farming into B&B and other interests. Their house and 70 acres, overlooking downland and the Lambourne gallops, amazingly close to the M4 (some traffic noise outside), is all polished country-house comfort: rugs on gleaming floors, well-loved antiques, good china. Bedrooms are comfortably traditional; bathrooms snug with endless hot water. Breakfasts will set you up for the day whether race-visiting, walking or visiting Stonehenge. The Cooks will point you to the best pubs, walks and viewpoints.

rooms	3: 1 double, 1 twin, 1 family, all with bath/shower.
price	£55. Singles from £35.
meals	Good pubs/restaurants 2–5 miles.
closed	Rarely.
directions	M4 exit 14. A338 to Wantage for 300 yds, then 1st left; signs to Baydon. Pass the Pheasant pub & The Hare restaurant later on; on right 1 mile before Baydon.

Sally & John Cook
Lodge Down,
Lambourn,
Hungerford,
Berkshire RG17 7BJ
tel   01672 540304
fax   01672 540304
e-mail lodgedown@hotmail.com
web   www.lodgedown.co.uk

Map 3 Entry 13

Berkshire

Fishers Farm

Ask if you may swim: there's an indoor pool; if you like to walk, there are acres of farmland and a dog for company. Both hosts are multilingual and enjoy their guests: Henry works less on the farm now and has turned his hand to preparing breakfasts in the beamed kitchen. Some of the guest rooms date back to the 16th century and are large, bright, simply and attractively decorated, with views of the well-tended garden and surrounding fields. The sitting room has a big open fire and a vast selection of books and classical CDs. Close to the M4 yet utterly tranquil – a treat.

Wilton House

The documented history of "the most ambitious house in Hungerford" (Pevsner) pre-dates 1470 and the early 18th-century façade conceals medieval origins. It is a classic townhouse with a Queen Anne frontage and, inside, wood panelling and beams, wonky floors, period furniture and family portraits. Bedrooms are fresh, traditional, perfect with exceptionally big beds; so is breakfast in the 18th-century dining room. The Welfares look after you brilliantly and give a terrific welcome. Antique shops to the front and a walled garden with cordon-trained fruit trees behind. *Children over eight welcome.*

	Fishers Farm
rooms	3: 2 twins/doubles, both with bath/shower; 1 twin/double with separate bath/shower.
price	£60–£62. Singles £45–£50.
meals	Good pub 0.5 miles.
closed	Rarely.
directions	From M4 junc. 14, A338 north for Wantage. After 0.5 miles, 1st left (B4000). 1st farm road on right after Pheasant Inn to house.

	Wilton House
rooms	2: 1 double, 1 twin/double, both with bath.
price	From £64. Singles from £45.
meals	Packed lunch £5. Pubs & restaurants an easy walk.
closed	Christmas.
directions	M4 exit 14; A338 to A4; right for Marlborough, turning at Bear Hotel onto Salisbury road (A338). Over canal bridge into High St. House 200 yds past Town Hall on right.

	Mary & Henry Wilson
	Fishers Farm,
	Shefford Woodlands,
	Hungerford,
	Berkshire RG17 7AB
tel	01488 648466
fax	01488 648706
e-mail	mail@fishersfarm.co.uk
web	www.fishersfarm.co.uk

	Deborah & Jonathan Welfare
	Wilton House,
	33 High Street,
	Hungerford,
	Berkshire RG17 0NF
tel	01488 684228
fax	01488 685037
e-mail	welfares@hotmail.com
web	www.wiltonhouse-hungerford.co.uk

Map 3 Entry 14

Map 3 Entry 15

Berkshire

Field Farm Cottage

Be greeted with tea or wine by Anne and her decorous labrador Rosie; if you're lucky, you'll sit in the bewitching garden. Borders spill over with flowers, an arch in the beech hedge beckons, and there's a pond fed by a natural spring. Parts of the house date back 350 years. Bedrooms are simple, sloping-ceilinged and inviting; breakfast in the kitchen is informal and good. Take as much time as you like over it for Anne is most accommodating and friendly. There's a whole range of places to visit nearby, including Oxford, while Roman Silchester has a little 12th-century church.

Brighton

Brighton City B&B

With beautiful houses and interesting people, Brighton should be a B&B mecca. But we have, strangely, no full-time Special Places here. We have, however, found some lovely 'part-time' places to join our City B&B scheme. Simply call the number below; you will immediately be offered somewhere to stay and your host will later contact you. We have sought out people with a spare room or two at home – inspired amateurs happy to do B&B. Most of them live in the loveliest parts of the city; we've visited them all and their houses are as special as you might expect.

rooms	2: 1 double with shower; 1 double with separate bath.
price	£50-£60. Singles £35-£40.
meals	Pubs/restaurants 1 mile. Dinner occasionally available.
closed	Rarely.
directions	Junc. 12 off M4, A4 for Newbury. 3 miles, left at The Spring Inn; on for 1 mile, cottage 100 yds past 2nd left hand turning & 30mph sign.

rooms	Call for details.
price	£60-£80. Singles £30-£50.
meals	Discuss with the owners, but Brighton has many restaurants.
closed	Rarely - we usually have rooms.
directions	Call for details.

	Pat & Anne Froom Field Farm Cottage, Sulhamstead, Reading, Berkshire RG7 4DA
tel	0118 9302735
mobile	07786 746323
e-mail	annefroom@knowall.co.uk

	Brighton City B&B
tel	07891 452683

Map 4 Entry 16

Map 4 Entry 17

Bristol

Park House

The first house to be built in Clifton Park in 1797 – now surrounded by busy streets – it is imposing, delightful, ivy-clad. Fight your way past an engaging muddle – books, pictures, shells, fossils and pre-war sports gear – to pretty, old-fashioned bedrooms. The upstairs one has views over one of the walled gardens where two white Call ducks plod; the downstairs twin is next to a library stuffed with books. A light sitting room has a large table for breakfast and a view of the other garden. Delia is wise, friendly and kind and you are within walking distance of everything.
Children over 12 welcome.

rooms	2: 1 double, 1 twin, both with shower.
price	£75. Singles £55.
meals	Excellent restaurants an easy walk.
closed	24 December-2 January; 1 week over Easter.
directions	Directions given when booking. From Temple Meads station, take 8 or 9 bus to Student Union, Queens Road, Clifton.

Mrs Delia Macdonald
Park House,
19 Richmond Hill,
Clifton,
Bristol BS8 1BA
tel   0117 973 6331

🐈 👞

Map 3 Entry 18

Bristol City B&B

Our City B&B scheme (see opposite) extends to Bristol. If our Bristol special place is full, call the number below and you will be offered a new place to stay. We have, as in Brighton, sought out people who are happy to do B&B when they have an empty spare room (or two) at home. These, for the most part, inspired amateurs live in the most attractive parts of the city – some in Georgian Clifton, others in Redland close to the Downs, another by the harbourside. All the houses and hosts are known to us and are as interesting as our 'main' houses throughout the UK. Just call the number below.

rooms	Call for details.
price	£60-£80. Singles £30-£50.
meals	Some owners serve meals, but Bristol is rich in restaurants.
closed	Rarely.
directions	Call for details.

Bristol City B&B
tel   07891 452673

🍴 🍷

Map 3 Entry 19

Buckinghamshire

Field Cottage

Sue, relaxed and friendly, is the consummate professional: the fitted bedrooms are immaculate, the bathrooms pristine, the towels fluffy. She has also created a horticultural haven amid open fields (old-fashioned roses, a willow tunnel, 40 varieties of clematis) and green fingers have been at work in the conservatory, too. The peachy guest sitting room is neat and comfortable – doors swing open onto the garden and your own patio suntrap – and you tuck into homemade muffins at breakfast surrounded by pastoral views. It's walking distance to the Ridgeway National Trail, Britain's oldest road.

rooms	3: 1 double with shower; 1 twin with separate shower; 1 single with separate bath/shower.
price	£60-£65. Singles £35-£50.
meals	Pub 0.5 miles.
closed	Christmas & New Year.
directions	South on A413 from Wendover. Pass Jet station, left to Kings Ash; 2 miles on, left at x-roads, pass pub; 0.5 miles on, sharp left onto bridlepath; 2nd gate along.

	Mike & Sue Jepson
	Field Cottage,
	St Leonards,
	Tring,
	Buckinghamshire HP23 6NS
tel	01494 837602
fax	01494 837137
e-mail	michael.jepson@lineone.net

Map 9 Entry 20

Cambridgeshire

Springfield House

A happy mix of town and country: you are in a small rural town yet wonderfully close to Cambridge. The former school house hugs the bend of a river, its French windows opening to delicious gardens. The conservatory, draped with a huge mimosa, is an exceptional spot for summer breakfasts. Beds and bedrooms are large, comfortable and comforting, with thick curtains, books, flowers and garden views. This is a cheerful and old-fashionedly elegant home; there's Charlie the flat-coated retriever, a family bustle in the holidays, and Judith, a quietly nurturing, ever-thoughtful hostess. Brilliant value.

rooms	2: 1 double with bath; 1 double with bath/shower.
price	£55-£65. Singles £35-£40.
meals	Good pubs 150 yds.
closed	Rarely.
directions	A1307 from Cambridge, left into High St. 1st right after The Crown (on left) into Horn Lane. House on right next to chapel, before ford.

	Judith Rossiter
	Springfield House,
	14-16 Horn Lane,
	Linton,
	Cambridgeshire CB1 6HT
tel	01223 891383
web	www.springfield-house.co.uk

Map 9 Entry 21

Cambridgeshire

Model Farm

You will unwind quickly, as the Barlows' relaxed 'take-us-as-you-find-us' approach pervades this house. One cosy and private bedroom in a separate wing is up its own circular metal stair — and is a sure contender for the Loo With A View competition. In the main house is a fresh, pretty, blue and white bedroom, and a functional, newly-converted room on the ground floor with its own entrance — even more private. All are spotless. There's homemade jam for breakfast, fruit trees outside and bees and, although this is an arable farm, sheep still graze the land. Beautifully quiet, and close to Cambridge.

Abington Pigotts Hall

Roman remains, Saxon hamlet, 13th-century church, Georgian house… The ancient estate has been in the family for nearly 600 years but the present house was built in 1820. A family home, it's big, comfortably furnished, informal and friendly, with two dogs and an African grey parrot. You eat in the impressive dining room, under the gaze of oil-painted ancestors, and are welcome to use the cosy family sitting room, too. Pleasant bedrooms look out over big gardens to peaceful Cambridgeshire countryside; the only sound is the cawing of rooks in the ancient trees nearby.

rooms	3 doubles, all with shower.
price	£55. Singles £33.
meals	Pub/restaurant 3 miles.
closed	Rarely.
directions	From A1198 at Longstowe onto B1046. House on right after 3 miles, before Little Gransden.

rooms	2: 1 double with shower; 1 twin with bath.
price	£60-£65. Singles £45.
meals	Dinner, 3 courses, £18. Good pub 300 yds.
closed	Christmas & New Year.
directions	From Royston A505 towards Baldock. Right to Litlington; at church, fork right to Abington Pigotts. After Pig & Abbott Pub, left up Church Lane; on left of church.

	Sue Barlow
	Model Farm,
	Little Gransden,
	Cambridgeshire SG19 3EA
tel	01767 677361
e-mail	suebarlow@modelfarm.org.uk
web	www.modelfarm.org.uk

	Guy & Eleanor Sclater
	Abington Pigotts Hall,
	Royston,
	Cambridgeshire SG8 0SH
tel	01763 852310
e-mail	sclaterg@aol.com

Map 9 Entry 22

Map 9 Entry 23

Cheshire

Lower Key Green Farm

Aga-cooked breakfasts with home-baked bread, home eggs and sausages, Staffordshire oatcakes: just the thing to set you up for a day's walking in the Peak District. A solid, unpretentious farmhouse – David's family have farmed here for generations – whose flagged floors, beamed ceilings, scrubbed tables and throws on chairs create an easy comfort. The bedroom has a cottagey simplicity; a Victorian washstand and a slipper bath add delight. Help yourself to homemade biscuits and sherry. There are good food pubs with pretty views nearby, and Janet and David are welcoming and down to earth.

The Mount

This is Britain at its best: rare trees planted in 1860, flowers everywhere, a pond, a fruitful vegetable garden and Rachel – delightful, warm and friendly. The Victorian house, built for a Chester corn merchant, furnished in elegant and traditional style, has garden views from every window. You get a light-filled drawing room, a high-ceilinged dining room and bedrooms that are truly inviting – bright, big, with attractive fabrics, art and lovely furniture. A haven for garden buffs, walkers, birdwatchers and tennis players. Easy access to Chester, North Wales and two airports. *Arrivals from 5pm.*

	Lower Key Green Farm	The Mount
rooms	1 twin/double with shower; extra shared bath.	3: 2 twins/doubles, both with bath; 1 double with shower.
price	£60. Singles £35.	From £55. Singles from £37.
meals	Supper, 3 courses, £15. Excellent pub a 10-minute drive.	Good pub/restaurant 0.5 miles.
closed	Rarely.	Christmas & New Year.
directions	From A54, A523 towards Leek. Through Bosley village, turn right, after 40mph and Queen's Arms sign, onto Tunstall Rd; 2nd farm on left after 0.5 mile.	A5104 to Broughton; left at 2nd r'bout to A5104 Pennyfordd; through Broughton, cross over A55; 1st left to Higher Kinnerton down Lesters Lane. On right, on bend, 0.75 miles down.

Janet Heath
Lower Key Green Farm,
Bosley,
Macclesfield,
Cheshire SK11 0PB

tel   01260 223278
fax   01260 223278
e-mail   lowerkeygreen@hotmail.com
web   www.lowerkeygreen.co.uk

Jonathan & Rachel Major
The Mount,
Higher Kinnerton,
Chester,
Cheshire CH4 9BQ

tel   01244 660275
fax   01244 660275
e-mail   major@mountkinnerton.freeserve.co.uk
web   www.bandbchester.com

Map 8 Entry 24

Map 7 Entry 25

Cheshire

Cotton Farm

Only a four-mile hop from Roman Chester and its 900-year-old cathedral to the attractive sprawl of this red brick farmhouse. And there are 250 acres to roam, populated by geese, beef cattle and sheep. Nigel and Clare are committed, hard-working hosts, farmers and conservationists: parts of the farm are under the Countryside Stewardship Scheme. Bedrooms are 'stylish farmhouse' with lovely fabrics and touches of luxury – bath towels are huge – but best of all is the relaxed, family atmosphere created by the Hills. Breakfasts are excellent.

rooms	3: 2 doubles, 1 twin, all with bath/shower.
price	From £58. Singles £38.
meals	Pub 1.5 miles.
closed	Rarely.
directions	From Chester, A51 east, signed Nantwich. 1.5 miles from city outskirts, right, down Cotton Lane, signed Cotton Edmunds. 1.5 miles, on sharp right-hand bend, left. Farm 2nd drive on right.

Clare & Nigel Hill
Cotton Farm,
Cotton Edmunds,
Chester,
Cheshire CH3 7PG
tel   01244 336616
fax   01244 336699
e-mail info@cottonfarm.co.uk
web   www.cottonfarm.co.uk

Map 7 Entry 26

Ardmore

Bright, sizeable rooms are furnished with style and restraint; the views at the back reach over five counties. A graceful hall runs from one end of the house to the other, past old prints, alcoves of china and a spinet. Polished stairs lead to delightful bedrooms overlooking the Welsh hills; bathrooms are new. Ardmore is in a leafy, rural setting (two good pubs to walk to), built in the 1930s in the Arts & Crafts style. The lovely gardens in the same idiom are being restored by Flossy and yield fresh fruit for breakfast; there's home-baked bread, too. Fascinating Chester is nearby. *Children over eight welcome.*

rooms	2: 1 double with bath/shower; 1 twin with shower.
price	£70. Singles from £35.
meals	Pubs & fish restaurant within walking distance.
closed	Christmas & occasionally.
directions	A51 from Chester; at Stamford Bridge traffic lights, left to Barrow (B5132); house 1.5 miles, on left with pointed oak gateposts.

Neil & Flossy Dixon
Ardmore,
Station Lane,
Great Barrow,
Chester,
Cheshire CH3 7JN
tel   01829 740257
mob   07765 634188
e-mail fdixon@ardmore2000.freeserve.co.uk

Map 7 Entry 27

Cornwall

Carmelin

The setting is sensational: you are perched on the last strip of land before the Atlantic which swirls around the Lizard at England's most southerly point. Breakfasts – hearty, continental, delicious – have to fight for your attention, so all-encompassing are the views. The bedroom has them too, from two big windows; they overlook your own patio and the sea beyond… waking is sheer delight. Note there is also a ladder to an attic room ideal for children aged over eight. John and Jane are gentle, relaxed people who enjoy their guests; walk the coastal path and return to a lovely home-cooked meal.

rooms	1 double with separate bath/shower.
price	£55. Singles by arrangement.
meals	Dinner, 3 courses, £19. Supper £11. BYO. Pub within walking distance.
closed	Rarely.
directions	From Helston to the Lizard; at Lizard Green, right, opp. Regent Café (head for Smugglers Fish & Chips); immed. right, pass wc on left. Road unmade; on for 500 yds; double bend; 2nd on right.

	Jane & John Grierson
	Carmelin,
	Pentreath Lane,
	The Lizard,
	Helston,
	Cornwall TR12 7NY
tel	01326 290677
e-mail	pjcarmelin@aol.com
web	www.bedandbreakfastcornwall.co.uk

Map 1 Entry 28

Chydane

All that separates you from the sand and sea is the coastal path. At the far end of the spectacular, three-mile beach is Porthleven; beyond, West Penwith stretches magically into the distance. You can see all this, and lighthouses, basking sharks, dolphins. Its stunning position is combined with rooms of utter luxury. One elegant double bedroom, with gorgeous linen, a superb bed and a chesterfield, opens onto a French balcony overlooking the waves. The bathrooms, too, are sybaritic in the extreme. Up steep little stairs to the attic is a second, good-sized room that children will find entrancing.

rooms	2 doubles both with separate bathroom.
price	£100. Singles £75.
meals	Pub/restaurant nearby.
closed	Never.
directions	From Helston A3083 to The Lizard. After 2 miles right to Gunwalloe. Right before Halzephron Inn. Chydane on right above beach.

	Karla & John Caslin
	Chydane,
	Gunwalloe Fishing Cove,
	Helston,
	Cornwall TR12 7QB
tel	01326 241232

Map 1 Entry 29

Cornwall

The Gardens

Two old miners' cottages combine to create this small, modest, well-tended home. Irish Moira, a retired midwife, adores flowers and her posies brighten every corner; Goff, a potter, tends the vegetables. Both are charming and kind. Sweet snug bedrooms have patchwork quilts, cotton sheets, antique linen runners and plenty of books. One is on the ground floor overlooking the pretty cottage garden, two are up a narrow stair. Aga-cooked breakfasts and homemade jams are brought to the sun-streamed conservatory; in the sitting room a woodburner belts out the heat. Great value B&B.

rooms	3: 2 doubles, both with bath & shower; 1 twin/double with separate bath.
price	£50–£54. Singles £25–£28.
meals	Packed lunch from £6.50. Pubs & restaurants a 10-minute drive.
closed	Christmas & New Year.
directions	A394 Helston to Penzance, 2nd right after Ashton Post Office for Tresowes Green. After 0.25 miles, sign for house on right.

Moira & Goff Cattell
The Gardens,
Tresowes,
Ashton,
Helston,
Cornwall TR13 9SY
tel   01736 763299
mobile   07881 758191
e-mail   thegardens@amserve.com

Map 1 Entry 30

Ednovean Farm

There's a terrace for each immaculate bedroom – one truly private – with views to the wild blue yonder and St Michael's Mount Bay: an enchanting outlook that changes with the passage of the day. Come for peace, space and the best of 'boutique B&B': eclectic fabrics and colours, pretty lamps, gleaming copper, fluffy bathrobes and handmade soaps. The beamed, open-plan sitting/dining area is an absorbing mix of exotic, rustic and elegant; have full breakfast here, or continental in your room. A footpath through the field leads to the village; walk to glorious Prussia Cove and Cudden Point, too.

rooms	3: 1 double with bath; 1 double with bath/shower; 1 four-poster with bath.
price	£80–£90. Singles £70–£80.
meals	Dinner available within walking distance.
closed	Christmas.
directions	From A30 after Crowlas r'bout, A394 to Helston. 0.25 miles after next r'bout, 1st right for Perranuthnoe. Drive on left, signed.

Christine & Charles Taylor
Ednovean Farm,
Perranuthnoe,
Penzance,
Cornwall TR20 9LZ
tel   01736 711883
e-mail   info@ednoveanfarm.co.uk
web   www.ednoveanfarm.co.uk

Map 1 Entry 31

Cornwall

Burnewhall House

Kenneth's talent and enthusiasm bubble over; he was a professional baritone and still occasionally sings. He also cooks superbly and unexpectedly (gunpowder sauce!), and lives with his vintage Mama in a rented, windswept farmhouse back from the cliffs near the exquisite hamlet of Penbirth. Breakfast is served from silver and family china in a gracious dining room. The bedroom is traditional with smart old Victorian beds and electric blankets; breathtaking panoramic sea views stretch to the Lizard. Don't expect perfection: just enjoy yourself. *Children over 12 welcome.*

Ennys

Prepare to be spoiled. A fire smoulders in the sumptuous sitting room, afternoon tea is laid out in the farmhouse kitchen, and bedrooms are luxurious: the four-poster with pretty toile de Jouy, a powerful shower and fat pillows, and elegant family suites too. Everywhere there are fascinating artefacts and curios from Gill's travels, designer fabrics and antique pieces. The road ends at Ennys, so the rural bliss is entirely yours. Walk down to the river and along the old towpath, or simply stay here; play tennis, or swim in the heated pool sunk deep into the tropical gardens. *Children over three welcome.*

rooms	1 twin with bath/shower.
price	£75. Singles £45. Christmas breaks available.
meals	Occasional dinners (min 4 people). Pubs/restaurants 2-6 miles.
closed	Rarely.
directions	A30 to Land's End; 3 miles from Penzance left at Catchall, onto B3283. Thro' St Buryan (for Porthcurno); 0.5 miles, left for Lamorna by phone box on green; 2nd right 0.75 miles on, on left-hand bend by woods; right into drive.

rooms	5: 1 double/twin, 1 four-poster, both with shower; 1 double with bath. Barn: 2 family suites, both with bath.
price	£70-£95. Singles from £55.
meals	Good pub 3 miles.
closed	November-February.
directions	2 miles east of Marazion on B3280, look for sign & turn left leading down Trewhella Lane between St Hilary & Relubbus. On to Ennys.

	Kenneth Fraser Annand
	Burnewhall House,
	St Buryan,
	Penzance,
	Cornwall TR19 6DN
tel	01736 810650
e-mail	burnewhall@btconnect.com

	Gill Charlton
	Ennys,
	St Hilary,
	Penzance,
	Cornwall TR20 9BZ
tel	01736 740262
fax	01736 740055
e-mail	ennys@ennys.co.uk
web	www.ennys.co.uk

Map 1 Entry 32

Map 1 Entry 33

Cornwall

Jamies

Breathe in the sweeping ocean views from this stylish 1920s villa. Airy bedrooms are hotel-smart with white bed linen, striped or checked curtains and fresh new bathrooms; all rooms have a great feeling of space. Crisp linen and silver at the dining table creates an elegant mood at breakfast — enjoy a delicious fruit salad while taking in the views, or admire some of artist Felicity's inspiring, bold work. There's also a sitting room for guests. Felicity and Jamie are generous hosts, ex-hoteliers with a great sense of fun, and can tell you about all the local restaurants and galleries.

Bosmorva

The bold South American colours in this Arts & Crafts home exude warmth — as do the owners, who worked and travelled in Mexico and Venezuela. Fresh creams and pink flowers sit well with crisp white linen, sage panelling and dark-wood furniture in the bedrooms; the roll-top bath in the big bathroom begs you to indulge. Wendy is a keen gardener and her maze-like garden reveals tropical planting and diverse views of the Hayle estuary. Take the coastal train to St Ives — it's a five-minute walk to the tiny station. Or stay put and luxuriate in the ever-changing light and scenery.

	Jamies		Bosmorva
rooms	4: 3 twin/doubles, 1 suite, all with bath.	rooms	2: 1 twin/double with bath/shower; 1 double with shower.
price	£80. Singles £60.	price	From £65. Singles from £45.
meals	Excellent restaurants within a 25-minute walk.	meals	Good pubs & restaurant 5-minute walk.
closed	Rarely.	closed	Rarely.
directions	A30, then A3704 for St Ives. At Carbis Bay, Marshalls estate agents & Methodist church on left. Next right down Pannier Lane; 2nd left is Wheal Whidden; 1st on left.	directions	After A30 Hayle bypass, A3047 to St Ives. In Lelant, before brow of hill, right into Vicarage Lane. House 80 yds downhill on right.

Felicity & Jamie Robertson
Jamies,
Wheal Whidden,
Carbis Bay,
St Ives,
Cornwall TR26 2QX
tel   01736 794718
e-mail   info@jamiesstives.co.uk
web   www.jamiesstives.co.uk

Wendy & Colin Grapes
Bosmorva,
Vicarage Lane,
Lelant, St Ives,
Cornwall TR26 3EA
tel   01736 755185
mobile   07774 126448
e-mail   colin@grapes3.wanadoo.co.uk
web   www.bosmorva-st-ives.com

Map 1 Entry 34

Map 1 Entry 35

Cornwall

1 Sea View Terrace

Sea-loving style-seekers look no further. This is a perfect seaside B&B run by the charming John who, until recently, ran the perfect country-house hotel. Meticulous attention to detail has made this St Ives house what it is. There are just two bedrooms and, in each, a bay window and a table set with fresh flowers for breakfast brought to your room. The feel is luxurious and contemporary, colours are muted and pebble-pale and the captivating harbour views will launch dreams of living by the sea. Designer bathrooms, organic soaps and shampoos, and the Tate a short stroll.

House at Gwinear

An island of calm — it sits, as it has for 500 years, in its own bird-trilled acres a short drive from St Ives. The mood is now artistic for the Halls are devoted to the encouragement of the arts and crafts which is reflected in their lifestyle. There's no stuffiness — just fresh flowers on the breakfast table, a piano in the corner, rugs on polished floors and masses of books. You have a cosy bedroom and sitting room in a separate wing and a fine view of the church from the bath. The big, lawn-filled gardens are there for bare-footed solace, and your interesting hosts couldn't be nicer.

rooms	2 twins/doubles, both with bath/shower.
price	£95.
meals	Pubs/restaurants 5-minute walk.
closed	Rarely.
directions	Fom Carbis Bay, on to St Ives. At Porthminster Hotel, continue left until sharp left, then first right to Sea View Terrace. Private parking.

rooms	1 twin/double with bath & separate sitting room.
price	From £65.
meals	Dinner sometimes available. Pub 1.5 miles.
closed	Rarely.
directions	From A30 exit Hayle (Pickfords r'bout); 100 yds left at mini-r'bout; 400 yds left for Gwinear; 1.5 miles, top of hill, driveway on right, just before 30mph Gwinear sign.

John Charlick
1 Sea View Terrace,
St Ives,
Cornwall TR26 2DH

tel   01736 798001
fax   01736 791802
e-mail oneseaviewterrace@hotmail.com
web   www.seaview-stives.co.uk

Charles & Diana Hall
House at Gwinear,
Gwinear,
St Ives,
Cornwall TR27 5JZ

tel   01736 850444
fax   01736 850031

Map 1 Entry 36

Map 1 Entry 37

Cornwall

Drym Farm

Rural, but not too deeply: the Tate at St Ives is a 15-minute drive. The 1705 farmhouse, beautifully revived, is surrounded by ancient barns, a dairy and a forge, fascinating to Cornish historians. Jan arrived in 2002, with an enthusiasm for authenticity and simple, stylish good taste. French limestone floors in the hall, striking art on the walls, a roll-top bath on seagrass matting, a *bateau lit*, an antique brass bed. Paintwork is fresh cream and taupe. There are old fruit trees and young camellias, a sitting room stocked with books and organic treats at breakfast. Charming and utterly peaceful.

Scorrier House

The grounds are full of delight: an oval walled garden, camellia walks, a Cornish garden, magnolias… And beyond, parkland, woods and farmland, the peace broken only by the occasional whinny from one of Richard's racehorses. The house is similarly grand – weddings with up to 100 guests can be catered for – and very lovely. A double stone staircase leads to big elegant bedrooms (night storage heaters, so you might want to bring a hottie), and there's a sitting room for guests (with a log fire). The Williams family have lived here since George III's reign; you will be greeted with old-style kindness.

rooms	3: 1 double with bath; 1 double with bath & shower; 1 twin sharing bath.
price	£60-£80. Singles from £45.
meals	Pubs/restaurants nearby.
closed	Rarely.
directions	From A30 to Hayle; through Hayle to r'bout signed left to Helston. At Leedstown, left towards Drym. Follow road until right turn to Drym. Farm fourth on lane, on right after Drym House.

rooms	2: 1 double with bath; 1 twin with separate bath.
price	£60-£70. Singles £35-£45.
meals	Pubs a 2-minute walk.
closed	Rarely.
directions	A30, then A3047 to Scorrier. On for 0.5 miles to mini-r'bout; left. Large drive on right (about 200 yds); signed.

Jan Bright
Drym Farm,
Drym,
Praze-an-Beeble,
Camborne,
Cornwall TR14 0NU

tel 01209 831039
e-mail drym_farm@onetel.com
web www.drymfarm.co.uk

Richard & Caroline Williams
Scorrier House,
Scorrier,
Redruth,
Cornwall TR16 5AU

tel 01209 820264
e-mail rwill10442@aol.com
web www.scorrierhouse.co.uk

Map 1 Entry 38

Map 1 Entry 39

Cornwall

Tregew Vean

Once the home of a packet skipper, this pretty Georgian slate-hung house stands in a sunny spot above Flushing. From the garden you glimpse the Fal estuary through the trees. There are palms, of course – de rigueur down here – but Sandra has started a mediterranean garden too: agapanthus, olive trees, figs. The house, newly smart from its recent renovation, is fresh and elegant, with tenderly cared-for antiques and an entertaining straw hat collection in the hall. The double has a brass bed and a view of Falmouth. If you're a family party, a smaller double room is also available, sharing the bathroom.

Trevilla House

The sea and the peninsula wrap themselves around you – an enviable position – and the King Harry ferry gives you an easy reach into the glorious Roseland peninsula. Frog stencils add a humourous touch to the bathroom, and the freshly-decorated bedrooms with Edwardian basketwork beds are faded though comfortable; the twin has double-aspect garden views and a sofa; from the double gaze out on expansive sea views. Jinty is a dear and rustles up delicious breakfasts, usually served in the sunny conservatory that looks south over the sea. Trelissick Gardens and the Copeland China Collection are just next door.

	Tregew Vean		Trevilla House
rooms	2: 1 double, 1 small double, sharing bath.	rooms	2: 1 double with sitting room & separate bath/shower, 1 twin with bath/shower. (Extra single for members of same party)
price	From £60.	price	From £65. Singles by arrangement.
meals	Pubs/restaurants within walking distance.	meals	Restaurants/pubs 1-2 miles.
closed	Christmas.	closed	Christmas & New Year.
directions	From Penryn towards Mylor. After 1 mile right to Flushing. Entrance 1 mile down road on right, 30 yds before T-junction.	directions	A390 to Truro; A39 to Falmouth. At double r'bout with garage, left off 2nd r'bout (B3289); pass pub on left; at x-roads, left (B3289); 200 yds on, fork right to Feock. On to T-junc., then left; 1st on right.

Sandra & Rodney Myers
Tregew Vean,
Flushing,
Falmouth,
Cornwall TR11 5TF
tel   01326 379462
e-mail   tregewvean@aol.com
web   www.tregewvean.co.uk

Jinty & Peter Copeland
Trevilla House,
Feock,
Truro,
Cornwall TR3 6QG
tel   01872 862369
fax   01872 864157
e-mail   jinty@trevilla.com
web   www.trevilla.clara.net/bed.html

Map 1 Entry 40

Map 1 Entry 41

Cornwall

Polsue Manor

Graham and Annabelle are a young, dynamic couple who run their B&B and their inn, the Port Gaverne, with a breezy enthusiasm. Life is busy, so don't expect over-solicitousness or a constantly hovering hostess, but the independent will appreciate the easiness and the sense of space; rooms are huge and bedrooms have eiderdowns and good beds. There are floral sofas in the traditional sitting room and windows give onto countryside views, big trees, camellias and a pond. It's over a mile along a pretty footpath from the garden to a big sandy beach; this is a great spot for coastal walking.

rooms	3 twins/doubles, all with bath.
price	£80. Singles £50.
meals	Pub 1 mile.
closed	November–March.
directions	A3078 south from Tregony. In Ruan High Lanes, 2nd right (for Philleigh & King Harry Ferry). House 1 mile up on left.

Graham & Annabelle Sylvester
Polsue Manor,
Ruan High Lanes,
Truro,
Cornwall TR2 5LU
tel   01872 501270
fax   01872 501177
web   www.polsuemanor.co.uk

Map 1 Entry 42

Pine Cottage

The Cornish sea laps the steep quay of this narrow inlet's port, its blue horizon just visible from the window of one of the elegant bedrooms high up on the coveside. A perfect spot to wake on a summer's morn. The house is as sunny as its owner, the rooms charmingly informal with their rose-strewn wallpaper and shelves brimming with tempting books. A handful of small open-top fishing boats slips out at dawn to bring back catches of crab and lobster. Clare crafts them and local sea bass, brill, mullet and sole into masterpieces that smack of her days as a restaurateur – delicious.

rooms	3: 1 double with bath/shower; 1 double with separate bath/shower; 1 single (Let to same party only)
price	£80–£90. Singles from £40.
meals	Dinner by arrangement. Packed lunch £7.50. Excellent pub 100 yds.
closed	Rarely.
directions	From Tregony, A3078 to St Mawes. After 2 miles, at garage, left to Portloe. Through village to Ship Inn. Right fork after pub car park. Cottage immed. on left between white gate posts up drive.

Clare Holdsworth
Pine Cottage,
Portloe,
Truro,
Cornwall TR2 5RB
tel   01872 501385
web   www.pinecottage.net

Map 1 Entry 43

Cornwall

Hay Barton

The giant windows ovelook many acres of farmland – cattle, lambs, rabbits, bantams – and Jill and Blair cheerfully involve you in their family life. Breakfast on locally-sourced treats in the smart dining room with its giant flagstones and family antiques; at the end of the day, retire to the guest sitting room. Bedrooms are pretty with fresh garden flowers, soft white linen, floral green walls and stripped floors. Gloriously large panelled bathrooms have roll-top baths and are painted in soft, earthy colours. A wholesome place, perfect for children, and lots of gardens and restaurants to explore nearby.

Oxturn House

A corner of peace and quiet from which to explore the surrounding area; French windows from the sitting room lead to a terrace with good views and the house, purpose-built for the Holts, sits in a delightful position above Ladock. It is big and light and set out with guests in mind – its furniture and fittings are new, bedrooms have plenty of cupboard space and a sitting room that is clutter-free and large. There are keys to the bedrooms. Barbara is a B&B professional and is the fourth generation of her family to have done B&B. She welcomes guests with an assured efficiency and kindness.

rooms	2 twins/doubles both with bath.
price	£70. Singles £45.
meals	Good pubs 3-4 miles.
closed	Rarely.
directions	A3078 from Tregony village towards St Mawes. After 1 mile, house on left.

rooms	2: 1 twin/double with bath/shower; 1 twin/double with separate bath/shower.
price	£50-£62. Singles by arrangement.
meals	Good village pub 200 yds; excellent restaurant 3 miles.
closed	December.
directions	From A30, B3275 south to Ladock. There, turn opposite Falmouth Arms & follow road uphill for 200 yds. Right 70 yds after 'End 30mph' sign. House on right.

	Jill & Blair Jobson
	Hay Barton,
	Tregony,
	Truro,
	Cornwall TR2 5TF
tel	01872 530288
mobile	07813 643028
e-mail	jill@haybarton.com
web	www.haybarton.com

	Ian & Barbara Holt
	Oxturn House,
	Ladock,
	Truro,
	Cornwall TR2 4NQ
tel	01726 884348
fax	01726 884248
e-mail	oxturnhouse@hotmail.com
web	www.oxturnhouse.co.uk

Map 1 Entry 44

Map 1 Entry 45

Cornwall

Creed House

Lally and William have transformed a jungle into one of Cornwall's loveliest gardens, where secret paths tempt you into the woodland's dappled delights. Inside the lovely, big, rambling 1730s rectory, shimmering wooden floors are covered with Persian rugs and light pours into every elegant corner; large guest bedrooms are gloriously furnished with antiques. Breakfasts (feasts of organic and local produce) often turn into an early morning house party, such is Lally's sense of spontaneity and fun. You are in deep, tranquil countryside, and the Eden Project and Heligan are close. *Minimum stay two nights.*

Bosillion

A special set up. Beautiful rooms in your part of the house lead onto a pretty, tiered garden – take out your breakfast and revive gently in the sun. Come for cool calm colours, elegant antiques, a big bedroom and a real sense of privacy. The farmhouse has been in the family since the 1600s and Annabel and Jonathon have renovated thoughtfully and with flair. Your pretty bathroom has Floris soaps and your fridge is filled with all you need: raspberries, walnut bread, local produce. Cooked breakfasts are sometimes available. You are close to Heligan and the beaches of the Roseland peninsular. Wonderful.

rooms	3: 1 twin/double with bath/shower; 2 twins/doubles, both with separate bath.
price	£90. Singles by arrangement.
meals	Pub/restaurant 1 mile.
closed	Christmas & New Year.
directions	From St Austell, A390 to Grampound. Just beyond clock tower, left into Creed Lane. After 1 mile left at grass triangle opp. church. House behind 2nd white gates on left.

rooms	1 suite (twin/double & breakfast room) with bath.
price	£70-£80.
meals	Excellent local restaurants.
closed	Christmas & New Year.
directions	From Truro, A390 for St Austell. 6 miles on, through Grampound; on leaving village, at top of hill, right at speed limit sign into Bosillion Lane. House 150 yds on left.

Lally & William Croggon
Creed House,
Creed,
Grampound,
Truro,
Cornwall TR2 4SL
tel   01872 530372

Jonathon & Annabel Croggon
Bosillion,
Bosillion Lane,
Grampound,
Truro,
Cornwall TR2 4QY
tel   01726 883327

Map 1 Entry 46

Map 1 Entry 47

Cornwall

Tregoose

Surrounded by a two-acre garden full of treasures (open to the public, by appointment and under the National Gardens Scheme), a classical late-Regency English country house that contains the occasional hint of eastern promise. Alison, charming and unstuffy, serves you tea in the drawing room where a Chinese cabinet graces one wall. In the dining room is a Malaysian inscribed silk-screen – a thank-you present from Empire days. Light, roomy bedrooms have elegance and style, gorgeous garden views and super bathrooms. The Eden Project and Heligan are nearby.

Bodrugan Barton

Everything's just right – the setting, the windy lanes, the gentle activity of the farm, the delightful hosts who look after you with such enthusiasm. What's more, there are freshly decorated bedrooms, good bathrooms, family antiques and the promise of good food. The dining room is huge: even with sofas and a woodburner, you could turn a cartwheel. An ancient lane leads to Colona Bay: small, secluded and full of rock pools. There's an indoor pool and sauna, too, and Heligan and the Eden Project nearby. Blissful. *Children over 12 welcome. Guided walks by arrangement.*

rooms	3: 1 twin, 1 four-poster, both with bath; 1 double with separate bath.
price	£74–£98. Singles by arrangement.
meals	Dinner, 4 courses, £27. BYO. Good pub & restaurant within 4 miles.
closed	Christmas & Easter.
directions	A30 for Truro, at Fraddon bypass left for Grampound Rd. After 5 miles, right onto A390 for Truro; 100 yds, right where double white lines end. Between reflector posts to house, 200 yds down lane.

rooms	3: 1 double with shower; 1 double, 1 twin, both with separate bath/shower.
price	£75. Singles £37.50.
meals	Supper £15. BYO wine. Good pubs/restaurants a 10-minute walk.
closed	Christmas & New Year.
directions	St Austell B3273 for Mevagissey. At x-roads on hill, right to Heligan, avoiding Mevagissey. Through Gorran, bend left to Portmellon. After 1.5 miles, right at grass triangle into farm, before hill.

	Alison O'Connor
	Tregoose,
	Grampound,
	Truro,
	Cornwall TR2 4DB
tel	01726 882460
fax	01872 222427
web	www.tregoose.co.uk

	Sally & Tim Kendall
	Bodrugan Barton,
	Mevagissey,
	Cornwall PL26 6PT
tel	01726 842094
e-mail	bodruganbarton@ukonline.co.uk
web	www.bodrugan.com

Map 1 Entry 48

Map 1 Entry 49

Cornwall

The Old Library

Follow wiggly streets to the centre of Fowey and this classical townhouse. Step off the street, through the elegant front door and all changes. Inside is big, white and open-plan: stripped floors, clean lines, modern art and period pieces. The bedroom is a calm space of white with pretty linen and antiques, and there's a double-ended bath. Breakfasts are organic and Aga-cooked, and you may return to find Cecilia baking with her children. Close to beaches, Cornish gardens and places to eat, this is comfortable, relaxed and stylish shared living. And there's a peaceful walled garden.

rooms	1 twin/double with shared bath.
price	£60. Singles from £30.
meals	Pubs & restaurants nearby.
closed	Rarely.
directions	From A3082 to Fowey, follow signs to town centre. Left at 'Safe Harbour' pub steeply down Brown's Hill. House at bottom before church, 2 white lions outside.

Cecilia & Tom Varcoe
The Old Library,
Church Avenue, Fowey,
Cornwall PL23 1BU
tel   01726 833532
fax   01726 555920

Map 1 Entry 50

Collon Barton

Come for the position, the breakfasts round the large Cornish slate table, and the family. High up on a grassy hillside, with phenomenal views over unspoiled countryside and the pretty creekside village of Lerryn, lies this most intriguing and unusual 18th-century farmhouse. It is a working sheep farm and an artistic household, with cheerful bedrooms on the second floor and an elegant drawing room for guests. Anne sells huge dried hydrangeas and, on sunny days, welcomes you with tea in the summerhouse. Walks are fantastic, and the Eden Project 20 minutes away. *Children & pets by arrangement.*

rooms	2: 1 twin with shower; 1 twin/double with bath/shower.
price	£66-£70. Singles from £40.
meals	Pub 5-minute walk; restaurants a 10-minute drive.
closed	Christmas.
directions	From Plymouth A38; A390 to Lostwithiel. Ignore Lerryn signs until 500 yds *after* Lostwithiel sign, then left signed 'Lerryn, 3'; left after 300 yds, signed Lerryn. Left for Couch's Mill, 1st left into cul-de-sac, up lane for 0.25 miles.

Anne & Iain Mackie
Collon Barton,
Lerryn,
Lostwithiel,
Cornwall PL22 0NX
tel   01208 872908
fax   01208 873812
e-mail   iainmackie@btconnect.com

Map 1 Entry 51

Cornwall

Allhays

A 1939 dower house built by the artist Sir Francis Cook; he was a frequent exhibitor at the Royal Academy and married seven times. He chose the plot well: other houses have a sea view but these have you rooted to the spot. The Rosiers were hoteliers once upon a time, and their home is a smart retreat; in the bedrooms are pretty fabrics and soft creams, mineral water, bathrobes and wild flowers. Breakfasts in the conservatory overlooking the bay are a feast of home-baked breads and brioche, homemade marmalade and jams, eggs Benedict courtesy of their hens, smoked haddock from the Aga.

Sheviock Barton

This is Cornwall's 'Forgotten Corner' and the countryside is gorgeous. The house is opposite the church, rooted in time and space, its massive walls echoing their 400 years of history. All is welcoming and comfortable within, from the farmhouse kitchen, with its blue Aga and Welsh dresser, to the elegant and flagstoned sitting room. There, Library Red walls contrast with heavy calico curtains, off-white sofas and church candles. Bedrooms have crisp cotton and great comfort. Your hosts are relaxed and fun and there is a games room too, with bar billiards and table tennis. Good value.

rooms	4: 1 double, 1 twin/double, both with bath; 1 double, 1 twin/double, both with shower.
price	£60-£90. Singles from £45.
meals	Good restaurants within 5 miles.
closed	Christmas.
directions	From Looe towards Polperro; 2nd turning to Talland, on left after 2 miles; on down lane for 1 mile.

rooms	3: 1 double with bath & shower; 1 double with shower; 1 family/twin with shower (extra bed).
price	From £60. Singles £35.
meals	Pub/restaurant 0.5 miles.
closed	Christmas & Boxing Day.
directions	To Sheviock on A374. House opposite church.

Mr & Mrs B Rosier
Allhays,
Porthallow,
Talland Bay,
Looe,
Cornwall PL13 2JB
tel   01503 273188/272434
e-mail info@allhays.co.uk
web   www.allhays.co.uk

Carol & Tony Johnson
Sheviock Barton,
Sheviock,
Torpoint,
Cornwall PL11 3EH
tel   01503 230793
e-mail thebarton@sheviock.freeserve.co.uk
web   www.sheviockbarton.co.uk

Map 1 Entry 52

Map 1 Entry 53

Cornwall

Erth Barton

Everyone is bowled over by this house and its approach; open to three tidal estuaries, it makes your heart leap. The listed manor, casually grand, has its own chapel; a 14th-century fresco still clings to the walls. The rooms are stuffed with interesting books, pictures and some comfortably faded, fine antiques. Guy is an easy, affable host and passionate about horses and books. Bedrooms, reached via a choice of four staircases, are not swish, but bright with a lived-in feel, beautiful carved and cane bedheads, old rugs. Come with a bunch of friends, stay for dinner, have a ball. *Children over 12 welcome.*

Lantallack Farm

Life and art exist in happy communion: Nicky loves playing the piano and runs courses in landscape painting and sculpture. This is a heart-warming place – hens in the orchard, fine breakfasts in the walled garden, a super outdoor pool, a straw-yellow sitting room with a log fire… and bedrooms with delicious beds and books galore. The gorgeous old Georgian farmhouse has breathtaking views over countryside, streams and wooded valleys. Set off to discover the Walkers' leat-side trail, and make a fuss of Polly, the Gloucester Old Spot pig, on the way. You will be inspired.

rooms	3: 2 doubles, both with bath; 1 twin with separate bath.
price	£80. Singles £50.
meals	Dinner £25. BYO.
closed	Rarely.
directions	From Plymouth A38, cross Tamar Bridge. Thro' bypass tunnel over r'bout. At top of next hill left to Trematon; thro' village. Right at fork. After 2 miles, white cottage with post box, signed right.

rooms	2: 1 double with shower; 1 twin with separate bath.
price	£70–£80. Singles by arrangement.
meals	Good pubs & restaurants 1 mile.
closed	Very occasionally.
directions	A38 through Saltash & on for 3 miles. At Landrake 2nd right at West Lane. After 1 mile, left at white cottage for Tideford. House 150 yds on, on right.

	Guy Bentinck
	Erth Barton,
	Saltash,
	Cornwall PL12 4QY
tel	01752 842127
fax	01752 842127
e-mail	erthbarton@aol.com

	Nicky Walker
	Lantallack Farm,
	Landrake,
	Saltash,
	Cornwall PL12 5AE
tel	01752 851281
fax	01752 851281
e-mail	lantallack@ukgateway.net
web	www.lantallack.co.uk

Map 1 Entry 54

Map 2 Entry 55

Cornwall

Hornacott

The garden, in its lovely valley setting, has seats in little corners poised to catch the evening sun – perfect for a pre-dinner drink. The peaceful house is named after the hill and you have a private entrance to your wonderfully fresh and airy suite: a twin-bedded room and a large, square, high sitting room with windows that look down onto the wooded valley. You also have a CD player, music, chocolates and magazines and feel beautifully self-contained. Jos, a kitchen designer, and Mary-Anne clearly enjoy having guests, and give you fresh local produce and free-range eggs for breakfast.

North Tamerton House

Overlooking the upper reaches of the Tamar, peacefully poised between two counties, this fine old Cornish rectory has stunning views to Dartmoor 25 miles away yet is only 10 miles from the dramatic Atlantic coast. It is surrounded by lawned gardens with clematis and roses, a camellia walk and ancient beeches which lead to a grassed tennis court, now used for croquet. Inside are large, well-proportioned rooms where period colours set off fine furniture and sumptuous fabrics. Your welcoming hosts – Jane, an art historian, Stephen, a keen golfer – can tell you about interesting places to visit.

	Hornacott		North Tamerton House
rooms	1 suite (twin) with bath/shower; child single next door, if required.	rooms	2: 1 double with bath & shower; 1 twin with separate shower.
price	From £70. Singles £45.	price	£65-£75. Singles £40-£45.
meals	Dinner, 3 courses, £18. BYO.	meals	Dinner, 3-4 courses, £19.50-£22.50.
closed	Christmas.	closed	Rarely.
directions	B3254 Launceston-Liskeard. Through South Petherwin, down steep hill, last left before little bridge. House 1st on left.	directions	From Launceston, B3254 towards Bude. After 9 miles, right signed North Tamerton. After 2 miles, at small x-roads with phone box, right signed Boyton; entrance 50 yds on right.

Jos & Mary-Anne Otway-Ruthven
Hornacott,
South Petherwin,
Launceston,
Cornwall PL15 7LH
tel   01566 782461
fax   01566 782461
e-mail   stay@hornacott.co.uk
web   www.hornacott.co.uk

Stephen & Jane Rhodes
North Tamerton House,
North Tamerton,
Cornwall EX22 6SA
tel   01409 271284
e-mail   smrhodes@btinternet.com

Map 1 Entry 56

Map 2 Entry 57

Cornwall

The Old Vicarage

The first sight of quirky chimneys – the spires of former owner Reverend Hawker's parish churches – sets the scene for a house of theatricality. Jill, Richard and their home burst with knowledge on the eccentric vicar, local history and Victoriana. Rooms are casually grand, dotted with *objets* – brass gramophone, magic lantern, policemen's helmets. Browse books in the study, play the drawing room grand piano, sip brandy over billiards. Bedrooms are country-house pretty, bathrooms clean if cheerfully dated. Views reach to the sea. Walk off breakfast along the cliffs. Mobiles don't work. Bliss.

Manor Farm

The Domesday-listed property of William the Conqueror's half-brother sits alongside fine outbuildings in a glorious garden with manicured lawns: the setting is stunning, and totally surprising. Inside there is sober luxury. Muriel runs the house with irreproachable efficiency and you're welcome to use the music and drawing rooms and help yourself to a drink at the honesty bar. There are fine paintings, stone-silled windows onto garden views, carefully decorated rooms. An immaculate, peaceful, totally English home. Magnificent coastal walks and beaches abound.

	The Old Vicarage
rooms	3: 1 double with bath; 1 twin with bath & shower; 1 single with shower.
price	£70. Single £35.
meals	Dinner, 3 courses, £25. Suppers available. Good pubs nearby.
closed	December–January.
directions	From A39 at Morwenstow, follow signs towards church. Small turning on right, just before church, marked 'public footpath'. Drive down to house.

	Manor Farm
rooms	2: 1 twin, 1 double, both with bath/shower.
price	£70–£80. Singles £40–£45.
meals	Pub 1 mile.
closed	Christmas Day.
directions	From Wainhouse Corner on A39, follow sign to Crackington Haven. At beach, turn inland, uphill, for 1 mile, left into Church Park Rd & 1st right into lane.

	Jill & Richard Wellby The Old Vicarage, Morwenstow, Cornwall EX23 9SR
tel	01288 331369
fax	01288 356077
e-mail	jillwellby@hotmail.com
web	www.rshawker.co.uk

	Muriel Knight Manor Farm, Crackington Haven, Bude, Cornwall EX23 0JW
tel	01840 230304

Map 1 Entry 58

Map 1 Entry 59

Cornwall

Trevigue

Built around a cobbled courtyard and tucked into a sheltered hollow, Trevigue hunkers down against the gustiness of the North Cornish coast. Inside, dark polished country furniture, stone mullions, flagstones and slate: a timeless feel. Bedrooms are white-walled, carpeted and beamed, bedcovers floral and breakfasts local, generous and good. Step across the courtyard to the family's restaurant for fresh, seasonal dinners. The family is passionate about the area; head for Strangles Cove for seclusion and Crackington beach – big at low tide – for buckets and spades. *Children over 12 welcome.*

Upton Farm

A restored farmhouse set back from the rugged coastline with unrivalled views, from Tintagel to Port Isaac and the Rumps beyond… the sunsets are unforgettable. Bedrooms are smart yet fresh and restful and your hosts wonderful. Slate slabs in the hall, gentle colours throughout; from the depths of the sea-green sofa in your drawing room, breathe in those AONB views. Such seclusion! Yet 10 minutes across fields is the coastal path and, nearby, serious surfing, great pub, restaurant and more – over the best of breakfasts, just ask your hosts. *Children eight and over welcome. Safe storage for surfing equipment.*

	Trevigue
rooms	3: 2 doubles, 1 twin, all with shower.
price	£75. Singles £45.
meals	Dinner available Fri/Sat in farmhouse restaurant.
closed	December & January.
directions	From Crackington Haven follow coastal road keeping sea on right. Up hill & right for Trevigue. Farm 1.5 miles on left on top of cliffs.

	Upton Farm
rooms	3: 1 double with bath/shower; 1 double, 1 twin, both with shower.
price	£70-£80. Singles from £50.
meals	Good pub & restaurant 1 mile.
closed	Rarely.
directions	In Delabole, past Atlantic Garage on left; right into Treligga Downs Rd; 0.5 miles to T-junc; turn right. 1 mile on, pass Trecarne Farm on left; 100 yds, house on right.

	Janet Crocker
	Trevigue,
	Crackington Haven,
	Bude,
	Cornwall EX23 0LQ
tel	01840 230418
fax	01840 230418
e-mail	trevigue@talk21.com
web	www.trevigue.co.uk

	Elizabeth & Ricardo Dorich
	Upton Farm,
	Trebarwith,
	Delabole,
	Cornwall PL33 9DG
tel	01840 770225
fax	01840 770377
e-mail	ricardo@dorich.co.uk
web	www.upton-farm.co.uk

Map 1 Entry 60

Map 1 Entry 61

Cornwall

Porteath Barn

Fantastic walks start from the door and a path leads through woods to the delightful Epphaven Cove at the bottom of the valley. What a spot! This upside-down house is impeccable. It is elegantly uncluttered and cool, new seagrass contrasts with old oak and the downstairs bedrooms, though not vast, have fresh flowers, quilted bedspreads and doors to the garden. The shower room – a mix of rusty red and Italian marble – is magnificent. The Bloors have perfected the art of B&B-ing, being kind and helpful without being instrusive. You may well leave as friends.
Children over 12 or by arrangement.

Roskear

Rosina modestly refers to her "simple cottage B&B" but this is just perfect for families with all the attractions 10 minutes by car. A large guest sitting room with a log fire, a warm and smiling hostess, estuary views, happy dogs, clucking hens – this is country Cornwall at its most charming. There's a sunny spot in the garden for summer breakfasts served on blue china, 30 acres of woodland and 40 of grassland to explore – and space to unload sporting gear and gumboots. Note the Camel cycle trail is nearby and you can hire bikes in Padstow or Wadebridge. Uncomplicated, good value B&B.

rooms	3: 1 double, 2 twins/doubles, sharing 1 bath & 1 shower.
price	From £60. Singles by arrangement.
meals	Pub 1.5 miles.
closed	Rarely.
directions	A39 to Wadebridge. At r'bout follow signs to Polzeath, then to Porteath Bee Centre. Through Bee Centre shop car park, down farm track; house signed on right after 150 yds.

rooms	2: 1 double with separate bath; 1 double sharing bath (let to same party only).
price	From £60. Singles £30.
meals	Excellent pubs/restaurants 0.5-6 miles.
closed	Rarely.
directions	Bypass Wadebridge on A39 for Redruth. Over bridge, pass Esso garage on left; then first right to Edmonton. By modern houses turn immed. right to Roskear over cattle grid.

Jo & Michael Bloor
Porteath Barn,
St Minver,
Wadebridge,
Cornwall PL27 6RA

tel	01208 863605
fax	01208 863954
e-mail	mbloor@ukonline.co.uk

Rosina Messer-Bennetts
Roskear,
St Breock,
Wadebridge,
Cornwall PL27 7HU

| tel | 01208 812805 |
| e-mail | rosina@roskear.com |

Map 1 Entry 62

Map 1 Entry 63

Cornwall

Tremoren

Views stretch sleepily over the Cornish countryside. You might feel inclined to do nothing more than snooze over your book on the terrace, but the north coast beaches, surfing, cycling (the Camel Trail) and the Eden Project are all close by. The stone and slate former farmhouse has been smartly updated with light, airy rooms – all soft colours, pretty china and crisp bed linen – and swish, power-shower bathrooms. A panelled, red-walled sitting room, full of books and interesting maps, leads out on to the flower-filled terrace; perfect for that evening drink. Lanie is bubbly and engaging.

rooms	1 double with bath/shower.
price	£80.
meals	Dinner, 4 courses, £25.
closed	Rarely.
directions	A39 to St Kew Highway through village; left at Red Lion. Down lane, 1st left round sharp right-hand bend. 2nd drive on right; signed.

Philip & Lanie Calvert
Tremoren,
St Kew,
Bodmin,
Cornwall PL30 3HA

tel	01208 841790
fax	01208 841031
e-mail	la.calvert@btopenworld.com
web	www.virtually-there.net/tremoren

Map 1 Entry 64

Polrode Mill Cottage

A lovely, solid, beamy, 17th-century cottage in a birdsung valley. Inside, flagged floors, chesterfields, a woodburner and a light open feel. Your friendly young hosts live next door; they are working hard on the informal flower and vegetable garden, much of the produce is used in David's delicious homemade dinners, and there's pumpkin marmalade and eggs from the hens. Bedrooms are cottage-cosy with stripped floors, comfy wrought-iron beds and silver cast-iron radiators; fresh bathrooms have double-ended roll-top baths. A slight hum of traffic outside but no matter, inside it is blissfully peaceful.

rooms	3: 2 doubles with bath/shower; 1 double with bath.
price	£72–£90. Singles £55.
meals	Dinner, 3 courses, £25.
closed	Rarely.
directions	From A395 take A39 towards Camelford. Through Camelford; continue on A39 to Knightsmill. From there, 1.8 miles up on left-hand side.

Deborah Hilborne
& David Edwards
Polrode Mill Cottage,
Allen Valley,
St Tudy, Bodmin,
Cornwall PL30 3NS

tel	01208 850203
e-mail	polrode@tesco.net
web	www.polrodemillcottage.co.uk

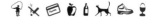

Map 1 Entry 65

Cornwall

Bokelly

Easy to see why Sir John Betjeman and historian A L Rowse loved this 16th-century manor – and the walks that surround it. It is so relaxed and unselfconsciously beautiful. Delightful hosts, an Elizabethan tithe barn, a wonderful garden with croquet, tennis and special trees add to the magic. The interior is an exhilarating mix of the traditional and the exotic, with more than a touch of luxury. Late afternoon sun streams into the drawing room, illuminating yellow stencilled walls, fine pictures and a vast fireplace. The Eden Project and the gardens of Pencarrow and Lanhydrock are an easy drive.

Lavethan

An exquisite house in a magical setting: 33 acres of ancient woods, Celtic crosses, a holy well and a delightful water garden. Catherine has decorated the house (part 15th-century) with flair, matching fabrics and antique pieces. One bedroom — part of the old chapel — has interesting stone lintels; all are sunny, with proper bathrooms and lovely old baths for wallowing at the end of the day. Catherine is a warm hostess and her guest sitting room full of books and flowers; there's a piano, too. In the walled garden, amid lavender, rosemary and yew, is a heated pool. *Children over 10 welcome.*

rooms	2: 1 double with bath; 1 twin with separate bath & shower.
price	From £70. Singles by arrangement.
meals	Excellent pub 1 mile.
closed	Rarely.
directions	On A39, 7 miles south of Camelford at St Kew Highway, through village on Trelill Rd (avoid St Kew); 1 mile; past white cottage on right, left over cattle grid past white bungalow; 0.25 miles down drive.

rooms	3: 2 doubles, both with separate bath; 1 twin/double with bath.
price	£70-£90. Singles £40-£50.
meals	Dinner £25. Pub 0.25 miles.
closed	Rarely.
directions	From A30, turn for Blisland. There, past church on left & pub on right. Take lane at bottom left of village green. 0.25 miles on, drive on left (granite pillars & cattle grid).

	Maggie Gordon Clark
	Bokelly,
	St Kew,
	Bodmin,
	Cornwall PL30 3DY
tel	01208 850325
e-mail	bokelly@gordonclark.freeserve.co.uk

	Christopher & Catherine Hartley
	Lavethan,
	Blisland,
	Bodmin,
	Cornwall PL30 4QG
tel	01208 850487
fax	01208 851387
e-mail	chrishartley@btconnect.com
web	www.lavethan.com

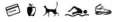

Map 1 Entry 66

Map 1 Entry 67

Cornwall

Higher Lank Farm
St Breward, Bodmin, Cornwall PL30 4NB

From January to October you may only come if you have a child under five! This is a marvellous, unpretentious haven for families. Children adore playing in the roofed sandpit and miniature farmyard, there are piglets and chicks, a pony to groom and eggs to collect. Nursery teas begin at 5pm (and don't miss cream teas in the garden) and Lucy will babysit while you slink off later to the local pub – the highest in Cornwall. One bedroom is modern with new pine; the other two are more traditional. Celtic crosses in the garden and original panelling hint at the house's 500 year history. A rare family treat.

Leave the nappies at home. Lucy can lend you re-usable nappies free of charge for your baby's holiday; she promotes them to reduce the amount of waste that is sent to landfill sites. Bio-degradable nappies are also composted. There's a laundry service, too. Recycling is taken seriously here, with special bins provided. The new 'nursery rhyme' barns are being completed using the highest-spec insulation available, underfloor heating saves on oil consumption and woodburning stoves use logs from their woods.

rooms	3 family rooms, all with bath/shower.
price	From £70. Singles by arrangement.
meals	Supper £14.75. Packed lunch £6.50. Nursery tea £3.75.
closed	November-Easter.
directions	From Launceston, A395, then A39 through Camelford. Left onto B3266 to Bodmin. 4 miles on, left signed Wenfordbridge Pottery; over bridge, past pottery & on brow of hill, left into lane; house at top.

Lucy Finnemore
tel 01208 850716
email a_finnemore@lineone.net
web www.higherlankfarm.co.uk

SPECIAL GREEN ENTRY
see page 12

Map 1 Entry 68

Cornwall

Cabilla Manor

Rich, exotic rugs, cushions and artefacts from around the world, and Louella's sumptuous hand-stencilled fabrics and furniture. There's a treasure round every corner of this fine old manor on the edge of Bodmin Moor, and an opera house in one of the barns. Huge beds, coir on the floors and garden flowers in your rooms, a dining room crammed floor to ceiling with books, many of them Robin's (a writer and explorer). A lofty conservatory for meals overlooks elegant lawns, garden and tennis court; the views are heavenly, the hosts wonderful and the final mile thrillingly wild.

Trewardale

Charles's ancestors built the house in 1744 — now a Grade II*-listed gem packed with detail and delight, whose owners are happy to share its faded, much-loved patina. Meet the relatives over breakfast — they look down from every wall — or relax over a game of backgammon by a log fire. Bathrooms are nicely old-fashioned with lovely new towels; bedrooms have space and glorious views across the sheep-dotted valley. The nine bird-sung acres, Victoria's delight, have a lake and 30 types of magnolia, and the village possesses a real ale pub and a beautiful church — one of John Betjeman's favourites.

rooms	4: 1 double with bath; 2 doubles, 1 twin, sharing 2 baths.
price	£80. Singles £40.
meals	Dinner, 3 courses, £20. Pub 4 miles.
closed	Christmas & New Year.
directions	6 miles after Jamaica Inn on A30, left for Cardinham. Through Millpool & straight on, ignoring further signs to Cardinham. After 2.5 miles, left to Manor 0.75 miles; on right down drive.

rooms	2: 1 twin with bath/shower; 1 double with separate bath/shower.
price	£60-£70. Singles £35.
meals	Packed lunch by arrangement. Pub 1 mile; good restaurants nearby.
closed	Rarely.
directions	A30 towards Bodmin, turn towards Blisland. At T-junction left (ignoring signpost to Blisland); down to bottom of hill, right up drive.

Robin & Louella Hanbury-Tenison
Cabilla Manor,
Mount,
Bodmin,
Cornwall PL30 4DW

tel	01208 821224
fax	01208 821267
e-mail	louella@cabilla.co.uk
web	www.cabilla.co.uk

Victoria & Charles Edward-Collins
Trewardale,
Blisland,
Bodmin,
Cornwall PL30 4HS

tel	01208 821226
fax	01208 821766
e-mail	vec@trewardale.com

Map 1   Entry 69

Map 1   Entry 70

Cornwall

Higher Tregawne

Micky and Gelda farm 450 acres at the head of the beautiful Ruthern Valley. There are stunning views, grassy fields, grazing cattle and gentle horses; laze in the garden hammock, drink in the peace. The farmhouse is as charming as its owners and Gelda has decorated with generosity and flair: fine fabrics hang at the windows, bathroom towels are soft, floors gleam and one of the bedrooms is in its own wing. Gelda is in her element running B&B and does it well; her meals have been highly praised, and breakfasts may be taken into the garden in summer. *Children by arrangement.*

The Old Vicarage

Tea in the garden or the drawing room when you arrive; Graham and Sarah are easy-going hosts and make you feel at home. The grandeur is soft: Empire sofa, good oils, faded rugs on wooden floors, lovely lamps, an old oak chest – just what you might hope for from a 1780s, creeper-smothered vicarage... not forgetting, in the dining room, Sydney the polar bear skin rug. Bedrooms have good period furniture, fresh flowers, a quilted bedspread; the children's room, off the twin, with its miniature beds, is charming. Breakfast on local produce, taken at your leisure. Rock and Polzeath are nearby.

rooms	2 doubles, both with separate bath.
price	£80. Singles £40.
meals	Dinner, 3 courses, £20-£25. Pubs & restaurants 4 miles.
closed	Rarely.
directions	From M5, A30 to r'bout south of Bodmin. On A30 for Redruth. 2.2 miles on, right to Withiel. Through Withiel, down hill, over bridge, left at T-junc., for Wadebridge. Drive on right, 0.5 mile on.

rooms	2: 1 double suite, 1 twin with children's room, both with bath.
price	£60-£65.
meals	Good pub 200 yds.
closed	Christmas Day.
directions	From Wadebridge, B3314 for Rock & Polzeath. After 3.5 miles, left for St Minver. In village, left into cul-de-sac just before Four Ways Inn. House at bottom on left.

Gelda Madden
Higher Tregawne,
Withiel,
Bodmin,
Cornwall PL30 5NS

tel   01208 831257
e-mail   highertregawne@btinternet.com

Graham & Sarah Tyson
The Old Vicarage,
St Minver,
Rock,
Cornwall PL27 6QH

tel   01208 862951
fax   01208 863578
e-mail   g.tyson2@tiscali.co.uk

Map 1 Entry 71

Map 1 Entry 72

Cornwall

Ballaminers House

Stone slabs, planked floors and deep sash windows with field views in this dear little house five minutes from Padstow. Generous, artistic Amanda serves delicious breakfasts in a duck-egg-blue room elegant with fresh flowers and small chandelier. Cottage-sized bedrooms are spotless and charming: the light, slopey-ceilinged double wears modern checks; the Cath Kidston-styled twin is snug; the bathroom spoils you with its roll-top bath, toileteries and Indonesian dressing gowns. In the garden is a series of hedged 'rooms' that provide flowers for every bedroom.

Mother Ivey Cottage

So close to the sea that there are salt splashes on the windows! Exceptionally lovely hosts here and a simple refuge from crashing surf and Atlantic winds. Look out of the window to the big blue below, swim to the lifeboat launch, barbecue on the beach. The coastal path is stunning and you can walk to magnificent surfing beaches or just drop down to the quiet bay beneath your window. The cottage, which has been in the family for four generations, was once a fish cellar for processing catches. Bedrooms really are unfrilly – it's the views that will rivet you, and your hosts' kindness. Families will love it.

rooms	3: 2 doubles, 1 twin, sharing 2 bathrooms.
price	£60-£70. Singles £55-£70.
meals	Excellent pubs/restaurants 5-minute drive.
closed	Never.
directions	A39 after Wadebridge, signed A389 Padstow. Reach Little Petherick; over hump bridge to whitewashed cottage at corner of unmarked lane; left up lane bearing right; on right, opp. pink house.

rooms	2 twins, both with bath (extra single bed optional).
price	From £60. Singles by arrangement.
meals	Dinner from £18. Packed lunch from £5.
closed	Rarely.
directions	From St Merryn, right for Trevose Head. Over sleeping policemen. After toll gate ticket machine, right through farm gate. On towards sea; cottage gate at end, on right.

Amanda Fearon
Ballaminers House,
Little Petherick,
Padstow,
Cornwall PL27 7QT

tel	01841 540933
fax	01841 540933
e-mail	pandafearon@aol.com
web	www.ballaminershouse.co.uk

Phyllida & Antony Woosnam-Mills
Mother Ivey Cottage,
Trevose Head,
Padstow,
Cornwall PL28 8SL

tel	01841 520329
e-mail	woosnammills@compuserve.com

Map 1 Entry 73

Map 1 Entry 74

Cumbria

The Kennels

At the end of a long, rough track, surrounded by Cumbrian miles, this double-winged house with immaculate lawns. It was built for a gamekeeper c.1745 and the wings are new additions. Here the bedrooms lie; fresh and well-presented with harmonious colours and pretty touches – a hand-painted Chinese table, an ornate mirror, feather duvets and embroidered pillow cases. And there's an elegant guest sitting room with powder-blue sofas and views that stretch to the Lakes and the Scottish Hills. Your hosts will fill you in on field sports, walks and horseracing... why not visit the course at Carlisle?

Sirelands

White, 18th-century and pretty, Sirelands was a gardener's cottage. It stands among spreading trees on a sunny, peaceful slope, lifting its eyes to the fells. A stream runs through the gardens, regularly visited by roe deer, red squirrels and an array of birds. The Carrs have lived here for over 35 years and the house has an attractive, lived-in feel. The pale green dining room is delightfully full of books and old, well-polished country furniture; the bedrooms are pleasant and comfortable. Angela loves cooking and much of the fruit and veg is home-grown. Game and venison are sometimes available.

rooms	2: 1 twin/double with bath/shower; 1 twin with separate bath.
price	£80. Singles £40.
meals	Supper, 2 courses, £15. Pub/restaurant 2 miles.
closed	Christmas & New Year.
directions	M6 exit 44; A7 to Longtown. There, 3rd right towards Netherby & Pentow; 2 miles to signed drive on right.

rooms	2: 1 double with separate bath/shower; 1 twin with bath/shower.
price	£70.
meals	Dinner, 2-3 courses, £20-£25. Two pubs 1.5 miles.
closed	Rarely.
directions	M6 north to junc. 43; A69 Newcastle; 3 miles to traffic lights. Right, on to Head's Nook; house 2 miles after village.

Serena Graham
The Kennels,
Netherby,
Longtown,
Cumbria CA6 5PD
tel   01228 791262
fax   01228 792959
e-mail   sj@graham-kennels.fsnet.co.uk
web   www.netherbyestate.co.uk

Angela Carr
Sirelands,
Head's Nook,
Brampton,
Carlisle,
Cumbria CA8 9BT
tel   01228 670389
mobile   07748 101513
e-mail   carr_sirelands@btconnect.com

Map 11 Entry 75

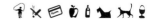

Map 12 Entry 76

Cumbria

The Old Rectory

The setting of this lovely old house could hardly be more pastoral. Many of its rooms face south and have superb views, with stunning mountains and fells beyond. History has created an intriguing house full of unexpected corners; the old rectory dates from around 1360 but bedrooms are big and airy and the beds huge. Gill cooks in imaginative 'bistro' style; David is a wine expert and has amassed a collection of corkscrews. They're relaxed, enthusiastic and full of plans: wine tasting and Aga-cookery weekends for a start. Outside, red squirrels, a croquet lawn and views of Skiddaw.

High Houses

Exceptional style in this 1669 yeoman's house, to a background of bare stone, inglenooks, flagged floors, chunky beams and wooden floors. Electricity is supplied by battery and generator, bedrooms are simple with unexpected touches. One has a four-poster, another a cerise velvet eiderdown and cream, gold and brown colourings; and there's a cockloft for children to play in. Jill is intent on your having a good time and gives you home-cured bacon, local sausages, free-range eggs, home-grown organic veg. There's a shoot on the farm and venison, game or trout may appear on the menu. Special.

	The Old Rectory	High Houses
rooms	3: 1 double, 1 twin/double both with shower; 1 double with separate bath.	3: 2 twins/doubles with mezzanine for children, sharing bath/shower; 1 four-poster with bath/shower.
price	From £84. Singles from £42.	£80. Singles £50.
meals	Dinner, 3 courses, £23. Good pub 15-20 minutes drive.	Dinner, 2-4 courses, £15-£25. Lunch £10-£15. Packed lunch £5.
closed	Christmas & New Year.	Rarely.
directions	B5305 to Wigton; at A595, left. After 5 miles, left to Boltongate. Left at T-junction; in village, signs for Ireby; down hill, last driveway on left.	On A591, 2 miles after Castle Inn Hotel right for Ireby. After 2 miles, steep hill & squirrel signs; right over cattle grid for Snittlegarth, bear right after 2nd grid; house 0.5 miles up lane; pass barn on left.

Gill & David Taylor
The Old Rectory,
Boltongate,
Ireby,
Cumbria CA7 1DA

tel	01697 371647
fax	01697 371798
e-mail	boltongate@talk21.com
web	www.boltongateoldrectory.com

Miss Jill Green
High Houses,
Snittlegarth,
Ireby,
Wigton,
Cumbria CA7 1HE

tel	01697 371549
e-mail	enquiries@highhouses.co.uk
web	www.highhouses.co.uk

Map 11 Entry 77

Map 11 Entry 78

Cumbria

Willow Cottage

Gaze across rooftops through tiny windows towards the towering mass of Skiddaw, the Lakes' third highest mountain. Here is a miniature cottage garden with sweet peas, herbs, vegetables and flowers... all suitably rambling. Lovely Roy and Chris have kept most of the old barn's features – wooden floorboards, wonderful beams. Dried flowers, pretty china, antique linen, glowing lamps and patchwork quilts, a collection of christening gowns... dear little bedrooms have panelled bathrooms and dreamy views. TV is delightfully absent, classical music plays and you are right in the village.

New House Farm

The large, comfortable beds, the linen, the fabrics, the pillows – everything pleases. You'll appreciate the sensitivity of the renovations, too – the plasterwork stops here and there to reveal old beam, slate or stone. Peaceful bedrooms are serenely luxurious and each is named after the mountain that it faces; Swinside brings the 1650s house its own spring water. The gorgeous breakfast room has a woodburner, hunting prints and polished tables for Hazel's breakfasts which will fuel your adventures. Mountain-weary walkers will fall gratefully into the hot spring spa. *Children over six welcome.*

	Willow Cottage
rooms	2: 1 double, 1 twin, both with bath.
price	£50-£55. Singles £35-£37.50.
meals	Inn 300 yds.
closed	December-January.
directions	From Keswick A591 to Carlisle (approx. 6.5 miles). Right at Bassenthwaite Chapel into village (0.5 miles). Straight on at village green for 170 yds.

	New House Farm
rooms	6: 3 doubles, 1 twin/double, 2 four-posters, all with bath/shower.
price	£108-£132. Singles by arrangement.
meals	Dinner £25. Packed lunch £7. Tea rooms next door (Mar-Nov). Pubs 2.5 miles.
closed	Rarely.
directions	From M6 junc. 40 west on A66. Past Keswick, on for Cockermouth. Left at Braithwaite, onto B5292, Whinlatter Pass. Through forest to Lorton. Left onto B5289; 1.5 miles to farm.

	Roy & Chris Beaty
	Willow Cottage,
	Bassenthwaite,
	Keswick,
	Cumbria CA12 4QP
tel	01768 776440
e-mail	chrisbeaty@amserve.com
web	www.willowbarncottage.co.uk

	Hazel Thompson
	New House Farm,
	Lorton,
	Cockermouth,
	Cumbria CA13 9UU
tel	01900 85404
fax	01900 85478
e-mail	hazel@newhouse-farm.co.uk
web	www.newhouse-farm.co.uk

Map 11 Entry 79

Map 11 Entry 80

Cumbria

Park House Farm

A bumpy track reminds you that you have left the everyday behind. Come for uncomplicated country hospitality at its best: communal dining, no standing on ceremony and a delightful hostess. Mary is great fun, down-to-earth and friendly, a real farmer's wife who gives you homemade biscuits in her simple farmhouse bedrooms. Wordsworth's brother-in-law lived here and the great man visited frequently; those views to Barton Fell are as glorious as ever. Bring your walking boots: there are 300 acres, 850 sheep and a lovely walled garden, all in the National Park.

Augill Castle

Huge and surprising – most people arrive unprepared for the scale of it. The 1841 Victorian folly comes with turreted rooms, soaring fairy-tale castle windows and vaulted ceilings. Grand, yes, but intimate too: you'll feel comfortably at home in the drawing room with its tumbling curtains, well-loved antiques, old rugs on polished floors and significant African touches. Bedrooms, too, are historic but homely. No uniforms, no rules, just Wendy, Simon and their staff who ply you with delicious food, scented hot water bottles, big pillows and massive tubs. Fancy getting married here? You can.

rooms	3: 1 double, 1 twin/double, both with shower; 1 double sharing bath.	
price	£52. Singles £26.	
meals	Pub 1 mile, restaurant 3 miles.	
closed	December-February.	
directions	M6 exit 40; A66 west. At r'bout, left on A592. Signs to Dalemain house, through car park into courtyard ignoring 'No Car' signs; right, 0.5 miles; right again, at farm building.	

rooms	10: 4 twins/doubles, 4 doubles, 2 four-posters.
price	£140. Singles £100.
meals	Dinner £35 (Fri/Sat only); can cater for groups.
closed	Never.
directions	M6 junc. 38; A685 through Kirkby Stephen. Just before Brough, right for South Stainmore; signed on left after 1 mile.

Mrs Mary Milburn
Park House Farm,
Dalemain,
Penrith,
Cumbria CA11 0HB
tel   01768 486212
e-mail   mail@parkhousedalemain.freeserve.co.uk
web   www.parkhousedalemain.co.uk

Simon & Wendy Bennett
Augill Castle,
Brough,
Kirkby Stephen,
Cumbria CA17 4DE
tel   01768 341937
e-mail   enquiries@augillcastle.co.uk
web   www.stayinacastle.co.uk

Map 11 Entry 81

Map 12 Entry 82

Cumbria

Coldbeck House

An old mill leat runs through the garden – elegant with trees, populated by woodpeckers and red squirrels. Belle's forte is her cooking and Richard assists with walks; both are natural hosts. The dignified 1820's house with Victorian additions has sanded and polished floors, antiques and splendid stained glass, a guest sitting room with a log-burning stove and a country-house feel. Bedrooms are delightful: expect fresh flowers, homemade biscuits and towels to match colourful walls. It's peaceful here, on the edge of a village with a green, and you are in unsurpassed walking country.

Low Jock Scar

As Low Jock Scar is folded into the leafy valley, so you are wrapped in the warmth of Philip and Alison's welcome. (The 'scar' is the escarpment on the far side of the stream.) This is a homely country guest house, built of stone, with a conservatory, cosy sitting area and bright, attractive bedrooms. The six acres of woodland and gardens are the Midwinters' pride and joy – a delight for guests to explore. Enjoy a feast at dinner – the food is wonderful: fresh with local produce – then wander down the garden to contemplate your life on the bank of the burbling beck.

	Coldbeck House
rooms	3: 2 doubles, 1 twin all with bath/shower.
price	£70. Singles £40.
meals	Dinner, 2-4 courses, £10-£25. Pubs within 5-minute walk.
closed	Christmas & New Year.
directions	M6 exit 38; A685 to Kirkby Stephen; 6 miles, then right to Ravenstonedale. 1st left opp. Kings Head pub; drive immed. on left.

	Low Jock Scar
rooms	4: 1 twin, 1 double, both with bath; 1 double with shower; 1 twin/double with separate bath.
price	£54-£66. Singles from £37.
meals	Dinner, 5 courses, £21. Packed lunch £4.
closed	November-mid-March.
directions	From Kendal, A6 to Penrith. After 5 miles, Plough Inn on left. After 1 mile turn into lane on left.

Belle Hepworth
Coldbeck House,
Ravenstonedale,
Kirkby Stephen,
Cumbria CA17 4LW
tel   015396 23407
e-mail   belle@coldbeckhouse.co.uk
web   www.coldbeckhouse.co.uk

Alison & Philip Midwinter
Low Jock Scar,
Selside,
Kendal,
Cumbria LA8 9LE
tel   01539 823259
fax   01539 823259
e-mail   ljs@avmail.co.uk

Map 12 Entry 83

Map 11 Entry 84

Cumbria

Fellside Studios

Two perfect studios in the tranquil Troutbeck valley: come for privacy, stylishness and breathtaking views. Make your own sandwiches – or candlelit dinners – get up when the mood takes you, come and go as you please. The flowerbeds spill with heathers and there's a secluded terrace for continental breakfast in the sun – delivered the night before for early risers; your hospitable hosts live in the attached house. Find oak floors, slate shower rooms, immaculate kitchenettes and designer touches, DVD players, comfortable chairs and luxurious towels. *Minimum stay two nights.*

Dorothy's Cottage

So pretty that artists have painted it; in 1626 it housed sheep. A dear little hideaway, with dry stone walls, tumbling roses and views that lift the soul. Perfect Troutbeck lies below: a post office, a couple of pubs, a National Trust property. The cottage is all yours, and if you don't fancy tumbling out of bed too early, Anne slips in quietly and leaves you a tray. (Or treats you to delicious full English and eggs from her hens.) A red rug on a stone floor, two cup chairs round the inglenook, a simple shower room, lovely quirky old-fashioned touches and a bed that faces the view. *Minimum stay two nights.*

rooms	2 studios: 1 double, 1 twin/double both with shower & dining/kitchen area.
price	£64-£76. Singles from £45.
meals	Excellent pub 10-minute walk.
closed	Open all year.
directions	From Windermere, A592 north for 3 miles; after bridge, immed. before church, left signed Troutbeck; 300 yds, 1st on right.

rooms	2: 1 double, 1 twin sharing shower.
price	£65. Singles £35.
meals	Good pub 0.5 miles.
closed	Christmas & New Year.
directions	Facing Post Office in Troutbeck up Robin Lane, left; 1st cottage on right, 100 yds from Post Office.

Monica & Brian Liddell
Fellside Studios,
Troutbeck,
Windemere,
Cumbria LA23 1PE
tel   015394 34000
e-mail   enquiry@fellsidestudios.co.uk
web   www.fellsidestudios.co.uk

Stephen & Anne Kelly
Dorothy's Cottage,
Robin Lane,
Troutbeck,
Cumbria LA23 1PF
tel   01539 432780
mobile   07774 549970
e-mail   skelly99@hotmail.com
web   www.robinlane.co.uk

Map 11 Entry 85

Map 11 Entry 86

Cumbria

Low House

A mile from Lakeland bustle, 17th-century Low House is a hidden gem. Generosity is key here; immense fires, capacious dressers, grand beds piled with duvets, coverlets and pillows. The bathrooms, too – hugely thick towels and opulent mirrors. Breakfast? Wonderful, in bed or downstairs. Curl up by the fire in the snug or the drawing room, dip into a book, take tea, pour yourself a sherry. Set off on sunny days on walks from the door. Best of all, you may 'hire' Johnnie to take you on the lake in his 1930s sailing boat, or on a grand tour in his classic Bentley. What a treat!

Gillthwaite Rigg

Such attention to detail in the magnificent Edwardian Arts & Crafts-style house. Vast airy rooms have leaded windows, panelled walls, oak floors, beautiful doors with wooden latches and motifs moulded into plaster. Bedrooms, reached via a spiral staircase, are simple; like the guest sitting room, they allow the architecture to breathe. Come for distant views of mountains and lakes and Rhoda's award-winning breakfasts (perhaps damsons from the garden). Your hosts are delightful, and passionate about conservation and the wildlife that populates their 14 acres. *Babies & children over six welcome.*

	Low House		Gillthwaite Rigg
rooms	3: 1 double, 1 twin/double both with bath; 1 double with shower.	rooms	2: 1 double with shower; 1 twin/double with bath.
price	£80–£100. Singles £50–£70.	price	£60. Singles £40.
meals	Dinner (party of 6) £30. Pubs/restaurants 1 mile.	meals	Excellent pubs/restaurants nearby.
closed	Christmas.	closed	Christmas & New Year.
directions	M6 exit 36; A590/591, past Kendal; 1st left at r'bout onto B5284 to Crook; 5 miles (past Windermere golf course); right signed Heathwaite; 100 yds on right.	directions	From M6, junc. 36, A590 & A591 to r'bout; B5284 (signed 'Hawkshead via ferry') for 6 miles. After Windermere golf club, right for Heathwaite. Bear right up hill past nursery. Next drive on right; central part of manor.

	Johnnie & Heather Curwen		Rhoda M & Tony Graham
	Low House,		Gillthwaite Rigg,
	Windermere,		Heathwaite Manor,
	Cumbria LA23 3NA		Lickbarrow Road,
tel	01539 443156		Windermere,
e-mail	info@lowhouse.co.uk		Cumbria LA23 2NQ
web	www.lowhouse.co.uk	tel	01539 446212
		fax	01539 446212
		e-mail	tony_rhodagraham@hotmail.com

Map 11 Entry 87

Map 11 Entry 88

Cumbria

Low Fell

Louise and Stephen are warm, fun, helpful, and their well-orchestrated house full of maps, lists, books and guides. Bedrooms are bright, sunny, pretty, with elegant patterned or checked fabrics, heavenly big beds, plump pillows and warm towels; the suite up in the loft is a super hideaway and you overlook trees animated with tunefeul birds. Enjoy warm home-made bread and Aga pancakes at breakfast, warm your toes by the fire in winter, relax in the secluded garden with a glass of wine in summer. The house a five-minute stroll from the lake and bustling Bowness. *Children over 10 welcome.*

Cockenskell Farm

Cockenskell goes back a thousand years but Sara has been here a mere half century. Come for sloped, beamed bathrooms and faded lemon quilts, old pine and patterned walls, idiosyncratic touches of colour and dashes of eccentricity. Relax with a book in the conservatory, stroll through the magical garden or tackle a bit of the Cumbrian Way which meanders through the fields to the back: hop over the dry stone wall. Sara, a delightful, energetic presence, serves you home-grown fruit from her orchard. History seeps from every pore, the place glows with loving care and to stay here is a treat.

	Low Fell		Cockenskell Farm
rooms	3: 1 twin/double with shower; 1 family suite (1 double, 1 twin) with bath.	rooms	3: 1 twin with bath; 1 twin with separate bath; 1 single sharing bath.
price	£64-£90. Half price for children.	price	£60. Singles from £30.
meals	Pubs/restaurants 5-minute walk.	meals	Lunch £10. Packed lunch £5. Good pubs 2 miles.
closed	Christmas & New Year.	closed	December-January.
directions	From Kendal, A591 to Windermere; signs to Bowness. Bear left at bottom of hill & 1st left opp. church. Follow road past Burneside Hotel on right; house 50 yds, on right.	directions	In Blawith, opp. church up a narrow lane, through farm yard. Right after cattle grid, over fell, right at fork through gates & up drive.

	Louise & Stephen Broughton Low Fell, Ferney Green, Bowness-on-Windermere, Windermere, Cumbria LA23 3ES		Sara Keegan Cockenskell Farm, Blawith, Ulverston, Cumbria LA12 8EL
tel	01539 445612	tel	01229 885217
fax	01539 448411	mobile	07909 885086
e-mail	louisebroughton@btinternet.com	e-mail	keegan@cockenskell.co.uk
web	www.low-fell.co.uk	web	www.cockenskell.co.uk

Map 11 Entry 89

Map 11 Entry 90

Derbyshire

Shaw House

They are the kindest, most gracious of hosts. Robert races vintage cars and Patricia is a more dedicated hostess than many you'll meet. Their splendid Georgian mansion, listed by Pevsner, was 'improved' in 1840 with pillars and, later, with a stunning great Victorian conservatory for sunny breakfasts and fresh coffee. It's a truly remarkable building, whose views stretch across the beautiful classic garden. Antique furniture works well with the elegant Georgian proportions and the bedrooms, wonderfully English in their pretty floral get-up, have superbly comfortable quilted beds.

Rose Cottage

Peaceful Rose cottage lies up a tiny country lane – and is brighter and airier than 'cottage' would suggest. The hall sets the tone: white tiles, Indian rugs, woodburning stove and ancestral paintings. Bedrooms are impeccable and there's a fine garden; from your bed you may gaze on long, dreamy views across the Dove valley and the Derbyshire Dales. Although elegant, the house is nevertheless a home and guests are treated as friends – no off-limits, and a small book-lined sitting room just for guests. Cynthia (Australian) and Peter are a delightful couple for whom nothing is too much trouble.

rooms	3: 2 doubles, both with bath/shower; 1 twin with shower.
price	£70-£80. Singles from £45.
meals	Several restaurants 0.5 mile.
closed	Christmas.
directions	Leave M1 at junc. 23a on to A453. At Isley Walton, right to Melbourne. Left in centre of village, then on Ashby road. Right at Melbourne Arms, on to Robinsons Hill.

rooms	2: 1 double with bath; 1 twin with separate bath.
price	£56-£60. Singles £38.
meals	Good pub 2 miles.
closed	Christmas.
directions	From Ashbourne, A515 Lichfield road. After 4 miles, right onto B5033. After 1 mile, 2nd lane on right. 0.5 miles on, on right.

Robert & Patricia Heelis
Shaw House,
Robinsons Hill,
Melbourne,
Derbyshire DE73 1DJ
tel   01332 863827
fax   01332 865201
e-mail   robert@heelis.streamlinenet.co.uk

Peter & Cynthia Moore
Rose Cottage,
Snelston,
Ashbourne,
Derbyshire DE6 2DL
tel   01335 324230
fax   01335 324651
web   www.rosecottageashbourne.co.uk

Map 8 Entry 91

Map 8 Entry 92

Derbyshire

Park View Farm

Daringly decadent, every inch of this plush Victorian farmhouse brims with flowers, sparkling trinkets, polished brass, plump cushions and swathes of chintz. The rooms dance in swirls of colour, frills, gleaming wood, lustrous glass, buttons and bows – it is an extravagant refuge after a long journey. New-laid eggs from the hens for breakfast, fresh fruits and homemade breads accompany the grand performance. The solid brick farmhouse sits in 370 peaceful acres and Kedleston Hall Park provides a stunning backdrop. A fair price for such an experience. *Children over eight welcome.*

Mount Tabor House

On a steep hillside between the Peaks and the Dales, a chapel with a peaceful aura and great views. Inside, the look is rustic contemporary: exposed stone walls, colourful church windows, ethnic touches, a metalwork chandelier. After a mouthwatering dinner, retire to a luxurious bed; your room is as inviting as can be – deep carpets, superb mattresses, good lighting. Bathrooms, too, are a treat. This is a relaxed and easy place to stay and breakfasts can be as carnivorous or as herbivorous as you wish, served on the balcony in summer. Fay is a delight and committed to her guests' comfort.

rooms	3: 1 double with bath; 1 double with shower; 1 double with separate bath.
price	£80-£90. Singles £50-£60.
meals	Good eating places within 20-minute drive; closest 1 mile.
closed	Christmas.
directions	From A52/A38 r'bout west of Derby, A38 north. 1st left for Kedleston Hall. House 1.5 miles past Park on x-roads in Weston Underwood.

rooms	2: 1 double with bath; 1 twin/double with shower.
price	£75. Singles from £40.
meals	Dinner by arrangement. Pubs 2 miles.
closed	Christmas & New Year.
directions	From junc. 26 on M1 A610 towards Ripley. At Sawmills, right under r'way bridge, signed Crich. Right at market place onto Bowns Hill. Chapel 200 yds on right. Can collect from local stations.

Linda & Michael Adams
Park View Farm,
Weston Underwood,
Ashbourne,
Derbyshire DE6 4PA

tel   01335 360352
fax   01335 360352
e-mail   enquiries@parkviewfarm.co.uk
web   www.parkviewfarm.co.uk

Fay Whitehead
Mount Tabor House,
Bowns Hill,
Crich, Matlock,
Derbyshire DE4 5DG

tel   01773 857008
mobile   07813 007478
e-mail   mountabor@msn.com
web   www.mountabor.co.uk

Map 8 Entry 93

Map 8 Entry 94

Derbyshire

The Dower House

How could the rooms of this 16th-century house match the beauty of its façade? But they do: Marsha has great flair, and the white-painted beams, vibrant colours and interesting pictures give her house a wonderfully stylish and contemporary feel. There's an elegant dining room that looks onto a walled garden, a pretty guest sitting room with part-flagged floor, and big warm comfortable bedrooms with conservation-village views; Winster (near Bakewell and Chatsworth) is a gem. Big, fluffy towels, farm-cured bacon for breakfast, delightful hosts – perfection.

Horsleygate Hall

The gardens are vibrant and fascinating, with terraces of stone walls, hidden patios, sculptures, streams and seats in every corner; the Fords, attentive and kind, encourage you to explore. Hens, ponies and doves animate the charming old stable yard and, inside the 1783 house, Margaret has created more magic. There is a warm, timeless, harmonious feel, with worn kilims on pine boards, striped and floral wallpapers, deep sofas and pools of light. Breakfast is served round a big table in the old schoolroom – homemade jams and oatcakes, home eggs, garden fruit. *Children over five welcome.*

rooms	3: 1 double with bath/shower; 1 double, 1 twin, both with separate bath.	rooms	3: 1 double with bath/shower; 1 family, 1 twin sharing bath & separate wc.
price	£90. Singles £65.	price	£55-£65. Singles from £35.
meals	Packed lunch £4. Pub/restaurant 300 yds.	meals	Pub 1 mile.
closed	Christmas & New Year.	closed	23 December-4 January.
directions	3 miles from Matlock on A6 for Bakewell. Left on B5057 signed Winster for 3 miles. House at end of Main Street.	directions	M1 exit 29; A617 to Chesterfield; B6051 to Millthorpe; Horsleygate Lane 1 mile on, on right.

John & Marsha Biggin
The Dower House,
Main Street,
Winster,
Derbyshire DE4 2DH
tel   01629 650931
fax   01629 650932
e-mail   fosterbig@aol.com

Robert & Margaret Ford
Horsleygate Hall,
Horsleygate Lane,
Holmesfield,
Derbyshire S18 7WD
tel   0114 289 0333
fax   0114 289 0333

Map 8 Entry 95

Map 8 Entry 96

Derbyshire

The Hollow

Elisabeth is an avid gardener and bird lover and has designed her garden to encourage wildlife. She also bakes bread, buys 'best-local' and has generally made this big country house a delight to stay in. The bedrooms, large and south-facing, have wonderful views. The double is chintzy, with walnut furniture and silk flowers, and you bathe in a cast-iron bath tub; the twin has Victorian/Edwardian furniture to match this wing of the house (the rest is much older). Elisabeth's garden is a joy and she is immensely kind. This is inspirational walking country and Chatsworth is a 10-minute drive.

Cote Bank Farm

Farmhouse life at its prosperous best in the heady surroundings of the Peak District. Water from the spring, views in every direction and challenging local walks. The farm has been in the family since 1804 and the mellow old house is deftly and smartly decorated – rooms are carpeted, wallpapered and full of well-loved family pieces. Bedrooms are immaculate, beds very comfy, there are oodles of towels and one room looks to the Peaks. Pam, South African, open and generous, bakes bread and oatcakes in the Aga; breakfasts are a treat, with free-range eggs from the farm and soft fruits in season.

rooms	2: 1 double with separate bath/shower; 1 twin with separate shower.
price	£55. Singles £40.
meals	Pubs/restaurants 200 yds.
closed	Christmas & New Year.
directions	On A6, 1.5 miles from Bakewell, right to Ashford-in-the-Water. Immed. left; right to Monsal Head & right at Monsal Head Hotel into Little Longstone. Pass Pack Horse pub on left. House almost opposite.

rooms	3: 1 double with shower; 1 double, 1 twin, both with bath/shower.
price	£60-£80. Singles £40.
meals	Many pubs & restaurants within 3 miles.
closed	November-Easter.
directions	From A6 follow Chinley signs. At Chinley Lodge Hotel leave B6062, over bridge, left into Stubbins Lane. After 0.25 miles, left fork onto farm road, over cattle grid & almost 0.5 miles into farmyard.

Elisabeth Chadwick
The Hollow,
Little Longstone,
Bakewell,
Derbyshire DE45 1NN
tel   01629 640746

Pamela & Nick Broadhurst
Cote Bank Farm,
Buxworth,
Chinley,
Derbyshire SK23 7NP
tel   01663 750566
fax   01663 750566
e-mail   cotebank@btinternet.com
web   www.cotebank.co.uk

Map 8 Entry 97

Map 8 Entry 98

Devon

Goutsford

An estate cottage in a bird-filled, woodland setting; the estate's 5,000 acres run down to the sea. The woodpecker comes at 8.10 every morning (sometimes, in May, with its young), the robin joins you for tea and the cat may slink into your room. Bedrooms are big and bright with a lovely mix of old and new pieces and lots of beams; two are in a raftered barn where the estate's steam engine once lived. Carol and Peter are interesting hosts who cherish their guests: fabulous breakfasts, cream tea if you arrive before 5pm, gin and tonic after. Curry weekends are in the offing. Perfect.

Orchard Cottage

Tucked into a village corner, the last cottage in a row of three. Walk through the pretty garden, past seats that bask in the sun and down to your own entrance and terrace… you may come and go here as you please. Your bedroom is L-shaped and large, with wooden floors, comfortable brass bed and a super shower; it is spotless yet rustic. The Ewens are friendly and fun, their two spaniels equally so and you are brilliantly sited for Dartmoor, Plymouth, the sand and the sea. Breakfasts in the beamed dining room are generous and delicious; this is good value, too.

rooms	3: 2 doubles, 1 twin/double, all with bath/shower.
price	£60. Singles £30.
meals	Packed lunch £5. Good pubs 1-2 miles.
closed	Rarely.
directions	From A38 exit Modbury, left at Hollowcombe. Left onto A379, right to Orcheton, right after 40 yds. Cottage 3rd on right.

rooms	1 double with shower.
price	£50. Singles £30.
meals	Good inns 300 yds.
closed	Christmas.
directions	A379 from Plymouth for Modbury. On reaching Church St at top of hill, before Modbury, fork left at Palm Cross, then 1st right by school into Back St. Cottage 3rd on left, past village hall.

Peter Foster & Carol Farrand
Goutsford,
Ermington,
Ivybridge,
Devon PL21 9NY

tel	01548 831299
mobile	07977 200324
e-mail	carolfarrand@tiscali.co.uk

Maureen Ewen
Orchard Cottage,
Back Street,
Palm Cross Green,
Modbury,
Devon PL21 0QZ

| tel | 01548 830633 |
| fax | 01548 830633 |

Map 2 Entry 99

Map 2 Entry 100

Devon

Washbrook Barn

Hard not to feel happy here – even the blue-painted windows on rosy stone walls make you want to smile. Inside is equally sunny. The barn – decrepit until Penny bought it three years ago – rests at the bottom of a quiet valley. She has transformed it into a series of big, light-filled rooms with polished wooden floors, pale beams and richly coloured walls lined with fabulous watercolours: the effect is one of gaiety and panache. No sitting room as such, but armchairs in big, impeccable bedrooms from which one can admire the view. The beds are divinely comfortable and the fresh bathrooms sparkle.

Lower Norton Farmhouse

Travel by train and Peter will chauffeur you home in his vintage Bentley (you can book a tour, too); if sailing's your thing he can take you out on the yacht. You can ride one of their horses, bring your own… or just mooch around the house and garden all day. Whichever appeals, Peter and Glynis want you to enjoy your stay. The house is Georgian, though in parts much older, and stands at the head of a lovely green valley with great views. The entire place has been beautifully renovated and the Farrow & Ball colours are easy on the eye. Sleep in an antique French or Italian bed, and wake to breakfast on the terrace in summer.

rooms	3: 1 double with bath/shower; 1 twin, 1 double both with separate bath/shower.
price	£65-£70. Singles £42.
meals	Pubs/restaurants 10-minute walk.
closed	Christmas & New Year
directions	From Kingsbridge quay to top of Fore St; right into Duncombe St; over x-roads to T-junc; left to Church St. Right into Belle Cross Rd; 150 yds, right into Washbrook Lane; 100 yds left downhill; at bottom on right.

rooms	3: 1 double, 1 twin, both with shower; 1 double with bath/shower.
price	From £60. Singles from £45.
meals	Dinner, 3 courses, £21. Lunch £7.50. Packed lunches £6.
closed	Rarely.
directions	From A381 at Halwell, 3rd left signed Slapton; 4th right after 2.3 miles signed Valley Springs Fishery at Wallaton Cross. House down 3rd drive on left.

Penny Cadogan
Washbrook Barn,
Washbrook Lane,
Kingsbridge,
Devon TQ7 1NN

tel	01548 856901
mobile	07989 502194
e-mail	penny.cadogan@homecall.co.uk
web	www.washbrookbarn.co.uk

Peter & Glynis Bidwell
Lower Norton Farmhouse,
Coles Cross,
East Allington,
Totnes,
Devon TQ9 7RL

tel	01548 521246
fax	01548 521246
e-mail	lowernorton@tiscali.co.uk

Map 2 Entry 101

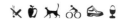

Map 2 Entry 102

Devon

Woodside Cottage

From a narrow decorative window, a charming vignette of Devon: a winding country lane edged by fat hedgerows, a hillside dotted with cows. The 18th-century former gamekeeper's cottage is folded into Devon's gentle green softness. Bedrooms are fresh and charming, the drawing and dining rooms formal and immaculate with fine furniture. Tim and Sally welcome you with tea and homemade cake; they used to run a clematis nursery; the terraced garden is lovely. An excellent pub and the sea are nearby; at night see the beam from Start Point lighthouse.

Minimum stay two nights in summer.

Rose Cottage

A cottage and former bakery, beautifully renovated with locally-sourced materials – beams salvaged from Plymouth docks and panelling in the bedrooms from Dartmouth church. Farmhouse breakfasts of local produce are served in a small book-filled, geranium-scented conservatory. Bedrooms are cosy and low ceilinged, the bathroom is tongue-and-groove panelled and you have your own entrance and key. You are on a narrow lane, less than a mile from the coastal path at Hope Cove (once a smugglers' den) and four from the magnificent Salcombe estuary. Paddy and Griselda are delightful.

rooms	3: 1 double, 1 twin/double, both with shower; 1 double with bath & shower.
price	From £65. Singles by arrangement.
meals	Packed lunch £5. Pub 800 yds.
closed	Christmas.
directions	A381 from Totnes to Halwell, A3122 for Dartmouth. After Dartmouth Golf Club, right at sign to house & Blackawton. 0.3 miles before Blackawton, cottage on right.

rooms	3: 2 doubles with bath; 1 double with shower.
price	£55-£65. Singles from £40.
meals	Pub/restaurant in Hope Cove, 1 mile.
closed	Christmas.
directions	From Kingsbridge on A381, right to Hope Cove. In Galmpton, cottage 200 yds on left, past village sign.

Tim & Sally Adams
Woodside Cottage,
Blackawton,
Dartmouth,
Devon TQ9 7BL

tel	01803 712375
mobile	07929 405812
e-mail	stay@woodsidedartmouth.co.uk
web	www.woodsidedartmouth.co.uk

Paddy & Griselda Daly
Rose Cottage,
Galmpton,
Salcombe,
Devon TQ7 3EU

tel	01548 561953
fax	01548 561953
e-mail	rosecottage@chattels.co.uk
web	www.rosecottagesalcombe.co.uk

Map 2 Entry 103

Map 2 Entry 104

Devon

Wig-wam

It's not much, but it works. This is for those of you who yearn for simple living. Rudyard Kipling wrote, oh so wisely: "Teach us delight in simple things/ and mirth that hath no bitter springs." There is, nevertheless, the ever-present danger here that whatever mirth you enjoy may have a bitter spring or two. But the strong-hearted will love it, love its symmetry, its purity of style, its gentle reach for the light above. It is our own culture's authentic response to the Indian tipi. As for meals, think upon Francis Bacon who wrote: "Hope is a good breakfast, but it is a bad supper".

rooms	1, complete with very open fire (and be prepared to rub two sticks together).
price	Trade a night's stay for moccasins, mirror or turquoise.
meals	Buffalo are scarce in Devon, so bring a can of emergency baked beans.
closed	For annual migration.
directions	Follow the smoke signals and the sound of tom-toms.

	Chief Hole-in-Roof
	Wig-wam,
	Buffalo Plain,
	Wilderness,
	Devon W1G W4M
tel	smoke signals only
e-mail	wobbly-wigwam@wilderness.co.uk
web	www.toppling-tipi.com

Map   Entry 105

Nonsuch House

The photo says it all! You are in your own crow's nest, perched above the flotillas of yachts zipping in and out of the estuary mouth: stunning. Kit, an ex-hotelier, smokes his own fish fresh from the quay and knocks out brilliant dinners. Further gastronomic delights lie across the water: a five-minute walk brings you to the ferry that transports you and your car to the other side. Breakfasts in the conservatory are a delight, bedrooms are big and comfortable and fresh bathrooms sparkle. But it's the position that will win your heart. *Children over 10 welcome. Minimum stay two nights at weekends.*

rooms	3: 2 twins/doubles with shower; 1 twin/double with bath.
price	From £90. Singles from £70.
meals	Dinner, 3 courses, £25. (Not Tues/Wed/Sat.) Good pub/restaurant 5-minute walk & short boat trip.
closed	Rarely.
directions	2 miles before Brixham on A3022, A379. After r'bout, fork left (B3205) downhill, through woods, left up Higher Contour Rd, down Ridley Hill. At hairpin bend.

	Kit & Penny Noble
	Nonsuch House,
	Church Hill,
	Kingswear, Dartmouth,
	Devon TQ6 0BX
tel	01803 752829
fax	01803 752357
e-mail	enquiries@nonsuch-house.co.uk
web	www.nonsuch-house.co.uk

Map 2 Entry 106

Devon

The White House

A great little place in a peaceful corner; gaze on the sparkling Dart estuary from the comfort of your deep bed.
A maritime theme plays throughout this relaxing, book-filled home, and there's classical music at breakfast. Fresh and cheerful bedrooms have tea, coffee, sherry, chocolates, bathrobes and views; more panoramas from the wide garden terrace by the river. In winter the guest sitting/breakfast room is cosy with open fire, comfortable chairs, masses of books. A ferry transports you to Dartmouth and Totnes, and Hugh and Jill are gracious and generous hosts.
Children by arrangement.

rooms	2: 1 double with bath & shower; 1 double with shower.
price	£80. Singles £55.
meals	Good pubs a short walk.
closed	Christmas.
directions	Downhill into Dittisham, sharp right imm. before Red Lion. Along The Level, up narrow hill & house entrance opp. at junc. of Manor St & Rectory Lane.

Hugh & Jill Treseder
The White House,
Manor Street,
Dittisham,
Devon TQ6 0EX
tel   01803 722355
fax   01803 722355

Map 2 Entry 107

Parliament House

The ancient rambling house (where William of Orange held his first Parliament) has blossomed – thanks to the care you'd expect from two designers. This is a fresh, stylish and charming cottage where wallpapers, napkins and toile de Jouy are Carole's own design. White walls and serene colours form a lovely backdrop for pretty touches. Breakfast are feasts – homemade marmalade, three sorts of bread – and bedrooms are supremely comfortable, one with a cast-iron fireplace and hand-stencilled paper. There's a sitting room with books and piano – and the garden is a joy.

rooms	2: 1 twin/double with separate bath/shower; 1 double, with separate shower.
price	From £70.
meals	Pubs/restaurants within 2 miles.
closed	Rarely.
directions	From Totnes, A385 Paignton road; 2 miles on, right at South Hams Motors. House 1st on right. Just past house to parking area on right.

Carole & Harry Grimley
Parliament House,
Longcombe,
Totnes,
Devon TQ9 6PR
tel   01803 840288
fax   01803 840288
e-mail   parliamenthouse@btopenworld.com

Map 2 Entry 108

Devon

Manor Farm

Sarah's a fanatical gardener – and a successful one, producing vegetables that will find their way onto your dinner plate, and fresh raspberries for your cereal. She keeps bees and hens too, so there are honey and eggs for breakfast, served in a smart red dining room. The farmhouse is part 14th-century, and twists and turns around unexpected nooks and crannies. Sarah is capable, breezy and well-used to looking after people. The two bedrooms are large and painted sunny yellow; each has a tray with pretty china, two types of tea, coffee and local spring water. More good food in the pub up the road.

rooms	2: 1 double with bath/shower; 1 twin with separate bath.
price	£50-£60. Singles £28-£35.
meals	Dinner £12-£15. Packed lunch £3-£4.
closed	Rarely.
directions	From Newton Abbot, A381 for Totnes. After approx. 2.5 miles, right for Broadhempston. Past village sign, down hill & 2nd left. Pass pub on right & left 170 yds on into courtyard.

Sarah Clapp
Manor Farm,
Broadhempston,
Totnes,
Devon TQ9 6BD
tel 01803 813260
fax 01803 813260
e-mail clappfamily@members.shines.net

Map 2 Entry 109

Avenue Cottage

The tree-lined approach is steep and spectacular; the cottage sits in 11 wondrous acres of rhododendron, magnolia and wild flowers with a lily-strewn pond and paths that dip down to the lovely river. Find a quiet spot in which to read or simply sit and absorb the tranquillity. Richard is a gifted gardener, and the archetypal gardener's modesty and calm have penetrated the house itself – it is sombre, uncluttered, comfortable. The old-fashioned twin room has a big bathroom with a faux-marble basin and a balcony with sweeping valley views; the pretty village and pub are a short walk away.

rooms	2: 1 double sharing shower; 1 twin with bath.
price	£50-£66. Singles £30-£38.
meals	Excellent pub in village.
closed	Rarely.
directions	A381 Totnes-Kingsbridge for 1 mile; left for Ashprington; into village, then left by pub ('Dead End' sign). House 0.25 miles on right.

Richard Pitts
Avenue Cottage,
Ashprington,
Totnes,
Devon TQ9 7UT
tel 01803 732769
mobile 07719 147475
e-mail richard.pitts@dial.pipex.com

Map 2 Entry 110

Devon

Higher Beneknowle

The 17th-century stone house, once three cottages, has a warm, modern feel and much aged character. A Tuscan red and polished oak hall opens to a beamed sitting room with family heirlooms, wood-burning stove; cottagey bedrooms with cushioned window seats overlook pretty gardens at the front. Hanging baskets, fruit trees and veggies, a small vineyard: Trina is a keen gardener and cook. Local organic produce where possible, a generous breakfast, a gourmet dinner or a simple supper (seared Brixham scallops, homemade pasta, ginger panacotta). Come for beaches and Dartmoor, village life and local walks.

rooms	2: 1 double with shower; 1 twin with separate bath/shower.
price	£70. Singles from £40.
meals	Dinner £22.50. Lunch £12.50. Picnic £7.50. Good pub 800 yds.
closed	Rarely.
directions	Leave A38 at Marley Head, follow Avonwick signs (ignore signs for Diptford); B3372 for 2 miles, garage on right, over narrow bridge, turn right. Sign to house 500 yds on left.

Trina & David Duncan
Higher Beneknowle,
Diptford,
Totnes,
Devon TQ9 7LU

tel	01364 649209
fax	01364 649203
e-mail	trinadad48@aol.com
web	www.higherbeneknowle.co.uk

Map 2 Entry 111

Penpark

Clough Williams-Ellis of Portmeirion fame did more than design an elegant house; he made sure it communed with nature. Light pours in from every window, and the enchanting woodland garden and farmland views lift the spirits. The big double has apricot walls, a comfy sofa and its own balcony; the private suite has arched French doors to the garden and an extra room for young children. Antiques and heirlooms, African carvings, silk and fresh flowers – it is deeply traditional and comforting. Your generous hosts have been doing B&B for years and look after you so well.

rooms	3: 1 twin/double with separate bath; 1 double with separate shower; 1 family suite with shower.
price	£60-£70. Singles from £40.
meals	Dinner occasionally available. Good pub 1 mile.
closed	Rarely.
directions	A38 west to Plymouth; A382 turn off; 3rd turning off r'bout, signed Bickington. There, right at junc. (to Plymouth), right again (to Sigford & Widecombe). Over top of A38; 1st entrance on right.

Madeleine & Michael Gregson
Penpark,
Bickington,
Newton Abbot,
Devon TQ12 6LH

tel	01626 821314
fax	01626 821101
e-mail	maddy@penpark.co.uk
web	www.penpark.co.uk

Map 2 Entry 112

Devon

Corndonford Farm

The bleat of sheep, the stamp of hooves – come to be engrossed in the routines of a wild, engagingly chaotic haven. Ann and William are friendly, kind and extrovert; guests adore them and keep coming back. There is comfort, too: warm curtains, a four-poster with lacy curtains, early morning tea… and a steep circular stair to rooms. Gentle giant shire horses live at the shippon end where the cows once stood; Bronze Age foundations add medieval magic. A place for those who love the rhythm of real country life – and the Two Moors Way footpath is on the doorstep.
Children over 10 by arrangement.

Bagtor House

Fires glow in granite fireplaces and the oak panelling in the breakfast room is remarkable. Yet among this ancient beauty – the house is 15th century and dramatist John Ford was born here in 1586 – there is no stinting on comfort. Generous bedrooms have lovely big beds and the double, red-painted and elegant, overlooks the gardens. Sue grows everything and makes her own bread, marmalade and jam. For families, a super big room at the top; outside, chickens, geese and ducks to be fed. (Your own pet may sleep by the Aga.) A leafy and lush retreat a 10-minute walk from the edge of the moor.

rooms	2: 1 twin, 1 four-poster, sharing bath.
price	£40-£50. Singles £20-£25.
meals	Pub 2 miles.
closed	Christmas.
directions	From A38 2nd Ashburton turn for Dartmeet & Princetown. In Poundsgate pass pub on left; 3rd right on bad bend signed Corndon. Straight over x-roads, 0.5 miles, farm on left.

rooms	2: 1 double, 1 family, both with separate bath.
price	From £60. Singles by arrangement.
meals	Excellent restaurant 1 mile; real-ale pub 0.75 miles.
closed	Christmas.
directions	From Bovey Tracy, B3387 for Widecombe-in-the-Moor; 2.5 miles, left for Ilsington; 0.75 miles, fork right to Bickington; next right to Bagtor; 0.75 miles, on right.

Ann & Will Williams
Corndonford Farm,
Poundsgate,
Newton Abbot,
Devon TQ13 7PP
tel   01364 631595
e-mail   corndonford@btinternet.com

Sue Cookson
Bagtor House,
Ilsington,
Dartmoor,
Devon TQ13 9RT
tel   01364 661538
fax   01364 661538
e-mail   sue@bagtor.freeserve.co.uk
web   www.bagtormanor.co.uk

Map 2 Entry 113

Map 2 Entry 114

Devon

Hooks Cottage

The seductive charm of this hideaway miner's cottage will soothe even the most stressed souls. At the end of a long bumpy track is a lush oasis carved out of woodland. Mary, gently spoken, loves to see guests unwind; both she and Dick have a finely judged sense of humour. There's a pretty American patchwork quilt on the brass double bed and a small bathroom off it which leads to the twin, and the sound of river and birdsong fill each room. Local sausages and bacon for breakfast, excellent dinners, a large pool, bluebells in spring and 12 acres to explore at ease. They even have their own water supply.

Vogwell Cottage

The house in the woods is small and unpretentious and fits around you like a well-worn glove. Christina is welcoming and plies you with tea and interested companionship. The walking and riding are outstanding in this fascinating corner of Devon – take your binoculars and catch the birds. Bedrooms are modest with pastel bedspreads and fabulous views: the garden and stream from one, the open moor from the other.
Come not for luxury but for the setting, the great hospitality (delicious country dishes), the hunting and riding, and the gentleness of it all. Treats for your dog, stabling for your horse.

rooms	2: 1 double, 1 twin, both with bath/shower.	rooms	2 twins/doubles, both with bath.
price	From £50. Singles from £25.	price	£50. Singles £25.
meals	Supper £15. BYO. Good pub/restaurant 2 miles.	meals	Dinner, 4 courses, £25. Supper £15. Packed lunch £5. Full-board available.
closed	Rarely.	closed	Occasionally.
directions	From A38, A382 at Drumbridges for Newton Abbot. 3rd left at r'bout for Bickington. Down hill, right for Haytor. Under bridge, 1st left & down long, bumpy track, past thatched cottage to house.	directions	From Bovey Tracey signs to Manaton & Becky Falls; on past Kestor Inn in Manaton for 3.3 miles, towards Moretonhampstead. On left down lane.

Mary & Dick Lloyd-Williams
Hooks Cottage,
Bickington,
Ashburton,
Devon TQ12 6JS
tel   01626 821312
e-mail   hookscottage@yahoo.com

John & Christina Everett
Vogwell Cottage,
Manaton,
Devon TQ13 9XD
tel   01647 221302
e-mail   john.everett03@ntlworld.com

Map 2 Entry 115

Map 2 Entry 116

Devon

Easdon Cottage

There is a peacefulness about Easdon Cottage that strikes you the moment you enter. Replenish your soul in this light and beautifully proportioned cottage; if the room in the house is taken, you may stay in the warm, peaceful barn. Both have delightful moor views. The interiors are an enchanting mix of good pictures, oriental rugs, books, plants and some handsome Victorian finds. Liza and Hugh are vegetarian and dedicated users of organic produce – veggie and vegan breakfasts are delicious. You are in a classic Devon valley yet the wilderness of Dartmoor lies just beyond the door.
Children and pets by arrangement.

The Gate House

A dear house in a dear village, grander inside than you might think.
The medieval longhouse (1460) has all the low beams and wonky walls you could hope for, and is properly looked after. Rose-print curtains and spruce quilts in the bedrooms, a woodburner and flowers in the sitting room – and robes, good soaps and soft towels… such care is taken you can't help but feel spoiled. John and Sheila are delightful attentive hosts who, serve you delicious Aga-side meals on white linen with candles. A small pool in the secluded gardens overlooks beautiful woodland and moors; you may not want to leave.

rooms	1 twin/double with bath/shower.
price	£56. Singles £28.
meals	Packed lunch £3-£5. Evening meals by arrangement. Good pub/restaurant 3 miles.
closed	Rarely.
directions	A38 from Exeter; A382 for Bovey Tracey. There, left at 2nd r'bout for Manaton. 2 miles beyond Manaton, right at x-roads for M'hampstead. 0.5 miles on, right, signed Easdon. On left up track.

rooms	3: 1 twin/double with bath/shower; 1 twin/double with shower; 1 double with separate bath/shower.
price	£66-£68. Singles £42.
meals	Dinner, 4-5 courses, £22. BYO. Packed lunch available. Good pub/restaurant 50 yds.
closed	Rarely.
directions	From Moretonhampstead via Pound St to North Bovey (1.5 miles). House 25 yds off village green, down Lower Hill past inn on left.

	Liza & Hugh Dagnall
	Easdon Cottage,
	Long Lane,
	Manaton,
	Devon TQ13 9XB
tel	01647 221389
fax	01647 221389
e-mail	easdondown@btopenworld.com

	John & Sheila Williams
	The Gate House,
	North Bovey,
	Devon TQ13 8RB
tel	01647 440479
fax	01647 440479
e-mail	gatehouseondartmoor@talk21.com
web	www.gatehouseondartmoor.co.uk

Map 2 Entry 117

Map 2 Entry 118

Devon

Cyprian's Cot

A charming terraced cottage of 16th-century nooks and crannies and beams worth ducking. The setting is exquisite: the garden leads into fields of sheep, the Dartmoor Way goes through the town and the Two Moors Way skirts it. Shelagh, a lovely lady, gives guests their own sitting room with a fire, lit on cool nights; breakfasts, served in the cosy dining room, are fresh, free-range and tasty. Up the narrow stairs and into flowery bedrooms – a small double and a tiny twin. A perfect house and hostess, and a perfect little town to discover, with its pubs, fine restaurant and delicatessen for picnickers.

rooms	2: 1 double with separate bath; 1 twin with shower.
price	£50. Singles fom £30.
meals	Good pubs & restaurants in village.
closed	Rarely.
directions	In Chagford leave church on left; 1st right beyond Globe Inn. House 150 yds on right.

Shelagh Weeden
Cyprian's Cot,
47 New Street,
Chagford,
Devon TQ13 8BB
tel   01647 432256
e-mail   shelagh-weeden@lineone.net
web   www.cyprianscot.co.uk

Map 2 Entry 119

Sampford Manor

History oozes from every cranny of this Devonshire manor farmhouse which pre-dates the Domesday Book: granite mullioned windows, slate floors and beamed ceilings are impressive. Rosalind gives a big welcome; she loves her ancient smallholding with its chickens and carthorse. Bedrooms have their own entrance and a modest feel – attractive fabrics and an aged sofa in the double, apricot walls and crocheted bedspreads in the twin. This is beautiful walking and riding country, and there's stabling and grazing for your horse. If you're after privacy and peace, and can see past the cracks, you'll be smitten.

rooms	2: 1 double with separate bath; 1 twin/double with separate shower.
price	From £60. Singles from £30.
meals	Dinner £20. Packed lunch £5. Pub 4 miles.
closed	Rarely.
directions	From Tavistock B3357 towards Princetown. 1st x-roads, right for Whitchurch Down. Next x-roads, left for S. Spiney; 2nd right turn (National Park sign), down hill, 1st drive on left.

Rosalind Spedding
Sampford Manor,
Sampford Spiney,
Yelverton, Tavistock,
Devon PL20 6LH
tel   01822 853442
fax   01822 855691
e-mail   manor@sampford-spiney.fsnet.co.uk
web   www.sampford-spiney.fsnet.co.uk

Map 2 Entry 120

Devon

Mount Tavy Cottage

An enchanted guest wrote: "There's no better place to recover from stress." Everything is geared to your comfort – pretty rooms, four-poster and half-tester beds, deep, free-standing baths. Joanna and Graham, a lovely Devon couple, have worked hard to restore this former gardener's bothy, Graham making much of the furniture himself. Two new bedrooms have been created in the potting shed across the courtyard: bed and breakfast in glorious seclusion. Outside are ponds, a stream, a walled Victorian garden... and Nelson, cheerfully retired from the rigours of the Pony Club.

rooms	3: 1 four-poster, 2 twins/doubles, all with separate bath.
price	From £60. Singles from £30.
meals	Dinner, 3 courses, £20.
closed	Rarely.
directions	From Tavistock B3357 towards Princetown. 0.25 miles on, after Mount House School, left. Drive past lake to house.

Mr & Mrs G H Moule
Mount Tavy Cottage,
Tavistock,
Devon PL19 9JL
tel   01822 614253
mobile   07776 181576
e-mail   graham@mounttavy.fsnet.co.uk
web   www.mounttavy.freeserve.co.uk

Map 2 Entry 121

South Hooe Mine

Quirky, delightful, fascinating! Pretty bedrooms have fresh wildflowers, beautiful linen, a quiet elegance. The lovely Trish makes fresh bread and Martha the donkey helps her win the battle with nature but prefers to have her front feet in the kitchen. Tartan curtains, polished antiques and paintings in the dining room, and a large terrace with soaring views. The Tamar is magnetic – sleep next to it in your own circular yurt (cook outside in the evenings); breakfast is lowered down by basket. Sail in, through the AONB – there's a jetty – or join a writing course. *Babes in arms and children over eight welcome.*

rooms	3: 1 double with bath; 1 twin/double with bath & single/dressing room; yurt for two sharing bathroom in house.
price	£60-£75. Singles from £30.
meals	Dinner £18, very occasionally available. Pub 3 miles.
closed	Rarely.
directions	Into Bere Alston on B3257, left for Weir Quay. Over x-roads. Follow Hole's Hole sign, right for Hooe. Fork left for South Hooe Farm; 300 yds on, turn sharply back to your left & down track.

Trish Dugmore
South Hooe Mine,
Hole's Hole,
Bere Alston,
Yelverton,
Devon PL20 7BW
tel   01822 840329
e-mail   southhooe@aol.com

Map 2 Entry 122

Devon

Burnville House

Granite gateposts, Georgian house, rhododendrons, beechwoods, views: that's the setting. But there's more. A working farm, heated pool, tennis court, riding, clay-pigeon shooting, easy trips to Eden or the sea. Lots of possible action! Or... just gaze at the moors and Brentor Church on the Tor, listen to sheep syncopating the silence... Your hosts left busy jobs in London to settle here. Their place breathes life – space, smiles, energy. And everywhere, hints of elegance: antique furniture, stylish bathrooms, delicious menus and subtle colour schemes giving warmth and light. Whatever, you'll love it.

Steeperton

Imagine being given this place as a wedding present! This is why it was originally built (in 1905); by the time the Osborns found it, it was sad and unloved. With the house now cheerful and cherished, Pippa is taming the garden. The position is wonderful: Dartmoor is all around you and the big, restful bedrooms look across to Belstone Tor. The village is pretty, too, with a 13th-century church and the highest cricket ground in England. Pippa is endlessly kind and accommodating; while away a wet afternoon with books and piano – she won't mind a bit – or set off on a hike.

rooms	2 doubles, both with bath.
price	£60-£70. Singles £35.
meals	Dinner from £14. Good pub 2-miles.
closed	Rarely.
directions	A30 from Exeter to Okehampton. A386 towards Tavistock. Right for Lydford opp. Dartmoor Inn. 4 miles (through Lydford) Burnville Farm on left (convex traffic mirror on right).

rooms	3: 2 doubles, 1 twin, all with bath & shower.
price	From £60. Singles from £40.
meals	Dinner, 3 courses, £25. Supper, 2 courses, £15. Good pubs/restaurants 5-10 minute walk.
closed	Rarely.
directions	Leave A30 (westbound) at Okehampton; signs to Belstone. On entering village, sharp left in middle of double bend; 200 yds on right.

Victoria Cunningham
Burnville House,
Brentor,
Tavistock,
Devon PL19 0NE
tel   01822 820443
fax   01822 820443
e-mail   burnvillef@aol.com
web   www.burnville.co.uk

Mr & Mrs R Osborn
Steeperton,
Belstone,
Okehampton,
Devon EX20 1RD
tel   01837 840270
e-mail   nights2remember@steeperton.fsnet.co.uk
web   www.steeperton.co.uk

Map 2 Entry 123

Map 2 Entry 124

Devon

Higher Eggbeer Farm

Over 900 years old and still humming with life: cows, ponies, cats, guinea fowl, rabbits and foxes share the rambling gardens. Sally-Anne and family are artistic, enthusiastic, zany and fun. It's an adventure to stay, so keep an open mind: the house is a historic gem and undeniably rustic. Huge inglenook fireplaces, interesting art, books, piano, wellies, muddle and charm; Sally-Anne will take children to collect eggs and may even babysit. Be wrapped in peace in your own half of the house (with beautiful drawing room), immersed in a magnificent panorama of forest, hills and fields of waving wheat.

Symonds

Watch hares cavort from your bedroom window in gentle, green Devon. The pretty thatched cottage has a calming, uncluttered mood of whitewashed walls, old pine and traditional chintz. There's a big, handsome conservatory, a flowered cottage garden and tennis to play; in winter, logs crackle in a huge hearth. Bedrooms have charming windows, white candlewick bedspreads and framed samplers on the walls. Judi looks after you with unflappable friendliness and her cooking is superb – breakfast is an ever-changing treat, and dinner worth staying in for. You will feel folded into the countryside and utterly content.

rooms	2 doubles/twins sharing bath (2nd room let to same party); 3rd double in main house sharing bath available.
price	£50–£60. Singles £30.
meals	Restaurants 0.5 miles.
closed	Christmas & New Year.
directions	A30 to Okehampton. After 10 miles left exit into Cheriton Bishop; 1st left after Old Thatch pub, signed Woodbrooke. Down & up hill; as road turns sharp left, fork right down private lane.

rooms	3: 1 double with bath/shower; 2 doubles, both with separate bath/shower.
price	From £80. Singles from £40.
meals	Dinner, 3 courses, £30. Supper £17.50. Pub/restaurant 1.5-7 miles.
closed	Rarely.
directions	B3212 to Dunsford; turn for Dunsford, follow road for 1.5 miles; on edge of village, turn for Cheriton Bishop. Right towards C. Bishop at Wild Banks; driveway 0.5 miles up lane on right.

Carter-Johnson Family
Higher Eggbeer Farm,
Cheriton Bishop,
Exeter,
Devon EX6 6JQ

tel   01647 24427

Judi Smith
Symonds,
Dunsford,
Exeter,
Devon EX6 7DR

tel   01647 24510
fax   01647 24084
e-mail   judismith@symondsdunsford.co.uk
web   www.symondsdunsford.co.uk

Map 2 Entry 125

Map 2 Entry 126

Devon

Rowhorne House

A gem of a setting: from the veranda, views sweep over green hills to the estuary beyond. The Edwardian house, 10 minutes from Exeter, is warm and gracious with soothing, successful colour schemes (russet, lichen-green), comfy sofas, piano, newspapers, books, an antique gong in the hall. Bedrooms come with homemade biscuits, good soaps, fabulous showers; tasty breakfasts include fresh fruit and eggs from the family hens. Your hosts are B&B naturals: interested in others and Jane is a great cook. Antique-hunting trips can be arranged and there's croquet.
Children and pets by arrangement.

The Garden House

An extraordinary restoration of a 1930s house, carried out with exuberance and passion. The exuberance reaches the beds, piled high with cushions, and the garden; Jane's energy among the many pots, quirky topiary and tulips is almost palpable. The chandelier has sparkling glass tears; the breakfast table and Lazy Susan groan under the weight of breakfast goodies; the sideboard under the weight of china; there's a vast choice of food beautifully served. Nothing is underdone; no stone is unturned. It may not be minimalist but it is deeply comfortable, good-humoured and an easy walk into the city.

rooms	2: 1 double with shower; 1 twin with separate shower.
price	From £60. Singles from £30.
meals	Dinner from £15. Lunch £10. Packed lunch £6.
closed	Christmas Day.
directions	A30 to Tedburn-St-Mary; towards Whitestone; after 2 miles pass Royal Oak; on to top of hill, sharp left for Rowhorne & Oldridge; on for 1.5 miles. On left.

rooms	3: 1 double with shower; 1 twin, 1 single sharing bath.
price	£75-£80. Singles £40.
meals	Pubs/restaurants nearby.
closed	Rarely.
directions	M5 junc. 30 for city centre & university. Behind Debenhams, Longbrook St into Pennsylvania Rd. Through lights, 2nd left into Hoopern Ave; house at end on left.

Jane Crosse
Rowhorne House,
Nadderwater,
Exeter,
Devon EX4 2LQ
tel   01392 274675
fax   01392 272473
e-mail rowhornehouse@hotmail.com

David Woolcock
The Garden House,
4 Hoopern Avenue,
Pennsylvania, Exeter,
Devon EX4 6DN
tel   01392 256255
fax   01392 256255
e-mail david.woolcock1@virgin.net
web   www.exeterbedandbreakfast.co.uk

Map 2 Entry 127

Map 2 Entry 128

Devon

Beach House

Lapping at the riverside garden is the Exe estuary, wide and serene. Birds and boats, the soft hills beyond, a gorgeous Georgian house on the river and kind hosts – silly to ask for more. The garden, too, is beautiful, full of topiary, old apple trees and box hedging; you may breakfast in the conservatory or in the dining room. No guest sitting room but comfy chairs in the bedrooms where a sweet simplicity prevails: peachy, soft, chintzy, with antique white bedspreads and charmingly old-fashioned bathrooms. A remarkable marriage of nature and human intervention.

Larkbeare Grange

Deep in the country, yet close to airport, cathedral and coast, the Georgian house exudes well-being – sparkling sash windows fill big rooms with light, stripped floors shine and the old grandfather clock ticks away the hours. Guests are spoiled with the best: goose down duvets on king-size beds, exceptional bathroom goodies and home-baked bread, contemporary luxury in fabric and fitting and bathroom mirrors mist-free! Charlie, Savoy-trained, and Julia are charming and easy – you are in perfect hands. Stylish, fun and without pretension.

rooms	2: 1 twin with bath; 1 double with bath & separate wc.
price	£70. Singles £40.
meals	Good pubs/restaurants 8-minute walk.
closed	Christmas & New Year; January-March.
directions	M5, junc. 30, signs to Exmouth. Right at George & Dragon. After 1 mile, immed. left after level crossing. At mini r'bout, left down The Strand. Last on left by beach.

rooms	3: 2 doubles, 1 twin/double, all with bath/shower.
price	£80-£95. Singles from £65.
meals	Supper from £15. Good pub 1.5 miles.
closed	Rarely.
directions	From A30 Exmouth & Ottery St Mary junction. At r'bouts follow Whimple signs. After 0.25 miles, right; 0.5 miles, then left signed Larkbeare. House 1 mile on left.

	Trevor & Jane Coleman
	Beach House,
	The Strand,
	Topsham,
	Exeter,
	Devon EX3 0BB
tel	01392 876456
fax	01392 873159
e-mail	janecoleman45@hotmail.com

	Charlie & Julia Hutchings
	Larkbeare Grange,
	Larkbeare,
	Talaton, Exeter,
	Devon EX5 2RY
tel	01404 822069
fax	01404 823746
e-mail	stay@larkbeare.net
web	www.larkbeare.net

Map 2 Entry 129

Map 2 Entry 130

Devon

Lower Marsh Farm

The round-headed oak door frame in the back bedroom hints at this listed farmhouse's 16th-century origins – James will tell you all the history. Orchards, paddocks and ponds outside; homeliness and comfort within. Sîan gives you homemade cake on arrival and is a lovely hostess. Pale-walled, carpeted bedrooms have charming old windows and deep sills; the cosy guest sitting room comes stacked with logs for the woodburner. The odd beam to be ducked, a soppy black labrador to be fussed over, eight miles from Exeter and a dream for walkers. Wholly delightful. *Children and pets by arrangement.*

West Colwell Farm

Privacy, peace and stylish comfort in stunning surroundings. After much travelling, these ex-TV producers had a clear vision of the perfect place to stay; they've achieved it here, using local craftsmen and materials in the renovations. Each bedroom feels self-contained, two with private terraces, one tucked under the roof beams. The beds are firm, the linen luxurious and the chrome shower heads are the size of dinner plates. Woodland, valley and bluebell walks start outside the door and the views are glorious. If Frank's teatime nut torte is anything to go by, breakfasts will be delicious.

	Lower Marsh Farm		West Colwell Farm
rooms	3: 1 double with bath; 1 double with separate bath/shower; 1 twin with shower.	rooms	3 doubles, all with shower.
price	£57–£63. Singles £36–£40.	price	From £70. Singles £45.
meals	Excellent pub 2 miles.	meals	Packed lunch from £7.50. Restaurants in Honiton.
closed	Rarely.	closed	Christmas.
directions	From A30, B3180 for Exmouth. 0.75 miles on, right at crossroads for Marsh Green. House 1st on left on entering village.	directions	3 miles from Honiton; Offwell signed off A35 Honiton-Axminster road. In centre of village, at church, down hill. Farm 0.5 miles on.

	Mr & Mrs J B Wroe		Frank & Carol Hayes
	Lower Marsh Farm,		West Colwell Farm,
	Marsh Green,		Offwell,
	Exeter,		Honiton,
	Devon EX5 2EX		Devon EX14 9SL
tel	01404 822432	tel	01404 831130
fax	01404 822062	fax	01404 831769
e-mail	lowermarshfarm@eclipse.co.uk	e-mail	stay@westcolwell.co.uk
web	www.lowermarshdevon.co.uk	web	www.westcolwell.co.uk

Map 2 Entry 131

Map 2 Entry 132

Devon

West Bradley

Total immersion in beauty – doves in the farmyard, hens in the orchard, fields on either side of the long drive. Privacy, too, in your 18th-century upside-down barn on the side of the owners' Devon longhouse – and views. A handmade oak staircase, oak floors, two freshly furnished bedrooms (one up, one down), a good big sitting room with a gas-fired woodburner and a kitchen you would be happy to use. Phillida can bring breakfast to you here, or you can tuck into full English in the farmhouse dining room. There will be homemade something on arrival, and Tiverton is a good source of ethnic restaurants.

Staghound Cottages

This is brilliant for walkers and cyclists: the cottage is a mile from Exmoor, half a mile from the Bristol to Padstow cycle route and Penny has space for bikes and wet clothes. *And* there's a bus stop outside. Built as an inn several centuries ago (there's a still-functioning pub next door), it overlooks meadows and rolling hills. The interior is not luxurious but simple, calm and appealing; the bedrooms, one big, one small, have wonky floors and beds with fresh cotton sheets. No guest sitting room but you'll be out exploring all day and Penny will start you off with a great breakfast.

rooms	1 double/twin with bath; 1 twin with separate shower.
price	£70-£75. Singles £40.
meals	Good pubs within 5 miles, restaurants 4 miles.
closed	Rarely.
directions	From Tiverton B3137 Witheridge road; on towards Rackenford & Calverleigh. After pink thatched cottage (2 miles), fork left to Templeton; West Bradley 2 miles; on left before village hall.

rooms	3: 1 double with bath/shower; 1 twin/double, 1 single sharing bath/shower.
price	£45-£55. Singles £25.
meals	Packed lunches £4. Good pubs & restaurants 2 miles.
closed	Christmas.
directions	M5 exit 27 for Tiverton; 7 miles, right at r'bout for Dulverton; left at next r'bout. At Black Cat junc. take middle road to Dulverton; in Exbridge, left at round house; 300 yds on left.

	Martin & Phillida Strong West Bradley, Templeton, Tiverton, Devon EX16 8BJ
tel	01884 253220
fax	01884 259504
e-mail	martin.strong@btinternet.com

	Penny Richards Staghound Cottages, Exebridge, Dulverton, Devon TA22 9AZ
tel	01398 324453
e-mail	penny@staghound.co.uk
web	www.staghound.co.uk

Map 2   Entry 133

Map 2   Entry 134

Devon

Sannacott

Bring your own horse! On the southern fringes of Exmoor you're in huntin' and shootin' country and the riding is great. And there's surfing at Croyde, 20 miles away. This is a stud farm – the Trickeys breed national hunt racehorses – and the house is a happy mix of 14th century and Georgian. It has an air of casual, comfortable elegance, with antiques, open fires and pictures. There are three pleasant bedrooms in the house, and a twin room in the annexe. Passion flowers rampage in the pretty garden; beyond are rolling hills and secret clusters of trees. Only the doves and distant sheep break the silent spell.

Catsheys

Folded into the Devon hills, the 30-year-old house is full of light and surprises. David is a designer, Rosie a florist and their home is a hymn to contemporary texture and colour. One bedroom is lilac, the other yellow – a French sleigh bed here, a chic 60s armchair there, new art, crisp linen, ethnic treasures. Bathrooms are pure delight. Surrounded by bluebell woods and badgers, the garden yields flowers for your room, vegetables for your table; there's even a solar-heated pool for summer swims. Surf the north Devon coast, ramble the two moors, walk the Tarka Trail... return for deep sleep.

rooms	3: 1 twin/double with bath; 1 twin with separate bath/shower; 1 double sharing bath.	rooms	2: 1 twin/double with bath; 1 double with shower.
price	£60-£70.	price	£95. Singles from £50.
meals	Dinner, 3 courses, £20 (occasionally available). Good pub 5 miles.	meals	Packed lunch from £7.50. Dinner from £17.50. BYO. Good pub 4 miles.
closed	Rarely.	closed	Rarely.
directions	M5 J27; A361 for Barnstaple, past Tiverton, 15.5 miles; right at r'bout (small sign Whitechapel). 1.5 miles to junc., right towards Twitchen & N. Molton; 1.5m to 3rd on left, black gates.	directions	From South Molton, B3137 for 4.5 miles; right at Odam Cross to Romansleigh; next left at Buckam Cross signed 'No through road'; steep hill, ford, 2nd right, house on left at top of hill.

	Mrs E C Trickey Sannacott , North Molton, Devon EX36 3JS		Rosemary Ames Catsheys, Romansleigh, South Molton, Devon EX36 4JW
tel	01598 740203		
fax	01598 740513	tel	01769 550580
e-mail	mctrickey@hotmail.com	fax	01769 550395
		e-mail	rose.ames@mailbox.co.uk
		web	www.catsheys.co.uk

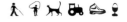

Map 2 Entry 135

Map 2 Entry 136

Devon

Lower Hummacott

Bright clear colours, antique furniture, charming decorative touches. There are fresh fruit and flowers in the bedrooms (one with a king-size bed) and two guest sitting rooms. Delicious, organic and traditionally-reared meat, veg and eggs, fresh fish, homemade cakes... As if that were not enough, the Georgian farmhouse has a stunning formal garden – spring-fed pools, lime walk, pergola, arches, herbaceous beds and ongoing *parterre* – which Liz, a weaver, and Tony, a painter, have created from a green field. A bold, grassy avenue leads to the three ponds which attract wildlife. Listen for the tawny owl.

rooms	2 doubles, both with bath.
price	£62. Singles £31.
meals	Dinner £25.
	Good pub/restaurant 1.5 miles.
closed	Rarely.
directions	0.5 miles east of Kings Nympton village is Beara Cross; straight over towards Romansleigh for 0.75 miles; Hummacott is 1st farm entrance on left.

Tony & Liz Williams
Lower Hummacott,
Kings Nympton,
Umberleigh,
Devon EX37 9TU

tel   01769 581177
fax   01769 581177

Map 2 Entry 137

Sea View Villa

The sea-captain's house gazes down from its wooded perch on beautiful Lynmouth below. There's a short, steep path up... then the pain is over and the pampering begins. Chris cooks, Steve does (sparkling) front of house, the attention to detail is wonderful. Perfumed candles, Indian cutlery and theatrical flourishes at every turn: from the copper vat stuffed with bottles of red to the 'finale' of the menu (... brandy zabaglione glace, maybe?) and the 'encore' (liqueurs, brandy, port). There's ochre and cream in curtain, carpet and stripe; the suite has a touch of French Empire, the bathrooms have luxury oils.

rooms	4: 1 double with bath; 1 double with shower; 2 twins sharing bath.
price	£72-£110. Single occupancy supplement £15.
meals	Dinner, 5 courses, £25.
closed	January.
directions	From M5 exit 23; A39 for Minehead; on to Porlock along coast to Lynmouth. Sea View Villa off Watersmeet Road, up path, directly opposite church.

Steve Williams & Chris Bissex
Sea View Villa,
6 Summerhouse Path,
Lynmouth,
Devon EX35 6ES

tel   01598 753460
fax   01598 753496
e-mail   reservations@seaviewvilla.co.uk
web   www.seaviewvilla.co.uk

Map 2 Entry 138

Devon

Coulsworthy House

Gaze over Exmoor or picture-book fields to the sea. At this generous farmhouse, Rachel's welcoming tea and homemade cake set the tone. Rooms have solid handsome furniture: pine table and red cushions in the breakfast room, tartan covered sofas and log-burning stove in the sitting room. Bedrooms are pretty with iron bedsteads, crisp linen and flashes of colour; bathrooms pamper with thick towels, robes and unguents. Breakfast on home produce – suppers also – and curative water from a private spring. Make friends with the pygmy goats and watch sunsets from the garden. Rachel is a natural homemaker.

Bratton Mill

Absolute privacy down the long, bumpy track to a thickly wooded valley and a rushing stream around which Viagra – a magnificent cock – struts with his happy hens. The house is long, painted traditional white and filled with treasure. Marilyn is excited about her part in the Good Life but still has enough of the city left in her to spoil you with elegant china, fresh flowers and oodles of comfort. Fine furniture abounds, meals are superb and can be eaten by the stream to almost deafening birdsong. Bracing walks from the door and the north coast beaches are near, if you can tear yourself away.

	Coulsworthy House		Bratton Mill
rooms	3: 1 double with bath/shower; 1 twin with shower; 1 twin with separate shower.	rooms	2: 1 double/twin with bath/shower; 1 four-poster with bath.
price	£70. Singles £35.	price	£75-£110. Singles from £40.
meals	Dinner, 3 courses, £22.50. Supper from £7.95. Good pub 4 miles.	meals	Dinner, 3 courses, £20.
closed	Christmas & New Year.	closed	Rarely.
directions	From A399, right at sign for Hunters Inn, Trentishoe & Heddons Mouth. First house, 170 yds on left.	directions	From Bratton Fleming High Street turn into Mill Lane. Down road for 0.5 miles through railway cutting, turn right.

	Toby & Rachel Hayward		Marilyn Holloway	
	Coulsworthy House,		Bratton Mill,	
	Combe Martin,		Bratton Fleming,	
	Devon EX34 0PD		Barnstaple,	
tel	01271 882813		Devon EX31 4RU	
e-mail	coulsworthy@tiscali.co.uk	tel	01598 710026	
web	www.coulsworthy.co.uk	e-mail	auntmazza@hotmail.com	
		web	www.brattonmill.co.uk	

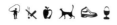

Map 2 Entry 139

Map 2 Entry 140

Devon

Bradiford Cottage

The Bradiford Valley is pretty and lush and runs down towards the glorious beaches of North Devon and the biosphere of Braunton Burrows. The 17th-century cottage – creaky, comfortable, deceptively big – is enveloped in a lovely garden. Old rugs give a warm passage over slate floors, and chintz and pretty wallpapers add to the snug feel. The main bedroom has wiggly walls and wicker furniture; the bathroom, with long sloping ceiling, has a huge bath. The house has been in the family for 200 years and your hosts are easy-going, unstuffy people who love and know the area well.

Southcliffe Hall

An Argentinian chandelier, antique French radiators, a Victorian jacuzzi, a telephone-box shower; we love this gorgeous, grandly idiosyncratic house overlooking Lee Bay. Eccentric owners have left their mark on what was originally the Manor House. Kate and Barry are young, enthusiastic – and sane! Vast bedrooms have rich carpets, big beds, antique flourishes. Bathrooms are fabulous one-offs – roll-top baths to porcelain loos. Tea in the drawing room or lawn, dinner in the panelled dining room; at breakfast, lots of local produce. Spot deer in the woodland, walk to the beach, hike along the coast. Great fun.

	Bradiford Cottage	Southcliffe Hall
rooms	3: 2 doubles, 1 twin, sharing bath & separate shower.	3: 2 doubles, 1 twin, all with bath.
price	£40–£50. Singles £20–£25.	£80–£100. Singles £50.
meals	Good pubs 400 yds & 1.5 miles.	Dinner, 3 courses, £20. Good pub 5-minute walk.
closed	Christmas & New Year.	Rarely.
directions	From Barnstaple, A361 for Braunton. At 2nd set of lights, right for Bradiford. Next T-junc., sharp left, over bridge, up hill for 100 yds, 2nd lane to right. 1st on left.	From A361, B3343 for Woolacombe. Right, through Lincombe, into Lee. Long drive to house on left, between village hall & Fuschia tearoom.

Jane & Tony Hare
Bradiford Cottage,
Bradiford,
Barnstaple,
Devon EX31 4DP

tel   01271 345039
fax   01271 345039
e-mail   holidays@humesfarm.co.uk
web   www.humesfarm.co.uk

Kate Seekings & Barry Jenkinson
Southcliffe Hall,
Lee,
Devon EX34 8LW

tel   01271 867068
mobile   07910 473725
e-mail   stay@southcliffehall.co.uk
web   www.southcliffehall.co.uk

Map 2 Entry 141

Map 2 Entry 142

Devon

Beara Farmhouse

The moment you arrive at the whitewashed farmhouse you feel the affection that Ann and Richard have for the place. Richard is a lover of wood and a fine craftsman – every room echoes his talent; he has also created the pond that's home to mallards and geese. Ann has laid brick paths, stencilled, stitched and painted, all with an eye for colour; bedrooms and guest sitting room are delectable and snug. Open farmland all around, sheep, pigs and hens in the yard, the Tarka Trail on your doorstep and hosts happy to give you 6.30am breakfast should you plan a day on Lundy Island. Exceptional. *Min. stay two nights June-Sept.*

Dorset

The Red House

Ask for breakfast on the balcony on a clear day: the views across Lyme Bay are stunning. Years of travel and naval lifestyle lie behind the Normans' meticulous and old-fashioned hospitality. Guest rooms under the eaves of the big 1920s house are carpeted, clean and comfortable; two have coastal views, one of the bathrooms is small. No living room but a good garden to relax in (take a peek at Vicky's studio: she handmakes wonderful dolls) and a sofa on the landing with games, guides and books galore. Such a pretty area – and coastal walks to die for. *Children over eight welcome.*

rooms	2: 1 double with shower; 1 twin with bath & shower.		rooms	3: 1 double, 2 twins, all with bath.
price	£60. Singles £35.		price	£46-£62. Singles £30-£42.
meals	Dinner £18, occasionally available. Good pub 1.5 miles.		meals	Supper tray £12 (1st night only). Pub/restaurant 400 yds.
closed	20 December-5 January.		closed	Mid-November-mid-March.
directions	From A39, left into Bideford, round quay, pass old bridge on left. Signs to Torrington; 1.5 miles, right for Buckland Brewer; 2.5, left; 0.5 miles, right over cattle grid & down track.		directions	From Lyme Regis, up Pound St & Sidmouth Rd, past 'Morgans Grave' & Somers Rd; house up 1st driveway on right, abreast of junction sign & 'Slow' sign on road.

<table>
<tr><td></td><td>Ann & Richard Dorsett
Beara Farmhouse,
Buckland Brewer,
Bideford,
Devon EX39 5EH</td><td></td><td>Tony & Vicky Norman
The Red House,
Sidmouth Road,
Lyme Regis,
Dorset DT7 3ES</td></tr>
<tr><td>tel</td><td>01237 451666</td><td>tel</td><td>01297 442055</td></tr>
<tr><td>web</td><td>www.bearafarmhouse.co.uk</td><td>fax</td><td>01297 442055</td></tr>
<tr><td></td><td></td><td>e-mail</td><td>red.house@virgin.net</td></tr>
</table>

Map 2 Entry 143

Map 2 Entry 144

Dorset

Seahill House

Spectacular views! Catch them from the bedrooms and the sweeping gardens. This handsome house stands up and away from the summer crowds above the World Heritage Jurassic coast, next to National Trust land – great walking country. Jane and Adrian, good company and well-travelled, have created a hugely comfortable home and B&B: antique furniture and books in the main rooms, bedrooms with colour-washed walls and pretty fabrics. You are in an Area of Outstanding Natural Beauty and a five-minute amble down to Seatown beach and the old Anchor Inn, great for a pint and a meal. *Children over 12 welcome.*

Champ's Land

An impeccably furnished 17th-century house so steeped in history that the Royal Commission included it in its inventory of historical monuments. A cherished home, too, with stacks of atmosphere. Attractive fabrics and paints complement the architectural charms of flagstones, window seats and original beams, and there is a fascinating collection of prints and china. Books, good beds and your own delightful sitting room with inglenook fire spoil you further. Absolute quiet – an orchard leads to a stream and the sea is one mile away. Mrs Tennant is a gentle, thoughtful hostess. *Children over 10 welcome.*

rooms	2: 1 double with separate bathroom; 1 twin/double (extra single) with shower.
price	From £60. Singles by arrangement.
meals	Good pub 5-minute walk. Restaurants in Chideock.
closed	Christmas & New Year.
directions	Into Chideock on A35, take Bridport & Honiton road. Left at sign to Seatown, then right fork. At top of hill take access road on right-hand side. Signed on right.

rooms	2: 1 double with separate bath; 1 twin sharing bath (let to same party only).
price	£60-£70. Singles by arrangement.
meals	Pubs & restaurants 0.75 miles.
closed	Christmas & New Year.
directions	From Bridport, A35 into Chideock; right at church; 0.75 miles up 'No Through Road' to T-junc. Right; house 7th on right (thatched with 2 porches); drive to end of house, through gate to yard.

	Jane & Adrian Tamone
	Seahill House,
	Seahill Lane,
	Seatown, Chideock,
	Dorset DT6 6JT
tel	01297 489801
fax	07989 940793
e-mail	jane@seahill.co.uk
web	www.seahill.co.uk

	Mrs Miranda Tennant
	Champ's Land,
	Brighthay Lane,
	North Chideock,
	Bridport,
	Dorset DT6 6JZ
tel	01297 489314

Map 3 Entry 145

Map 3 Entry 146

Dorset

Innsacre Farmhouse

Sydney and Jayne share a gift for unwinding stressed souls – and producing memorable food and wine. Secluded in its 21 acres of orchard, valley and wooded hills, wrapped in peace and quiet; inside, 17th-century stone walls, low-beamed ceilings and a warm gallic flair. Bedrooms have antique French beds, bold colours and crisp linen; in the sitting room are books, a log fire and soft, deep chairs. Breakfast on Jayne's orchard fruit compotes with cured sausage, pains au chocolat and American pancakes. Cliff-top walks, beaches and fields to explore – lovely. *Arrival after 4pm.*

Crosskeys House

A pub, cobbler's shop, blacksmith's, this handsome stone house, right on the village crossroads, has settled with ease into its new role. Robin and Liz, no strangers to running a B&B, are relaxed and efficient and help guests with the best pubs, walks and day-trip ideas. Rooms are softly traditional – plump sofas, family antiques – while portraits of Robin's ancestors keep a watchful eye. Crisply furnished bedrooms, not large, are indulgent with king-size beds, thick towels and interesting books. The house is near the road but there's a courtyard garden for breakfast and water fresh from the well.

rooms	4: 3 doubles, 1 twin, all with bath.
price	£80-£90.
	Singles, weekdays only, £60.
meals	Dinner, 3 courses, £19.50. Potage supper for late arrivals, £16.50. Good pubs/restaurants 1.5 miles.
closed	October, Christmas & New Year.
directions	From Dorchester A35 for Bridport. After 13 miles 2nd road signed left to Shipton Gorge & Burton Bradstock. 1st left up long drive to farmhouse.

rooms	2 doubles/twins both with bath/shower.
price	£65. Singles from £40.
meals	Packed lunches £5. Good pub 200 yds.
closed	Rarely.
directions	A35 to Bridport; A3066 to Beaminster. B3163 to Broadwindsor. House on one-way system.

Sydney & Jayne Davies
Innsacre Farmhouse,
Shipton Gorge,
Dorset DT6 4LJ
tel   01308 456137
e-mail   innsacre.farmhouse@btinternet.com
web   www.innsacre.com

Robin & Liz Adeney
Crosskeys House,
High Street, Broadwindsor,
Beaminster,
Dorset DT8 3QP
tel   01308 868063
fax   01308 868063
e-mail   robin.adeney@care4free.net
web   www.crosskeyshouse.com

Map 3 Entry 147

Map 3 Entry 148

Dorset

Gray's Farmhouse

The views from the ramparts of Eggardon's hill fort are superb: from here you can gaze down on the soft stone farmhouse and the sleepy flower-decked lanes. This former shooting lodge has huge flagstones, stripped floors, chunky pine doors, a cheerful, sunny dining room for excellent breakfasts and Rosie's vibrant paintings on several walls. The gardens and grounds join a network of footpaths through ancient meadows and woodland rich in wildlife; Rosie and Roger will advise on how to explore the secret valleys of Hardy country and the spectacular World Heritage coast. *Minimum stay two nights.*

rooms	3: 1 double/family with bath/shower; 1 double with bath; 1 double/twin with shower across courtyard.
price	£60–£70. Singles from £50.
meals	Excellent pub 3 miles.
closed	Rarely.
directions	On A37, A356 from Dorchester, left at 1st sign for T. Porcorum. Through, & up hill 1 mile. At x-roads, right for Powerstock, under bridge. Track 0.5 miles on left, opp. white post. At end, on left.

Rosie & Roger Britton
Gray's Farmhouse,
Toller Porcorum,
Dorchester,
Dorset DT2 0EJ

tel	01308 485574
e-mail	rosieroger@farmhousebnb.co.uk
web	www.farmhousebnb.co.uk

Map 3 Entry 149

Woodwalls House

Quiet seclusion among birds, badgers and wildflowers. The 1806 keeper's cottage sits in its own 12 acres in deepest Dorset where lovely walks lead in all directions. A pretty garden, a sheltered, wisteria-fringed terrace and two cosy bedrooms with lace bedspreads, garden views and a little cream sofa in the twin. It is all thoroughly comforting and welcoming, and your kind, wildlife-loving hosts rustle up fine breakfasts of Beaminster bangers and honey from their bees. Hone your skills for the vicious game that is croquet, and for tennis: the Major is a coach so why not book a lesson? *Minimum stay two nights.*

rooms	2: 1 double with bath & shower; 1 twin with separate bath/shower.
price	£70. Singles from £40.
meals	Excellent inn 500 yds.
closed	Christmas.
directions	Leave Yeovil on A37 to Dorchester. After 1 mile, right for Corscombe; 6 miles to Corscombe; left after village sign down Norwood Lane; 300 yds, 1st white gate on right.

Sally & Tony Valdes-Scott
Woodwalls House,
Corscombe,
Dorchester,
Dorset DT2 0NT

tel	01935 891477
fax	01935 891477
web	www.woodwallshouse.co.uk

Map 3 Entry 150

Dorset

Fullers Earth

The sash windows of your bedroom frame the Dorsetshire hills. Such an English rural feel: the village with pub, post office and stores, the walled garden with fruit trees beyond (source of your breakfast jams), the gentle church view. This listed house – its late-Georgian face added in 1820 – was where the Cattistock huntsmen lived; the unusual thatched stables alongside housed their steeds. Guests share a large and lovely sitting room in sand, cream and dove-blue; carpeted bedrooms have a lofty feel; the resplendent coastline – at times dramatic, at other times softly serene – is yours to discover.

Frampton House

A grand Grade II*-listed house in parkland landscaped by Capability Brown... and two labradors, Potter and Dodger to greet you as you scrunch up the gravel. Beyond the Georgian façade lies a delicious mix of English and Gallic styles. Bedrooms combine comfort with outstanding views; elegant antique iron bedsteads in one, a magnificent four-poster in the other, and everywhere, fine linen and plump pillows. Georgina is a food and arts writer and breakfasts, served in the conservatory, are true-blue English, with spectacular bangers. Dinners are accompanied by French wines.

rooms	2: 1 double with bath/shower; 1 double with separate shower.	rooms	2: 1 four-poster with bath; 1 twin with shower.
price	£56–£62. Singles from £35.	price	£65–£85. Singles £50.
meals	Good pub 500 yds.	meals	Dinner, 3 courses with wine, £18.50. Excellent pubs 2 miles.
closed	Christmas & New Year.	closed	Rarely.
directions	From A37 take Cattistock turning downhill to T-junction. Left through village. Pub on left. After 90 degree right hand bend, 5th house on right.	directions	A37 Dorchester-Yeovil; A356 for Crewkerne & Maiden Newton. In Frampton, left at green; over white bridge; left, opp. Frampton Roses. 'Private' track to house, signed 3rd on left.

	Wendy Gregory		Georgina & Nicholas Maynard
	Fullers Earth,		Frampton House,
	Cattistock,		Frampton,
	Dorchester,		Dorchester,
	Dorset DT2 0JL		Dorset DT2 9NH
tel	01300 320190	tel	01300 320308
mobile	07968 325698	fax	01300 321600
e-mail	stay@fullersearth.co.uk	e-mail	maynardryder@btconnect.com
web	www.fullersearth.co.uk	web	www.framptonhouse.com

Map 3 Entry 151

Map 3 Entry 152

Dorset

East House Cottage

Surrender to the warmth of Tricia and her sweet cottage in a village worth exploring – plus Cairn terrier Mousey who vets visiting pets. The thatched stone house, with a gorgeous terraced garden behind, has been remodelled to introduce modern comforts while leaving every drop of 18th-century charm intact. Upstairs, crisply cottoned twin beds await you, pretty antiques and hundreds of books; your hostess is a published author. Copious Aga-cooked breakfasts are eaten at a magnificent circular inlaid table. A gem – and the Cerne Abbas Giant and pretty Cattistock are close by.

Holyleas House

Breakfast by a log fire in the elegant dining room in winter – a feast of free-range eggs, homemade jams and marmalades. All the rooms in this Victorian house are stylish and well decorated, with lovely prints, many lamps and stunning views; bedrooms are full of light. After a day out or a good walk, relax beside the fire in the big drawing room with a pile of the family's books. This is a fabulous old house, comfortable and easy. Its walled half-acre garden with herbaceous borders is Tia's passion. She is genuinely welcoming – as are her two little terriers – and is happy to babysit.

rooms	2: 1 twin with separate bath; 1 single (let to same party)
price	£60. Singles £40.
meals	Good pubs 4-minute walk.
closed	Christmas & New Year.
directions	A37 from Dorchester; follow signs for village. Cottage on left of High Street, clipped box balls outside.

rooms	3: 1 double with bath/shower; 1 twin/double with shower; 1 single with separate bath.
price	£60. Single £30.
meals	Supper tray £8 on first night. Pub a short walk.
closed	Christmas.
directions	From Dorchester, B3143 into Buckland Newton over x-roads; Holyleas on right opposite village cricket pitch.

Mrs Christopher Davy
East House Cottage,
Sydling St Nicholas,
Dorchester,
Dorset DT2 9PB

tel   01300 341 229
e-mail   tdavy@sydling.f9.co.uk

Tia Bunkall
Holyleas House,
Buckland Newton,
Dorchester,
Dorset DT2 7DP

tel   01300 345214
mobile   07968 341887
e-mail   tiabunkall@holyleas.fsnet.co.uk
web   www.holyleashouse.co.uk

Map 3 Entry 153

Map 3 Entry 154

Dorset

Marren

On the Dorset coastal path, with spectacular views of Portland, a blissfully tranquil and bird-rich spot. Designers Peter and Wendy have transformed their 1920s house and the interiors sing with good taste; antique pine floors softened with kilims, colours contemporary. From six acres of terraced and wooded garden, step into your airy room, perfect with its own entrance, deep-mattressed bed, crisp sheets and luxurious bathroom. Breakfasts of farm produce and homemade bread will set you up for clifftop hikes – leave the low-slung Morgan at home: the track here is adventurously steep!

Muston Manor

The walled garden, with its ornamental ponds and lawns, rambles around this beautiful manor house that began its noble life in 1609 as the seat of the Churchills (the elegant red dining room bears the family's coat of arms). There's still a trace of grandeur along with flamboyant florals carefully chosen by your effusive host. The extravagant main bedroom, with its vintage wallpaper and padded headboards, has gorgeous antiques and its own sitting room with wonderful furniture. Complete privacy – and homemade marmalade and bantam eggs for breakfast. Come and explore the Piddle Valley.

rooms	1 twin/double with bath.
price	£75. Singles £60.
meals	Good pub 1 mile.
closed	Rarely.
directions	On A353 after Poxwell, left at Ringstead sign; up hill (not to Ringstead), over cattle grid into NT car park; cross & drive through gate 'No Cars'; 2 more gates; 100 yds after 3rd gate, sharp right down steep track.

rooms	2: 1 double with bath/shower; 1 double with separate bath/shower.
price	£50-£65. Singles £35-£40.
meals	Pub 1.5 miles.
closed	Rarely.
directions	Turn off A35 at Puddletown r'bout. Take B3142. Right towards Piddle Hinton after sharp right-hand corner. Left down farm track to house.

	Peter Cartwright
	Marren,
	Holworth,
	Dorchester,
	Dorset DT2 8NJ
tel	01305 851503
fax	01305 851504
e-mail	marren@lineone.net
web	www.marren.info

	Mrs Patricia Paine
	Muston Manor,
	Piddle Hinton,
	Dorchester,
	Dorset DT2 7SY
tel	01305 848242

Map 3 Entry 155

Map 3 Entry 156

Dorset

Whitfield Farm Cottage

The well-travelled Jackie and David make light of the practicalities of B&B; they and their 200-year-old cottage have much character and charm. Breakfast in the large, stone-tiled, beamed kitchen, or in the walled courtyard in summer. The twin with garden access is immaculate in its fresh white and blue checks; the sitting room is cosy with comfy sofas and pretty coral-checked cushions, inglenook fireplace and window seats. The River Frome – a chalk stream beloved by local fishermen – is 150 yards from the grounds; you can fish here for £20 a day. Convenient for the A35, yet peaceful.

rooms	3: 1 twin with separate (downstairs) shower; 1 twin with separate bath & shower; 1 single also available.
price	£60. Singles £40.
meals	Pub/restaurant 1.25 miles.
closed	Easter & Christmas.
directions	From r'bout at top of Dorchester, west on B3150 for 100 yds. Right onto Poundbury Rd (before museum). 1 mile; over another road; 2nd track on right by house sign. Cottage set back from road.

Jackie & David Charles
Whitfield Farm Cottage,
Poundbury Road,
Dorchester,
Dorset DT2 9SL
tel   01305 260233
fax   01305 260233
e-mail   dc.whitfield@clara.net
web   www.dc.whitfield.clara.net

Map 3 Entry 157

The Old Manor

Few B&Bs are as stately as this – Pevsner described the magnificent manor as being "refined to a point of perfection". Plush window seats at mullioned windows, Jacobean fireplaces, vast staircases: the splendours are varied and the grounds a fair match. There's something to delight at every turn: huge, carved, cup-and-cover four-posters, beautiful rugs on stone and wooden floors, lavish period fabrics, lush white bathrobes, lake views. Andrew and Mulu pamper you in great style; Mulu can even give you a professional massage or a beauty treatment in the salon. *Children by arrangement.*

rooms	3: 1 double with bath & shower; 1 twin, 1 four-poster, both with bath.
price	£96–£116. Singles £63–£73.
meals	Restaurant within walking distance.
closed	Mid-December-mid January.
directions	At r'bout on A35, 1 mile NE of Dorchester, follow sign to Kingston Maurward gardens & animal park. In grounds, follow estate road.

Andrew & Mulu Thomson
The Old Manor,
Kingston Maurward, Dorchester,
Dorset DT2 8PX
tel   01305 261110
fax   01305 263734
e-mail   thomson@kingston-maurward.co.uk
web   www.kingston-maurward.co.uk

Map 3 Entry 158

Dorset

Higher Came Farmhouse

It's a listed farmhouse of two halves, the front 100 years younger than the back. Inside, winding corridors, sloping floors and the odd wonky wall. Bedrooms are a good size, particularly the cream triple, which has its own dressing room and views of garden and paddock. All are comfortable with good mattresses, bottles of mineral water, thick bathrobes and a melée of patterns on walls, drapes, sofas and bed covers. Lisa and Tim, B&B pros, are terrific with guests and deliver great breakfasts. The place hums with birdsong, the garden is lovely and Dorchester is a five-minute drive.

Stickland Farmhouse

An encapsulation of much that is charming about Dorset... a soft, delightful thatched cottage in an enviably rural setting. Sandy and Paul have poured love into this listed farmhouse and garden, the latter bursting with lupins, poppies, foxgloves, clematis, delphiniums. Sandy, so welcoming, serves guests delicious breakfast in an Aga-warmed kitchen. Cottagey bedrooms have comfy mattresses and good pictures on the walls and one room opens to the garden. You are in a village with its own pub, and Cranbourne Chase, rich in barrows and hill forts, is close by. *Children over 10 welcome.*

rooms	3: 1 triple with bath; 1 triple, 1 twin/double, both with separate bath.
price	£60-£70. Singles £38.
meals	Packed lunch £3.50. Pub/restaurant 2.5 miles.
closed	Rarely.
directions	From Dorchester bypass A354 to Weymouth. 1st left to Winterbourne Herringston; at T-junc. right, on for 1 mile; look out for golf course, next left to house.

rooms	3: 2 doubles, 1 twin, all with shower.
price	From £60. Singles from £35.
meals	Pub in village.
closed	Christmas & New Year.
directions	Leave Blandford for SW, cross river Stour. Hard right after Bryanston school, for W. Stickland (4.5 miles). Down North St, right signed W. Houghton. House 150 yds on left with 5-bar gate.

Lisa Bowden
Higher Came Farmhouse,
Higher Came,
Dorchester,
Dorset DT2 8AP

tel	01305 268908
fax	01305 268908
e-mail	enquiries@highercame.co.uk
web	www.highercame.co.uk

Sandy & Paul Crofton-Atkins
Stickland Farmhouse,
Winterborne Stickland,
Blandford Forum,
Dorset DT11 0NT

tel	01258 880119
fax	01258 880119
e-mail	sticklandfarmhouse@sticklanddorset.fsnet.co.uk

Map 3 Entry 159

Map 3 Entry 160

Dorset

Lower Lynch House

On the glorious Isle of Purbeck, where the wind blows the trees sideways, this wisteria-strewn house (two 18th-century cottages woven together) sits in a tranquil fold. At the end of a long woodland track, a warm, clean and comfortable B&B. Your gentle hosts give you Aga-cooked breakfast at tables overlooking courtyard and garden; old-fashioned bedrooms with pale colours and florals are as peaceful as can be. No sitting room, but there is a small sofa in the double. You are minutes from the coastal path – and if you spot wild deer munching on the roses, tell Bron.

Gold Court House

Anthea and Michael have created a mood of restrained luxury and uncluttered, often beautiful, good taste in their Georgian townhouse. Bedrooms are restful in cream with mahogany furniture, sloping ceilings, beams, armchairs and radios. There's a large drawing room and good paintings. Your hosts are delightful – "they do everything to perfection," says a reader – and both house and garden are a refuge. Views are soft and lush yet you are in the small square of this attractive town; the house was rebuilt in 1762 after a great fire, and the Hipwells added their creative spin six years ago. *Children over 10 welcome.*

rooms	2: 1 double with separate bath/shower; 1 twin with shower.
price	From £60. Singles by arrangement.
meals	Good inn 0.75 miles.
closed	Christmas & New Year.
directions	A351 from Wareham to Corfe Castle. At end of village fork right on B3069 for Kingston. Left in 0.5 miles down track (sign on roadside).

rooms	3 twins/doubles, all with separate bath.
price	From £60. Singles £40.
meals	Dinner £15, available in winter. Good restaurants 50 yds.
closed	Christmas & New Year.
directions	From A35, A351 to Wareham. Follow signs to town centre. In North St, over lights into South St. 1st left into St John's Hill; house on far right-hand corner of square.

Bron & Nick Burt
Lower Lynch House,
Kingston Hill,
Corfe Castle,
Dorset BH20 5LG
tel   01929 480089
e-mail bronburt@tiscali.co.uk

Anthea & Michael Hipwell
Gold Court House,
St John's Hill,
Wareham,
Dorset BH20 4LZ
tel   01929 553320
fax   01929 553320
web   www.goldcourthouse.co.uk

Map 3 Entry 161

Map 3 Entry 162

Dorset

North Mill

It's the setting that does it. With the river Piddle mill-race rushing right outside the house, you can sit and enjoy the views across the water meadows and watch ducks, swans and Sally's chickens. This pretty 16th-century mill house, formed by two cottages set at right angles, is on the edge of Wareham and has been completely restored over the last four years. Neat, cosy bedrooms look down over the pretty little garden and the river; there's also a separate sitting/dining room with a woodburning stove, books, paintings, piano and antiques. The World Heritage coastline beckons.

Bering House

At the end of a quiet cul de sac, an immaculate retreat. Pretty little sofas, golden taps, coordinating drapes – Renate is justly proud. Gaze from the balcony of your sumptuous suite on sparkling Poole harbour, biscuits and sherry to hand; the garden room, too, has every little extra – dressing gowns, sweets, fruit, videos, bathroom treats. Summer breakfasts are served among the birds, the flowers and the breezes on blue and white Spode china, or in the dining room off a darkly wooden table. Fresh fruit, Parma ham, smoked salmon, kedgeree: the choice is superb. Amazing harbourside B&B.

rooms	2: 1 double with shower; 1 twin with separate bath/shower.
price	£65. Singles £45.
meals	Dinner, 3 courses with wine, £15. Pubs/restaurant 5 minute walk.
closed	Rarely.
directions	On entering Wareham, right up Shatters Hill just after garage. Right down footpath opposite Mill Lane.

rooms	2: 1 twin/double with bath & shower; 1 twin/double suite with kitchen, bath & shower.
price	£60-£75. Singles by arrangement.
meals	Pub 400 yds, good restaurants 1 mile.
closed	Rarely.
directions	From A35/A350 Upton, towards Blandford; B3068 for Hamworthy & Rockley Park. 1.5 miles on right at Red Lion into Lake Rd; under bridge past Yachtsman Pub; 2nd left down Branksea Ave; last on left.

	Sally Dubuis
	North Mill,
	Wareham,
	Dorset BH20 4QW
tel	01929 555142
mobile	07976 273385
e-mail	sallydubuis@northmill.wanadoo.co.uk
web	www.northmill.org.uk

	Renate & John Wadham
	Bering House,
	53 Branksea Avenue,
	Poole,
	Dorset BH15 4DP
tel	01202 673419
fax	01202 667260
e-mail	johnandrenate@tiscali.co.uk

Map 3   Entry 163

Map 3   Entry 164

Dorset

Thornhill

A large house kept in pristine condition by Sara and John – as is the huge and enchanting garden. Furnishings are sedate, and some newer pieces are well mixed with family antiques. The twin, with swirly-patterned carpet, has a good collection of books; the double has garden views from both windows. Sara is helpful and kind and pays great attention to detail: a toothbrush for the forgetful, linen table napkins, fruit in the rooms, a choice of teas. Every view is onto green Hardy Country... or the lovely garden. Bring your rackets and bounce a few balls around the tennis court.

Crawford House

Below, the River Stour winds through the valley and under the medieval, nine-arched bridge; above, an Iron Age hill fort; between is Crawford House. It's an elegant Georgian house, soft and pretty inside with an easy, old-fashioned feel. Carpeted bedrooms are homely and warm, with long curtains; one room has four-poster twin beds with chintz drapes. The sun streams through the floor-to-ceiling windows of the downstairs rooms, and charming 18th- and 19th-century oil paintings hang in the pale green dining room. The Poole ferries are 25 minutes away.

rooms	3: 1 double, 1 twin, 1 single sharing 2 baths. Possible use of separate bath.
price	From £54. Singles from £27.
meals	Pub/restaurant 400 yds.
closed	Rarely.
directions	From Wimborne B3078 to Cranborne. Right to Holt. After 2 miles Thornhill on right, 200 yds beyond Old Inn.

rooms	3: 1 twin/double with bath; 2 twins sharing bath.
price	£55. Singles £27.50.
meals	Pub in village, 0.5 miles.
closed	Mid-October-mid-April.
directions	1st gateway immed. on left after crossroads (B3075) on A350 going north after entering Spetisbury.

John & Sara Turnbull
Thornhill,
Holt,
Wimborne,
Dorset BH21 7DJ
tel   01202 889434
e-mail scturnbull@lineone.net

Andrea Lea
Crawford House,
Spetisbury,
Blandford,
Dorset DT11 9DP
tel   01258 857338
fax   01258 858152

Map 3 Entry 165

Map 3 Entry 166

Dorset

The Old Forge, Fanners Yard

Tim and Lucy are tangibly happy in this beautifully restored forge. It was built in the 1700s; the wheelwright and carriage-builder from the local estate used to work here. Tim is a classic car restorer and has rebuilt a 1934 Lagonda; Lucy rides long distance on her Arab horse. The attic bedrooms are snug, with Lucy's quilts, country antiques and sparkling bathrooms. Delicious Aga-cooked breakfasts include eggs from their own free-strutting hens, organic sausages and bacon, home-grown jams, apple juice straight from the orchard. The Downs beckon walkers; warm corners invite readers. Utterly genuine.

Oakdale House

It's modest, unfussy, quiet, decent and softening with age. The house is only five years old yet blends well with its surroundings here on the edge of the Cranborne Chase. There's a collection of books in the dining room and chairs decorated with Ella's tapestry work and, in your bedroom under the eaves, there are floral blinds at the windows and thoughtful extras such as spring water and flowers. This is good value, breakfasts are freshly cooked and Ella is kind and keen that you should enjoy your stay. The charming village is in an AONB and there's a good pub. *Children over 10 welcome.*

	The Old Forge	Oakdale House
rooms	3: 1 double/family with shower; 1 double, 1 single sharing bath (single for same party).	1 twin/double with separate bath.
price	£60–£85. Singles £40.	From £50. Singles from £35.
meals	Pub/restaurant 1 mile.	Excellent pub 3-minute walk.
closed	Rarely.	Rarely.
directions	From Shaftesbury, A350 to Compton Abbas. House 1st on left before Compton Abbas sign. Left; entrance on left.	From Shaftesbury, A30 east. Through Ludwell, then left at bottom of hill signed The Donheads. At T-junc. towards Donhead. Pass Foresters Inn on right, fork left after 150 yds. House on right after 300 yds.

Tim & Lucy Kerridge
The Old Forge,
Fanners Yard,
Compton Abbas,
Shaftesbury,
Dorset SP7 0NQ
tel   01747 811881
fax   01747 811881
e-mail   theoldforge@hotmail.com

Ella Humphreys
Oakdale House,
Donhead St Andrew,
Shaftesbury,
Dorset SP7 9EG
tel   01747 828767
e-mail   ella@oakdalehouse.co.uk
web   www.oakdalehouse.co.uk

Map 3 Entry 167

Map 3 Entry 168

Dorset

Strouds House

The house, named after the 16th-century farmer who built it, is full of old-style charm. A low-beamed sitting room, comfortably stylish and softly lit, has a big old fender across the fire. Honeysuckle hugs the window of the twin, with its own little door to the garden; the double, with books and big brass bed, looks to the hills. A delightful home, thanks to Sally, who brings guests together over supper and fills the house with flowers. Recline in the hammock as your children help collect eggs for breakfast (a feast of local and organic produce); then stride off into the green Dorset hills.

Golden Hill Cottage

Deep in the countryside lies Stourton Caundle and this charming thatched cottage. All yours are a carpeted twin room with pleasant village views and a downstairs sitting room cosy with antiques, paintings on the walls, a piano in the corner and a fire. In the morning Anna, courteous and kind, brings you splendid platefuls of local bacon and sausage, homemade jams and Dorset honey. There are glorious walks from the village, a good pub that serves real ales, and Sherborne, Montacute and Stourhead for landscape, culture and history. *Babes in arms welcome.*

rooms	2: 1 double with separate bath/shower; 1 twin with bath/shower.
price	£57–£60. Singles £30.
meals	Dinner, from £17.50. Picnic £8.
closed	Rarely.
directions	A350 Shaftesbury-Blandford. After 6 miles, right to Sutton Waldron; at T-junc., left; at 2nd T-junc, left. Over little bridge; road curves right; opp. chapel, take road to left; follow to end.

rooms	1 twin with shower & sitting room.
price	From £50. Singles fom £25.
meals	Good pubs/restaurants within 3 miles.
closed	Rarely.
directions	From Sherborne, A352 to Dorchester; after 1 mile, left onto A3030; on to far end of Bishops Caundle, left to Stourton Caundle; after sharp left into village street, house 200 yds on right.

	Sally Weldon
	Strouds House,
	Farrington,
	Blandford Forum,
	Dorset DT11 8RA
tel	01747 811412
e-mail	sallyweldon@hotmail.com

	Andrew & Anna Oliver
	Golden Hill Cottage,
	Stourton Caundle,
	Sturminster Newton,
	Dorset DT10 2JW
tel	01963 362109
e-mail	anna@goldenhillcottage.co.uk
web	www.goldenhillcottage.co.uk

Map 3 Entry 169

Map 3 Entry 170

Dorset

Tudor Lodge

The interior of this quiet Victorian townhouse is as immaculate as the garden outside. Classically English rooms are decorated in harmonious aqua and soft yellow, bedrooms are comfortable and inviting, bathrooms are white with a touch of chintz and the sitting room – where a dear little dachsund basks by the big Sixties' window – is warm, light and sunny. Your courteous hosts give you beds dressed with fine sheets and blankets and the best of produce at breakfast. Shops, restaurants, abbey are the shortest stroll, and the garden has views to Sherborne Castle Hill.
Children over 12 welcome.

The Old Vicarage

The 1872 house is handsome gothic outside, traditional English inside – with unusual oriental flourishes. With its huge, sunny, carpeted drawing room, impressively sofa-ed at each end, this would be an excellent place for a big family get-together. Bedrooms are large and light, pelmetted, flowered and draped; the three in the stables are smaller but almost as grand. All have super bathrooms and rolling views. Your ex-restaurateur hosts serve weekend dinners – a brilliant blend of east and west – in an orangery-style dining room at white-dressed tables.
Children over five welcome.

rooms	2: 1 twin/double with bath; 1 double with separate bath.
price	From £75. Singles from £47.50.
meals	Good pubs & restaurants an easy walk.
closed	December & January.
directions	From Yeovil A30, left into North Rd; left at first x-roads into Newlands, then sharp right at Castleton x-roads into Long St. House on left, 150 yds from x-roads.

rooms	6: 3 doubles, 3 family, all with bath/shower.
price	£68-£112. Singles £52-£84.
meals	Dinner £21-£29, Friday & Saturday only. Pub/restaurant 200 yds.
closed	January.
directions	From Sherborne A30 to Milborne Port. House 3rd on right on entering village.

Mrs Pamela Rae
Tudor Lodge,
Long Street,
Sherborne,
Dorset DT9 3ED

| tel | 01935 813970 |
| e-mail | rae-tudorlodge@tiscali.co.uk |

Mr Anthony Ma & Jorgen Kunath
The Old Vicarage,
Milborne Port,
Sherborne,
Dorset DT9 5AT

tel	01963 251117
fax	01963 251515
e-mail	theoldvicarage@milborneport.freeserve.co.uk
web	www.milborneport.freeserve.co.uk

Map 3 Entry 171

Map 3 Entry 172

Dorset

Windrush Farm

You breakfast in the farmhouse kitchen at a long, polished oak table beside French windows; beyond is the scented, rambler-strewn English garden. Walls are terracotta-washed and cupboards painted a pretty cream – the feel is French, natural, stylish. Upstairs is delightful, too, with creaky carpeted floors, sloping ceilings and a maze of corridors. Bedroom colours are soft yellows and blues, pinks and creams, with paintings, prints and books to catch your eye. On colder evenings, the Golds will light a fire for you in the sitting room which is snug and set about with comfy sofas.

rooms	2: 1 double, 1 twin with separate bath (2nd room let to same party).
price	From £60. Singles from £40.
meals	Dinner £15-£20. Good pub/restaurant 2 miles.
closed	Christmas.
directions	From Wincanton, A357 for Templecombe. 2nd signed turning to Stowell on right opp. entrance to Horsington House. Down hill past church. 0.5 miles on. House on left after phone box.

Richard & Jenny Gold
Windrush Farm,
Stowell,
Sherborne,
Dorset DT9 4PD
tel   01963 370799
e-mail   jennygold@amserve.com

Map 3 Entry 173

Durham

Ivesley Equestrian Centre

For lovers of horses this is special: there are 40 of them and you can learn to ride. Still with a hunting lodge feel, Ivesley stands at the end of an avenue of beeches planted in 1350 to commemorate the end of the Black Death. Half the house is new, discreetly so; the floorboards that creak are in the old part. Big bedrooms are 'country house' with antiques and panoramic views; dining and drawing rooms are warmly grand. Roger prepares flexible continental breakfasts, staff come in to do full English. Popular with university parents and handy for Beamish Museum. *Children over eight welcome.*

rooms	5: 3 twins/doubles, all with bath or shower; 1 double, 1 single sharing bath & shower.
price	£49-£60. Singles from £36.
meals	Cooked breakfast supp. £5. Dinner £26.
closed	Christmas Day.
directions	A1, then A68 to Tow Law. Right onto B6301, signed Lanchester. After 3.7 miles, right at sign. Avenue 0.7 miles up hill on left.

Roger & Pauline Booth
Ivesley Equestrian Centre,
Waterhouses,
Durham DH7 9HB
tel   0191 3734324
fax   0191 3734757
e-mail   ivesley@msn.com
web   www.ridingholidays-ivesley.co.uk

Map 12 Entry 174

Durham

Spring Lodge

The renovation of the 1825 Regency villa was an enormous task and Sarah-Jane has tackled it with good humour and energy. Within strolling distance from the delightful small town, this is a fine country house that has come alive since she took over: a rocking horse in the hall, comfy sofas in the guest sitting room, a fire lit on chilly evenings. Carpeted bedrooms are light and airy with fresh white bed linen and towels; ask for one with a view. A lovely walled rose garden – breakfast here in summer – envelopes the house and merges with a buttercup field. Beyond, the rolling dales and purple-clad moors.

rooms	3: 1 double with shower; 1 twin with bath; 1 twin with separate bath.
price	£65-£75. Singles from £40.
meals	Pubs & restaurants 3-minute walk.
closed	Christmas & New Year.
directions	From A1, Scotch Corner, A66 for B. Castle. 7 miles, before 1st section of dual carriageway, 1st right for B Castle to lights; right over bridge; at T-junc. left for B. Castle town. Pass school & museum, through gates on left.

Sarah-Jane Ormston
Spring Lodge,
Newgate,
Barnard Castle,
Durham DL12 8NW

tel	01833 638110
fax	01833 630389
e-mail	sarahjane7@btopenworld.com

Map 12 Entry 175

The Coach House

We loved this place – the cobbled courtyard that evokes memories of its days as a coaching inn (Dickens stayed here), the river running through the estate, the garden and potager, the fine breakfasts and home-grown produce, and Peter and Mary, your kind, unstuffy hosts who have three adorable, beautifully-behaved dogs. Every creature comfort has been attended to in this cosy, stylish house: crisp linen, soft lights and embroidered pillows in the bedrooms; big soft towels and heated rails in the bathrooms; a log fire in the drawing room. A perfect stepping stone to Scotland – or the south.

rooms	2: 1 twin/double with bath/shower; 1 twin/double with separate bath.
price	£75. Singles £45.
meals	Dinner, 3 courses, £22.50. Pubs & restaurants nearby.
closed	Rarely.
directions	A1(M) to Scotch Corner. A66 west for 8 miles until Greta Bridge turn-off. House on left just before bridge.

Peter & Mary Gilbertson
The Coach House,
Greta Bridge,
Barnard Castle,
Durham DL12 9SD

tel	01833 627201
fax	01833 627201
e-mail	info@coachhousegreta.co.uk
web	www.coachhousegreta.co.uk

Map 12 Entry 176

Durham

34 The Bank

In this impressive Georgian townhouse live Digby, Eva, Ian and Georgina. Digby's an Old English sheepdog and Georgina is the resident ghost whose manners are unfailingly polite; Eva and Ian merely run the place. Ian cooks the breakfasts and Eva arranges them artistically because that's her thing. They love their guests and provide beautiful rooms – white quilts, bold walls, easy chairs – and much comfort in the sitting room with open fire. Sally forth to see the rest of bonny Barney on the Tees: the castle, the antique shops and the restaurant next door where Cromwell really stayed. Marvellous.

rooms	3: 1 double, 1 twin, 1 four-poster, all with bath/shower.
price	From £50. Singles from £35.
meals	Good pubs/restaurants 50 yds.
closed	Rarely.
directions	At A1 Scotch Corner, A66 west for 14 miles. Then 1st dual carriageway; right for Barnard Castle. At lights right over bridge, left at T-junc. to Butter Market. Left down bank, house on left.

	Ian & Eva Reid
	34 The Bank,
	Barnard Castle,
	Durham DL12 8PN
tel	01833 631304
e-mail	evasreid@aol.com
web	www.number34.com

Map 12 Entry 177

Essex

Brook Farm

Lovely large Georgian windows fill the house with light, unpretentious family pieces warm the friendly bedrooms and the low carved cross beam in the family room is late medieval. Anne, country lover and B&B-er, has farmed here for over 30 years and her sheep and 'coloured' horses roam these 100 acres. You breakfast (well) at a long table on antique benches, and nod off, after a pub supper, on a comfy sofa. Logs fill the copper, hunting prints line the walls and there are magazines and books to delve into. The handsome bright farmhouse is full of country charm – yet 30 minutes from Stansted.

rooms	3: 1 double, 1 family both with separate bath; 1 twin with shower.
price	£55–£65. Singles from £30.
meals	Packed lunches £3-£5. Good pubs 1.5 miles.
closed	Rarely.
directions	House on B1053, 500 yds south of Wethersfield.

	Mrs Anne Butler
	Brook Farm,
	Wethersfield,
	Braintree,
	Essex CM7 4BX
tel	01371 850284
fax	01371 850284
e-mail	abutlerbrookfarm@aol.com

Map 9 Entry 178

Essex

The Old Rectory

Scrunch up to this Georgian-fronted, wisteria-wrapped family house. Six children are variously away or busying about tending all sorts of fowl and four-legged folk; Bella, gracious and easy, makes it all look a doddle. Come for lovely walks through an ancient woodland cleared to free bluebells and your own private 'studio' bolthole with duckpond deck. There are tall windows, a long sofa, free-range flowers, yards of books and beckoning beds, a spanking new kitchen (make your own organic breakfast and just taste those eggs) and a classy bathroom. Just 10 minutes from Colchester.

rooms	1 double with bath/shower.
price	From £75. Singles from £40.
meals	Good pubs/restaurants nearby.
closed	Christmas.
directions	A12; A1124 towards Halstead. After 1st r'bout, right at Brick & Tile pub, into Spring Lane then right on Argent's Lane; left uphill at T-junc., then 1st left Cooks Hall Road; blue gates at first bend.

Bella Huddart
The Old Rectory,
West Bergholt,
Colchester,
Essex CO6 3EX
tel   01206 241637
mobile   07768 511755
e-mail   bella_huddart@hotmail.co.uk

Map 10 Entry 179

Bromans Farm

The island of Mersea is secluded, surprising, and Bromans Farm is in the most tranquil corner; the sea murmurs across the saltings where the Brent geese wheel and the great Constable skies stretch. The house began in 1343 – nearly as old as the exquisite church. The Georgians added their bit, but the venerable beams and uneven old construction shine through. It is a sunny, comfortable house, with good bedrooms and warm bathrooms. There is a snug, book-filled sitting room, a beautiful Welsh oak dresser in the breakfast room, and a conservatory gazing over the large garden. Wild walks beckon.

rooms	2: 1 double, 1 twin, both with separate bath.
price	£60-£70. Singles £35.
meals	Restaurant 1 mile; pub 0.5 mile.
closed	Rarely.
directions	From Colchester B1025, over causeway, bear left. After 3 miles, pass Dog & Pheasant pub; 2nd right into Bromans Lane. House 1st on left.

Ruth Dence
Bromans Farm,
East Mersea,
Essex CO5 8UE
tel   01206 383235
fax   01206 383235
e-mail   bromansfarm@btopenworld.com
web   www.bromansfarm.co.uk

Map 10 Entry 180

Gloucestershire

Boyts Farm

A magnolia rambles around the wooden mullioned windows and an old oak door admits you to the 16th-century farmhouse. Stone flags, Georgian panelling and polished wooden stairs are softened by pale fabrics, comfortable sofas, books and flowers. The effect is simple, uncluttered, pleasing. The bedrooms are delightful, too, one with an original Thirties' bathroom. John and Sally are inspired gardeners in their Italianate two acres: orchards, ponds, ha-has, paddocks and canal. Breakfast on orchard stewed fruits and homemade jams. The house is handsome, the setting wonderful, the peace a balm.

Hillcourt

Off a snowdropped lane, a friendly Cotswolds house whose ha-ha leads to fields where polo ponies graze. Enter a hall resplendent with antiques, flowers and oil paintings of horses and family; beyond, a comfy, chintzy drawing room with a piano: a musical atmosphere prevails. Bedrooms are pale and restful, old beds have new mattresses and fine linen, there are books and pretty tea trays and big old-fashioned bathrooms. Breakfast on butcher's sausages, homemade bread and marmalade in a dining room with big garden views. Peace, space, seclusion – and Westonbirt Arboretum right next door.

rooms	2: 1 double, 1 twin, both with bath.
price	£75. Singles £35-£40.
meals	Pub with restaurant 3-minute walk.
closed	21 December-2 January.
directions	M5 junc. 16, A38 for Gloucester. After 6 miles, turn for Tytherington. From north, M5 exit 14; A38 for Bristol. Turn for Tytherington after 3 miles.

rooms	2 doubles, both with bath.
price	£80. Singles by arrangement.
meals	Dinner, 2 courses, £25.
closed	24 December-1 January.
directions	From Tetbury, A433 for Bath. 1st left to Shipton Moyne. After 1 mile 1st right to Westonbirt. House 0.8 miles on left.

John & Sally Eyre
Boyts Farm,
Tytherington,
Wotton-under-Edge,
Gloucestershire GL12 8UG
tel   01454 412220
e-mail   jve@boyts.fsnet.co.uk

Susie & Antony Brassey
Hillcourt,
Shipton Moyne,
Tetbury,
Gloucestershire GL8 8QB
tel   01666 880280
fax   01666 880570
e-mail   susieb@dial.pipex.com

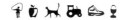

Map 3 Entry 181

Map 3 Entry 182

Gloucestershire

Drakestone House

A treat by anyone's reckoning. Utterly delightful people with wide-ranging interests (ex British Council and college lecturing; arts, travel, gardening) in a manor-type house full of beautiful furniture. The house was born of the Arts & Crafts movement and remains fascinating: wooden panels painted green, a log-fired drawing room for guests, quarry tiles on window sills, handsome old furniture, comfortable proportions... elegant but human. The garden's massive clipped hedges and smooth, great lawn are impressive, as is the whole place. Refined but nevertheless easy.

The Old Rectory

Behind the elegant Georgian façade, a ravishing interior. Large, light, sunny rooms glow in their finery: cut-glass on mahogany, paintings in gilt frames, cushions on deep sofas, pelmets, tie-backs and swags. Opulent bedrooms carpeted in palest cream have sweeping views of the Severn. Jane decorates houses for a living and was surely destined to do B&B: she thrives on meeting people – from babies to grannies – and cooks perfect roast dinners with organic trimmings. Ducks, dogs, pigs, sheep, horses and ha-ha share these 30 acres, in a lovely, undiscovered corner of Gloucestershire. *Horse B&B*.

rooms	3: 1 twin with separate shower; 1 double, 1 twin, sharing bath.
price	£68. Singles £44.
meals	Dinner £24. BYO.
closed	December-January.
directions	B4060 from Stinchcombe to Wotton-under-Edge. 0.25 miles out of Stinchcombe village. Driveway on left marked, before long bend.

rooms	3: 1 twin, 1 family room both with bath/shower; 1 four-poster with separate bath.
price	£70. Singles £40.
meals	Dinner occasionally available. Good pubs/restaurants 0.5-4 miles.
closed	Rarely.
directions	A48 from Chepstow for approx. 4 miles. At Woolaston, left after picnic area into Keynsham Lane. Road forks, take left at end, drive for house on left of church gates.

Hugh & Crystal Mildmay
Drakestone House,
Stinchcombe,
Dursley,
Gloucestershire GL11 6AS

tel	01453 542140
fax	01453 542140

Jane Bowyer
The Old Rectory,
Woolaston,
Lydney,
Gloucestershire GL15 6PR

tel	01594 528179
mobile	07771 656520
e-mail	jane@rectorydesign.co.uk

Map 8 Entry 183

Map 7 Entry 184

Gloucestershire

Cinderhill House

Coffee and homemade biscuits on arrival. Gillie, passionate about local produce, spoils you; a feast at breakfast, produce from the garden, home-baking, wines at dinner. The medieval hall house is a warren of low beamed ceilings, flagstone floors, oak doors and bulging walls. Plenty of space to relax and a conservatory with stunning views over the Wye valley to the Brecon Beacons. Country-style bedrooms are fresh with chintz, soft lamps, flowers; white and wood-panelled bathrooms have Neal's Yard soaps. Tintern Abbey is close, there are village walks and tea in the terraced garden to come home to.

rooms	3: 1 double, 1 twin/double, 1 family all with bath.
price	From £80. Singles from £45.
meals	Supper, 2-4 courses, £18.50-£26.50 excluding wine. Pub 300 yds.
closed	Christmas & New Year.
directions	A466 Chepstow-Monmouth. Cross Bipsweir Bridge and follow signs for St Briavels. House just below castle on left.

Gillian Peacock
Cinderhill House,
St Briavels,
Gloucestershire GL15 6RH
tel   01594 530393
mobile   07743 576368
e-mail   cinderhill.house@virgin.net
web   www.cinderhillhouse.co.uk

Map 7 Entry 185

Grove Farm

Boards creak and you duck – it is a farmhouse of the best kind: simple, small-roomed, stone-flagged, beamed, delightful. The walls are white, the furniture is good and there are pictures everywhere. In spite of great age (16th century), it's light, with lots of windows. You'll have a good breakfast, too; the 400 acres are farmed organically (cows and sheep) and you can bring your horse – some of the forest pubs have hitching posts. Stupendous views across the Severn estuary to the Cotswolds, and woodland walks, carpeted with spring flowers. And there is simply no noise – unless the guinea fowl are in good voice.

rooms	2: 1 twin/double with separate bath; 1 double with shower.
price	£60-£70. Singles £30.
meals	Packed lunch £3.50. Pub 2 miles.
closed	Rarely.
directions	2 miles south of Newnham on A48, opp. turn for Bullo Pill, large 'pull-in' with phone box on right; turn here; follow farm track to end.

Penny & David Hill
Grove Farm,
Bullo Pill,
Newnham,
Gloucestershire GL14 1DZ
tel   01594 516304
fax   01594 516304
e-mail   davidandpennyhill@btopenworld.com
web   www.grovefarm-uk.com

Map 8 Entry 186

Gloucestershire

Frampton Court

Deep authenticity in this magnificent, Grade I-listed house in a fascinating village. The manor of Frampton-on-Severn has been in the family since the 11th century and although Rollo looks after the estate, it is Gillian, the housekeeper, who looks after you (very well). Exquisite examples of carved wood and, in the hall, a Doric frieze. Bedrooms are solidly traditional with antiques and panelling and wonderful views. Beds have fine linen, bathrooms are delectably antiquated. Stroll around the Dutch ornamental canal, soak up the old-master views. An architectural masterpiece.

The Old School House

The perfect English scene: a late 18th-century house tucked down a lane off the country's longest village green; a garden alive with colourful posies. Bedrooms are large with fluffy towels, crisp linen, muted yellows and rich velvety plums. It's a wonderful house that feels freshly decorated and Carol wants you to treat it as home. When we visited, there was a jigsaw puzzle that invited a challenge, dogs and cats happily co-existed and the visitors book was inscribed: "We'll be back" (and return they do). At breakfast: fresh eggs, elegant china, pots of homemade jam. *Children over 10 welcome.*

rooms	3: 1 twin/double, 1 double both with bath; 1 four-poster with bath & separate wc.
price	£90–£100. Singles £60.
meals	Dinner £24. Pub across the green. Good restaurant 3 miles.
closed	Rarely.
directions	From M5 junc. 13 west, then B4071. Left down village green, then look to left! Entrance between two chestnut trees. 2nd turning left, 400 yds.

rooms	2: 1 twin/double, 1 twin, both with bath/shower.
price	£70. Singles £35.
meals	Pubs in village. Excellent restaurant 5 miles.
closed	Christmas & New Year.
directions	A38 for Bristol, west onto B4071. 1st left & drive length of village green. 300 yds after end, right into Whittles Lane. House last on right. 3 miles fom junc. 13 on M5.

Rollo & Janie Clifford
Frampton Court,
Frampton-on-Severn,
Gloucestershire GL2 7EU
tel   01452 740267
fax   01452 740698
e-mail   clifford@framptoncourt.wanadoo.co.uk
web   www.framptoncourtestate.uk.com

Carol Alexander
The Old School House,
Whittles Lane,
Frampton-on-Severn,
Gloucestershire GL2 7EB
tel   01452 740457
e-mail   theoldies@the-oldschoolhouse.co.uk
web   www.the-oldschoolhouse.co.uk

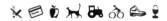

Map 8 Entry 187

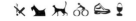

Map 8 Entry 188

Gloucestershire

The Pinetum Lodge

A year-round, Gloucestershire retreat. Come for sheets of snowdrops in January, the nightingale's song in spring, stunning foliage in autumn – and delightful hosts. Their home is a hunting lodge with views over the rolling Cotswold Hills. Enter an enchanted wood surrounded by a RSPB sanctuary and an arboretum planted by Thomas Gambier Parry in 1844 – the scent of pine wafts into the house. Carol and David are knowledgeable about organic gardening (home-grown seasonal veg for dinner) as reflected in the 13-acre grounds. Homely bedrooms have new beds and bathrooms and good views.

Heaven's Above at The Mad Hatters

Mike and Carolyn have opened a fully organic restaurant above which sits their equally excellent B&B. "We do it for spirit, not money," says Carolyn, the food is very good and it's a place that we are delighted to include. Your bedroom may share a bathroom but each room is wonderful – huge, like a studio, with oak floors or seagrass matting and lovely art on the walls. They've used local craftsmen to hand-make the beds, light fittings, fire baskets, tables and crockery and you have your own entrance opposite the Herb Wheel: you can come and go as you please. *Children by arrangement.*

rooms	3: 1 double, 1 twin/double, both with bath; 1 twin/double with shower.
price	£65–£70. Singles £35–£40.
meals	Dinner £22.50. Pub/restaurant 4 miles.
closed	Rarely.
directions	From Gl'cester A40 & A48 r'bout follow A40 (Ross) for 0.7 miles. Right into drive of black & white cottage at speed camera sign on left; track into woods; through gates. Drive round to front door.

rooms	3: 1 double with shower; 1 double, 1 twin sharing bath.
price	£60. Singles £35.
meals	Fully organic restaurant. Dinner, 3 courses, £27; Lunch, 3 courses,£20. Pub 0.5 miles.
closed	Rarely.
directions	M5, junc. 13, A419 to Stroud, A46 south to Nailsworth. Right at r'bout & immed. left; restaurant & house opp. Britannia Pub.

	David & Carol Wilkin
	The Pinetum Lodge,
	Churcham,
	Gloucestershire GL2 8AD
tel	01452 750554
fax	01452 750402
e-mail	carol@igeek.co.uk
web	www.pinetumlodge.ik.com

	Carolyn & Mike Findlay
	Heaven's Above at The Mad Hatters
	3 Cossack Square,
	Nailsworth,
	Gloucestershire GL6 0DB
tel	01453 832615
e-mail	mafindlay@waitrose.com

Map 8 Entry 189

Map 8 Entry 190

Gloucestershire

Nation House

Three cottages were knocked together to create this perfect little house, now listed and resplendent with wisteria in spring. Beams are exposed, walls are pale and hung with prints, floors are close-carpeted (pinky beige), curtains are floral, the sitting room is formally cosy and bedrooms are a dream: fat quilts, low beams, lattice windows. In summer gentle Brenda serves you breakfast – probably organic, always local – in the conservatory overlooking the ancient-walled garden. The village is a Cotswold treasure, full of lovely eating places and with walks from the door.

Well Farm

Perhaps it's the warm welcome from charming, intelligent young hosts. Or the unusual nature of the house – two 19th-century farm cottages newly connected by a single storey. Or the great position and glorious views across the valley. Whatever, you'll feel disarmed and invigorated by your stay here. It's a real family home and guests have their own wing, with a fresh, pretty bedroom and a sitting room that opens to a sunny courtyard. Kate, an inspired gardener, is establishing a garden and has a special interest in old roses. It's going to be terrific, and the area teems with good walks and pubs.

rooms	3: 2 doubles sharing bath; 1 suite with shower.
price	£60–£75. Singles £40.
meals	Excellent pubs 50 yds.
closed	Rarely.
directions	From Cirencester A419 for Stroud. After 7 miles right to Bisley. Left at village shop. House 50 yds on right.

rooms	1 twin/double with bath.
price	From £65.
meals	Dinner by arrangement, from £15. Excellent pubs nearby.
closed	Rarely.
directions	5.1 miles west of Cirencester on A419. Take first right to Frampton Mansell (unsigned) 300 metres before petrol/pub on left. 1st right into driveway, keep left to 2nd house.

Brenda & Mike Hammond
Nation House,
George Street,
Bisley,
Gloucestershire GL6 7BB
tel   01452 770197
e-mail   nation.house@homecall.co.uk

Kate & Edward Gordon Lennox
Well Farm,
Frampton Mansell,
Stroud,
Gloucestershire GL6 8JB
tel   01285 760651
e-mail   kategl@btinternet.com.
web   www.well-farm.co.uk

Map 8 Entry 191

Map 8 Entry 192

Gloucestershire

Lodge Farm

A plum Cotswolds position, a striking garden, stylish décor, exceptional linen – there are plenty of reasons to stay here. Then there are your hosts, who can throw a house party, help wedding groups, give you supper en famille next to the Aga, arrange dinners in the dining room with crystal and silver. The visitors' sitting room has fresh, elegant flowers, family photographs and lots of magazines; throughout are flagstones, Bath stone and wood. Home-produced (Hebridean) lamb for dinner, maybe, and excellent coffee at breakfast. The Salmons breed thoroughbreds and can stable your horse.

rooms	4: 2 twins/doubles with bath & shower; 1 twin/double, 1 family both with shared bath.
price	£50–£60. Family room £75. Singles from £40.
meals	Packed lunch £8.50. Dinner, 3 courses, £15.50. Good pub/bistro 2.5 miles.
closed	Rarely.
directions	From Cirencester A433 to Tetbury, right B4014 to Avening. After 250 yds, left onto Chavenage Lane. Farm 1.3 miles on right; left of barn.

Mrs Nicola Salmon
Lodge Farm,
Chavenage,
Tetbury,
Gloucestershire GL8 8XW

tel	01666 505339
fax	01666 505346
e-mail	nicky@lodgefarm.vianw.co.uk
web	www.lodgefarm.co.uk

Map 8 Entry 193

The Old Rectory

Old-fashioned authenticity here in historic Rodmarton, and much well-worn dignity. Mary is efficient and quietly kind; John is a company director and works from home. Beamed bedrooms lie on the older, 16th-century side of the house; they have wicker or padded headboards, coloured bathroom suites, formica-surround basins, mahogany chests, framed landscapes on walls. The staircase is listed in its own right. There are some excellent charcoal drawings by John's mother and a striking bust of Mary's uncle in the racing-green dining room. Roman history and good walks abound.

rooms	3: 2 doubles, both with bath; 1 twin with separate shower.
price	£60. Singles from £35.
meals	Dinner, 2-3 courses, £14–£17.50. BYO. Good pub/restaurant 2 miles.
closed	Christmas & New Year.
directions	From Cirencester, A433 towards Tetbury. After 6 miles, right, signed Rodmarton. 2nd right into village; house 3rd on right.

Mary FitzGerald
The Old Rectory,
Rodmarton,
Cirencester,
Gloucestershire GL7 6PE

tel	01285 841246
fax	01285 841246
e-mail	jfitz@onetel.com
web	www.rodmarton.com

Map 8 Entry 194

Gloucestershire

The Old House

A glorious 1600s house in Calmsden ('place of calm'). There's a delightful drawing room (log fire, squishy sofas), light, sunny bedrooms all of which face south, plump pillows and elegance and friendliness in equal measure. Floors creak, beams go the wrong way, views sail out of mullioned windows and the smell of home-baked bread entices you to a delicious panelled dining room for breakfast. Walkers have perfect countryside to explore, race-goers have Cheltenham. It's all very special and Bridget is lovely – she doesn't even mind last-minute bookings!

Children by arrangement.

Lady Lamb Farm

Light pours into perfectly proportioned rooms through windows hung with velvet and chintz; great sofas entice; china sits in alcoves on both sides of the fireplace. And chickens strut on the lawn – a manicured one for a working farm! Your charming hosts built the honey-stone house 22 years ago and have kept their Cotswold dream immaculately. After a scrumptious Aga-cooked breakfast – with eggs from those happy hens – you may baulk at the idea of swimming or tennis. Jeanie and James, farmers, inventors and hosts extraordinaires, can organise all the usual jaunts: fishing, cycling, golf.

rooms	3: 1 double with shower; 1 twin/double with bath/shower; 1 double with separate bath.
price	£65-£80. Singles £45-£50.
meals	Breakfast 8-9am. Excellent pub 1.5 miles.
closed	December-February.
directions	From Cirencester A429 north. After 5 miles, 2nd left for Calmsden, just before Hare & Hounds. On for 1.5 miles; 3rd house on right.

rooms	2: 1 twin with bath; 1 twin/double with separate bath.
price	£64. Singles £40.
meals	Pubs/restaurants 1-4 miles.
closed	Christmas & New Year.
directions	A417 Cirencester-Fairford road. Pass Meysey Hampton sign & entrance on right opp. sign for Waitenhill & Cherry Tree House. Approx 1 mile from Meysey Hampton, 0.5 miles from Fairford.

Bridget Baxter
The Old House,
Calmsden,
Cirencester,
Gloucestershire GL7 5ET
tel   01285 831240
e-mail   baxter@calmsden.freeserve.co.uk

Jeanie Keyser
Lady Lamb Farm,
Meysey Hampton,
Cirencester,
Gloucestershire GL7 5LH
tel   01285 712206
fax   01285 712206
e-mail   jekeyser1@aol.com

Map 8 Entry 195

Map 8 Entry 196

Gloucestershire

The Old Rectory

English to the core – and to the bottom of its lovely garden, with a new woodland walk and many places to sit. You sweep in across the circular driveway to a golden labrador welcome. The house, despite its magnificent age, throbs with family energy and conviviality – Caroline is calmly competent, friendly and warm, with a talent for understated interior décor. The two ample, airy bedrooms are furnished with antiques, very good beds, a chaise longue or an easy chair, even a bottle opener and wine glasses. Elsewhere, old furniture and creaky floorboards complete the sense of well-being in a very special place.

Clapton Manor

Like Wilde's reformed Selfish Giant, the house chuckles 'under the influence' of children. Relaxed and inviting, the 16th-century manor is as all homes should be: loved and lived-in. Yet, with three-foot-thick walls, a flagstoned hall, sit-in fireplaces and stone mullioned windows, it's an impressive pile. (The garden, too, is quite something.) One bedroom has a secret door that leads to an unexpected fuchsia-pink bathroom; the other, smaller, has wonderful garden views. Gaze over the garden wall as you breakfast on home-laid eggs and homemade jams. A lovely family house – worth at least a weekend stay.

	The Old Rectory		Clapton Manor
rooms	2: 1 double, 1 twin, both with bath/shower.	rooms	2: 1 double, 1 twin/double, both with bath/shower.
price	From £70. Singles £45.	price	From £80. Singles £60.
meals	Excellent pub within walking distance.	meals	Pub/restaurants 5-15-minute drive.
closed	December-January.	closed	Christmas & New Year.
directions	South through village from A417. Right after Masons Arms. House 200 yds on left.	directions	From Cirencester, A429 for Stow. Right at construction site, signed Clapton. Follow signs. In village, pass triangular green on left & house straight ahead on left on corner.

Roger & Caroline Carne
The Old Rectory,
Meysey Hampton,
Cirencester,
Gloucestershire GL7 5JX
tel   01285 851200
fax   01285 850452
e-mail   carolinecarne@cotswoldwireless.co.uk

Karin & James Bolton
Clapton Manor,
Clapton on the Hill,
Bourton on the Water,
Gloucestershire GL54 2LG
tel   01451 810202
mobile   07967 144416
e-mail   bandb@claptonmanor.co.uk
web   www.claptonmanor.co.uk

Map 8 Entry 197

Map 8 Entry 198

Gloucestershire

Grove Farm House

Masses of charm and style here – the 1789 Cotswold farmhouse is much loved and is a restful place to stay. Outbuildings, courtyards and granary are in the same warm stone as the house, and your hosts are friendly, fun and terrific cooks. Angela is Cordon Bleu trained. Breakfasts and dinners are served in the oak-beamed dining room, where lovely oils complement the beams and flagged floors. Country bedrooms are stylish with curtains in Colefax florals and there are robes in the bathrooms. Walking and riding all around, a good village pub and a pool for summer swims.

Rectory Farmhouse

The farmhouse was a monastery, then Henry VIII took it over and gave it to Christ Church College, Oxford; it has had only two private owners since. Passing a development of converted farm buildings to reach the warm Cotswold stones of this place makes the discovery doubly exciting. More glory within: Sybil, a talented designer, has created something immaculate, fresh and uplifting. Bed linen is white, walls cream; beds are superb, baths deep. Sybil used to own a restaurant and her breakfasts – by the Aga or in the conservatory, under the rampant vine – are a further treat.

rooms	3: 1 double, 1 double with extra single, 1 twin, all with bath.
price	£80. Singles £40-£45.
meals	Dinner £25. Good pub in village.
closed	Christmas.
directions	In middle of village, pass Plough Inn on left; look for gates on right.

rooms	3: 1 double with bath/shower; 1 double with bath; 1 suite with sitting room & shower.
price	From £76. Singles £50.
meals	Pub/restaurant 1 mile.
closed	Christmas & New Year.
directions	B4068 from Stow to Lower Swell, left just before Golden Ball Inn. Far end of gravel drive on right.

Angela Storey
Grove Farm House,
Cold Aston,
Cheltenham,
Gloucestershire GL54 3BJ

tel	01451 821801
fax	01451 821108
e-mail	angela@cotswoldbedandbreakfast.com
web	www.cotswoldbedandbreakfast.com

Sybil Gisby
Rectory Farmhouse,
Lower Swell,
Stow-on-the-Wold,
Gloucestershire GL54 1LH

tel	01451 832351
e-mail	rectory.farmhouse@cw-warwick.co.uk

Map 8 Entry 199

Map 8 Entry 200

Gloucestershire

Lower Farm House

The impression of tranquil England in good order is all around. Once the Home Farm of the Leigh estate, Lower Farm House has a perfect Georgian feel – high ceilings, sash windows, elegantly proportioned rooms – and, although graciously furnished, is not dauntingly formal. The pale-carpeted guest bedrooms are softly serene and have views of a restful garden that is a joy to sit out in in summer. Nicholas and Zelie are charming, articulate and love entertaining. Meals – everything as organic and locally sourced as possible – sound superb: cooking and gardening are Zelie's passions.

Wren House

Speckled brown-and-gold and dating from the 15th century, Kiloran's cottage oozes style and charm. Open the wrought-iron gates flanked by hollies, walk through the pretty garden and into the hall. Wren House was built before the English Civil War, Kiloran has spent two years renovating it and the results are a joy. Downstairs, light-filled, elegant rooms with glowing rugs on pale Cotswold stone; upstairs, fresh, sunny bedrooms, good bathrooms and a doorway to duck. Luscious breakfasts include cream from the Jersey cows in the fields over the wall. Dinners are equally fine. *Children over ten welcome.*

rooms	2: 1 double with shower; 1 twin with separate bath.
price	£80-£84. Singles £50.
meals	Dinner £20-£25. Pub/restaurant 1 mile.
closed	Rarely.
directions	A436 from Stow; after 3 miles, left to Adlestrop; right at T-junc; after double bend, drive 50 yds on right; sign at end of drive.

rooms	2: 1 twin/double with bath; 1 twin/double with separate bath/shower.
price	£90. Singles £55.
meals	Dinner, 3 courses, £20-£25. Good pubs 2.5 miles.
closed	November-Easter.
directions	A429 between Stow & Moreton; turn to Donnington; 400 yds, fork left; 100 yds, sign on right: entrance in wall marked by holly trees.

Nicholas & Zelie Mason
Lower Farm House,
Adlestrop,
Moreton-in-Marsh,
Gloucestershire GL56 0YR

tel   01608 658756
fax   01608 659458
e-mail   zelie.mason@talk21.com

Kiloran McGrigor
Wren House,
Donnington,
Moreton-in-Marsh,
Gloucestershire GL56 0XZ

tel   01451 831 787
e-mail   enquiries@wrenhouse.net
web   www.wrenhouse.net

Map 8 Entry 201

Map 8 Entry 202

Gloucestershire

Neighbrook Manor

You are on the site of an extinct medieval village, mentioned in the Domesday Book; until 1610 this was the village church. The ground floor is stone-flagged with rugs for colour and delightful touches of exotica everywhere. One bedroom is massive and the whole house is a treasure trove of things to look at and read – luxurious and stylish. The 37 acre gardens are beautiful, with sweeping views, trout lake, tennis court and pool; medieval stones have been used in the courtyard borders. John and Camilla are wickedly funny with a laid-back approach to B&B. *Children over seven welcome.*

rooms	3: 2 doubles, both with bath; 1 single with separate bath.
price	£85. Single £52.50.
meals	Supper £24. Excellent pub & restaurant nearby.
closed	Christmas.
directions	4 miles north of Moreton on A429, left to Aston Magna. At 1st building, immed. right. House 0.75 miles on right, up drive.

John & Camilla Playfair
Neighbrook Manor,
Aston Magna,
Moreton in Marsh,
Gloucestershire GL56 9QP
tel   01386 593232
fax   01386 593500
e-mail info@neighbrookmanor.com
web   www.neighbrookmanor.com

Map 8 Entry 203

Windy Ridge

Astonishing! It feels palpably Elizabethan, with superb mullioned windows, gables, great expanses of stoned, slated and thatched roofs and those unexpected corners that make old buildings so fascinating. Yet, unbelievably, it was started in 1951. Retired builder Cecil and his family have opened their home and prize-winning gardens to guests with generosity and bonhomie. There's an outdoor swimming pool flanked by a folly, an all-weather tennis court, croquet, a snooker/billiard room and an arboretum with almost 300 species of trees. It's immaculate and sumptuous, fun and special.

rooms	3: 1 double with bath; 1 double, 1 twin, both with separate bath.
price	From £80. Singles from £60.
meals	Excellent pub 100 yds, restaurant 2 miles.
closed	Rarely.
directions	From Stow, north for Broadway on A424 for 2 miles to Coach & Horses Pub on left. Opposite, turn right by post box & 30mph signs down single track lane. Entrance 100 yds down on left.

C J Williams
Windy Ridge,
Longborough,
Moreton-in-Marsh,
Gloucestershire GL56 0QY
tel   01451 832328/830465
fax   01451 831489
e-mail cjw@windy-ridge.co.uk
web   www.windy-ridge.co.uk

Map 8 Entry 204

Gloucestershire

Hyde Farm

Rex and Julia enjoy horses – bring yours and it won't want to leave! There's an honest decency about the Bovills, who are passionate about farming and the rural environment. The Cotswold stone farmhouse stands in an AONB with views to the hills above Stow; 180 green acres are home to a suckler herd of Limousin cattle. Rex rustles up breakfast: eggs from their Sussex hens, Gloucestershire Old Spot sausages and bacon, homemade marmalade. A wide oak staircase leads to a twin and a fresh double – both are quiet and homely, and the pink bath is huge. Good walks and gardens to visit nearby.

Westward, Sudeley Lodge

Susie and Jim are a bundle of energy and good humour, juggling teenage children, horses and B&B. She's also a great cook (Leith-trained). The house sits above Sudeley Castle surrounded by its own 600 acres; all bedrooms look west to long views. Colours, fabrics and furniture are in perfect harmony, beds and linen are luxurious, and the easy mix of elegant living and family bustle is delightful. There's tea on the terrace in summer and by a log fire in winter… your hosts delight in sharing this very English home. Wonderful walks on your doorstep and all those honey-hued Cotswold villages just beyond.

rooms	2: 1 double, 1 twin sharing bath/shower.
price	£70. Singles from £45.
meals	Dinner occasionally available. Good pubs 1 mile.
closed	Rarely.
directions	From Stow-on-the-Wold, B4077 towards Tewkesbury. After 6 miles, left to Temple Guiting. Through village, right at T-junc. opp. schoolhouse. 1 mile on left on upper side of road.

rooms	3: 1 double with bath & shower; 2 twins/doubles, both with bath/shower.
price	From £70. Singles £45.
meals	Good pubs/restaurants 1 mile.
closed	December-January.
directions	From Abbey Sq, Winchcombe, go north; after 50 yds, right into Castle St. Follow for 1 mile; after farm buildings, right for Sudeley Lodge; follow for 600 yds. House on right; first oak door.

Rex & Julia Bovill
Hyde Farm,
Temple Guiting,
Cheltenham,
Gloucestershire GL54 5RT

tel   01451 850665
e-mail   rajsbovill@hotmail.com

Susie & Jim Wilson
Westward,
Sudeley Lodge,
Winchcombe, Cheltenham,
Gloucestershire GL54 5JB

tel   01242 604372
fax   01242 604640
e-mail   jimw@haldon.co.uk
web   www.westward-sudeley.co.uk

Map 8 Entry 205

Map 8 Entry 206

Gloucestershire

Upper Court

Everything you'd want from a glorious English country house. A splendid Georgian manor in acres of landscaped grounds (National Gardens Scheme) and a two-acre lake alive with wildfowl. Bring friends for a party, get married, or come for a weekend of pure romantic indulgence. Antique furniture, floral flourishes, sumptuous four-poster beds with yards of drapery, kind hosts... and you can play tennis, croquet, billiards, swim in the outdoor pool, hill-walk, ride or clay pigeon shoot on Bredon Hill. Groups can book dinner or there's a good pub in the village. *Minimum stay two nights at weekends, unless late booking.*

rooms	5: 1 twin/double, 1 twin, 3 four-posters, all with bath.
price	£95–£120. Singles £75.
meals	Breakfast served in bed at no extra cost! Dinner, for parties only, £35. Pubs/restaurants 3-minute walk.
closed	Christmas.
directions	M5 junc. 9, A46 to Teddington Hands; left & follow signs for Kemerton. Left at War Memorial. House directly behind parish Church (not Catholic Church).

Bill & Diana Herford
Upper Court,
Kemerton,
Tewkesbury,
Gloucestershire GL20 7HY

tel	01386 725351
fax	01386 725472
e-mail	herfords@uppercourt.co.uk
web	www.uppercourt.co.uk

Map 8 Entry 207

Hampshire

Bay Trees

Hard to believe this was once a Poor House! Step in from the village street and you find yourself in a striking hall where Indian rugs gleam on a dark slate floor and cream walls are hung with good pictures. Bedrooms too have a grace and comfort beyond the dreams of any pauper – there's even a sumptuous, violet-draped four-poster. Breakfast is in the conservatory, overlooking captivating gardens where a giant willow grows beside the brook. Robert, humorous and down-to-earth, makes you feel at ease the moment you arrive. The shingle beach with great views of the Isle of Wight is a five-minute walk.

rooms	3: 1 double, 1 four-poster, both with bath; 1 family & extra single room sharing bath.
price	£70–£100. Singles from £40.
meals	Pub close by.
closed	Rarely.
directions	From Lymington follow signs for Milford-on-Sea (B3058). On left, just past village green.

Robert Fry
Bay Trees,
8 High Street,
Milford-on-Sea,
Lymington,
Hampshire SO41 0QD

tel	01590 642186
e-mail	rp.fry@virgin.net
web	baytreebedandbreakfast.co.uk

Map 3 Entry 208

Hampshire

Sandy Corner

Stride straight onto open moorland from this smallholding on the edge of the New Forest – a great spot for anyone who loves walking, cycling, riding, wildlife and outdoor space. And there's plenty of room for wet clothes and muddy boots. Cattle graze within 10 feet of the window, you may hear the call of a nightjar in June, Dartford warblers nest nearby, happy hens cluck around the yard. Sue also keeps a horse, two cats, a few sheep. You have a little guest sitting room, lovely fresh bedrooms, good home cooking and a marvellous, away-from-it-all feel. You can walk to one pub; others are nearby.

rooms	2: 1 double with bath/shower; 1 double with bath.
price	From £62. Singles from £40.
meals	Dinner from £15. Packed lunch £6. Good pub/restaurant 2.5 miles.
closed	Christmas & New Year.
directions	On A338, 1 mile S of Fordingbridge, at small x-roads, turn for Hyde & Hungerford. Up hill & right at school for Ogdens; left at next x-roads for Ogdens North; on right at bottom of hill.

	Sue Browne Sandy Corner, Ogdens North, Fordingbridge, Hampshire SP6 2QD
tel	01425 657295

Map 3 Entry 209

Ranvilles Farm House

The herringbone brickwork is just one of the features that grants this unusual house Grade II* listing. It dates from the 13th century – Richard de Ranville sailed here from Normandy with his family. A large bed in a big room overlooks a courtyard of old barns, and two further rooms are in the newer courtyard wing: modern and with level access, perfect for the less mobile. Delicious breakfasts are served in the palest grey dining room, grand with long table and paintings. There are five acres of garden, a paddock, lovely prints, lots of books and an easy atmosphere. Bill and Anthea are dynamic and fun.

rooms	3 twins/doubles, all with bath/shower; one could be a family room.
price	£50-£65. Singles from £35.
meals	Pub/restaurant 1 mile.
closed	Rarely.
directions	Exit M27 junc. 2; A3090 for Romsey. Climb hill; Gardener's Lane on left; on 100 yds, on south side of dual carriageway; house marked by flagpole. Crossing marked with 2 white posts.

	Bill & Anthea Hughes Ranvilles Farm House, Romsey, Hampshire SO51 6AA
tel	02380 814481
fax	02380 814481
e-mail	info@ranvilles.com
web	www.ranvilles.com

Map 3 Entry 210

Hampshire

Yew Tree House

The views, the house and the villagers are said to have inspired Charles Dickens, who escaped London, wisely, for the peace of this valley. The warm red brick was there 200 years before him; the rare dovecote (to which you may have the key) at the end of the herbaceous border 300 years before that. Delightful artistic hosts, generous with their time, have created a house of understated elegance: a yellow-ochre bedroom with Descamps bed linen, cashmere/silk curtains designed by their son, a view onto an enchanting garden, a profusion of flowers. The village is as tranquil as the house.

rooms	2: 1 double with separate bath; 1 twin with shower.
price	£56. Singles £35.
meals	Good pub in village; restaurants 5 miles.
closed	Rarely.
directions	From A30 west of Stockbridge for 1.5 miles, left at minor x-roads. After 2 miles left at T-junc. House on left at next junction opp. Greyhound pub.

Philip & Janet Mutton
Yew Tree House,
Broughton,
Stockbridge,
Hampshire SO20 8AA
tel   01794 301227
e-mail   pandjmutton@onetel.com

Map 3 Entry 211

Old Fullerton Station

Yes, it was a station – built in 1865 and serving the 'Sprat and Winkle' line from Andover to Southampton. Stroll along the platform, admire the original fretwork, enter the old waiting room where a marble fire-surround installed for a visit by Queen Victoria is still a striking feature. The whole of this sunny, delightful, very comfortable house is full of such talking points. Terance is a photographer and designer, Jane is charming and likeable and will tell you all you want to know about the area. She can organise fishing – Fullerton is in the lovely Test valley – and even provide a hamper. *Children over 8 welcome.*

rooms	2: 1 double, 1 twin, both with shower.
price	£60-£65. Singles £40-£45.
meals	Good pub 500 yds.
closed	Rarely.
directions	From A303, A3057 to Stockbridge. After 3 miles, left immed. after Fullerton sign on left. House down track though double gates on right.

Mrs Jane Dixon
Old Fullerton Station,
Fullerton,
Andover,
Hampshire SP11 7JZ
tel   01264 860202
fax   01264 860885
e-mail   jane@oldfullertonstation.co.uk
web   www.oldfullertonstation.co.uk

Map 3 Entry 212

Hampshire

Brymer House

Complete privacy in a B&B is rare. Here you have it, a 12-minute walk from town, cathedral and water meadows. Relax in your own half of a Victorian townhouse immaculately furnished and decorated with a garden to match. Fizzy serves sumptuous breakfasts and fresh flowers abound – guests have been delighted. You are also left with an 'honesty box' so you may help yourselves to drinks. Bedrooms are small and elegant, with antique mirrors, furniture and bedspreads; bathrooms are first class. There's a log fire in the sitting room and a small garden, too. *Children over 7 welcome.*

rooms	2: 1 double, 1 twin, both with shower & bath.
price	£65-£75. Singles £50-£54.
meals	Pubs/restaurants nearby.
closed	Christmas.
directions	M3 junc. 9; A272 Winchester exit, then signs for Winchester Park & Ride. Under m'way, straight on at r'bout signed St Cross. Left at T-junc. St Faith's Rd 100 yds ahead.

Guy & Fizzy Warren
Brymer House,
29/30 St Faith's Road,
St Cross,
Winchester,
Hampshire SO23 9QD
tel   01962 867428
fax   01962 868624
e-mail   brymerhouse@aol.com

Map 4 Entry 213

The Old School House

A galleried landing joins the addition to the Victorian flint-and-brick schoolhouse and you can't see the join! Susie is a natural, easy, courteous host and a welcoming atmosphere surrounds you. The kitchen is a pure country-life retreat, all old oak and terracotta, the nerve centre of the vivacious Susie's cooking and entertaining, plainly a matter of pride to her. You have your own delightful sitting room with open fire and piles of books; the double has three windows facing south to the garden, the twin two, so both feel light and airy. There are five acres and a vegetable plot.

rooms	2: 1 double with shower; 1 twin/double with separate bath.
price	£70. Singles £45.
meals	Good pubs within 5 miles.
closed	Christmas.
directions	From M3 exit 9, A272 to Petersfield. After 2 miles, fork right to Warnford & Preshaw, over x-roads. House 2nd on left after 300 yds.

Susie Lintott
The Old School House,
Lane End,
Longwood,
Winchester,
Hampshire SO21 1JZ
tel   01962 777248
fax   01962 777744
e-mail   dereklintott@hotmail.com

Map 4 Entry 214

Hampshire

Little Ashton Farm

Part 18th-century farm cottage, part extended Victorian extension, this is a quirky, friendly house and Felicity loves having guests. She's a china restorer and a keen cook with a burgeoning kitchen garden: plums, peaches, figs for bottling and jamming. You eat in the dining room; delicious "everything's local" breakfasts and dinners that are hard to resist. Separate staircases lead to the large triple under the rafters and the smaller cottage double; both have garden views, good furniture, linen, books and paintings. Country walks from the doorstep and a mile to Bishop's Waltham, of William of Wyckham fame.

Little Shackles

Gaze upon the pretty Arts & Crafts house from the comfort of the hammock or solar-heated pool: this is a charming place to stay. Rosemary advises on local gardens to visit (her own two acres are also special) and is the loveliest of hosts. Your bedroom has an elegant country air – firm beds, gingham and fine florals – and a spring-like bathroom with fluffy bathrobes and views to fresh green fields. Breakfast is plentiful, dinner at the lovely old drover's pub down the sleepy lane is a simple treat, and the walks on the South Downs are marvellous.

rooms	2: 1 double, 1 triple, both with bath & shower.
price	£60. Singles £35.
meals	Dinner from £18. Lunch £10. Packed lunch £5. Pubs/restaurants nearby.
closed	Mid-December-28 February.
directions	B2177 Winchester to Portsmouth. Just after 40mph sign into Bishop's Waltham, left into Ashton Lane. 0.75 miles up on left, black wrought-iron gates into drive.

rooms	2: 1 twin/double with bath; 1 single sharing bath, for child only.
price	£60. Single £20-£35.
meals	Packed lunches £5. Good pub 0.5 mile.
closed	Rarely.
directions	From London, A3/A272 junction Petersfield; right at r'bout, over level crossing; immed. left into Harrow Lane. House 2nd driveway on left.

	Felicity & David Webb-Carter
	Little Ashton Farm,
	Ashton Lane,
	Bishop's Waltham,
	Hampshire SO32 1FR
tel	01489 894055
mobile	0760 221785
e-mail	flossywebb@hotmail.com
web	www.littleashtonfarm.20m.com

	Rosemary Griffiths
	Little Shackles,
	Harrow Lane,
	Petersfield,
	Hampshire GU32 2BZ
tel	01730 263464
fax	01730 263464
e-mail	martgriff@freenet.co.uk

Map 4 Entry 215

Map 4 Entry 216

Hampshire

Mizzards Farm

Wow! The central hall is three storeys high, its vaulted roof open to the rafters. This is the oldest (and medieval) part of this lovely, rambling, mostly 16th-century farmhouse. Contemporary colours and fine antiques look splendid alongside ancient flagstones. There's a drawing room for concerts and an upstairs conservatory that catches the evening sun. The four-poster is on a raised dias with electric curtains; rooms ooze modern comfort. The garden is magnificent with lake, heated and covered swimming pool, outdoor chess, croquet and sculpture garden. *Children over eight welcome.*

rooms	3: 1 double, 1 four-poster, both with bath/shower; 1 twin with bath.
price	£66-£78. Singles by arrangement.
meals	Good pubs within 10-minute drive.
closed	Christmas & New Year.
directions	From A272 at Rogate, turn for Harting & Nyewood. Cross humpback bridge; drive signed to right after 300 yds.

Harriet & Julian Francis
Mizzards Farm,
Rogate,
Petersfield,
Hampshire GU31 5HS

tel	01730 821656
fax	01730 821655
e-mail	julian.francis@hemscott.net

Map 4 Entry 217

Park Farm

Gates sweep open to a gravelled forecourt and a super home: Nigel and Cathy's 18th-century dairy farmhouse and your annexe. Bedrooms, let to one party only, are pale and pretty, deeply comfortable and huge: one with elegant family pieces, both with field views. There are soft carpets, fat duvets and – luxury – your own sitting/dining room with books, music and TV. Blue polka dots frame French windows, a patio leads to a garden with wild areas and paddocks. Your friendly and humorous hosts know all about walking and wine, and there are good places to eat nearby. *Children over eight welcome.*

rooms	2: 1 twin with separate bath; 1 twin/double let to members of same party.
price	From £60. Singles £35.
meals	Good pub within walking distance.
closed	Christmas–mid-January.
directions	From x-roads in centre of Milland by the Rising Sun pub, take Petersfield road; Park Farm 0.25 miles on right on leaving village.

Nigel & Cathy Johnson-Hill
Park Farm,
Milland,
Liphook,
Hampshire GU30 7JT

tel	01428 741389
fax	01428 741368
e-mail	cathy@vintry.co.uk

Map 4 Entry 218

Hampshire

Land of Nod

A 1939 house of character with hosts to match and one of the greatest gardens in the book... seven tended acres within 100 acres of woodland. There are azaleas and camellias, specimen trees, croquet, tennis and wildlife. Breakfast in the chinoiserie dining room, designed by Jeremy – the allegorical tableau is charming. Both bedrooms have garden views; one has a fireplace with Beatrix Potter tiles, the other a blue and pink check bedspread; original baths have vast taps. Flexible breakfasts are locally sourced and seasonal fruit and preserves come from the garden. *Children over 10 welcome.*

The Manor House

Gracious yet informal, a crisp Regency house in this little corner of Hampshire where Jane Austen wrote most of her books and the great naturalist Gilbert White recorded the wildlife. Clare will spoil you, even collect you from the station if you come without a car. The bedrooms are airy and light with space for chairs, knick-knacks and family pictures. Eat a delicious breakfast in the elegant dining room whose French windows overlook a lovely garden and imagine you are living in a dreamier age – or take a look at the collection of contemporary art and bring yourself bang up to date.

rooms	2: 1 twin with bath; 1 twin with separate bath.
price	From £70. Singles from £45.
meals	Good restaurants 5-minute drive.
closed	Rarely.
directions	South on A3 to lights at Hindhead. Straight across & after 400 yds, right onto B3002. On for 3 miles. Entrance (signed) on right in a wood.

rooms	2: 1 double with bath; 1 twin with separate bath.
price	£65.
meals	Good pub 0.5 mile.
closed	Never.
directions	Exit A31 north of Alton, signed for Alton, Bordon & Holybourne. Over r'way; 1st right to Holybourne. After 300 yds road dips, look for church lane to left, turn; 100 yds on left up gravel drive without gate.

Jeremy & Philippa Whitaker
Land of Nod,
Headley,
Bordon,
Hampshire GU35 8SJ

| tel | 01428 713609 |
| fax | 01428 717698 |

Clare Whately
The Manor House,
Holybourne,
Alton,
Hampshire GU34 4HD

tel	01420 541321
mobile	07711 655450
e-mail	clare@whately.net

Map 4 Entry 219

Map 4 Entry 220

Hampshire

The Old Post House

A handsome Georgian cottage and an easy place to stay. Chintz at the windows, pictures on the walls, a generous oak dresser lined with blue and white china... hard to believe this was the village post office! The twin has polished walnut beds and a dressing table laid with silver-backed brushes; the smaller double has fresh white walls and a scarlet bedcover. Jollyon dashes off bacon and eggs on the Aga, Ruthie runs the village shop, source of some fine breakfast jams. Your sitting room looks onto a colourful cottage garden and it is all wonderfully homely and relaxing.

Manor House

Outside is a courtyard with a dovecote: pretty for breakfasts in the sun. This remarkable manor house was built in 1546 with timber from the forest that supplied the wood for the *Mary Rose*. The place is full of intriguing and fascinating features: dark beams, diamond leaded windows and witches' marks on the fireplace to ward off evil. But this is no museum – kind, friendly Wren and Rhydian make you comfortably at home aided by their well-mannered spaniel. The rooms have a warm, peaceful elegance and much of the impeccable upholstery has been fashioned by Wren.

rooms	2: 1 twin, 1 twin/double, sharing bath.
price	From £60. Singles from £35.
meals	Packed lunch by arrangement. Good pub next door.
closed	Christmas & New Year.
directions	M3, exit 5 to North Warnbrough & sign to Upton Grey (approx. 3 miles). House on left between pub & duckpond.

rooms	2: 1 double, 1 single sharing bath.
price	£70. Singles from £45.
meals	Supper £15–£20. Good pubs 2 miles.
closed	Christmas & New Year.
directions	M4 junc 11; A33 to Bramley, 14 miles. House at western end of village in Vyne Road, close to junction with The Street.

Jollyon & Ruthie Coombs
The Old Post House,
Upton Grey,
Basingstoke,
Hampshire RG25 2RL
tel   01256 862574
fax   01256 862025
e-mail jcpartnership@btopenworld.com

Wren & Rhydian Vaughan
Manor House,
Bramley, Tadley,
Basingstoke,
Hampshire RG26 5DE
tel   01256 881141
fax   01256 881141
e-mail info@manorhouse.biz
web   www.manorhousebramley.co.uk

Map 4 Entry 221

Map 4 Entry 222

Herefordshire

The Grove House

Surrounded by 13 acres of gardens and pastures, Grove House is warmly cosseting, its beams and furniture gleaming richly in the winter firelight. The guests' drawing room is large, elegant and generously furnished with plump sofas, and you sleep in the house's heart, among 14th-century timbers and 18th-century additions. Relax on the terrace in summer with a tea or cool Pimms, play tennis, swim in the neighbour's pool, spin off on a bike, walk the Malvern Hills. There's a games area in the barn, and the market town of Ledbury draws visitors from around the world.

The Barn House

A paean to carpentry: the hall open to the roof is beautiful, with Chippendale panels in the staircase, and oak beams and timber crucks on bold display. Breakfast under more beams, at a long table, on fresh fruits and compotes made by the warm, easy-going Judi. The bright yellow bedroom is the largest, with comfortable chairs and art from around the world. The other double is small and the twin, with toe-to-toe beds, would be best for friends sharing. Fluffy white robes are given for the quick flit to the vast bathroom with huge antique bath. Relax in your own sitting room, or take tea in the garden.

rooms	3: 1 twin/double, 2 four-posters, all with bath/shower.		rooms	3: 1 double with shower; 1 double, 1 twin, sharing bath.
price	From £79.50. Singles £51.50.		price	£75-£85. Singles £55.
meals	Dinner £27.50 (min. 6 people). Pubs/restaurants 3 miles.		meals	Pubs & restaurants 50 yds.
closed	Christmas.		closed	Christmas & New Year.
directions	M50 exit 2, for Ledbury; 1st left to Bromsberrow Heath; right by post office, up hill, house on right.		directions	From Ledbury bypass, A449 for Worcester & town centre. House on left just past Somerfield but before central town crossroads.

	Michael & Ellen Ross			Judi Holland
	The Grove House,			The Barn House,
	Bromsberrow Heath,			New Street,
	Ledbury,			Ledbury,
	Herefordshire HR8 1PE			Herefordshire HR8 2DX
tel	01531 650584		tel	01531 632825
mobile	07960 166903		e-mail	barnhouseledbury@lineone.net
e-mail	ross@the-grovehouse.co.uk		web	www.thebarnhouse.net
web	www.the-grovehouse.com			

Map 8 Entry 223

Map 8 Entry 224

Herefordshire

Hall End House

Classic English elegance on these 420 farmed acres – and a livery of polo ponies. The Jeffersons have devoted an enormous amount of care and energy to the restoration of Hall End and welcome you kindly. You have two drawing rooms to choose from, a conservatory resplendent with scented geraniums, a handsome staircase to wide landings and big bedrooms, tennis and an outdoor pool. The twin is elegant with a fabulous bathroom, fine linen and peachy touches; the four-poster is a delight. Lamb and beef from this well-managed farm is used when in season, served off Spode china. *Children over 12 welcome.*

Moor Court Farm

The buildings, about 500 years old, ramble and enfold both gardens and guests. This is an honest, authentic farmhouse with only the bleating of sheep to disturb the peace. Elizabeth, a busy farmer's wife, manages it all efficiently with husband Peter; they were lambing when we were there. They also dry their own hops and in September you can watch the lovely old oast house at work. Elizabeth is a good, traditional cook – make the most of the home-produced meat, preserves and vegetables. Cottagey bedrooms have been newly decorated and the smallest sits under the eaves.

rooms	2: 1 four-poster with shower; 1 twin with bath/shower.
price	£80-£90.
meals	Supper, 2 courses, £17.50. Dinner, 4 courses, £27.50. Good pub 2.5 miles.
closed	Christmas & New Year.
directions	From Ledbury, A449 west. Right for Leominster on A4172. 1 mile on, left for Aylton. 1.25 miles to junc. Left, towards National Fuschia Collection; cont. to junc. with Hall End Farm; keep left; drive 1st right.

rooms	3: 1 double, 2 twins all with shower.
price	From £50. Singles £30.
meals	Dinner, 3 courses, £15.
closed	Rarely.
directions	From Hereford, east on A438. A417 into Stretton Grandison. 1st right past village sign, through Holmend Park. Bear left past phone box. House on left.

Angela & Hugh Jefferson
Hall End House,
Kynaston,
Ledbury,
Herefordshire HR8 2PD

tel	01531 670225
fax	01531 670747
e-mail	khjefferson@hallend91.freeserve.co.uk
web	www.hallendhouse.com

Elizabeth & Peter Godsall
Moor Court Farm,
Stretton Grandison,
Ledbury,
Herefordshire HR8 2TP

| tel | 01531 670408 |
| fax | 01531 670408 |

Map 7 Entry 225

Map 7 Entry 226

Herefordshire

Dovecote Barn

Super people – natural hosts – and an easy atmosphere. This is an exceptional B&B and good value, too. There's much of architectural interest: a copse of 17th-century oak beams and timbers above and masses of light. Judy, an artist, created a beautiful conversion, then decorated with style. Bedrooms are simple and charming, with fresh flowers, good soaps, books, magazines, electric blankets to ensure the deepest sleep. Breakfasts are lavish and include homemade bread and jams. There's the freshest produce for dinner, and you can also eat at the local pub – Judy or Roger will ferry you.

Lower Bache House

A sense of honest industry pervades this special place. The Wiles have created a B&B that introduces you to all that they – and we – hold dear: they smoke their own meat and fish, bake bread daily and have a fully organic wine list. It's a fascinating place – 17th-century with cider house, dairy, butterfly house and 14-acre nature reserve; perched at the top of a small valley the views are tremendous. The private suites — one across the courtyard, the others in the granary annexe – all are timber-framed, snug and have their own sitting rooms. Breakfasts are superb. *Children over 12 welcome.*

rooms	3: 1 double with bath/shower; 1 twin/double with separate bath & shower; 1 double with travel cot & toddler bed.
price	£60. Singles £40.
meals	Dinner, 3 courses, £23. BYO. Pub 1 mile.
closed	Rarely.
directions	At Burley Gate r'bout on A417, A465 for Bromyard. At Stoke Lacy church, on right; right; then 2nd right to entrance.

rooms	3: 2 suites with bath; 1 suite with shower.
price	£69. Singles £44.50.
meals	Dinner £19.50–£24.50.
closed	Rarely.
directions	From Leominster, A49 north; right onto A4112, signed Leysters. Lower Bache signed after village of Kimbolton; look out for white butterfly sign.

Roger & Judy Young
Dovecote Barn,
Stoke Lacy,
Herefordshire HR7 4HJ

tel	01432 820968
fax	01432 820969
e-mail	dovecotebarn@mail.com
web	www.dovecotebarn.co.uk

Rose & Leslie Wiles
Lower Bache House,
Kimbolton,
Leominster,
Herefordshire HR6 0ER

tel	01568 750304
e-mail	leslie.wiles@care4free.net
web	www.smoothhound.co.uk/hotels/lowerbache.html

Map 7 Entry 227

Map 7 Entry 228

Herefordshire

The Old Vicarage

There are 11 fireplaces in the part-17th-, part-19th-century house, and bedrooms are large and airy, with perfect white linen and carpets soft underfoot. If you enjoy the luxuries of space and tranquillity, this immaculate house, full of old paintings and fine furniture, will make your heart sing. The double is fit for a king and the bathrooms are equally lavish. In the grounds, handsome lawns, mature trees and two kitchen gardens: Guy not only makes bread but also grows fruit and vegetables. Share the fruits of his labours with these kind and generous hosts at the grand dining table: Amanda loves to entertain.

rooms	2: 1 twin with bath; 1 double with bath/shower.
price	£80. Singles £50.
meals	Dinner, 3 courses with wine & pre-dinner drink, £28. Good pub/restaurant 4 miles.
closed	Rarely.
directions	From Tenbury Wells to Leysters, on A4112, left at crossroads in village. Ignore sign to Leysters church. House on left, with wooden gate (after postbox in wall).

Guy & Amanda Griffiths
The Old Vicarage,
Leysters,
Leominster,
Herefordshire HR6 0HS

tel	01568 750208
fax	01568 750208
e-mail	enquire@oldvicar.co.uk
web	www.oldvicar.co.uk

Map 7 Entry 229

Bunns Croft

The timbers of the medieval house, and there are many, are probably 1,000 years old. Little of the structure has ever been altered and it is an absolute delight: stone floors, rich colours, a piano, books and cosy chairs. Cruck-beamed bedrooms are snugly small, the stair to the family rooms is steep – this was a yeoman's house – and the twin's bathroom has its own sweet fireplace. The countryside is 'pure', too, with 1,500 acres of National Trust land five miles away. Anita is charming, loves her garden and her guests, grows her own fruit and veg and makes fabulous dinners. Just mind your head.

rooms	4: 1 twin with bath; 1 double, 2 singles, sharing bath, for family group.
price	£60-£68. Singles £30.
meals	Dinner, 3 courses, £20. Pub 4 miles.
closed	Rarely.
directions	From Leominster, A49 towards Ludlow. After approx. 4 miles, in village of Ashton, left & house on right behind postbox after 1 mile.

Mrs Anita Syers-Gibson
Bunns Croft,
Moreton Eye,
Leominster,
Herefordshire HR6 0DP

| tel | 01568 615836 |

Map 7 Entry 230

Herefordshire

Staunton House

The Georgian rectory's well-proportioned rooms, painstakingly restored, brim with beautiful furnishings and fine furniture. The original oak staircase leads to peaceful bedrooms with comfortable beds; the blue room looks onto garden and pond. It's a house that matches its owners – traditional and country-loving. Rosie and Richard are talented cooks and serve delicious dinners in the new kitchen, or in the dining room, elegant with portraits. You will feel as well tended as the three-acre garden. The highest 18-hole golf course in England is at nearby Kington, near Offa's Dyke.

Pear Tree Farm

Steve and Jill, young and well-travelled, enjoy opening up their home and spoiling you rotten. Fir-apple potatoes and orchard fruit often end up on the dinner table... food is taken seriously here and dinner is a sumptuous affair. So too is breakfast. Much panache in the décor, too, with delightful drapes and medieval-style chairs, tan leather sofas and polished boards, a Mexican hammock in the garden and masses of space to chill. The upstairs bedrooms are fresh and lovely, bathrooms candlelit and seductive. The old farmhouse is perfectly quiet at night. *Children over 10 welcome.*

rooms	2: 1 double with bath; 1 twin/double with bath/shower.
price	From £60. Singles £36.
meals	Dinner, 2-4 courses, £15-£25. Good pub/restaurant 2.5 miles.
closed	Rarely.
directions	A44 Leominster-Pembridge; right to Shobdon. After 0.5 miles, left to Staunton-on-Arrow; at x-roads, over into village. House opp. church, with black wrought-iron gates.

rooms	3: 1 double with separate bath; 1 twin, 1 double, both with shower.
price	From £80.
meals	Dinner £25.
closed	Rarely.
directions	A4110 north to Wigmore. At 'Welcome' sign on for 150 yds, then right. Drive 1st on left.

	Rosie & Richard Bowen
	Staunton House,
	Staunton-on-Arrow,
	Pembridge, Leominster,
	Herefordshire HR6 9HR
tel	01544 388313
mobile	07780 961994
e-mail	rosbown@aol.com
web	www.stauntonhouse.co.uk

	Steve Dawson & Jill Fieldhouse
	Pear Tree Farm,
	Wigmore,
	Herefordshire HR6 9UR
tel	01568 770140
fax	01568 770140
e-mail	info@ptf.me.uk
web	www.peartree-farm.co.uk

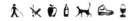

Map 7 Entry 231

Map 7 Entry 232

Herefordshire

Church House

This is more like staying in a home than a B&B. Your hosts are delightful, she a concert singer, he a wine merchant, and you may buy his excellent wines. You have all the advantages of being in a small, rural town: on one side the church, on the other a garden that disappears into the rolling hills. Bedrooms are prettily wallpapered, carpeted and cosy and share a big bathroom with a roll-top bath. You breakfast at a big polished table in the Georgian, shuttered dining room on Andrew's excellent marmalades and jams. A charming place to stay with glorious walks all around.

Hall's Mill House

A cosy and unpretentious house in a wonderful setting. The sitting room may be snug with woodburner and sofas but the kitchen is the hub of the place – delicious breakfasts and dinners are cooked on the Aga. Grace, chatty and easy-going, obviously enjoys living in her modernised mill house. Rooms are small, with exposed beams and slate window sills; only the old mill interrupts the far-reaching, all-green views. Drift off to sleep to the sound of the Arrow river burbling nearby – a tonic for frenzied city-dwellers. Excellent value, too. *Children over four welcome.*

rooms	2: 1 double, 1 twin, sharing bath.
price	£50. Singles £30.
meals	Pubs/restaurants 400 yds.
closed	Christmas & New Year.
directions	Coming into Kington, follow signs for town centre. Through middle of town & up long steady hill to St Mary's church. House on left opposite.

rooms	3: 1 double with shower; 1 double, 1 twin, sharing bath & wc.
price	£36-£50. Singles £18-£25.
meals	Dinner from £15. Good pub/restaurant 3 miles.
closed	Christmas.
directions	A438 from Hereford. After Winforton, Whitney-on-Wye & toll bridge on left, sharp right for Brilley. Left fork to Huntington, over x-roads & next right to Huntington. Next right into 'No through' road, then 1st right.

Andrew & Lis Darwin
Church House,
Church Road,
Kington,
Herefordshire HR5 3AG
tel   01544 230534
fax   01544 231100
e-mail darwin@kc3.co.uk
web   www.churchhousekington.co.uk

Grace Watson
Hall's Mill House,
Huntington,
Kington,
Herefordshire HR5 3QA
tel   01497 831409

Map 7 Entry 233

Map 7 Entry 234

Herefordshire

Winforton Court

Dating from 1500, the Court is dignified in its old age — undulating floors, great oak beams, thick walls. It is a light, airy, colourful home with exceptional timber-framed bedrooms; the four-poster has an Indian-style bathroom with huge roll-top bath, the 'suite' a sitting area with two sofas. You have your own sitting room and a small library, too, for restful evenings. Your hosts are delightful and spoil you with decanters of sherry and wine, even chocolates on special occasions. Walk down to the Wye, relax in the garden in summer, or visit nearby Hay-on-Wye. *Fishing can be arranged.*

Bollingham House

The views alone might earn the house a place in this book. But there's more… a beautifully furnished interior and an interesting four-acre garden with a perfumed rose walk. Stephanie and John, working unobtrusively to make your stay enjoyable, are natural hosts. Bedrooms are large, bright and comfortable, and Stephanie has cleverly brought vibrant colours, fine furniture and paintings together with a dash of elegance. Gaze from your windows across the Wye Valley to the Malvern Hills, and west to the Black Mountains. Stephanie's cooking is worth a detour.

	Winforton Court		Bollingham House
rooms	3: 1 double, 1 four-poster, 1 four-poster suite, all with bath.	rooms	2: 1 twin with bath; 1 double with separate bath.
price	£66-£84. Singles from £48.	price	From £70. Singles from £35.
meals	Pub/restaurant 3.5 miles.	meals	Dinner £20. Packed lunch £5. Pub 2 miles.
closed	Christmas.	closed	Occasionally.
directions	From Hereford, A438 into village. House on left with a green sign & iron gates.	directions	A438 Hereford to Brecon road, towards Kington on A4111; through Eardisley; house 2 miles up hill on left, behind long line of conifers.

	Jackie Kingdon		Stephanie & John Grant
	Winforton Court, Winforton, Herefordshire HR3 6EA		Bollingham House, Eardisley, Herefordshire HR5 3LE
tel	01544 328498	tel	01544 327326
fax	01544 328498	fax	01544 327880
web	www.winfortoncourt.co.uk	e-mail	grant@bollinghamhouse.com
		web	www.bollinghamhouse.com

Map 7 Entry 235

Map 7 Entry 236

Herefordshire

The Old Vicarage

An ecclesiastic entrance hall sweeps you into an imposing former Victorian vicarage built for a 'gentleman' priest. The stunning carved staircase leads to a galleried landing where light and well-proportioned bedrooms have been traditionally decorated; you'll find period furniture, good fabrics and attractive, plain colours. The Gallimores enjoy entertaining and there's a sitting room for you to relax in; there's also a super garden with Wellingtonia, potager and hedges of laurel and yew. Come for peace and elegance in a rural setting — and exceptional views to Hay and the Radnor Hills.

rooms	2: 1 double with bath & shower; 1 twin with separate bath/shower.
price	From £65. Singles by arrangement.
meals	Dinner from £20. Packed lunch from £5. Good pubs/restaurants 4 miles.
closed	Rarely.
directions	A438 from Hereford, A480 to Stretton Sugwas. After 10 miles from Hereford, left to Norton Wood & church. House 1st on right, entrance 2nd on right.

Jill & Julian Gallimore
The Old Vicarage,
Norton Canon,
Weobley,
Hereford,
Herefordshire HR4 7BQ
tel   01544 318146
e-mail   galli@gallimore.me.uk

Map 7 Entry 237

The Great House

Wordsworth visited and King Charles II danced on the landing: history comes alive at this gracious 16th-century manor house. On the edge of a charming black and white village, it is surrounded by beautiful gardens that open for the National Gardens Scheme. The ornate gates, dating from 1720, were admired by Pevsner. There are period furnishings throughout and you sleep in high brass beds under linen sheets. Bathrooms are large and comfortable, and the sunny guest sitting room leads into the garden. In winter a fire blazes in the flagstoned hall, in summer sit out by the ornamental canal.

rooms	2: 1 double, 1 twin, both with bath & shower.
price	From £70. Singles from £40.
meals	Dinner from £20. Good pubs/restaurants 3 miles.
closed	Rarely.
directions	From Leominster, A44 & follow signs for Brecon. After 6 miles, left into Dilwyn. Round 3 sharp bends. House set back on right behind stone gate piers & wrought-iron railings.

Tom & Jane Hawksley
The Great House,
Dilwyn,
Hereford,
Herefordshire HR4 8HX
tel   01544 318007
web   www.thegreathouse-dilwyn.co.uk

Map 7 Entry 238

Herefordshire

Lower House

I was in the equatorial forest, surely. The view reached over a pattern of tree tops to a distant hill, whose mist hovered as it awaited the day's heat. The house, itself a forest of old timber, is almost lost within the beautiful garden. It is old, but restored with affection. Stairs twist and creak, the unexpected awaits you. Bedrooms are panelled or timber-clad, bathrooms are neat, there is a handsome room where you eat a superb breakfast, read or play the piano. Nicky and Pete are unpretentious and easy, steeped in good taste and this exquisite project, next to Offa's Dyke path and on the Welsh border.

rooms	2: 1 double with shower; 1 double with separate bath.
price	From £60.
meals	Good pubs & restaurants 1 mile.
closed	Rarely.
directions	East through Hay on B4348 for Bredwardine. On the edge of Hay, right into Cusop Dingle; 0.75 mile, old mill house on left; drive on right, across stone bridge over stream.

Nicky & Peter Daw
Lower House,
Cusop Dingle,
Hay-on-Wye,
Herefordshire HR3 5RQ
tel   01497 820773
e-mail   nicky.daw@btinternet.com

Map 7 Entry 239

Ladywell House

Snuggling in the Golden Valley, wrapped by ancient oaks, with badgers, curlews, lambs and Hereford cattle for neighbours, you will breathe a sigh of relief even before stepping inside. The whitewashed dower house is welcoming and informal with understated good taste: soft colours, family paintings, antiques; this is very much open house. The four-poster bedroom is regal, the bathrooms are stylish. Breakfast in the conservatory, take drinks in the garden, dine under candlelight on locally-sourced produce, including rare-breed and traditionally farmed meats. Sarah and Charles are warm and generous.

rooms	2: 1 double with bath/shower; 1 twin with separate bath/shower.
price	£50-£65. Singles from £35.
meals	Dinner, 3 courses, from £20. Good pub 10-minute drive.
closed	Rarely.
directions	From A465 Hereford-Abergavenny, B4348 towards Hay-on-Wye. In Vowchurch, left towards Michaelchurch. Through hamlet of Turnastone, house 0.5 mile on right.

Charles & Sarah Drury
Ladywell House,
Turnastone,
Vowchurch,
Herefordshire HR2 0RE
tel   01981 550235
mobile   07970 510110
e-mail   sarahjdrury@amserve.com
web   www.ladywellhouse.com

Map 7 Entry 240

Herefordshire

Corner House

Their Dexter cattle provide beef; sausages and bacon are from their pigs; cream, eggs and honey are home-produced too. Such good, simple living is reflected in your white-walled, white-bedded room with its double bed, pale blue check curtains, modern pictures and simple furniture. The bathroom is neat, wooden-floored, white-curtained; the small sitting room, all yours, has a log-burning stove, books, CD-player, breakfast table, no TV. You are in remote and lovely countryside, but collectable from the railway station, and cyclists have a second night free! Easy-going and generous.

rooms	1 double with bath.
price	£50. Singles £25.
meals	Dinner, 3 courses, £15.
closed	Rarely.
directions	A465 Abergavenny-Hereford, then B4347 towards Hay-on-Wye. Through Ewyas Harold & Abbeydore; left at Bacton. Right at top of hill; 0.5 mile; house on right at x-roads opp. phone box.

Tim & Fiona Start
Corner House,
Newton St Margarets,
Herefordshire HR2 0QP

tel   01981 510283
e-mail   timstart@yahoo.co.uk
web   www.golden-valley.co.uk/cornerhouse

Map 7 Entry 241

Hertfordshire

The Old Rectory

Bright, fresh bedrooms lie across a flower-filled, cobbled courtyard and there's an ivy-clad squash court in the garden for the energetic. This is a handsome Grade II*-listed rectory in the village where George Bernard Shaw lived – his house is now owned by the National Trust. Relax on the sun-drenched terrace for breakfast or settle by the log fire in the ancient dining room with its deep red walls. Helen and Dick are kind and relaxed; they will tell you of wonderful walks and bike rides and introduce you to their enchanting local inn. All this 35 minutes from London. *Children by arrangement.*

rooms	3 twins/doubles, all with bath & shower.
price	£85. Singles by arrangement.
meals	Supper trays or dinner, £8-£20. Pub in village.
closed	Christmas.
directions	Exit A1 junc. 4. Follow signs to B653, towards Wheathampstead. At r'bout on to B653; 1st right for Codicote & Ayot St Lawrence. Left up Bride Hall Lane, signed Shaws Corner. Right into drive before red phone box in village.

Helen & Dick Dunn
The Old Rectory,
Ayot St Lawrence,
Welwyn,
Hertfordshire AL6 9BT

tel   01438 820429
fax   01438 821844
e-mail   ayotbandb@aol.com

Map 9 Entry 242

Hertfordshire

Homewood

Lutyens built this wonderful 1901 house for his mother-in-law, Lady Lytton. It is set down a long drive in six acres of beautiful gardens and fields, and each elevation is different. Architectural peculiarities – such as internal octagonal windows – abound, and Samantha has applied her considerable artistic skills to the interior. The downstairs rooms are particularly elegant and formal. Unusual colour schemes offset magnificent antiques, tapestries and chinoiserie. The family are happy to share their home with guests, can converse in a clutch of languages and will book tables and taxis if required.

rooms	3: 1 double with shower; 1 family suite (1 double, 1 twin) with bath; 1 double with separate shower sometimes available.
price	£80. Singles £50. Suite £80–£110.
meals	Pub 15-minute drive. Dinner (min. 4) by arrangement.
closed	20 December–3 January.
directions	Into Knebworth B197, into Station Rd (becomes Park Lane); 300 yds after m'way bridge, left into public footpath; 300 yds; bear left through gates; house at end.

Samantha Pollock-Hill
Homewood,
Old Knebworth,
Hertfordshire SG3 6PP

tel	01438 812105
fax	01438 812572
e-mail	sami@homewood-bb.co.uk
web	www.homewood-bb.co.uk

Map 9 Entry 243

Isle of Wight

North Court

The Harrisons bought this glorious Jacobean house for its matchless grounds: 15 acres of pathed terraced gardens, exotica and subtropical flowers. The house, too, is magnificent, with 80 rooms, its big, comfortable guest bedrooms in two wings. The library houses a full-size snooker table (yes, you may use it) and the vast music room a grand piano (yours to play). The dining room has separate tables and delightful Nina Campbell wallpaper. Step back in time – in a quiet, untouristy village in lovely downland, this large house, very much a family home, has softly-spoken and intelligent hosts and acres of space.

rooms	6 doubles/twins, all with bath/shower.
price	£60–£80. Singles £38–£45.
meals	Light meals sometimes available. Pub 3-minute walk through gardens.
closed	Christmas.
directions	From Newport, drive into Shorwell; down a steep hill, under a rustic bridge & right opp. thatched cottage. Signed.

John & Christine Harrison
North Court,
Shorwell,
Isle of Wight PO30 3JG

tel	01983 740415
fax	01983 740409
e-mail	christine@northcourt.info
web	www.northcourt.info

Map 4 Entry 244

Isle of Wight

Gotten Manor

Ancient peace, miles from the beaten track, bordered by beautiful stone barns; stylishness too. There's a refreshing simplicity to this unique 'first-floor' Saxon house where living space was above, and downstairs was reserved for storage. Stunning bedrooms have limewashed walls, polished wooden floors, A-frame beams and sofas; one is up a steep open stairs. You sleep on a French rosewood bed, and there's a huge cast-iron bath in each room — wallow by candlelight with a glass of wine. The garden bursts with magnificent fruit trees; breakfasts include smoked salmon and smoothies. Superb.

rooms	2: 1 double with bath; 1 double with bath/shower.
price	£60-£80. Singles by arrangement.
meals	Good pub 1.5 miles.
closed	Rarely.
directions	0.5 miles south of Chale Green on B3399. After village, left at Gotten Lane. House at end of lane.

	Caroline Gurney-Champion
	Gotten Manor,
	Gotten Lane,
	Chale,
	Isle of Wight PO38 2HQ
tel	01983 551368
mobile	07746 453398
e-mail	as@gottenmanor.co.uk
web	www.gottenmanor.co.uk

Map 4 Entry 245

Kent

Olde Moat House

Cross the moat into an arcadia of fields, birdsong and bleating sheep. The 15th-century house has a storybook elegance from its white walls and pitched roof to its beamed ceilings and canopied beds. The sitting room, with its inglenook, rug-scattered floor and big sofas, is perfect for Dianna's afternoon tea. Dreamy bedrooms — lush fabrics, striking wallpaper, canopied beds, a roll-top bath — have top-notch extras, and Aga-cooked breakfasts include homemade breads, muesli & preserves. Doze among the garden's fruit trees after exploring Rye, Sissinghurst or Great Dixter. The Eptons are affable and gracious.

rooms	2: 1 double with bath/shower; 1 suite with shower;
price	£90-£100. Singles from £60.
meals	Dinner, 2-3 courses, £20-£25. Good pub 3 miles.
closed	Rarely.
directions	M20 exit 10, then A2070 towards Brenzett; left to Ivychurch. From Rye A259 to Brenzett. A2070 for 1 mile; right to Ivychurch. House 0.75 miles on left.

	Dianna Epton
	Olde Moat House,
	Ivychurch,
	Romney Marsh,
	Kent TN29 0AZ
tel	01797 344700
e-mail	oldemoathouse@hotmail.com
web	www.oldemoathouse.co.uk

Map 5 Entry 246

Kent

The Old Rectory

On a really good day (about once every five years) you can see France. But you'll be more than happy to settle for the superb views over Romney Marsh, the Channel in the distance. The big, friendly house, built in 1850, has impeccable bedrooms and good bathrooms; the large, many-windowed sitting room is full of books, pictures and flowers from the south-facing garden. Marion and David have been here for years; she's an organist, he gardens and tinkers with boats; both make you welcome. It's remarkably peaceful – perfect for walking, cycling and birdwatching. *Children over 10 welcome.*

rooms	2: 1 twin with bath; 1 twin with separate bath/shower.
price	£60-£70. Singles £35-£40.
meals	Two excellent pubs within 4 miles.
closed	Christmas & New Year.
directions	M20, exit 10 for Brenzett on A2070. After 6 miles, right for Hamstreet; immed. left; in Hamstreet, left B2067. After 1.5 miles, left (Ash Hill); 700 yds on right.

Marion & David Hanbury
The Old Rectory,
Ruckinge,
Ashford,
Kent TN26 2PE
tel   01233 732328
e-mail   oldrectory@hotmail.com
web   www.oldrectoryruckinge.co.uk

Map 5 Entry 247

The French House

So robust is the building that it survived intact when it slid 50 feet down the escarpment in a dramatic subsidence in 1726! High on a hill overlooking Romney Marsh and the sea, the house is impressively ancient in parts. Life is lived to the full here and you'll be swept along by Matty and Peter's joie de vivre; don't come if you're a fervent anti-smoker or averse to unbridled enjoyment. Bedrooms are for sleeping rather than entertaining but each has its own 40-gallon cast-iron bath and wonderful view. France is so close you can see it, so take off on a wine run – Peter will help you organise it, take you, even!

rooms	3: 2 doubles, both with bath/shower, 1 with adjoining twin.
price	£70. Singles £40.
meals	Restaurants 10-minute drive.
closed	Christmas & New Year.
directions	M20 junc. 11, A20 south, then B2068 (Stone St), to Lympne. 0.25 mile on, County Members pub & school sign on right. Left opposite convex mirror. House at end of lane.

Peter & Matty Gaston
The French House,
Lympne,
Hythe,
Kent CT21 4PA
tel   01303 265974
fax   01303 262545
e-mail   gastons@frenchhouse.freeserve.co.uk
web   www.frenchhouse.freeserve.co.uk

Map 5 Entry 248

Kent

Stowting Hill House

A classic Georgian manor house in an idyllic setting close to the North Downs Way. This warm, civilised home mixes Tudor with Georgian styles and the friendly owners welcome you with tea and flowers from the garden. There's a large conservatory full of blooms and greenery, a comforting guest sitting room with sofas, log fire and views, Aga-cooked breakfasts and dinner if required. Carpeted bedrooms are cheerfully traditional, one has a pretty dressing table and a rich ethnic bedspread. You are 10 minutes from the Chunnel but this is worth more than one night. *Children over 10 welcome.*

Woodmans

Not only are you in the depths of the countryside but you feel wonderfully private too: your ground-floor bedroom is reached via a corner of the garden all your own. Step past greenery to the breakfast room, cosy with old pine table, dresser and flowers, for bacon and eggs; if you don't feel like emerging Sarah will kindly bring breakfast to your room. You can eat delicious dinner here, too. This is a good stopover point for trips across the Channel — and you're no more than a 15-minute drive from Canterbury and its glorious cathedral. *Babies welcome.*

rooms	3: 2 twins, both with bath/shower; 1 double sharing bath (let to same party only).
price	From £70. Singles £45.
meals	Dinner £20-£25. Excellent pub 1 mile.
closed	Christmas & New Year.
directions	From M20 junc. 11, B2068 north. After 4.6 miles, left opp. Jet garage. House at bottom of hill on left, after 1.7 miles. Left into drive.

rooms	1 double with bath/shower.
price	£60. Singles £30.
meals	Dinner, 3 courses, £20. Packed lunch £5.
closed	Rarely.
directions	From A2, 2nd exit to Canterbury. Follow ring road & B2068 for Hythe. Over A2, through Lower Hardres, past Granville pub. Right for Petham & Waltham. 1.5 miles after Waltham, right into Hassell St. 4th on left.

	Richard & Virginia Latham Stowting Hill House, Stowting, Ashford, Kent TN25 6BE
tel	01303 862881
fax	01303 863433
e-mail	vjlatham@hotmail.com

	Sarah Rainbird Woodmans, Hassell Street, Hastingleigh, Ashford, Kent TN25 5JE
tel	01233 750250

Map 5 Entry 249

Map 5 Entry 250

Kent

Park Gate

Who would not love it here? Peter and Mary make a delightful team and their conversation is informed and easy. Behind the wisteria-clad façade are two sitting rooms (one with chesterfield, one TV-free), ancient beams and polished wood. Bedrooms are freshly comfortable with views over the glorious garden to the fields beyond; bathrooms gleam; meals are delicious. More magic outside: croquet, tennis, foxgloves, wildlife and roses – and nine sheep to mow the paddock. Sir Anthony Eden lived here during WWII to be close to the Channel defences; now you have Channel Tunnel and ferry convenience.

rooms	3: 1 double, 1 twin with bath/shower; 1 single with separate shower.
price	£65. Singles £35.
meals	Dinner £20. Good pubs & restaurants 1 mile.
closed	Christmas.
directions	A2 Canterbury to Dover road; Barham exit. Through Barham to Elham. After Elham sign 1st right signed Park Gate 0.75 miles. Over brow of hill; house on left.

	Peter & Mary Morgan
	Park Gate,
	Elham,
	Canterbury,
	Kent CT4 6NE
tel	01303 840304

Map 5 Entry 251

Hornbeams

A heavenly setting: rolling hills and woodland, long views over luscious Kent and a sweet-scented garden that Alison has created herself. This is a sturdy Swedish bungalow, brilliant for wheelchair users and altogether easy and comfortable. Floral sofas and chairs, repro beds, carpets underfoot and masses of light. Alison, beauty therapist and engaging hostess, offers you fine toiletries and towels and has bags of local and walking knowledge. The house is beautifully remote yet so close to Dover it is worth staying at least one night before tackling the ferry.

rooms	3: 1 double with bath/shower; 1 twin with separate bath/shower; 1 single (let to same party only).
price	£70. Singles £40.
meals	Dinner, £20. Pubs 1.5 miles.
closed	Christmas.
directions	From A2 Canterbury-Dover, towards Barham & Kingston. Right at bottom of hill by shelter, into The Street, Kingston to top of hill & right fork. 1st left on sharp right bend. Left into farm, keep right of barn.

	Alison Crawley
	Hornbeams,
	Jesses Hill,
	Kingston, Canterbury,
	Kent CT4 6JD
tel	01227 830119
mobile	07798 601016
e-mail	alison@hornbeams.co.uk
web	www.hornbeams.co.uk

Map 5 Entry 252

Kent

Little Mystole

All is reassuringly traditional and peaceful in this lovely corner of Kent. The small Georgian house graced by an ancient mulberry tree has extremely neat outer and walled gardens with fine delphiniums and climbing roses. These well-travelled hosts give you cosy, comfortable bedrooms with touches of chintz and frill and the most inviting beds. A handsome dining room, beamed ceilings, antiques, plump sofas, gilt-framed portraits, pretty flower arrangements and... great scrambled eggs! Golf at Royal St George's and other courses can be arranged. *10 minutes from Canterbury, 30 from ferries and tunnel.*

Sylvan Cottage

The value is terrific and the feel is of a family home; Jac and Chris work, but nevertheless manage guests with helpful efficiency. Jac can babysit if you ask in advance, and prepare simple suppers. There's a guest sitting room and you feel private in your bit of the house. Chris, an umpire, runs a hockey and cricket shop and the two grown-up boys play county/national level sport. Breakfasts with all the trimmings, cooked by Chris, are very good, bedrooms are spotless and fresh with floral borders, and bathrooms are modern. *Bookings not accepted from smokers.*

rooms	3: 1 double with shower, 1 single in adjoining dressing room; 1 twin with bath & shower.
price	£75. Singles £15–£46.
meals	Dinner occasionally. Pubs & restaurants 1.5 miles.
closed	Christmas & Easter.
directions	A28 Canterbury-Ashford. Left to Shalmsford Street; right immed. after Post Office at Bobbin Lodge Hill. Road bends left, then right at T-junc.; 2nd drive on left at junction with Pickelden Lane.

rooms	4: 1 double, 1 twin/double, both with shower; 1 double & adjoining twin, with bath (let to same party).
price	From £48. Singles by arrangement. Children £5–£15.
meals	Dinner £12.
closed	Rarely.
directions	From M20 exit 11, B2068 for Canterbury. After crossing A2, house, with postbox in wall, 100 yds on right.

Hugh & Patricia Tennent
Little Mystole,
Mystole Park,
Canterbury,
Kent CT4 7DB

tel	01227 738210
fax	01227 738210
e-mail	little_mystole@yahoo.co.uk

Chris & Jac Bray
Sylvan Cottage,
Nackington Road,
Canterbury,
Kent CT4 7AY

| tel | 01227 765307 |
| e-mail | sylvan5@btinternet.com |

Map 5 Entry 253

Map 5 Entry 254

Kent

Great Weddington

An enchanting home in a peaceful setting, and the garden a treat even in winter. The listed house of perfect proportions was built by a Sandwich brewer of ginger beer... the drawing room is gorgeous, bedrooms are desirable and cosy, bathrooms are small, snug and spotless, and Katie has decorated, sponged and stencilled to perfection. Much-loved antiques, shelves of books, fine watercolours, fresh flowers. Outside, stunning hedges and lawns and a terrace for tea and drinks in the summer. You are surrounded by farmland and the area hums with history. *Children over eight welcome.*

rooms	2 twins/doubles, both with bath/shower.
price	£96. Singles £65.
meals	Dinner £29.50. Light suppers on request.
closed	Christmas & New Year.
directions	From Canterbury A257 for Sandwich. On approach to Ash, stay on A257 (do not enter village), then 3rd left at sign to Weddington. House 200 yds down on left.

Katie & Neil Gunn
Great Weddington,
Ash,
Canterbury,
Kent CT3 2AR
tel   01304 813407
fax   01304 812531
e-mail traveltale@aol.com
web   www.greatweddington.co.uk

Map 5 Entry 255

Forstal House

Where to begin – the house or garden? Both are a rare delight. The house started life as a bailiff's cottage around 1620 but was extended in 1789 to make a dower house. It is beautiful, quietly traditional, all muted colours, paintings and books. Cosy, welcoming bedrooms, one up, one down, look onto the gardens – graceful, formal, tantalising. Duncan, a painter, sculptor and printmaker, redesigned much of it after the 1987 hurricane. Fruit from the orchards goes into crumbles and pies and delicious breakfast jams. Your hosts enjoy their guests and could not be nicer. *Children over seven welcome.*

rooms	2: 1 twin/double with bath/shower; 1 double with shower.
price	£60. Singles from £35.
meals	Dinner, 3 courses, £20.
closed	Christmas.
directions	From A257, Canterbury to Sandwich; left at Wingham, north towards Preston. In Preston, the Forstal is 2nd left; 500 yds to house.

Elizabeth Scott
Forstal House,
The Forstal,
Preston,
Canterbury,
Kent CT3 1DT
tel   01227 722 282
e-mail emscott@forstal.fsnet.co.uk

Map 5 Entry 256

Kent

Frith Farm House

Eight immaculate acres of garden with pond, obelisk and orchards. Magnificent views, too – this is an AONB – and a very pretty indoor pool that is heated all year round. The house is large, traditional, luxurious. Bold fabrics and vividly coloured walls make a fine background for antiques; a Chinese carpet and oriental pictures hang in the hall. There's a music room with an organ, too. Markham occasionally gives concerts for charity – why not join in? He and Susan enjoy meeting new people over breakfast – local and delicious – and are lovely hosts. Canterbury and Leeds Castle are easily reached.

Dadmans

This listed dower house has two winding stairs: two Tudor cottages were joined to make one. Amanda enthuses about art history and her rare-breed hens – your breakfast eggs are the best. There's good local food for dinner, too, served in the dining room on polished mahogany. Bedrooms have patterned fabrics, firm beds and flowers, bathrooms are delightful: one heavily beamed with a claw-foot bath, the other blue-and-white-tiled. Ancient trees in the walled garden, orchards and fields all around, and Doddington Place with its gardens (and opera in summer) a five-minute drive. *Children over four welcome.*

rooms	3. 1 double, 1 twin, 1 four-poster, all with shower.
price	£70. Singles £40.
meals	Dinner, 2 courses, £19.50.
closed	Christmas.
directions	From A2 at Faversham, Brogdale road to Eastling. 1.5 miles past Carpenters Arms, right (by postbox). House 0.5 miles on right.

rooms	2: 1 double with separate bath; 1 twin with bath.
price	£65-£75. Singles £40.
meals	Dinner, 3 courses, £25. Light snacks £10.
closed	Rarely.
directions	M20 junc. 8, then east on A20; left in Lenham towards Doddington. At The Chequers in Doddington, left; house 1.7 miles on left before Lynsted.

	Susan & Markham Chesterfield
	Frith Farm House,
	Otterden,
	Faversham,
	Kent ME13 0DD
tel	01795 890701
fax	01795 890009
e-mail	enquiries@frithfarmhouse.co.uk
web	www.frithfarmhouse.co.uk

	Amanda Strevens
	Dadmans,
	Lynsted,
	Sittingbourne,
	Kent ME9 0JJ
tel	01795 521293
e-mail	amanda.strevens@btopenworld.com

Map 5 Entry 257

Map 5 Entry 258

Kent

Hartlip Place

The house resonates with a faded, funky grandeur. Family portraits and lovely pieces, a drawing room to die for, an antique table shimmering with potted hyacinths, sash windows with sweeping views and a garden intricate and special. After candlelit dinner, up the circular stair to your bedroom, delightful with big bed, garden views, decanter for sherry, proper old-fashioned bathroom and – huge treat – real winter fire. John is unflappable and a touch mischievous, Gillian cooks, daughter Sophie greets – you'll like the whole family. *Children over 12 welcome.*

Little Dane

Acres of enchanting garden with pheasants and moorcocks roaming the lawn and a church next door... blissfully peaceful. It wasn't always so; built as a rectory in the 1830s, the house was taken over by the RAF in the war, turned into a market garden and finally run as a school. Now fresh flowers scent the air and light floods in through long windows revealing fine rugs, antique beds and comfy sofas. Bedrooms glow with bold colours and fabrics, bathrooms are full of goodies. The Ashdowns have achieved a gracious, traditional look with a crisp modern slant – and Sonia's bread comes fresh from the Aga.

rooms	1 double with bath.
price	From £90. Singles £50.
meals	Dinner £25.
closed	Christmas & New Year.
directions	From Dover, M2 to Medway Services. Into station, on past pumps. Ignore no exit signs. Left at T-junc., 1st left & on for 2 miles. Left at next T-junc. House 3rd on left.

rooms	2: 1 double with bath & shower; 1 double with shower.
price	£80-£95. Singles from £65.
meals	Supper occasionally available. Pub 3-minute walk. Excellent restaurant 1 mile.
closed	Rarely.
directions	M20 exit 7 for Maidstone. At 2nd r'bout, follow signs for Bearsted. At shops, sharp left into Thurnham Lane. 1 mile up lane, after sign for church, house on left.

	Gillian & John Yerburgh & Sophie & Richard Ratcliffe Hartlip Place, Place Lane, Sittingbourne, Kent ME9 7TR
tel	01795 842323
e-mail	jyerburgh@aol.com

	Sonia Ashdown Little Dane, Thurnham Lane, Thurnham, Maidstone, Kent ME14 3LG
tel	01622 730908
e-mail	info@thurnhamoldrectory.co.uk
web	www.thurnhamoldrectory.co.uk

Map 5 Entry 259

Map 5 Entry 260

Kent

Clock House

Fresh raspberries for breakfast at this 200-acre fruit farm in the Kentish Weald. Antonia and Brian are elegant hosts with a lively sense of humour and a Grade II*-listed house. Painted in warm colours, filled with portraits and family antiques, it is a wonderfully comfortable place to stay. Your bedrooms are in their own wing: a twin, deliciously cosy; a double with an extra room for a child and views onto paddock and fields. There are dogs, chickens, a tennis court and a pool, and apple blossom magnificent in spring. Two minutes drive from a good pub, 20 from Sissinghurst, and not much further for a trip to France.

Barclay Farmhouse

Breakfast on fresh fruits, warm croissants, banana bread, eggs en cocotte; Lynn's good food welcomes you. The weatherboarded guest barn has a solid, been-here-for-ever feel and is in perfect trim. A cosy, oak-floored dining room, a patio for summer, views onto a big peaceful garden and a bird-happy pond. Gleaming bedrooms have brocade bedspreads, French oak furniture, lotions, potions and flat-screen TVs; shower rooms are spot-on. Lynn has a young family and welcomes all, from honeymooners to garden-lovers: glorious Sissinghurst is down the road. Immaculate, warm-hearted B&B.

rooms	2: 1 twin with bath; 1 double with separate bath/shower & extra child's room.
price	From £65. Singles £35.
meals	Pub 15-minute walk.
closed	Christmas & New Year.
directions	From Maidstone, A229 towards Hastings. After 4.5 miles, right at lights onto B2163 Coxheath. After 0.5 miles, drive on left; house at top of drive.

rooms	3 doubles, all with shower.
price	£60. Singles from £55.
meals	Good pubs/restaurants 1 mile.
closed	Rarely.
directions	From Biddenden centre, south on A262: Tenterden Rd. 0.7 miles, bear right (signed Par3 Golf, Vineyard and Benenden). Immed. on right.

	Brian & Antonia Allfrey
	Clock House,
	Linton,
	Maidstone,
	Kent ME17 4PG
tel	01622 743679
mobile	07775 745580
e-mail	antonia@allfrey.net

	Lynn Ruse
	Barclay Farmhouse,
	Woolpack Corner,
	Biddenden,
	Kent TN27 8BQ
tel	01580 292626
fax	01580 292288
e-mail	info@barclayfarmhouse.co.uk
web	www.barclayfarmhouse.co.uk

Map 5 Entry 261

Map 5 Entry 262

Kent

West Winchet

Annie goes the extra mile: homemade compotes and jams with local croissants and brioches on the breakfast table, treats in your room. The house is spotless but infectiously informal, the Parkers are great company and Annie is a treasure. Light, bright, ground-floor bedrooms are in the post-Edwardian wing, one with French windows which open on to the gardens; all is polished, nothing looks out of place: traditional fabrics, soft carpeting, fresh flowers and towels changed every day. Breakfast in the splendid drawing room with garden views – or in bed. *Children over five welcome.*

rooms	2: 1 double with bath; 1 twin with shower.
price	From £65. Singles from £45.
meals	Good pubs 2 miles.
closed	Christmas & New Year.
directions	A262 to Goudhurst. There, B2079 to Marden. House 2 miles from village, on left.

Annie Parker
West Winchet,
Winchet Hill,
Goudhurst,
Cranbrook,
Kent TN17 1JX
tel   01580 212024
fax   01580 212250
e-mail   annieparker@jpa-ltd.co.uk

Map 5 Entry 263

Blundeston

A new surprise in the heart of the old town: a period home that's just 14 years old. Timothy does architectural conversions using reclaimed timbers and tiles; Gillie fills rooms with the prettiest things. It is charmingly English, informal and easy, with plenty to please the eye inside and out. Your hosts, huge fun, serve you breakfasts on mahogany, there are teak seats by a summer pool, and bedrooms big enough for an armchair. The one on the ground floor has a patchwork quilt on a bed hand-painted by Gillie, the one upstairs, sprigged walls and a bedcover to match. Tempting Tunbridge waits outside the door.

rooms	2: 1 double, 1 twin/double, both with bath.
price	£54-£64.
meals	Pubs/restaurants 5-minute walk.
closed	December-January.
directions	From High Street, turn up Mount Zion with Pizza Express to left; 100 yds, right into Eden Road. 3rd house on left through white gates.

Timothy & Gillie Day
Blundeston,
Eden Road,
Tunbridge Wells,
Kent TN1 1TS
tel   01892 513030
fax   01892 540255
e-mail   daysblundeston@excite.com

Map 5 Entry 264

Kent

40 York Road

Slap bang in the centre of Royal Tunbridge Wells, a five-minute walk from the delightfully preserved Pantiles and its clutter of tiny shops, is this attractive Regency townhouse. Patricia recenty moved here, having been in charge of cooking up delights for hungry skiers coming off the French mountains. She is a gentle presence and leaves you to come and go as you please, but she will work her culinary magic on you if you prefer to stay in. Bedrooms are straightforward and comfortable, and in the summer you can breakfast outside in the pretty courtyard garden. *Children over 12 welcome.*

rooms	2: 1 twin/double with bath/shower; 1 twin/double with shower.
price	£56. Singles £32.
meals	Dinner, 4 courses with wine, £20. Picnics available.
closed	23 December-2 January.
directions	From M25 junc. 5 onto A21, then A26 through Southborough to Tunbridge Wells. Take sign for Lewes, incline left taking 4th road left. Half way along, on left. Car parks nearby, from £3.50 per 24 hours.

Patricia Lobo
40 York Road,
Tunbridge Wells,
Kent TN1 1JY

tel	01892 531342
fax	01892 531342
e-mail	yorkroad@tiscali.co.uk
web	www.yorkroad.co.uk

Map 5 Entry 265

Hoath House

Mervyn and Jane live in a fascinating house which creaks under its own history, twisting, turning, rising and falling, and takes you on a journey through medieval, Tudor and Edwardian times. Breakfast in what was a medieval hall, all heavy panelling, low ceilings and small, leaded windows, entertained by your local historian and film extra host. Ancestors gaze down from the walls; dark staircases wind up to big bedrooms with views to Ashdown Forest. There are few modern embellishments – other than an unexpected Art Deco bathroom. For the curious and the robust.
Minimum stay two nights atweekends.

rooms	3: 1 twin, 1 family, 1 double, all with separate bath.
price	£60-£70. Singles £30-£35.
meals	Light supper/dinner £12.50-£20.
closed	Christmas & New Year.
directions	From A21, Hildenborough exit. Signs to Penshurst Place; pass vineyard; right at T-junc. for Edenbridge; through village, bear left, for Edenbridge. House 0.5 miles on left.

Mr & Mrs Mervyn Streatfeild
Hoath House,
Chiddingstone Hoath,
Edenbridge,
Kent TN8 7DB

| tel | 01342 850362 |
| e-mail | jstreatfeild@hoath-house.freeserve.co.uk |

Map 5 Entry 266

Kent

Charcott Farmhouse

The 1750 brick farmhouse is home to a charming family — guests love it here. You share a beamed sitting room in the old Bake House with a piano and TV, while ample bedrooms are simple but fresh, with country views; one has a forest of oak beams, another its own stair. Nicholas and Ginny enjoy the buzz of company, but understand you need privacy too. Make the most of their knowledge of the historic houses and gardens of Kent, many of which are a 20-minute drive. Breakfast is a happy affair with heaps of homemade bread and marmalade and free-range eggs. Best of all, you may come and go as you please.

Worples Field

Sue is a gifted garden-designer and bursting with ideas for making her three acres even more special: currently she is creating a 'planet' garden with sparkling surprises. Not many gardens have mown worples to tread: the ancient, wave-like ridge-and-furrows are a most unusual feature in Kent. All the rooms in this wonderfully traditional house are light, airy and comfortable, towels are soft, colours restful and the rooms that share the bathroom have pastoral views. Play tennis or croquet, discover the magical garden; stroll into historic Westerham. Sue, full of fun and sparkle, knows how to spoil you.

rooms	3: 1 twin with shower; 1 twin with bath; 1 twin with separate bath.		rooms	3: 1 twin, 1 double, sharing bath; 1 double with separate bath.
price	£55–£60. Singles £40–£45.		price	£60. Singles £50.
meals	Breakfast 7.30-9.30am. Excellent pub 5-minute walk.		meals	Excellent pubs/restaurants 0.25 miles.
closed	Christmas Day & very occasionally.		closed	Rarely.
directions	B2027 0.5 miles north of Chiddingstone Causeway. Equidistant between Tonbridge, Sevenoaks & Edenbridge.		directions	From M25 junc. 6 to Westerham (A25). After town sign & 30mph sign, 1st left into Farley Lane. After 200 yds, left at top, then left again.

	Nicholas & Ginny Morris Charcott Farmhouse, Charcott, Leigh, Tonbridge, Kent TN11 8LG		Sue & Alastair Marr Worples Field, Farley Common, Westerham, Kent TN16 1UB
tel	01892 870024	tel	01959 562869
e-mail	nicholasmorris@charcott.freeserve.co.uk	e-mail	marr@worplesfield.com
		web	www.worplesfield.com

Map 5 Entry 267   Map 4 Entry 268

Kent

Field of Dreams

Runner up in this year's Country Loving Green Bedroom of the Year competition, here is the UK's first genuinely al-fresco bedroom. Eat your heart out, Farrow and Ball; you are, frankly, irrelevant. The fool who proposed astro-turf was shown the door and fed to the pigs. Where now the heating, the frivolous add-ons like running water and kettle? Irrelevant too – and good riddance. This is a cool, reflective, revisionist approach to B&B, paring comfort back to its essentials: what else do you really need?? Wordsworth, especially ('The winds come to me from fields of sleep'), would have loved this.

rooms	1 large open-plan bedroom.
price	A damp bed.
meals	Forage from the comfort of your own room.
closed	Tricky without a door.
directions	Through woods, left at stile. From there it should stand out.

Al Fresco
Field of Dreams,
Sleepy Hollow,
Kent 5LE 3PY
tel   00110 123456
e-mail   al-fresco@greatoutdoors.co.uk

Lancashire

Northwood

The Victorian façade conceals a houseful of riches and light. Lofty rooms are a bold mix of traditional and modern – a red leather sofa, a polished stair, an original tiled floor. Your hosts happily find babysitters, advise on restaurants (then drive you there) and offer you maple syrup pancakes at breakfast, along with other treats; the whole place radiates humour and warmth. Bedrooms are generous: a palette of white, chocolate and grey, or a rich violet quilt and a view of the sea. Expect coir floors, baskets of blankets and towels, DVDs, tranquillity. Delightful St Annes lies outside the door.

rooms	2: 1 double, 1 double/family, both with bath.
price	£75. Singles from £65.
meals	Restaurants 5-minute walk.
closed	Christmas & New Year
directions	M6 exit 32 then M55 to Blackpool. Follow signs for Lytham St Annes then St Annes. Head for the promenade.

Shannon Kuspira
Northwood,
24 North Promenade,
St Annes on Sea,
Lancashire FY8 2NQ
tel   01253 782356
e-mail   skuspira@hotmail.com
web   www.24northwood.co.uk

Map 11 Entry 270

Lancashire

Sagar Fold House

Helen transformed this 17th-century dairy and created the perfect studio apartment: self-contained, all mod cons, very here and now. Your own entrance leads up to a large beamed space that brings together comfort, immaculate efficiency and unusual beauty. A carved Indian doorframe serves as half-tester: like a four-poster without the pomp. Pretty touches – Chinese rug, butterfly-embroidered curtains, blue-green sofa – lift the spirit. Now, gaze out over Helen's Italian knot garden, which ties in lines of a lovely landscape. Take wonderful walks! Such peace and it's not far to top-notch eateries.

rooms	1 double with extra single, with shower.
price	£65. Singles £50.
meals	Pubs and restaurants very close by.
closed	Rarely.
directions	A59 through centre of Whalley. At 2nd mini r'bout left to Mitton; 3 miles, Three Fishes pub on left. Right to Whitewell Chaigely; 1 mile, left to W. Chaigely; 0.5 mile, 3rd drive left to house.

Helen & John Cook
Sagar Fold House,
Higher Hodder,
Clitheroe,
Lancashire BB7 3LW
tel   01254 826844
e-mail   cookj@thomas-cook.co.uk

Map 12 Entry 271

Peter Barn Country House

Wild deer roam – this is the Ribble Valley, an AONB that feels like a time-locked land. In this former 18th-century tithe barn, where old church rafters support the guest sitting room, you settle in among plump sofas and antiques. Your bedrooms and sitting room are on the top floor, so feel private; bathrooms are huge. The Smiths couldn't be more helpful and breakfast is a feast: jams and muesli are homemade, stewed fruits are from the lovely gardens. Step outside to see them: Jean has transformed a field into a riot of colour and scent, there's a meandering stream and water lilies bask in still pools.

rooms	3: 1 double with bath/shower; 1 double with separate bath; 1 twin/double with shower.
price	From £58. Singles £35.
meals	Good restaurants 1.5 miles.
closed	Christmas & New Year.
directions	M6 junc. 31, A59 to Skipton, left to Clitheroe. Through Clitheroe & Waddington, on for 0.5 miles, left along Cross Lane. 0.75 miles on, past Colthurst Hall, house on left.

Jean & Gordon Smith
Peter Barn Country House,
Cross Lane/Rabbit Lane,
Waddington,
Clitheroe,
Lancashire BB7 3JH
tel   01200 428585
mobile   07970 826370
e-mail   jean@peterbarn.co.uk

Map 12 Entry 272

Lancashire

Herris's Farm

A luxurious slice of peace and quiet in the Forest of Bowland — an Area of Outstanding Natural Beauty. Your hosts are full of friendly enthusiasm and their home glows with comfort and warmth. The private sitting room has three charming sofas, logs, books and art; the flagstoned shippon — the oldest part — guards a country table to which delectable breakfasts are brought. In summer, step onto the patio for eye-stretching views over the village and valley beyond. Up a stone stair past shelves full of maps and historic guides are cottagey bedspreads on luxurious beds. Brilliant value.

rooms	2: 1 double with shower; 1 twin with separate bath/shower.
price	£55. Singles £35.
meals	Excellent pubs in village.
closed	Christmas & New Year.
directions	From A59 at Chatburn follow signs to Grindleton. In village, left at Duke of York pub. Follow Slaidburn road for 1.5 miles; pass Hayloft Country Kitchen; next right over cattle grid.

	Vivien Leslie
	Herris's Farm,
	Smalden Lane,
	Grindleton,
	Lancashire BB7 4RX
tel	01200 440725
e-mail	info@herrisesfarm.co.uk
web	www.herrisesfarm.co.uk

Map 12 Entry 273

Leicestershire

The Grange

Behind the mellow brick exterior (Queen Anne in front, Georgian at the back) is a real family home. Log fires brighten chilly days and you are greeted with warmth and courtesy by Mary and Shaun, their two young children and a sweet dog called Marmite. Beautifully quiet bedrooms are hung with strikingly unusual wallpapers and furnished with excellent beds and pretty antiques, bathrooms are simple yet impeccable and there's a fireplace in the big, flagstoned hall decorated with sporting prints and deeds. The generous garden has shrubs, flowerbeds and a summer croquet lawn.

rooms	2: 1 twin, 1 double both with bath/shower.
price	£70. Singles £40.
meals	Pubs/restaurants 0.5-1.5 miles.
closed	Christmas & New Year.
directions	M1 exit 20; A4304 towards Market Harborough. First left after Walcote marked 'Gt Central Cycle Ride'. 2 miles, then right into Kimcote, pass church on left. On right after Poultney Lane.

	Shaun & Mary Mackaness
	The Grange,
	Kimcote,
	Leicestershire LE17 5RU
tel	01455 203155
fax	01455 203155
e-mail	shaunandmarymac@hotmail.com
web	www.thegrangekimcote.co.uk

Map 8 Entry 274

Leicestershire

Littlefield Farm

A pond to picnic by, 850 acres to roam, a field for your horse, a games room for the children, an indoor pool, a newly-laid tennis court – there's something to delight everyone at this 1860 traditional farmhouse. Luxurious bathrooms encourage hot soaks; big, comfortable bedrooms have sweeping views.
The house is an Aladdin's cave of special things: oriental rugs, tapestry cushions, rich drapes, paintings old and new. Nicky splits her time between Market Harborough and London, leaving her efficient housekeeper to look after you.
Children over 12 welcome.

The Gorse House

Passing traffic is less frequent than passing horses – a truly peaceful spot. The lasting impression of this 17th-century cottage is of lightness and brightness: the house is filled with laughter and the Cowdells are terrific hosts. There's a fine collection of paintings and furniture, and double oak doors lead from dining room to guest sitting room. Bedrooms are restful and fresh; one has three-way views. The garden was designed by Bunny Guinness, the stables accommodate up to six horses and the village of Grimston is delightful. An excellent base if travelling from East Midlands airport.

rooms	3: 1 double with bath & shower; 1 twin with separate bath; 1 double with bath.
price	£70-£80. Singles £45.
meals	Pubs/restaurants nearby.
closed	Rarely.
directions	From A427 (Market Harborough to Corby) follow sign for East Carlton. House last on left in village.

rooms	3: 1 twin/double with bath & extra single; 1 twin/double with shower; 1 family with bath & shower.
price	From £50. Singles £30.
meals	Packed lunch £5. Good pub 100 yds.
closed	Rarely.
directions	From A46 Newark-Leicester; B676 for Melton. At x-roads, straight for 1 mile; right to Grimston. There, up hill, past church. House on left, just after right-hand bend at top.

	Nicky Chaplin
	Littlefield Farm,
	East Carlton,
	Market Harborough,
	Leicestershire LE16 8YA
mobile	07860 201395
fax	0207 736 0456

	Mr & Mrs R L Cowdell
	The Gorse House,
	33 Main Street, Grimston,
	Melton Mowbray,
	Leicestershire LE14 3BZ
tel	01664 813537
mobile	07780 600792
e-mail	cowdell@gorsehouse.co.uk
web	www.gorsehouse.co.uk

Map 9 Entry 275

Map 9 Entry 276

Lincolnshire

The Old Farm House

Hidden in the Lincolnshire wolds, a demure, 18th-century, ivy-covered house. Nicola was born and bred in the county and her father still farms the fields beyond the ha-ha. The stone-flagged, terracotta-washed hall gives a hint of warm colours to come; creamy walls show off tawny fabrics, prints and antiques; the beamed sitting/breakfast room has a big, rosy brick inglenook fireplace and tranquil views. Although it's so quiet, the hamlet is a 10-15-minute drive from shops, golf and racing in the nearby towns. Excellent value – and perfect if you fancy privacy and space. *Children over eight welcome.*

Knaith Hall

This intriguing place, medieval church at its gate, dates from the 16th century. You enjoy breakfast in the kitchen alcove, lawns slope down to the river Trent. Daffodils, lambs, a passing barge and waterfowl pattern the serenity. And the skyscapes are terrific! At night, a distant power-station shines, actually enhancing that 'great rurality of taste' referred to in Pevsner. Indoors, diamond-paned windows, domed dining room and fine furniture are softened by easy décor and a log fire. A lovely family home, with a relaxed atmosphere. Your own room offers real rest, and the very best of old-fashioned bedding.

	The Old Farm House		Knaith Hall
rooms	2: 1 double with bath; 1 triple with separate bath.	rooms	2: 1 double with separate shower; 1 twin with separate bath.
price	£60. Singles £40.	price	£60. Singles £30.
meals	Pubs/restaurants less than 5-minute drive.	meals	Dinner, 3 courses with wine, £20. Pub 4 miles.
closed	Christmas, New Year & occasionally.	closed	Christmas & New Year.
directions	M180 exit 5; A18 past airport; right 2.5 miles after A46 r'bout. From Lincoln, A46 to Grimsby; right at A18; 2nd right to Hatcliffe.	directions	Knaith 3 miles south of Gainsborough on A156 Lincoln-Gainsborough road. After Knaith signs, look for white gateposts on west side with sign for St Mary's Church.

	Nicola Clarke The Old Farm House, Low Road, Hatcliffe, Lincolnshire DN37 0SH		John & Rosie Burke Knaith Hall, Knaith, Gainsborough, Lincolnshire DN21 5PE
tel	01472 824455	tel	01427 613005
e-mail	nicola@hatcliffe.freeserve.co.uk	fax	01427 613005
		e-mail	jandrburke@aol.com

Map 13 Entry 277

Map 13 Entry 278

Lincolnshire

The Manor House

One guest's summing up reads: "Absolutely perfect – hostess, house, garden and marmalade." Ann loves having people to stay and makes you feel truly at home. You have the run of downstairs: neat, traditional, all family antiques, fresh flowers and space. Chintzy, carpeted bedrooms have dreamy views of the pretty gardens and duck-dabbled lake, and dinners are good value and delicious: game casserole, ginger meringue bombe... Perfect stillness at the base of the Wolds and a lovely one-mile walk along the route of the old railway that starts from the front door. Very special.

rooms	2: 1 twin with shower; 1 double with bath.
price	From £55. Singles by arrangement.
meals	Dinner from £15. BYO. Excellent pub 4-5 miles.
closed	Christmas.
directions	From Wragby A157 for Louth. After approx. 2 miles, at triple road sign, right. Red postbox & bus shelter at drive entrance, before graveyard.

Ann Hobbins
The Manor House,
West Barkwith,
Lincolnshire LN8 5LF
| tel | 01673 858253 |
| fax | 01673 858253 |

Map 9 Entry 279

The Grange

Wide open Lincolnshire farmland on the edge of the Wolds. This immaculately kept farm has been in the family for five generations; their award-winning farm trail helps you explore. Listen to birdsong, catch the sun setting by the trout lake, have supper before the fire in a dining room whose elegant Georgian windows are generously draped. Sarah is a young and energetic host and brings you delicious homemade cake on arrival. Comfortable bedrooms have spick and span bathrooms and fabulous views that stretch to Lincoln Cathedral. A delightful couple running good, honest, farmhouse B&B.

rooms	2: 1 double with bath; 1 double with shower.
price	£54. Singles £37.
meals	Dinner, 3 courses, from £16. Supper from £12. Packed lunch £6. BYO. (No meals at harvest time.) Pub/restaurant 1 mile.
closed	Christmas & New Year.
directions	Exit A157 in East Barkwith at War Memorial, into Torrington Lane. House 0.75 miles on right after sharp right-hand bend.

Sarah & Jonathan Stamp
The Grange,
Torrington Lane,
East Barkwith,
Lincolnshire LN8 5RY
tel	01673 858670
e-mail	jonathanstamp@farmersweekly.net
web	www.thegrange-lincolnshire.co.uk

Map 9 Entry 280

Lincolnshire

Churchfield House

The little house was built in the Sixties and inside glows with character and charm. Bridget is an interior decorator whose eye for detail and sense of fun inform the light-filled rooms. Small, snug bedrooms sport fresh checks, warm colours, firm mattresses, down pillows, interesting pictures, even a gilt-trimmed copy of a Louis XIV chair. The bathroom is spotless and inviting, and there's a conservatory mood to the brick-walled, stone-tiled dining room, where glass doors open to a large, lush garden in summer. Bridget cooks and chats with warmth and humour. A gem.

The White House

Right on the green in this fine conservation village is a tall, gravely beautiful Georgian house. It is even lovelier inside. Victoria and David, understandably passionate about the place, have filled the rooms with gorgeous things. Feel free to slop on chaise longues in the library; admire the fine moulded fireplace and the etchings, the watercolours and the English and Chinese porcelain. The bedrooms, too, are striking, one with an antique four-poster canopied in green silk; bathrooms are fresh and appealing. Your charming hosts serve breakfast in the pretty little walled garden in summer.

rooms	2: 1 twin, 1 double sharing bath (2nd room let to same party).
price	£55. Singles £30.
meals	Dinner from £15. Excellent pubs/restaurants 3 miles.
closed	Christmas & New Year.
directions	A607 Grantham to Lincoln road. On reaching Carlton Scroop 1st left for Hough Lane. Last house on left.

rooms	3: 1 twin/double with separate bath/shower; 1 four-poster sharing bath with extra single room (single let to same party).
price	£60. Singles £35.
meals	Dinner, 2-3 courses with wine, £15-£20. Pubs/restaurants within 3 miles.
closed	Rarely.
directions	A15 to Folkingham; on village green.

Mrs Bridget Hankinson
Churchfield House,
Carlton Scroop,
Grantham,
Lincolnshire NG32 3BA

tel	01400 250387
fax	01400 250241
e-mail	info@churchfield-house.co.uk
web	www.churchfield-house.co.uk

Victoria & David Strauss
The White House,
25 Market Place,
Folkingham,
Sleaford,
Lincolnshire NG34 0SE

tel	01529 497298
e-mail	victoria.strauss@btinternet.com

Map 9 Entry 281

Map 9 Entry 282

Lincolnshire

The Barn

Simon and Jane have farmed for 30 years and are the nicest people. Breakfasts are local and delicious, there are endless little extras and nothing is too much trouble. In this light-filled barn conversion old beams go well with new walls, floors, windows and the odd antique; a brick-flanked fireplace glows and heated flagged floors keep toes warm. Above the high-raftered main living/dining room is a comfy, good-sized double; in the adjoining stables, two further rooms, a crisp feel, sparkling showers, restful privacy. Views are to sheep-dotted fields and the Georgian village is a charmer.

Cawthorpe Hall

Built in 1819, embellished later by Gardner of the RA, filled with original, unusual art, African carvings and swimming with light, it is a fascinating house. Gardner's remarkable studio has now been transformed into a vast sitting room, heated by a great woodburning stove. The rest of the house is full of oddities such as the boat-shaped windows that open onto the garden. The double rooms, a mix of traditional and floral with great bay windows and plenty of space, overlook fields of roses (Ozric makes the only genuine English rose oil and water). He and Chantal are extremely friendly and warm.

	The Barn		Cawthorpe Hall
rooms	3: 1 twin/double, 1 double, both with shower; 1 single with separate bath/shower.	rooms	3: 1 double with bath; 1 twin, 1 double, both with separate shower.
price	£60. Singles £30.	price	£70. Singles £35.
meals	Supper, 2 courses, £15. Dinner, 3 courses, £20. Good pub 2 miles.	meals	Pub/restaurant 1 mile.
closed	Rarely.	closed	Christmas & New Year.
directions	Midway between Lincoln & Peterborough. From A15, in Folkingham, turn west into Spring Lane next to village hall; 200 yds on right.	directions	From Bourne, A15 north for Sleaford, 1st hamlet on left signed to Cawthorpe. House last on right before road becomes track.

Simon & Jane Wright
The Barn,
Spring Lane,
Folkingham, Sleaford,
Lincolnshire NG34 0SJ
tel   01529 497199
mobile   07876 363292
e-mail   sjwright@farming.co.uk
web   www.thebarnspringlane.co.uk

Ozric & Chantal Armstrong
Cawthorpe Hall,
Bourne,
Lincolnshire PE10 0AB
tel   01778 423830
fax   01778 426620
e-mail   chantal@cawthorpebandb.co.uk
web   www.cawthorpebandb.co.uk

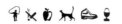

Map 9 Entry 283

Map 9 Entry 284

Lincolnshire

Rose Cottage

The chaps who serviced Model T-4s here in the 1920s would be amazed at the transformation. The 1760s cottage with its limestone extension has much comfort: family memorabilia in the sitting room, a piano in the dining room, floral themes in bedrooms, brand new beds and pristine tiled bathrooms. Veronica, who couldn't be more helpful and chatty, grows fruit and vegetables for the table; in winter, Bob can arrange hunting and beagling parties followed by candlelit dinner. Two acres of paddock are home to the providers of breakfast eggs, and the fenced-off lawn is perfect for small children.

rooms	3: 1 double with shower; 1 twin/double with separate bath & shower; 1 family room with bath.
price	£55-£75. Singles £35-£45.
meals	Supper, 2-3 courses, £18-£25. Good pubs 5-minute drive.
closed	Rarely.
directions	North on A1; exit after Ram Jam Inn towards South Witham. From south exit, immed. after Fox Inn upon reaching High Street. After village sign, cottage 2nd on left.

Veronica & Bob Van Kimmenade
Rose Cottage,
7 High Street,
South Witham,
Lincolnshire NG33 5QB
tel   01572 767757
fax   0870 1368319
e-mail   veronica@rosecottage-southwitham.co.uk
web   www.rosecottage-southwitham.co.uk

Map 9 Entry 285

London

78 Albert Street

In the heart of vibrant Camden Town, well set back in a quiet, wide, tree-lined street, moments from Regent's Park, a superb central London base. The large and stylish kitchen where you breakfast was designed by Peter (an architect and lighting specialist) and every room in the modernist house has had the best brought out of it – small rooms have been cleverly planned and there's a really super large double. All is distinctive and understated with cool colours and fresh flowers. The Bells run this established B&B with a cool professionalism.
Near to Camden Lock and market.

rooms	2: 1 twin/double, 1 room with bunkbeds, sharing bath.
price	£90-£100. Singles £45-£60.
meals	Pubs/restaurants nearby.
closed	Occasionally.
directions	From Camden Town tube (Northern Line), up Parkway. Albert St 2nd on left. House on left. Parking free Sunday; otherwise meters.

Joanna & Peter Bell
78 Albert Street,
Camden Town,
London NW1 7NR
tel   020 7387 6813
e-mail   joanna@peterbellarchitects.co.uk

Map 4 Entry 286

London

66 Camden Square

An unusual, interesting house made of African teak and glass. The open-plan living area makes good use of space and is decorated with ethnic pieces from far-flung travels. It opens to a courtyard garden; halogen lights and a pyramid of glass on the roof brighten the space still further. Climb the wooden stair to bedrooms decorated in Japanese style with low platform beds and modern chairs; the double has two walls of glass. Camden's market and plenty of good places to eat are close by. Sue and Rodger are excellent hosts, and Peckham the parrot completes the picture.
Children by arrangement.

rooms	2: 1 double, 1 single sharing bath (single for same party).
price	£90. Singles from £45.
meals	Pubs/restaurants nearby.
closed	Occasionally.
directions	From Camden Town tube, Camden Rd towards Holloway. Pass Camden Road train station; 4th right into Murray St. House on corner of Murray St & Camden Mews. Parking free at weekends; meters during week.

Sue & Rodger Davis
66 Camden Square,
Camden Town,
London NW1 9XD

tel	020 7485 4622
fax	020 7485 4622
e-mail	rodgerdavis@btopenworld.com

Map 4 Entry 287

30 King Henry's Road

The luxury of a country-house hotel – grand bathroom, great bed, all mod cons – yet here you have the personal touch we so like. Breakfast is a feast of bagels, croissants, yogurts, fruits, jams in a lovely large kitchen/dining room with real fire and views to the garden. No lounge, but your room on the top floor has a brass bed, a sisal floor, good pictures, fine pieces of furniture and a wall of books. The shops, restaurants and sublime views of Primrose Hill are a five-minute stroll, and there's open-air theatre in Regent's Park in summer. Carole and Ted know London and will happily advise.

rooms	1 double with bath/shower.
price	£100. Singles £80.
meals	Good pubs & restaurants 2-minute walk.
closed	Occasionally.
directions	Five-minute walk from Chalk Farm tube (Northern Line): cross Adelaide Rd, right for 20 steps, then left into Bridge Approach. Cross bridge, turn right. No. 30 on right. Free parking weekends, ticket parking nearby.

Carole Cox
30 King Henry's Road,
Primrose Hill,
London NW3 3RP

tel	020 7483 2871
fax	020 7483 2871
e-mail	mail@carolecox.co.uk

Map 4 Entry 288

London

26 Hillgate Place

You are in luxurious, bohemian Notting Hill: a movie at the Coronet, a pint at the Windsor Castle, the best Thai at the Churchill and the chic-est shops. Whatever you do, roll back to Hilary's easy-going home for a bit of eastern spice; Indian textiles, old teak dressers, the odd wooden elephant, wildly colourful art (Hilary paints). The bigger double has a Caribbean influence and shares a bathroom up a flight of stairs; the smaller is smarter – immaculate, actually – with a sofa and a claw-foot bath. Both rooms come with bathrobes and small fridge, and there are two gardens to choose from, one on a roof.

rooms	2: 1 double with bath/shower; 1 double sharing family bath.
price	£70-£90. Singles from £60.
meals	Pubs/restaurants nearby.
closed	Occasionally.
directions	At Coronet Cinema on south side of Notting Hill Gate turn into Hillgate Street; at 2nd junction, right into Hillgate Place; next to Hillgate pub.

Hilary Dunne
26 Hillgate Place,
Notting Hill Gate,
London W8 7ST

tel	020 7727 7717
fax	020 7727 7827
e-mail	hilary.dunne@virgin.net
web	www.26hillgateplace.co.uk

Map 4 Entry 289

101 Abbotsbury Road

The area is one of London's most sought-after and Sunny's family home is right opposite the park – well placed for Kensington High Street, Notting Hill and Olympia. The whole top floor is generally given over to visitors. Bedrooms are in gentle yellows and greens, with pale carpets, white duvets, pelmeted windows, big porcelain table lights, treetop views. The bathroom is marble-tiled and sky-lit, with a cast-iron bath and shower. Near to Kensington Gardens, the Albert Hall, Knightsbridge or Piccadilly. The independently-minded will particularly like it. *Children over 10 welcome.*

rooms	2: 1 double, 1 single, sharing bath.
price	£100. Singles £55-£75.
meals	Continental breakfast included. Many places to eat nearby.
closed	Occasionally.
directions	Tube: Holland Park (7-min walk); Bus: 148, 94 to West End/Victoria from Kensington High Street; 9 & 10 to Knightsbridge/Piccadilly. Off-street parking sometimes available.

Sunny Murray
101 Abbotsbury Road,
Holland Park,
London W14 8EP

tel	020 7602 0179
mobile	07768 362562
e-mail	sunny@101abb.freeserve.co.uk

Map 4 Entry 290

London

37 Trevor Square

A fabulous find, luxury in the middle of Knightsbridge. The square is impossibly pretty, unexpectedly peaceful and a three-minute walk from Hyde Park or Harrods. Margaret runs an interior design company – rather successfully, by the look of things. You breakfast in the dining room (smoked salmon with scrambled eggs, if you wish) with its toile de Jouy walls, stone busts, warm rugs and fire in winter. Upstairs: an electric blanket, a cashmere duvet, a maple table, a gorgeous marbled bathroom, DVDs and CDs. There's a snug conservatory/sitting room you're welcome to use, too.

Off Kensington Road

Just about everything in this delectable home is Welsh, including Mary. Take the lift – or navigate your way up one floor in this Art Deco mansion block that's a little like a 1920s P&O steamer and quietly grand. Inside you find antique china, a beautiful dresser, a rosewood dining table for breakfast by the window. Very pretty windows wrap around the flat, flooding it with light. The bedroom is equally lovely (a Louis XIV sofa, big porcelain lamps, fresh flowers) with a tiny balcony, and a lovely compact bathroom with a trompe-l'oeil door. So peaceful, and Hyde Park a five-minute walk.

rooms	2: 1 double, 1 twin sharing bath & shower (2nd room let to same party).
price	£130.
meals	Restaurants 200 yds.
closed	Occasionally.
directions	Tube: Knightsbridge. Bus: 9, 10, 14, 19, 22, 52, 74, 137. Nearest car park £25 per 24 hrs (closed overnight).

rooms	1 double with bath/shower.
price	£80–£90. Singles £60.
meals	Restaurants nearby.
closed	Occasionally.
directions	Directions given on booking. Parking meters (free 6.30pm-8.30am & Sunday); car park £1.50 hour. Tube: Knightsbridge. Buses: 9, 10, 52.

	Margaret & Holly Palmer
	37 Trevor Square,
	Knightsbridge,
	London SW7 1DY
tel	020 7823 8186
fax	020 7823 9801
e-mail	margaret@37trevorsquare.co.uk
web	www.37trevorsquare.co.uk

	Mary Williams
	Off Kensington Road,
	Knightsbridge,
	London SW7
tel	020 7581 0395
mobile	07767 261667
e-mail	maryeleanorwilliams@hotmail.co.uk

Map 4 Entry 291

Map 4 Entry 292

London

21 Barclay Road

The grand piano is a magnet for esteemed conductors and music professors from around the world. Charlotte, who does something unspeakably high-powered by day, happily advises on the best London sites. You pretty much get the run of the house: a large sitting room with an open fire, two small but well laid out double bedrooms with waffle bathrobes and a book-filled bathroom. Breakfast is a feast of homemade cranberry muffins, French toast, fresh fruit salad, Swiss coffee – eat on the tree-top terrace in summer. Very special, a great city find.

Use of grand piano by arrangement.

rooms	2 doubles, both with separate bath.
price	£80. Singles £65.
meals	Many restaurants 2-minute walk. Music & food evenings Thursdays.
closed	Occasionally.
directions	From Fulham Broadway tube, right into Effie Road, then right into Barclay Road. Parking free 8pm-9am & all Sunday. 9am-8pm Pay & Display.

	Charlotte Dexter
	21 Barclay Road,
	Fulham,
	London SW6 1EJ
tel	020 7384 3390
e-mail	info@barclayhouselondon.com
web	www.barclayhouselondon.com

Map 4 Entry 293

15 Delaford Street

A lovely terraced home: small, but decidedly pretty. In a tiny, sun-trapping courtyard you can breakfast on croissants, smoothies and tropical fruits in good weather; a second garden bursts with life at the back. The bedroom, up a spiral staircase, looks down on it all. Expect pure cotton linen, a quilted throw, books in the alcove, a three-quarter bath and fluffy white towels. The tennis at Queen's is on your doorstep and takes place in the second week of June. Tim and Margot – she's from Melbourne – are fun, helpful and happy to pick you up from the nearest tube. Oh, and there's Poppy the dog.

rooms	1 double with bath.
price	£80. Singles £55.
meals	Great restaurants on Fulham Road and King's Road.
closed	Occasionally.
directions	Left outside West Brompton tube (District Line); cont. 0.75 miles; left into Rylston Rd; Delaford St 1st right. Parking free eves/weekends; otherwise Pay & Display.

	Margot & Tim Woods
	15 Delaford Street,
	Fulham,
	London SW6 7LT
tel	020 7385 9671
fax	020 7385 9671
e-mail	margotwoods@telco4u.net

Map 4 Entry 294

London

8 Parthenia Road

Caroline, an interior designer, mixes the sophistication of the city with the human warmth of the countryside and her handsome big kitchen is clearly the engine-room of the house. It leads through to a light breakfast room with doors onto a pretty brick garden with chairs and table – hope for fine days. The house is long and thin – Fulham style – and reaches up to the bedroom in the eaves, which needs no more explanation than the picture below. A warm, beautiful place to stay in an accessible part of the metropolis – and near the King's Road with all its antique and designer shops. *Broadband connection.*

rooms	1 twin/double with shower & separate bath.
price	£80–£100. Singles from £75.
meals	Pubs/restaurants nearby.
closed	Rarely.
directions	Public transport: 4-minute walk to Parsons Green tube. Parking: £15.40 per day in street.

Caroline & George Docker
8 Parthenia Road,
Fulham,
London SW6 4BD
tel   020 7384 1165
fax   020 7371 8819
e-mail   carolined@angelwings.co.uk

Map 4 Entry 295

22 Marville Road

Smart railings help a pink rose climb, orange lilies add a touch of colour and breakfast is in the back garden in good weather, with lavender, rose and clematis for company. Tess – the spaniel – and Christine – music lover, traveller, rower – make you feel at home. A generous single on the first floor shares the main bathroom (claw-foot bath, huge shower). The big ensuite room in elegant French grey comes with a chaise longue; it was tested and vacated with regret. Treasures from Chrisine's travels, crisp linen, good mattresses… and the famous White Horse at Parsons Green only a five-minute stroll.

rooms	2: 1 twin/double with bath/shower; 1 single with shared bath/shower.
price	£75–£85. Singles from £35.
meals	Meals by special arrangement. Good pubs nearby.
closed	Rarely.
directions	At Fulham Rd junc. with Parsons Green Lane, turn down Kelvedon Rd. Cross Bishop Rd into Homestead Rd; 1st left into Marville Rd.

Christine Drake
22 Marville Road,
Fulham,
London SW6 7BD
tel   020 7381 3205
fax   020 7381 0234
e-mail   christine.drake@btinternet.com
web   www.londonguestsathome.com

Map 4 Entry 296

London

Paddock Lodge

Two acres of formal rose beds, borders, lawns and orchards sweep down to the Thames – a magical, secluded London base. This exceptional Palladian house has fine moulded ceilings, portraits, books and fresh flowers. Bedrooms have sumptuous fabrics, exquisite furniture, lovely views. Louis is a film producer; Sonia serves delicious cooked breakfasts; dinners include a fine repertoire of Jewish and continental recipes. For garden enthusiasts, Hampton Court Palace (home to the International Flower Show) is next door and Windsor, Wisley and Kew a short drive. *French & Italian spoken. Minimum stay two nights.*

20 St Philip Street

Come for peace and undemanding luxury: the 1890 Victorian cottage with delightful courtyard garden protects you from the frenzy of city life. You breakfast in the dining room – the full English works (unusual for London); across the hall is the sitting room, with gilt-framed mirrors, wooden blinds, plump-cushioned sofas and a piano you are welcome to play. Upstairs is a bright and restful bedroom with pretty linen and a goose down duvet (worth the trip alone!). Your bathroom next door is fabulous with its porthole windows and huge mirror. Nothing has been overlooked.

rooms	2: 1 double with bath; 1 double with separate bath.
price	£90–£110. Singles by arrangement.
meals	Dinner £30. Good pub/restaurant 5-minute walk.
closed	Occasionally.
directions	From Hampton Court r'bout, A308, west, for 300 yds. Hampton Court station 5 minutes; 30 minutes Waterloo.

rooms	1 double with separate bath & shower.
price	£90. Singles £60.
meals	Good restaurants 200 yds.
closed	Occasionally.
directions	Near r'way stations (6 mins Waterloo/3 mins Victoria) or 137 bus (Sloane Sq) 156 bus (Vauxhall) 10 mins. Parking £10 per day, 9.30-5.30 Mon-Fri. Otherwise free.

Dr Louis & Mrs Sonia Marks
Paddock Lodge,
The Green,
Hampton Court,
London KT8 9BW

tel	020 8979 5254
e-mail	paddocklodge@compuserve.com
web	www.paddocklodge.co.uk

Barbara Graham
20 St Philip Street,
Battersea,
London SW8 3SL

tel	020 7498 9967
fax	020 7498 9967
e-mail	stay@bed-breakfast-battersea.co.uk
web	www.bed-breakfast-battersea.co.uk

Map 4 Entry 297

Map 4 Entry 298

London

33 Barmouth Road

Good value, family-friendly B&B in a smart 1880s terraced house of which only the exterior walls survive. Everything else is new, from the four flights of stairs to the Farrow & Ball paints. Expect neutral colours, a clipped cosy elegance, old pine dressers and Aga-cooked breakfasts. Uncluttered bedrooms at the top have good linen and all mod cons, the kitchen's floors are warm underfoot, there's a pretty Arts & Crafts feel and curtains made by Nessie. She, a fashion designer, and Duncan, a sports editor on a national paper, are most welcoming and full of enthusiasm for their B&B.

rooms	2: 1 twin/double with bath; 1 double with shower.
price	From £50. Singles from £35.
meals	Excellent pubs, restaurants & cafés nearby.
closed	Occasionally.
directions	From A217 at Wandsworth r'bout into Trinity Road; under bypass & right at lights into Windmill Road; right at lights into Heathfield Road; 1st left into Westover Road; Barmouth Road 3rd right.

	Nessie & Duncan Maclay
	33 Barmouth Road,
	Wandsworth Common,
	London SW18 2DT
tel	020 8877 0331
mobile	07885 379136
e-mail	beds@maclayworld.com
web	www.maclayworld.com

Map 4 Entry 299

The Coach House

A rare privacy: you have your own Coach House, separated from the Notts' home by a stylish terracotta-potted courtyard with Indian sandstone paving and various fruit trees (peach, pear, necturine). Breakfast in your own sunny kitchen, or let Meena treat you to an all-organic full English in hers (she makes a fine porridge, too). The big but cosy main attic bedroom has toile de Jouy bedcovers, cream curtains, rugs on dark polished floors; the brick-walled ground-floor twin is pleasant, light and airy. An exceptionally quiet south London B&B. *Minimum stay three nights; two nights in January/February.*

rooms	2: 1 family with bath & shower, 1 twin with separate shower. Same-party bookings only.
price	£75-£165.
meals	Pub/restaurant 200 yds.
closed	Occasionally.
directions	From r'bout on south side of Wandsworth Bridge, head south down Trinity Rd on A214. At 3rd set of traffic lights, 1.7 miles on, left into Upper Tooting Park. 4th left into Marius Rd, then 3rd left.

	Meena & Harley Nott
	The Coach House,
	2 Tunley Road,
	Balham,
	London SW17 7QJ
tel	020 8772 1939
fax	0870 133 4957
e-mail	coachhouse@chslondon.com
web	www.coachhouse.chslondon.com

Map 4 Entry 300

London

108 Streathbourne Road

It's a handsome house in a conservation area that manages to be both elegant and cosy. The cream-coloured double bedroom has an armchair, a writing desk, delightful curtains and a big, comfy walnut bed; the twin is light and airy. The dining room overlooks a secluded terrace and garden and there are newspapers at breakfast. Dine in – David, who works in the wine trade, always puts a bottle on the table – or eat out at one of the trendy new restaurants in Balham. A delightfully friendly city base on a quiet, tree-lined street – maximum comfort and good value for London. *Minimum stay two nights.*

113 Pepys Road

Anne and Tim, full of life, well-travelled, live on the side of a hill above a carpet of London lights. Hats on the hat stand, batiks on the walls, orchids… the place sparkles. The downstairs room has plush carpets, a huge bed, bamboo blinds; pad into your gorgeous marble bathroom kimono-clad. Upstairs, two more lovely rooms, one in country-house style, the other in elegant yellow. Anne also cooks brilliantly and will do you a steaming hot oriental cooked breakfast or the 'full English'. The garden has two splendid magnolias and it's a short walk downhill to buses, tubes and trains. Special.

	108 Streathbourne Road		113 Pepys Road
rooms	2: 1 double with separate bath; 1 twin sharing bath (let to same party only).	rooms	3: 1 double, 1 twin/double, both with bath; 1 twin with separate bath.
price	£75-£85. Singles £60-£70.	price	£90-£100. Singles from £55.
meals	Dinner £25. Good restaurants 5-minute walk.	meals	Dinner £26. BYO.
closed	Occasionally.	closed	Occasionally.
directions	From Tooting Bec tube, along Balham High Rd towards Balham. 3rd road on right. 7 minutes' walk from tube. Free parking weekends, otherwise meters or £5 daily.	directions	From Elephant & Castle r'bout, A2 (New Kent, Old Kent, New Cross Rd) to junc. with Queens Rd; right for Queens Rd; 1st left into Erlanger Rd, left into Sherwin Rd; right into Pepys Rd up hill. House opp. Telegraph Hill Park.

	Mary & David Hodges		Anne & Tim Marten
	108 Streathbourne Road,		113 Pepys Road,
	Balham,		New Cross,
	London SW17 8QY		London SE14 5SE
tel	020 8767 6931	tel	020 7639 1060
fax	020 8672 8839	fax	020 7639 8780
e-mail	mary.hodges@virgin.net	e-mail	annemarten@pepysroad.com
web	www.streathbourneroad.com	web	www.pepysroad.com

Map 4 Entry 301

Map 4 Entry 302

London

The Bowling Hall

Once an Irish drinking den, now a wonderland of cool lines and soothing colours. The mix of old and new is delicious: rugs on limestone tiles, a satin wood chest, wonderful old prints – Peter has renovated with style. Stand at the front door and look through the house: the view floats seamlessly through each room, 160-feet deep. On the walls, dazzling art, much of it Katherine's. Bedrooms are simpler, with maple wood floors, linen curtains, light colours, the odd piece of art. You get the front of the house, including a sitting room that opens onto a courtyard garden stuffed with lavender and bamboo.

rooms	2: 1 double, 1 single sharing bath/shower (single let to same party).
price	£80. Singles £45-£50.
meals	Continental breakfast included.
closed	Occasionally.
directions	Ask for details when booking.

Peter Camp & Katherine Virgils
The Bowling Hall,
346 Kennington Road,
London SE11 4LD

tel	020 7840 0454
fax	020 7840 0454
e-mail	bowlinghall@freenet.co.uk

Map 4 Entry 303

Norfolk

Rushall House

Blue-shelled eggs for breakfast, homemade cake for tea. Plenty to delight eyes and tummy at this comfortable Victorian rectory. High rooms are classically decorated with a contemporary touch, airy bedrooms have pale walls, rich fabrics, crisp bed linen and simple but choice furniture; radios and books are pleasing touches. Sink into the sitting room's sofa in front of a crackling fire. Walk off breakfast – a feast of local produce – around the garden, or cycle, antiques browse, birdwatch… children will love collecting eggs from the hens. Jane and Martin are relaxed but efficient hosts.

rooms	3: 1 double with bath; 1 double, 1 twin, sharing bath/shower.
price	From £55. Singles £35.
meals	Dinner, £20, by arrangement. BYO. Pubs/restaurants 0.5-3 miles.
closed	Rarely.
directions	Turn off A140 at r'bout to Dickleburgh; right at village store. Two miles pass Lakes Rd & Vaunces Lane, on right. Shortly after z-bend sign, drive to house on right.

Martin Hubner & Jane Gardiner
Rushall House,
Dickleburgh Road,
Rushall, Diss,
Norfolk IP21 4RX

tel	01379 741557
fax	01379 740418
e-mail	janegardineruk@aol.com
web	www.rushallhouse.co.uk

Map 10 Entry 304

Norfolk

Conifer Hill

A house on a hill – unusual for Norfolk; the lawns fall away and views stretch out to the farmland beyond. Richard and Patricia are utterly charming and easy to talk to; their respective passions are fishing and gardening and the garden is superb. Inside: fresh flowers, family photographs, agricultural prints, a feeling of light and space. The guest sitting room is generously furnished and Patricia will light a fire for you. The double, predominantly green, is the biggest; both have thick carpets and a Victorian elegance. *Children over six welcome. Dogs by arrangement. Complementary therapies nearby*

The Old Rectory

Soft pale brick, striking ogee arched windows, curtains of wisteria and acres of garden. This Victorian rectory is as handsome out as in. High-ceilinged rooms are flooded with light, furnished with a comfy contemporary and traditional mix and Lucy's paintings catch the eye. Large bedrooms have pale colours and Portuguese embroidered bedspreads. Pick your spot in the garden, perhaps the bench by the pond or the vine-covered pergola, as John and Lucy whip up supper. Fruit and vegetables from the garden, beef from their own herd, homemade bread: great food in a rural oasis.

rooms	2: 1 twin/double with separate bath. Further double let to same party only. Extra wc available.
price	From £50. Singles £30.
meals	Pub/restaurant 1 mile.
closed	Rarely.
directions	A143 Diss/Yarmouth for 9 miles. At r'bout left for Harleston; immed. left to Starston. Over x-roads, into village, over bridge, immed. right. After 0.5 miles, drive on left by white railings.

rooms	3: 1 double with bath; 1 twin with shared bath; 1 twin with separate bath.
price	£60-£70. Singles £40.
meals	Dinner, 4 courses, £27.50. Good pub 2.5 miles.
closed	Rarely.
directions	A143 Harleston bypass to Beccles/Yarmouth. 3rd left after 2nd r'bout; up Station Rd; right at T-junc; right at x-roads opp. pillar box up School Rd. Left up driveway just before T-junc.

Mrs Patricia Lombe Taylor
Conifer Hill,
Low Road,
Starston,
Harleston,
Norfolk IP20 9NT
tel   01379 852393
fax   01379 852393
e-mail richard.taylor55@virgin.net

Lucy & John Hildreth
The Old Rectory,
Alburgh,
Harleston,
Norfolk IP20 0BW
tel   01986 788408
fax   01986 788192
e-mail lucy@alburgholdrectory.com
web   www.alburgholdrectory.com

Map 10 Entry 305

Map 10 Entry 306

Norfolk

Le Grys Barn

Light pours into this 17th-century threshing barn – a jewel of a conversion in peaceful Norfolk. Julie lived in Hong Kong and her house glows with warmth, colour and oriental touches. Glass-topped tables increase the sense of space, Persian carpets beautify beech floors, golden buddhas rest in quiet corners. Across a courtyard, the two, very private, beamed and raftered bedrooms are stunningly equipped: guidebooks and glossies, easy chairs and Thai silk, music, flowers and mini fridge. Bathrooms have Italian tiles and breakfast, served on a Chinese altar table, is as delicious as all the rest.

Sallowfield Cottage

So many family treasures, it takes time to absorb the splendour: in the drawing room, gorgeous prints and paintings (many of carriage ponies: Caroline's passion), unusual furniture and decorative lamps. One bedroom has a Regency-style canopied bed and decoration to suit the era of the house (1850); the attic room is huge; all have views. And the garden is just as fascinating, with hedged rooms and a huge, jungly pond that slinks between the trees. Caroline loves cooking and can seat up to 10 at her candlelit dinner table. *Children over nine welcome.*

rooms	2: 1 double/twin, 1 double, both with bath.	rooms	3: 1 double with bath; 1 double with separate bath; 1 single with separate shower.
price	£60-£65. Singles from £45.	price	From £55. Singles £35.
meals	Packed lunch by arrangement. Pub 5-minute drive.	meals	Dinner from £17.50. Lunch £10.
closed	Christmas & New Year.	closed	Christmas & New Year.
directions	From A140 at Long Stratton, take Flowerpot Lane (opp. Shell garage) to Wacton; at x-roads left by phone box, past swings; 500 yds to telegraph pole with sign: left turn up 'Private Rd'.	directions	A11 Attleborough to Wymondham road. Take Spooner Row sign. Over x-roads by Three Boars pub. After 1 mile left at T-junc. to Wymondham for 1 mile. Look for rusty barrel on left. Turn into farm track.

	Mrs Julie Franklin Le Grys Barn, Wacton Common, Long Stratton, Norfolk NR15 2UR		Caroline Musker Sallowfield Cottage, Wattlefield, Wymondham, Norfolk NR18 9PA
tel	01508 531576	tel	01953 605086
fax	01508 532124	e-mail	caroline.musker@tesco.net
e-mail	jm.franklin@virgin.net		
web	www.norfolkbroads.co.uk/legrysbarn		

Map 10 Entry 307

Map 10 Entry 308

Norfolk

Washingford House

Tall octagonal chimney stacks and a Georgian façade give the house a stately air. In fact, it's the friendliest of places to stay: Paris and Nigel love entertaining and give you a delicious breakfast (dinner too, if you're lucky). The house, originally Tudor, has been freshly decorated and is a delightful mix of old and new. Big, light bedrooms look out over the lovely four-acre garden, a favourite haunt for local birds. Beyond, sheep graze equably on acres of green. Bergh Apton is a conservation village seven miles from Norwich and you are in the heart of it.
Children over 12 welcome.

The White House

Peace, tradition and unassuming good taste in this dignified old house. A large tapestry hangs in the stairwell and foot-square stone slabs make up the ground floor, softened by rugs from Persia. In the sitting room, a beautiful grand piano, which musical guests are welcome to play; in the mature garden a gazebo, a delightful place to read a book. Traditional bedrooms are comfortable with colourful bedcovers and garden views, and the double and twin can make a self-contained flat, with private sitting room and kitchen. Marvellous value, a good welcome and home-laid eggs for breakfast.

rooms	2: 1 twin with bath; 1 single with separate bath.
price	£70. Singles £40.
meals	Dinner with wine, £15-£25, occasionally available. Packed lunch £4.50. Pubs/restaurants 4-6 miles.
closed	Rarely.
directions	A146 from Norwich to Lowestoft for 4 miles. Right after Gull Pub signed Yelverton & Alpington. First left, left at T-junc for 1 mile. House on left past Post Office.

rooms	2: 1 double with bath; 1 twin with separate bath.
price	£60. Singles by arrangement.
meals	Dinner £15. BYO. Excellent pub 1.5 miles.
closed	Rarely.
directions	10-15 minute drive from Norwich & University. Bramerton signed from A146, 1st left (Norwich-Lowestoft Rd). House opp. church, with white 5-bar gate.

Paris & Nigel Back
Washingford House,
Cookes Road,
Bergh Apton,
Norwich,
Norfolk NR15 1AA
tel   01508 550924
mobile   07900 683617
e-mail   parisb@waitrose.com

Elizabeth Perowne
The White House,
Bramerton,
Norwich,
Norfolk NR14 7DW
tel   01508 538673
e-mail   e.perowne@amserve.net

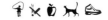

Map 10 Entry 309

Map 10 Entry 310

Norfolk

The Buttery

A thatched, self-contained, octagonal former dairy. Built on the Berry Hall Estate – designated as being of national, historic and scenic importance – it has been beautifully restored by the best local craftsmen. Outside are 126 acres to roam, half of which are woodland, but you may be tempted to stay in and finish that book. You get a little kitchen and a fridge stocked with delicious things for a full breakfast, a terracotta-tiled sitting room and a luxurious sofabed, a magical mezzanine bedroom, reached by a steep stair, a jacuzzi and a private sun terrace. Sheer indulgence.

White House Farm

A creeper-clad farmhouse, a chandelier-hung dining hall, afternoon tea overlooking landscaped gardens: you're in for a treat. Come for country-house elegance – soft colours, fine antiques, polished silver – 10 minutes from town. Bedrooms are restful with pretty wallpapers, gorgeous curtains and heaps of books. Enjoy home-grown fruit and eggs and local sausages at breakfast; in the evenings, take your book into the garden, play tennis, slip into the pool, relax in the sauna, paint in the studio. Woodland walks, golf and Norwich are on the doorstep. Huge comfort, green views, relaxed, gracious hosts.

	The Buttery
rooms	1 double with bath; mezzanine bed available.
price	£70-£80.
meals	Excellent pub in village.
closed	Rarely.
directions	From A47 Barnham Broom/Weston Longville x-roads, south towards Barnham Broom. After 150 yds, 1st drive on right. Left at T-junc., left again, house on left.

	White House Farm
rooms	3: 1 double with bath; 1 twin with separate bath; 1 single (let to same party only).
price	£90. Singles £45-£60.
meals	Dinner, 3 courses, £25. Good pub within walking distance.
closed	Rarely.
directions	At traffic lights on A1042, turn for New Rackheath; 0.7 miles left at lights into Blue Boar Lane; 0.5 miles, right into 'White House Farm'. House 0.5 miles on.

Deborah Meynell
The Buttery,
Berry Hall,
Honingham,
Norwich,
Norfolk NR9 5AX
tel   01603 880541
fax   01603 880887
e-mail   thebuttery@paston.co.uk

Jane & Simon Macfarlane
White House Farm,
Rackheath,
Norwich,
Norfolk NR13 6LB
tel   01603 788533
mobile   07767 352233
e-mail   simonmacfarlane@btopenworld.com
web   www.whitehousefarmnorfolk.com

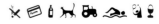

Map 10 Entry 311

Map 10 Entry 312

Norfolk

Manor Farmhouse

The best of both worlds: a family buzz in the farmhouse where you breakfast, privacy in the stylish 16th-century barn where you stay. All rooms lead off its beautifully vaulted sitting room. A kitchen and four-poster room with compact shower room on the ground floor, then a little stair to more bedrooms – small but lofty with a cosy, tucked-up-in-the-roof feel and views to Happisburgh's red and white striped lighthouse. A courtyard garden, billiards in the stable, lovely hosts, and you may come and go as you please. Ideal for friends or a family, with a contemporary feel. *Children over seven welcome.*

rooms	3: 1 double, 1 twin/double both with bath; 1 four-poster with shower.
price	From £50. Singles by arrangement.
meals	Dinner, 3 courses, £15. Pubs 1 mile.
closed	Christmas & New Year.
directions	From Norwich, A1151/A149 almost to Stalham. Left, for Walcott. At T-junc. left again. 1 mile on, right for H'burgh. Next T-junc., right. Next T-junc., left. Road bends right, look for house sign by fence.

David & Rosie Eldridge
Manor Farmhouse,
Happisburgh,
Norfolk NR12 0SA

tel	01692 651262
fax	01692 650220
e-mail	manorathappisburgh@hotmail.com
web	www.northnorfolk.co.uk/manorbarn

Map 10 Entry 313

The Old Rectory

Conservation farmland all around; acres of wild heathland busy with woodpeckers and owls; the coast two miles away. Life in the handsome 17th-century rectory revolves around the great kitchen and the draw of the Aga is irresistible on bread-baking days: Fiona loves to cook and food is seasonal and good. Comfortable bedrooms have *objects* from diplomatic postings, and the larger double has armchairs so you can settle in with a good book. Super views, three friendly dogs, a drawing room to share, masses of space and a family buzz when the teenagers come home.

rooms	2: 1 double/twin with bath; 1 double sharing bath & shower.
price	From £50. Singles £35.
meals	Dinner from £12.50. Good pubs 2 miles.
closed	Rarely.
directions	From Norwich A1151 for Stalham. Just before Stalham, left to Happisburgh. Left at T-junc; 3 miles; 2nd left after E. Ruston church, signed by-way to Foxhill. Right at x-roads; 1 mile on right.

Peter & Fiona Black
The Old Rectory,
Ridlington,
Norfolk NR28 9NZ

tel	01692 650247
fax	0870 1335719
e-mail	blacks7@email.com
web	www.oldrectory.northnorfolk.co.uk

Map 10 Entry 314

Norfolk

Holly Grove

Elegance and prettiness in equal measure. Light, airy, stylish rooms with long Georgian windows hung with beautiful fabrics – checks, toile de Jouy and ochre stripes. The bedrooms are most attractive too (the family room is one of the best we've seen and opens onto a delightful sleeping area for children, with toys and books). Bibby, a Cordon Bleu cook, uses local produce and vegetables from the walled kitchen garden. There's also a large heated pool. Worstead, the birthplace of worsted cloth, is charming – only a stroll away. Come at the end of July and you can join in the fun of the village festival.

Stable Cottage

In a privately owned village stands one of Norfolk's finest Elizabethan houses, Heydon Hall. In the Dutch-gabled stable block, fronted by Cromwell's Oak (a frequent visitor, he once scaled it while escaping a bull!), is this cottage – fresh, sunny and enchanting. Each room is touched by Sarah's warm personality and love of country things; seagrass floors and crisp linen, toile de Jouy walls and pretty china. Bedrooms are cottagey and immaculate, there are fresh fabrics, baskets of toiletries in the bathrooms, delicious food on your plate. All this in a serene parkland setting: a rare treat.

rooms	2: 1 twin/double with separate shower; 1 family with bath.
price	From £55. Singles from £37.50.
meals	Dinner, 2-3 courses, £14.50-£18. Packed lunch available. Pub 500 yds.
closed	Christmas & New Year.
directions	From Norwich, B1150 (N. Walsham road). At Westwick, right for Worstead. In village square, left into School Rd. On right opp. pond.

rooms	2 twins/doubles, both with bath.
price	£80. Singles £45.
meals	Dinner, 3 courses, from £18. BYO. Good pub 1 mile.
closed	Christmas.
directions	From Norwich, B1149 for 10 miles. 2nd left after bridge, for Heydon. 1.5 miles, right into village, into park, left over cattle grid, into stable courtyard.

Michael & Bibby Horwood
Holly Grove,
Worstead,
North Walsham,
Norfolk NR28 9RQ

tel	01692 535546
fax	01692 535400
e-mail	stay@hollygrovehouse.co.uk
web	www.hollygrovehouse.co.uk

Sarah Bulwer-Long
Stable Cottage,
Heydon Hall,
Heydon,
Norfolk NR11 6RE

| tel | 01263 587343 |

Map 10 Entry 315

Map 10 Entry 316

Norfolk

Burgh Parva Hall

Sunlight bathes the Norfolk longhouse on summer afternoons; the welcome from the Heals is as warm. The listed house is all that remains of the old village of Burgh Parva, deserted after the Great Plague. It's a handsome house and warmly inviting... old furniture, rugs, books, pictures and Magnet the terrier/daschund. Large guest bedrooms face the sunsets and the garden annexe makes a sweet hideaway. Breakfast eggs are from the garden hens, vegetables are home-grown, fish comes fresh from Holt and the game may have been shot by William. Settle down by the fire and tuck in.

The Old Vicarage

Norfolk at its best in this fine Georgian vicarage... huge skies, views that stretch forever, absolute peace. An elegant staircase springs from the flagstoned inner hall lit by a glass pyramid high above. Two delightful bedrooms (one capturing sunsets) have good furniture, books, china and pictures. Breakfast in the sunlit dining room on homemade bread and eggs from the home flock; for dinner, let Rosie treat you to mussels, crab and game in season. Five miles from the coast – sail, walk, cycle, visit the seals... and close to five National Trust properties. *French spoken.*

rooms	3: 1 twin with separate bath; 1 double with bath/shower; 1 garden flat (1 twin with bath/shower).
price	From £50-£70. Singles from £30.
meals	Dinner £20. Good pub/restaurant 4 miles.
closed	Rarely.
directions	Fakenham A148 for Cromer. At Thursford B1354 for Aylsham. Just before Melton, speed bumps, left immed. before bus shelter; 1st house on right after farmyard.

rooms	2: 1 double with separate bath; 1 twin/double with bath.
price	From £55. Ask for singles' rates.
meals	Dinner, 2-3 courses, £16.50-£20. BYO. Good pub 2 miles.
closed	Christmas & New Year.
directions	From Fakenham to Cromer for 6 miles. Left at Crawfish pub into Hindringham, down hill & left; before church, into Blacksmith's Lane. Follow lane, bear right, house on left at top of hill; flint-wall entrances.

Judy & William Heal
Burgh Parva Hall,
Melton Constable,
Norfolk NR24 2PU

tel   01263 862569
fax   01263 862569
e-mail   judyheal@burghparvahall.wanadoo.co.uk

Rosie & Robin Waters
The Old Vicarage,
Blacksmith's Lane,
Hindringham,
Norfolk NR21 0QA

tel   01328 878223
fax   01328 878223
e-mail   watersrobin@hotmail.com

Map 10 Entry 317

Map 10 Entry 318

Norfolk

Tylers Barn

The luxury of a hotel and the friendliness of a B&B – this is a gem. Tucked into a hollow, enfolded by gardens, the 1820 barns have been decorated in huge style. In the vast North Wing, the suite: floor-to-ceiling windows, opulent colours, velvet sofas, candles in the bathroom, a baby grand and a mezzanine bed. Allan, a trained chef, welcomes you with scones from the Aga and serves you seasonal breakfasts and dinners on polished mahogany. Books, magazines and Mozart in the sitting room, Tuscan murals in the conservatory, a fabulous welcome all round.

Highfield Farm

Elizabeth is capable and funny – a winning combination. She got the local church bells ringing again after years of silence: tractor grease did the trick. Reached by a long lane and wonderfully quiet, this is a mainly arable farm, with hens, geese and horses, yet the house is unusually elegant inside – antiques, silver, porcelain and paintings. There's a sitting room for guests and the bedrooms have high ceilings and pretty details: hand-painted tiles above the basins, padded headboards, lovely prints. Their own Soil Association-approved farm eggs for breakfast and Elizabeth's excellent lemon cake for tea.

rooms	1 suite with bath.
price	Suite £90.
meals	Dinner £25. BYO. Picnic £12.50.
closed	Rarely.
directions	From A1067 south of Fakenham towards Stibbard. There, right into Wood Norton Rd, then left split (not to Guist); Tylers Barn signed 2nd on left after split.

rooms	2: 1 double with separate bath; 1 twin with bath.
price	£52-£56. Singles in high season, £30-£40.
meals	Dinner, winter only, 3 courses, £15. Pub 2.5 miles.
closed	Christmas & New Year.
directions	From Fakenham B1146 for East Dereham. After 2 miles, left to Gt. Ryburgh. In village, 2nd left up Highfield Lane opp. pink cottage & on for 0.5 miles; house on right.

Allan Urquhart
Tylers Barn,
Wood Norton Road,
Stibbard, Fakenham,
Norfolk NR21 0EX

tel	01328 829260
fax	01328 829643
e-mail	allan@tylersbarnholidaycottages.co.uk
web	www.tylersbarnholidaycottages.co.uk

Elizabeth Savory
Highfield Farm,
Great Ryburgh,
Fakenham,
Norfolk NR21 7AL

tel	01328 829249
fax	01328 829422
web	www.broadland.com/highfield

Map 10 Entry 319

Map 10 Entry 320

Norfolk

Manor Farm Barn

Extraordinarily kind and generous hosts – a guest wrote to tell us so – and they really enjoy having people in their 200-year-old converted barn/smithy, with its wildflower garden and farmland views. It's light and open, with a large kitchen where candles are suspended above the table and dried flowers hang from the beams. There are bees, free-range hens and home-grown organic vegetables and fruit; Jane's an imaginative cook and gives you fresh juice before breakfast. One bedroom is carpeted; the other has seagrass matting. Walsingham is close by and there's plenty to inspire artists. Jane paints and can organise trips.

rooms	2: 1 twin/double with separate bath; 1 twin/double with separate shower.
price	£50. Singles from £25.
meals	Dinner, 3 courses, £15. BYO.
closed	Christmas.
directions	From A148 Fakenham for King's Lynn, then left for Dunton. Straight through Dunton. Keep on main country lane. Barn on left before phone box.

Michael & Jane Davidson-Houston
Manor Farm Barn,
Tatterford,
Fakenham,
Norfolk NR21 7AZ
tel   01485 528393

Map 10 Entry 321

Bagthorpe Hall

Among the wholesomeness of Norfolk – all birdwatching, boats, salt marshes and crab nets – beats the heart of this dynamic household. Tid is a pioneer of organic farming and good things from his 700 acres wing their way monthly to the farmers' market. Gina's passions are music, dance and gardens and she organises open days and concerts for charity. Theirs is a large, elegant house with a mural in the hall chronicling their family life. It's fascinating, and beautiful. Wonderful colours, good beds, generous curtains and excellent food – maybe fresh raspberries for breakfast, and local and home produce for dinner.

rooms	2: 1 double with separate bath; 1 twin with separate shower.
price	£50–£60. Singles £35.
meals	Dinner £20–£25. Pubs/restaurants nearby.
closed	Rarely.
directions	From King's Lynn for A148 to Fakenham. Left at East Rudham by Cat & Fiddle Pub. 3.5 miles to Bagthorpe. Pass farm on left, wood on right, white gates set back from trees. At top of drive.

Gina Morton
Bagthorpe Hall,
Bagthorpe,
King's Lynn,
Norfolk PE31 6QY
tel   01485 578528
fax   01485 578151
e-mail   dgmorton@hotmail.com

Map 10 Entry 322

Norfolk

Lower Farm

This house reflects its farming owners – delightful, warm and natural. Relaxed, comfortable and lived-in, it has touches of real elegance: the drawing room has a grand piano and gilt cornicing. Bedrooms are neither designery nor lavish, but homely and generous with towels, bathrobes, hotties and other extras, even a fridge and sofa. Two are vast and high-ceilinged, with chairs to relax in and good views from long windows. The garden is lovely and there are dogs and horses galore (stabling available); the walls bear the proof of success at point-to-points and shows. Breakfasts are lavish.

rooms	3: 1 double with shower; 1 double with bath/shower; 1 twin with separate bath & wc.
price	£50-£56. Singles £30-£35.
meals	Pub/restaurant 800 yds.
closed	Rarely.
directions	From King's Lynn, A148 for Cromer. 3 miles after Hillington, 2nd of 2 turnings right to Harpley (no signpost) opp. Houghton Hall sign. 200 yds on; over x-roads, house 400 yds on left.

Amanda Case
Lower Farm,
Harpley,
King's Lynn,
Norfolk PE31 6TU
tel   01485 520240
fax   01485 520240

Map 10 Entry 323

Admiral's House

Fronted by a village green, encircled by a tended garden, the Admiral's House is a serene Georgian home and a fine B&B. Penelope loves to cook and is Cordon Bleu trained – breakfasts alone are worth the trip (eggs from Welsummer hens, honey from orchard bees, coffee from the espresso machine, muffins from the oven). There's a lovely fresh sitting room with grey and rose colours and a pale planked floor, and big comfortable bedrooms upstairs; choose between views over the pretty garden or the perfect green. A Norfolk treat – especially for gardeners and foodies. *Children over 12 welcome.*

rooms	3: 1 twin/double, 1 double, both with bath; 1 single let to same party only.
price	£50-£60. Singles £35.
meals	Cooked breakfast supp. £5. Dinner, 4 courses, £22. Good pub 4 miles.
closed	Rarely.
directions	From A1065 turn left at Fox & Hounds. In Weasenham, right, then left onto track across village green.

Penelope Hands
Admiral's House,
The Green,
Weasenham St Peters, King's Lynn,
Norfolk PE32 2TD
tel   01328 838240
e-mail penelope.hands@btopenworld.com

Map 10 Entry 324

Norfolk

Manor House Farm

Vines clamber across ancient walls, lawns stretch to neat hedges, a limpid pond here, sprays of roses there. In the stables of this traditional Norfolk farmhouse are two beautiful, bright, fresh rooms with their own deeply comfortable sitting room; antiques, colourful rugs on seagrass matting, fresh flowers and "wildly comfortable beds" add to the luxury. Breakfast is home-grown and delicious and served in the cheery dining room of the main house, or in the lavish, plant-filled greenhouse. Libby and Robin have won conservation awards for the farm – and the coast is 20 minutes away. *Children over 10 welcome.*

Litcham Hall

For the whole of the 19th century this was Litcham's doctor's house; the red-brick Hall is still at the centre of the community. The big-windowed guest bedrooms look onto the stunning garden where church fêtes are held in summer. This is a thoroughly English home with elegant proportions – the hall, drawing room and dining room are gracious and beautifully furnished. The hens lay the breakfast eggs, the garden fills the table with soft fruit in season and John and Hermione are friendly and most helpful. *Children & dogs by arrangement.*

rooms	2: 1 double, 1 twin/double in stable annexe, both with bath.
price	£70-£80. Singles £40-£45.
meals	Pub 1.5 miles.
closed	Rarely.
directions	A1065 Swaffham-Fakenham road. 6 miles on, through Weasenham. After 1 mile, right for Wellingham. House on left, next to church.

rooms	3: 1 double, 1 twin, both with bath; 1 twin with separate bath. Sitting room available.
price	£55-£70. Singles by arrangement.
meals	Dinner, 3 courses, £25. Pub/restaurant nearby.
closed	Christmas.
directions	From Swaffham, A1065 north for 5 miles, then right to Litcham on B1145. House on left on entering village. Georgian red brick with stone balls on gatepost.

Elisabeth Ellis
Manor House Farm,
Wellingham,
Fakenham,
King's Lynn,
Norfolk PE32 2TH

tel	01328 838227
fax	01328 838348
e-mail	l.ellis@farming.co.uk

John & Hermione Birkbeck
Litcham Hall,
Litcham,
King's Lynn,
Norfolk PE32 2QQ

tel	01328 701389
fax	01328 701164
e-mail	h.birkbeck67@amserve.com

Map 10 Entry 325

Map 10 Entry 326

Norfolk

College Farm

Mrs Garnier has done B&B for years and looks after her stupendous Grade II*-listed house single-handedly. Over afternoon tea, she tells colourful stories of the house and her family's long local history: from 1349 until the Dissolution of the Monasteries the house was a college of priests; in 1975 it was saved from ruin and given the Laura Ashley facelift. There's a stunning panelled dining room, big, lived-in bedrooms (the sky-blue one is particularly pretty) and great views. Good value and very good locally sourced breakfasts. *Children over seven welcome.*

Northamptonshire

Colledges House

Liz clearly derives pleasure from sharing her 300-year-old stone thatched cottage, heavenly garden, pretty conservatory and converted barn with guests. And there is something special wherever you turn: a Jacobean trunk, a Bechstein piano, a beautiful bureau in the bathroom. Beds are hugely comfortable, and Cordon Bleu dinners are elegant affairs, and fun and jolly, too – Liz has a lovely sense of humour. Previous guests have said that staying here is like "staying with a good friend". Stroll around the conservation village of Staverton – delightful. *Children over eight and babes in arms welcome.*

rooms	3: 1 double with separate bath; 1 twin, 1 twin/double, both with bath. Extra shower & wc.
price	From £55. Singles £27.50.
meals	Afternoon tea included. Pub 1 mile.
closed	Rarely.
directions	From Thetford, A1075 north for Watton. After 9 miles, left to Thompson at 'Light Vehicles Only' sign. After 0.5 miles, 2nd left at red postbox on corner. Left again, house at end.

rooms	4: 2 doubles, 1 twin, all with bath/shower; 1 single with bath.
price	£95. Singles £59.50.
meals	Dinner, 3 courses, £28.50.
closed	Rarely.
directions	From Daventry, A425 to Leamington Spa. 100 yds past Staverton Park Conference Centre, right into village, then 1st right. Keep left, & at 'Give Way' sign, sharp left. House immed. on right.

	Mrs Garnier
	College Farm,
	Thompson,
	Thetford,
	Norfolk IP24 1QG
tel	01953 483318
fax	01953 483318
e-mail	collegefarm@amserve.net

	Liz Jarrett
	Colledges House,
	Oakham Lane,
	Staverton, Daventry,
	Northamptonshire NN11 6JQ
tel	01327 702737
fax	01327 300851
e-mail	liz@colledgeshouse.co.uk
web	www.colledgeshouse.co.uk

Map 10 Entry 327

Map 8 Entry 328

Northamptonshire

Nobottle Grange

A grand avenue of limes leads to this former farmhouse, built in the 1840s and part of the Althorp estate. Valerie and Ian are great company — easy and natural — and welcome guests with afternoon tea and cakes; they also collect and sell Staffordshire pottery. Meals are enjoyed by a log-burning stove in the deep-blue dining room in winter, and on the terrace on warm summer nights. Bedrooms are large and simple, with sofas and armchairs. The garden reveals traces of medieval ridge-and-furrow farming, the views of the countryside are magnificent and it's a great area for riding — livery is available.

rooms	3: 1 double with bath; 1 twin with separate bath; 1 extra twin (let to same party only).
price	£55–£65. Singles £40–£45.
meals	Dinner £17.50. BYO.
closed	Rarely.
directions	From N'hampton, A45 for Daventry. After 1.5 miles, 3rd exit at r'bout for Althorp. After 1 mile, 1st exit at r'bout for Nobottle. House just beyond Nobottle on left, on brow of hill.

Valerie Cocks
Nobottle Grange,
Nobottle,
Northampton,
Northamptonshire NN7 4HJ

tel	01604 759494
mobile	07887 850965
e-mail	stay@nobottlegrange.co.uk
web	www.nobottlegrange.co.uk

Map 8 Entry 329

Haselbech House

The 1970s exterior belies the formal interior — there are family antiques, gilt-framed oils of ancestors and much military and horsey memorabilia. Tessa and her ex-Army husband David have lived all over the world, yet feel rooted here and the views are stunning. The twin comes with decorative dark wooden bedsteads and yellow floral curtains; the double has a family feel, framed military photos and good paintings. Delicious breakfasts, with eggs from the hens and bantams that wander the garden, and plenty of walking in beautiful countryside. You'll feel at peace.

rooms	2: 1 twin, 1 double, sharing bath.
price	£80. Singles £45.
meals	Dinner £25. Packed lunch £5. Good pubs locally.
closed	Rarely.
directions	From A14, A508 for Northampton, 1st right to Haselbech. At sharp r-h bend, left to Cottesbrooke, 0.25 miles. Left between 2 red cottages; 1st right between fields. Tarmac drive to house.

Tessa Le Sueur
Haselbech House,
Haselbech Hill,
Northampton,
Northamptonshire NN6 9LL

tel	01604 686266
e-mail	tess@lesueur.co.uk
web	www.haselbechhousefarm.co.uk

Map 9 Entry 330

Northamptonshire

Old Vicarage

A big, rambling, Regency house on the border of the ancient county of Rutland, its 10 acres home to an assortment of animals, horses and hens. It is unsmart, engagingly eccentric and you may get up when you please. Dogs jump on sofas, there are books and toys, croquet on the lawn and their own smellies by the bed. Your hosts are irresistible – David runs the herbal beauty company, Susan supports Compassion in World Farming; both are amusing company. A haphazard collection of furniture, paintings in gilded frames, oddities at every turn and Susan's generous organic breakfasts fresh from the Aga.

rooms	3: 1 twin, 1 double, both with separate bath; 1 family with shower.
price	£49. Singles £32.
meals	Pubs/restaurants 1.5 miles.
closed	Rarely.
directions	From Corby to Stamford, left to Laxton (1 mile); with the Green on right, house on left up drive.

	Susan Hill-Brookes
	Old Vicarage,
	Laxton,
	Corby,
	Northamptonshire NN17 3AT
tel	01780 450248
fax	01780 450259
e-mail	susan@marthahill.co.uk
web	www.old-vicarage-laxton.co.uk

Map 9 Entry 331

Northumberland

Chain Bridge House

The kitchen is the hub of Livvy's home, and the house, mid-19th century, is the last in England. The old Union Chain Bridge over the river Tweed is yards away, anglers fish for salmon and the riverside walks are wonderful. Log fires in the sitting room, a revolving summer house in the garden to relax in – bring your own champagne! – white towels on heated rails and goose down duvets in lovely bedrooms (or sheets and soft blankets should you prefer). Breakfasts and dinners are as local, seasonal and organic as can be, Livvy is a fantastic cook and babies and children get as big a welcome as all the rest.

rooms	2: 1 double with shower; 1 twin with bath.
price	£60. Singles £35.
meals	Dinner, 2-3 courses, £15-£20. Packed lunch £5. Good pub 3 miles.
closed	Rarely.
directions	A698; exit from A1 at East Ord, west of Berwick. After 1 mile, right for Horncliffe; follow signs for Honey Farm; past farm 200 yds; house on right.

	Livvy Cawthorn
	Chain Bridge House,
	Horncliffe,
	Berwick-upon-Tweed,
	Northumberland TD15 2XT
tel	01289 386259
fax	01289 386259
e-mail	info@chainbridgehouse.co.uk
web	www.chainbridgehouse.co.uk

Map 16 Entry 332

Northumberland

West Coates

Slip through the gates of this Georgian townhouse and you're in the country. Two acres of leafy gardens, with shady or sunny spots to relax, belie the closeness of Berwick's centre. As surprising are the indoor pool and hot tub tucked in the corner. From the lofty ceilings and sash windows to the soft colours, gleaming furniture and handsome sporting prints, the house has a calm, ordered elegance. Bedrooms have antiques and garden views; two have roll-top baths; fruit, homemade cakes, flowers welcome you. Warm, friendly Karen is a stunning cook, inventively using local produce and spoiling you.

Hethpool

Spot wild goats on the hills of this valley, whose private roads are virtually car-free: vehicles are restricted. It's remote, rugged and breathtakingly beautiful. Inside, old family pieces, honeysuckle chintz, hunting gear, milling dogs – and Martin and Eildon who have lived here for years and look after you with ease. Bedrooms, neat and tidy, comfy and clean, share a sitting room; after one of Eildon's fine dinners, settle in in front of the fire. There's a 16th-century peel tower in the garden and the National Park beyond. Bring your horse and let your hosts be your guide!

rooms	3: 1 twin/double with bath/shower; 1 double with shower; 1 twin/double with separate bath/shower.
price	£90-£100. Singles from £50.
meals	Dinner £30.
closed	Christmas & New Year.
directions	From A1 take A6105 into Berwick. House 300 yds on left. Stone pillars at end of drive.

rooms	2: 1 twin with shower, 1 double with separate bath.
price	£60. Singles £35.
meals	Dinner, 2-3 courses, £15-£20.
closed	Rarely.
directions	From Wooler A697 towards Coldstream; 2 miles left onto B6352. After 4 miles left to Hethpool; 1.5 miles, left at 'Private Drive' sign; 3rd on right.

	Karen Brown
	West Coates,
	30 Castle Terrace,
	Berwick-upon-Tweed,
	Northumberland TD15 1NZ
tel	01289 309666
mobile	07814 282973
e-mail	karenbrownwestcoates@yahoo.com
web	www.westcoates.co.uk

	Eildon & Martin Letts
	Hethpool,
	Wooler,
	Northumberland NE71 6TW
tel	01668 216232
e-mail	eildon@hethpoolhouse.co.uk
web	www.hethpoolhouse.co.uk

Map 16 Entry 333

Map 16 Entry 334

Northumberland

Broome

A totally surprising one-storey house, full of beautiful things. It is an Aladdin's cave and sits in the middle of a coastal village with access to miles of sandy beaches. The garden/breakfast room is its hub and has a country cottage feel; enjoy locally-smoked kippers here, award-winning 'Bamburgh Bangers' and home-cured bacon from the village butcher. There's also a sun-trapping courtyard full of colourful pots for breakfasts in the sun. Guests have a cheerful sitting/dining room and bedrooms fresh flowers and good books. Mary is welcoming and amusing and has stacks of local knowledge.

North Charlton Farm

Sylvia is a doyenne of farmhouse B&B, with 25 years' experience under her belt. She received an MBE for her Household and Farming Museum and is justly proud of her gong. She has a wonderful sense of community and Charlie, even if he's been up since dawn with his sheep, will come and chat over breakfast. It's warm, cosy, comfortable – big fires, family furniture, knick-knacks and photos. Breakfasts are as generous as you'd expect, and there are fresh flowers everywhere. Bedrooms are large, with long views, fine cotton sheets and patchwork quilts. The quintessence of farmhouse B&B. *Children over 10 welcome.*

rooms	2: 1 double, 1 twin, sharing separate bath/shower (2nd room let to same party).
price	£60–£70. Singles £40–£45.
meals	Dinner occasionally available. Excellent pubs/restaurants 2-minute walk.
closed	1 November–1 March.
directions	From Newcastle north on A1; right for Bamburgh on B1341. To village, pass 30mph sign & hotel; 1st right at Victoria Hotel; 400 yds on right.

rooms	3: 2 doubles, both with shower; 1 twin with separate bath.
price	£70. Singles £40.
meals	Restaurants 4 miles.
closed	Christmas & New Year.
directions	5 miles north of Alnwick on A1, left on reaching dual carriageway, for North Charlton. House 300 yds up on left through trees.

	Mary Dixon
	Broome,
	22 Ingram Road,
	Bamburgh,
	Northumberland NE69 7BT
tel	01668 214287
mobile	07971 248230
e-mail	mdixon4394@aol.com

	Charles & Sylvia Armstrong
	North Charlton Farm,
	Chathill,
	Alnwick,
	Northumberland NE67 5HP
tel	01665 579443
fax	01665 579407
e-mail	stay@northcharltonfarm.co.uk
web	www.northcharltonfarm.co.uk

Map 16 Entry 335

Map 16 Entry 336

Northumberland

Bilton Barns

A solidly good farmhouse B&B whose lifeblood is still farming. The Jacksons know every inch of the countryside and coast that surrounds their 1715 home; it's a pretty spot. They farm 400 acres of mixed arable land that sweeps down to the coast, yet make time to greet and get to know their guests. Dorothy takes pride in creating an easy and sociable atmosphere – three couples who were introduced to each other one weekend returned for a reunion! Bedrooms are big, carpeted and comfortable, a conservatory leads onto the garden and there's an airy guests' sitting room with an open fire and views to the sea.

The Orchard House

A blissful surprise, to step off the bustling street of this old-world market town into a stylish, welcoming B&B. Large, finely proportioned rooms have lost none of their Georgian character; the drawing room, palest yellow and cream, sports a gilt mirror above a marble fire and a Persian carpet on an antique floor. Bedrooms, in their taupe and cream makeover, are civilised havens: duckdown on big beds, white towelling robes, modish bathrooms. Up for sumptuous breakfasts at immaculately dressed tables… then all of Northumberland to explore. *Minimum stay two nights at holidays and weekends.*

rooms	3: 1 four-poster, 1 double, 1 twin, all with shower. Bath also available.
price	£60-£70. Singles £30-£40.
meals	Dinner £16. Packed lunch from £4. Good pub/restaurant 1.5 miles.
closed	Christmas & New Year.
directions	From Alnwick, A1068 to Alnmouth. At Hipsburn r'bout follow signs to station & cross bridge. 1st lane to left, 0.3 miles down drive.

rooms	5: 2 doubles with shower; 1 family room with bath; 1 suite with bath.
price	£65-£150. Singles £50.
meals	Good pub nearby.
closed	December-March.
directions	From A1 onto A697, Coldstream exit; on to A6344, signs into Rothbury. On main street on right.

Brian & Dorothy Jackson
Bilton Barns,
Alnmouth,
Alnwick,
Northumberland NE66 2TB
tel   01665 830427
fax   01665 833909
e-mail   dorothy@biltonbarns.com
web   www.biltonbarns.com

Graham Stobbart
The Orchard House,
Rothbury,
Northumberland NE65 7TL
tel   01669 620 684
mobile   07837 578962
e-mail   info@orchardhouserothbury.com
web   www.orchardhouserothbury.com

Map 16 Entry 337

Map 16 Entry 338

Thistleyhaugh

Enid thrives on hard work and humour, her passions are pictures, cooking and people and if she's not the perfect B&B hostess, she's a close contender. Certainly you eat well – eggs from the farm hens at breakfast and their own beef at dinner. Choose any of the five large, lovely bedrooms and stay the week; they are awash with old paintings, silk fabrics, crisp white linen and views. But if you do stray downstairs, past the log fire and the groaning table, there are 600 acres of farmland to discover and a few million more of the Cheviots beyond that. Wonderful hosts, house and region.

Shieldhall

You stay in recently converted 18th-century farm buildings, each with an entrance into a central courtyard. Stephen and his sons make and restore antique furniture and there are examples of their artistry throughout. Bedrooms are compact and named after the wood used within, bathrooms are spacious and there's a sitting room/library that's shared. Meals are taken in the beamed dining room of the main house – once home to the family of Capability Brown. Celia is friendly and attentive and loves cooking – and most ingredients are locally sourced. There's also a secret bar and a small but varied wine list.

rooms	5: 4 doubles, 1 twin, all with bath/shower.
price	£65. Singles £42.
meals	Dinner, 3 courses, £17.
closed	Christmas & New Year.
directions	Leave A1 for A697 for Coldstream & Longhorsley; 2 miles past Longhorsley, left at Todburn sign; 1 mile to x-roads, then right; on 1 mile over white bridge; 1st right, right again, over cattle grid.

rooms	3: 1 double, 1 four-poster, 1 twin, all with bath/shower.
price	£76. Singles £45-£55.
meals	Dinner, 4 courses, £22.50. Good pub 7 miles.
closed	Rarely.
directions	From Newcastle A696 (for Jedburgh). 5 miles north of Belsay, right onto B6342. On left after 500 yds (turn into front courtyard).

Henry & Enid Nelless
Thistleyhaugh,
Longhorsley,
Morpeth,
Northumberland NE65 8RG
tel   01665 570629
fax   01665 570629
web   www.thistleyhaugh.co.uk

Celia & Stephen Robinson-Gay
Shieldhall,
Wallington,
Morpeth,
Northumberland NE61 4AQ
tel   01830 540387
fax   01830 540490
e-mail   robinson.gay@btinternet.com
web   www.shieldhallguesthouse.co.uk

Map 16 Entry 339

Map 16 Entry 340

Northumberland

Charlton House

The countryside is breathtaking and you could walk forever – perhaps to Hadrian's Wall. The solid old manor house, dating to the lawless days of the Border Reivers, used to house the cattle downstairs; now there's a restful sitting room instead – blue armchairs, coal fire, pretty china. After an excellent pub dinner return to ample, traditional bedrooms that are peacefully TV-free: one with a white bed and pale blue touches, the other with pink quilts and chintz drapes. Bathrooms are pristine. Gaze on swans from sash windows – the pretty garden has a wetland across the road. Charming Ann was born here.

The Hermitage

A magical setting, only three miles from Hadrian's wall. Through ancient woodland – owls, birdsong, deer – up the long drive and over the burn to this supremely comfortable, country-elegant home. Large, carpeted and delightful bedrooms are furnished with antiques, prints and superb beds; bathrooms have large roll-top baths. There is a walled garden, and breakfasts (delicious) can be served on the terrace. Katie grew up in this lovely house, looks after you brilliantly and knows all there is to know about the area. *Katie prefers guests to be in by 11pm. Children over seven and babes in arms welcome.*

rooms	2: 1 double with separate bath; 1 twin with separate bath/shower.
price	£56. Singles from £30.
meals	Excellent pubs 5-minute drive.
closed	November-February.
directions	Exit A68, 12 miles north of Corbridge, onto road for Bellingham; 2 miles, then road to Kielder; right to Charlton (no sign): house 1st on left.

rooms	3: 1 double, 1 twin, both with bath; 1 twin with separate bath.
price	From £75. Singles from £45.
meals	Good pubs 7 miles.
closed	October-February.
directions	7 miles north of Corbridge on A68. Left on A6079 for 1 mile, then right through lodge gates with arch. House 0.5 miles down drive.

Mrs Ann Pearson
Charlton House,
Charlton,
Hexham,
Northumberland NE48 1PE
tel   01434 240232

Simon & Katie Stewart
The Hermitage,
Swinburne,
Hexham,
Northumberland NE48 4DG
tel   01434 681248
fax   01434 681110
e-mail   katie.stewart@themeet.co.uk

Map 16 Entry 341

Map 16 Entry 342

Northumberland

Bog House

It's too quiet for some townies – and thank goodness! If you've had it with bustle, bury yourself in the depths of Northumberland, two miles from Hadrian's Wall. Here is an immaculate barn conversion that's mercifully free from the usual modern furniture; what you have is a contemporary, airy feel and an open-raftered space stuffed with antiques. The delightful Rosemary has created a stunning place. Breakfast sausages are local (organic where possible), the peace total and the welcome disarming; you have your own entrance and may come and go as you please. An indulgent, wonderful retreat.

Matfen High House

Bring the wellies! You are 25 miles from the border and the walking is a joy. Struan and Jenny are amusing company, love country pursuits and will drive you to Matfen Hall for dinner. Expect tasselled lampshades and festoon blinds in comfortable bedrooms, white towels in white bathrooms, pictures, books and choice pieces in the drawing room; the sturdy stone house of 1735 is a pleasant, pretty place to stay. You are served delicious breakfast at a mahogany table and may try out French and Spanish on your fluent hostess. The Roman Wall and the great castles of Alnwick and Bamburgh beckon.

rooms	3: 1 double, 1 single sharing bath (single for same party); 1 twin with bath.
price	£80-£90. Singles £40-£45.
meals	Dinner, 2 courses,£15-£18. Pubs/restaurants 8 min drive.
closed	Rarely.
directions	A68; 5 miles north of Corbridge, right onto B6318. After 3.5 miles, left signed Moorhouse. On for 1 mile, right; left to Bog House after 1 mile. Last farm on left.

rooms	4: 1 double, 1 twin both with bath/shower; 1 double, 1 twin with shared bath.
price	£60-£70. Singles £30-£35.
meals	Packed lunches £3.50. Restaurant 2 miles.
closed	Rarely.
directions	A69 at Heddon on the Wall, onto B6318 past Robin Hood Inn; 500 yds, right to Moorhouse; right at next junction; past Hadrian Pet Hotel; 300 yds, right, opp. cottages.

	Rosemary Stobart
	Bog House,
	Matfen,
	Northumberland NE20 0RF
tel	01661 886776
mobile	07850 375535
e-mail	rosemary.stobart@btinternet.com
web	www.boghouse-matfen.co.uk

	Struan & Jenny Wilson
	Matfen High House,
	Matfen,
	Corbridge,
	Northumberland NE20 0RG
tel	01661 886 592
fax	01661 886 847
e-mail	struan@struan.enterprise-plc.com

Map 16 Entry 343

Map 12 Entry 344

Northumberland

Ovington House

Friendly Lynne has made many improvements to this 1730 gentleman's residence. Bedrooms have original Georgian shutters, some have waxed floors with rugs. Shower rooms are large and modern and guests love the comfy beds. Substantial breakfasts are served in the delightful dining room, so inviting with chesterfield, piano and chess. A pretty garden, a newly-built stable block, an outdoor arena set in five acres – and views of Northumberland countryside to enchant the walker, the naturalist and the stressed city soul. Wonderful.

Old Ridley Hall

The topiary is magnificent! And the old dovecote fascinates foreigners. Much-extended over the years, this started as a solid, Victorian farmhouse but now sits in expansive, breathtaking Northumbrian scenery – a magnet for walkers and naturalists. Your gentle, hospitable hostess welcomes families now that her children have flown the nest, though the house hasn't lost its familial warmth. The bedrooms are straightforward and lived-in, but are large and perfectly adequate, with wonderful views. The huge, attractive drawing room is yours to wallow in, and the breakfasts are as local and organic as possible.

rooms	3: 2 doubles, both with shower; 1 family with bath/shower.
price	£60. Singles £35.
meals	Restaurants within walking distance.
closed	Never.
directions	A69 signed Ovington, on left if travelling to Hexham. Through Ovington. House signed on left, after sharp corner.

rooms	3 twins sharing 2 baths.
price	£60. Singles from £30.
meals	Good pubs/restaurants 2 miles.
closed	Rarely.
directions	From A68, south of Tyne at r'bout, east for Stocksfield. B6309 right, signed Hindley. 1st left, then biggest house at end.

Lynne Moffitt
Ovington House,
Ovington,
Prudhoe,
Northumberland NE42 6DH
tel   01661 832442
e-mail   stay@ovingtonhouse.co.uk
web   www.ovingtonhouse.co.uk

Mrs J Aldridge
Old Ridley Hall,
Stocksfield,
Northumberland NE43 7RU
tel   01661 842816
e-mail   oldridleyhall@talk21.com

Map 12 Entry 345

Map 12 Entry 346

Nottinghamshire

The Yellow House

A butter-yellow 30s semi in a quiet, tree-lined street. Suzanne, a well-travelled ex-model, is as immediately engaging as her home, and great company. Colour schemes are cool with the occasional oriental touch. Your bedroom in the loft – a self-contained hideaway with a good, big bed – is carpeted and crisply decorated in bold cream-and-green florals. Suzanne encourages you to enjoy your eggs and bacon on the terrace in fine weather; she is also happy to pick you up from the station. Nottingham's attractions are only three miles away, the great oaks of Sherwood Forest 12 miles north.

The Old Vicarage

Jillie's grandmother studied at the Slade and her paintings line the walls; glass and china adorn every surface. This wisteria-clad Victorian vicarage next to the 12th-century church was falling down when the Steeles bought it; now it's an elegant, traditional country home. Long windows are generously draped, bedrooms are large, baths have claw feet and a number of friendly cats and dogs wait to welcome you. Jerry bakes the bread and all the vegetables come from the garden, where you may play tennis or croquet. Mary Queen of Scots is reputed to have stayed at Langford as guest of the Earl of Shrewsbury.

rooms	1 double with shower.
price	£55. Singles £35.
meals	Good pubs/restaurants 1 mile.
closed	Rarely.
directions	From main Mansfield Rd at junc. with Vale Pub, going North, right onto Thackerey's Lane; at r'bout straight on; after 100 yds right into Whernside Rd. Left at x-roads into Littlegreen Rd; house on left.

rooms	3: 1 double, 1 twin, both with bath & shower; 1 small double with shower.
price	£70–£80. Singles £45–£50.
meals	Dinner, for 4 or more, £22.50.
closed	Rarely.
directions	From A1, A46 to Lincoln & left onto A1133 for Gainsborough. Through Langford, 0.5 mile on, & left for Holme. House 100 yds on, on right, by church.

Suzanne Prew-Smith
The Yellow House,
7 Littlegreen Road,
Woodthorpe,
Nottingham,
Nottinghamshire NG5 4LE
tel   0115 926 2280
e-mail   suzanne.prewsmith1@btinternet.com

Jerry & Jillie Steele
The Old Vicarage,
Langford,
Newark,
Nottinghamshire NG23 7RT
tel   01636 705031
fax   01636 708728
e-mail   jillie.steele@virgin.net

Map 8 Entry 347

Map 9 Entry 348

Oxfordshire

Hernes

Stunning, pre-Raphaelite Aunt Connie looks down on you in the subtly-lit hall and family portraits dot every room. The rambling farmhouse has been in the family for over a century and has a warmly individual flavour thanks to your delightful hosts – helpful, friendly, with a great sense of fun. Small brown dogs scamper among the antiques and childhood toys; the high-ceilinged bedrooms have country-house elegance and endearing personal touches. The garden is wonderful, the surroundings peacefully rural and there's home-produced honey for breakfast.

Holmwood

The grounds are captivating and the late Georgian interior makes a stately bow to light, height and space. The hall is galleried and the staircase, elegantly delicate, sweeps you regally up to the bedrooms. These are big, carpeted and comfy, four with lovely long views; bathrooms sport powerful showers. You have a huge, traditional drawing room, an impressive dining room for excellent breakfasts and, outside, tennis, croquet and 30 acres of woodland and immaculate gardens to explore. A warm, peaceful, relaxing place to stay, with delightful and entertaining hosts.

rooms	3: 1 twin/double with shower; 1 double with separate bath; 1 four-poster with bath.
price	£80-£95. Singles from £55. (£20 bank holiday surcharge.)
meals	Pub & restaurants within 1 mile.
closed	December-mid-January & occasionally.
directions	At lights in Henley, into Duke St; next lights, right into Greys Rd for 2 miles; 300 yds after 30mph zone, 2nd drive on right, signed.

rooms	5: 1 twin/double, 2 twins, 1 single, 1 four-poster, all with bath/shower.
price	From £70. Singles £50-£60.
meals	Pub 0.5 miles.
closed	Christmas & occasionally.
directions	From Henley, A4155 for Reading. After 2.5 miles, College on left & pub on right. Before pub turn right into Plough Lane. House 1 mile on left. Beware tight turn.

Richard & Gillian Ovey
Hernes,
Henley-on-Thames,
Oxfordshire RG9 4NT

tel	01491 573245
fax	01491 574645
e-mail	oveyhernes@aol.com
web	www.bed-breakfast-henley.co.uk

Brian & Wendy Talfourd-Cook
Holmwood,
Shiplake Row,
Binfield Heath,
Henley-on-Thames,
Oxfordshire RG9 4DP

tel	0118 947 8747
fax	0118 947 8637
e-mail	wendy.cook@freenet.co.uk

Map 4 Entry 349

Map 4 Entry 350

Oxfordshire

Cowdrays

Birdsong and sunlight find their way into every room and Margaret, genuinely welcoming, bends to the needs of all guests; the suite, complete with piano, is perfect for wheelchair-users. There are chickens, geese, dogs and, in the lovely garden – a corner of which is Gertrude-Jekyll-inspired – a tennis court and pool. This is a treasured family home, not smart or designery, but with good furniture, masses of books, sparkling bathrooms, a little sitting room… even a kitchen area in which to prepare a snack if you prefer not to walk to the historic village's pubs.

The Craven

Roses and clematis cover this pretty 16th-century thatched cottage where breakfast in the farmhouse kitchen is served at a long pine table by a dresser laden with china. The beamed bedrooms have embroidered sheets and pillow slips and lovely views. The four-poster room is charming with cabbage-rose chintz drapes; the Primrose Room in the 17th-century stable block has a Victorian half-tester. Yet more beams in the sitting room, where you sip tea or wine around a winter log fire. Daughter Katie makes prize-winning food using as much local produce as possible. Good walks from the door.

rooms	5: 2 doubles with bath/shower; 1 twin with separate shower; 1 twin & 1 single sharing bath/shower.
price	From £60. Singles £30-£35.
meals	Packed lunch £5. Pubs 7-minute walk.
closed	Rarely.
directions	Off A417, 3 miles from Wantage going east. Right into East Hendred; 3rd right into Orchard Lane; past pub; at x-roads, left into Cat St; house behind wall/gates.

rooms	3: 1 double and 1 four-poster, both with bath; 1 double with shower.
price	£75-£95.
meals	Dinner, 3 courses, from £24.50.
closed	Rarely.
directions	From M4, junc. 14, north on A338. Left onto B4001. Through Lambourn, 1 mile north of village, fork left. 3 miles to Kingston Lisle, left to Uffington. Through village, right after church. House 0.3 miles out, on left.

	Margaret Bateman
	Cowdrays,
	Cat Street, East Hendred,
	Wantage, Oxford,
	Oxfordshire OX12 8JT
tel	01235 833313
mobile	07799 622003
e-mail	cowdrays@virgin.net
web	www.cowdrays.co.uk

	Carol Wadsworth
	The Craven,
	Fernham Road,
	Uffington,
	Oxfordshire SN7 7RD
tel	01367 820449
fax	01367 820351
e-mail	carol@thecraven.co.uk
web	www.thecraven.co.uk

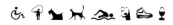

Map 4 Entry 351

Map 3 Entry 352

Oxfordshire

Rectory Farm

Come for the happy buzz of family life: it's relaxed and informal and you settle in easily, welcomed with tea and homemade shortbread by Mary Anne. The date above the entrance stone to the Tudor farmhouse reads 1629 and bedrooms, light and spotless, have beautiful stone-arched and mullioned windows. The huge twin has ornate plasterwork and views over the garden and church, the green and peach double is cosier. Both have good showers and large fluffy towels. The pedigree North Devon cattle are Robert's pride and joy and his family has farmed here for three generations. It's a treat to stay.

rooms	2: 1 double, 1 twin, both with shower.
price	£54-£60. Singles £40-£45.
meals	Good pub 2-minute walk.
closed	Mid-December-mid-January.
directions	From Oxford, A420 for Swindon for 8 miles & right at r'bout, for Witney (A415). Over 2 bridges, immed. right by pub car park. Right at T-junc.; drive on right, past church.

Mary Anne Florey
Rectory Farm,
Northmoor,
Witney,
Oxfordshire OX29 5SX

tel	01865 300207
mobile	07974 102198
e-mail	pj.florey@farmline.com
web	www.oxtowns.co.uk/rectoryfarm

Map 8 Entry 353

The Glebe House

Come pad about in your woollen socks: this is a relaxed place. Beyond the idyllic garden and the honey-stone walls are beautifully renovated rooms, the friendliest people and the character and elegance you'd expect from a couple with art and architecture running through their veins. A comfortable sitting room, sweet bedrooms (one with sitting room), flowers from a garden that is Clare's delight, glorious views and a delightful, peaceful hamlet. There are children's arts and crafts workshops, a tree "fort" to discover, ponies to ride and masses to see and do.

rooms	3: 1 twin/double with bath & sitting room; 1 double, 1 twin, both with separate bath.
price	£58-£80. Singles £44-£55.
meals	Dinner from £20. Good pubs & restaurants 2 miles.
closed	Rarely.
directions	From Burford, A40 for Cheltenham. 1st left, for Westwell. 2 miles to T-junc., then right, through village. Right to Aldsworth then 1st right onto drive. On to end.

Clare & Robin Dunipace
The Glebe House,
Westwell,
Burford,
Oxfordshire OX18 4JT

tel	01993 822171
fax	01993 824125
e-mail	clare.dunipace@amserve.net
web	www.oxford-cotswold-holidays.com

Map 8 Entry 354

Oxfordshire

Manor Farmhouse

Helen and John radiate pleasure and good humour. Blenheim Park is a short walk down the lane and this soft old stone house is perfect for any delusions of grandeur: good prints and paintings, venerable furniture, gentle fabrics, nothing cluttered or overdone. Shallow, curvy, 18th-century stairs lead past grandfather's bronze bust to the splendid double; the tiny twin beyond the fine green shower room has its own challenging spiral stair down to a cobbled courtyard. Breakfast is by the rough-hewn fireplace and the ancient dresser. A delight of a garden and a quiet village complete the picture.

rooms	2: 1 double, 1 twin, sharing shower.
price	£57–£68. Singles from £40.
meals	Pub within walking distance.
closed	Christmas.
directions	A44 north from Oxford's ring road. At r'bout, 1 mile before Woodstock, left onto A4095 into Bladon. Last left in village; house on 2nd bend in road, with iron railings.

Helen Stevenson
Manor Farmhouse,
Manor Road, Bladon,
Woodstock,
Oxfordshire OX20 1RU
tel   01993 812168
fax   01993 812168
e-mail   helstevenson@hotmail.com
web   www.oxlink.co.uk/woodstock/manor-farmhouse/

Map 8 Entry 355

Gower's Close

All the nooks, crannies and beams you'd expect from an ancient thatched cottage in a Cotswold village… and more besides: music, fun, laughter and lots of inside information about gardens to visit. Judith is a keen gardener who writes books on the subject (her passion for plants is evident from her own glorious garden) and her style and intelligence are reflected in her home. Pretty, south-facing and full of sunlight, the house has an elegant sitting room that opens onto the garden and a terrace to eat out on in summer. Bedrooms are light, charming and cottagey. A thoroughly relaxing place to stay.

rooms	2: 1 double, 1 twin, both with bath.
price	£70. Singles £45.
meals	Dinner, 4 courses, £25. Excellent restaurant 150 yds.
closed	Christmas & New Year.
directions	In Sibford Gower, 0.5 miles south off B4035 between Banbury & Chipping Campden. House on Main Street, same side as church & school.

Judith Hitching & John Marshall
Gower's Close,
Sibford Gower,
Banbury,
Oxfordshire OX15 5RW
tel   01295 780348
mobile   07776 231588
e-mail   j.hitching@virgin.net

Map 8 Entry 356

Oxfordshire

Mill House

There's a marvellous glow to this lovingly restored house. A rare, original and fine example of a large 1650s Yeoman farmhouse, it has more than its fair share of oak beams, stone-mullioned windows, big fireplaces and bread ovens. What's more, there are fine antiques, paintings and, in the attic, a games room with a full-size billiard table; beamed bedrooms are large, light and airy, with views to valley or church. This is an exceptionally pretty Cotswold village with a proper green. Breakfasts are generous, the Hainsworths are excellent hosts, and their two lovely dogs are "weird-haired" pointers, apparently!

Buttermilk Stud

Right at the top of an avenue of limes, surrounded by 70 acres, a rambling farmstead with orchards and vegetables, wildlife and roses. George teaches art and paints, Victoria manages the small farm and fills the house with flowers. Inside is a happy assemblage of family furniture, vibrant art, children, pets and harmonious colours. Bedrooms are flowery but not fussy with pastoral views, the twin being the bigger of the two. Outside are ducks, hens, horses and a stonemason in one of the stables; the delightful Falkland Arms at Great Tew is an hour's stride across fields. Wonderful.

rooms	2: 1 double, 1 twin, both with bath.
price	From £75.
meals	Excellent pub & restaurant in village.
closed	Rarely.
directions	From A422, 7 miles north-west of Banbury, left down hill through Alkerton, then up hill. 1st left by church. House on right.

rooms	2: 1 double, 1 twin both with bath.
price	£75. Singles £50.
meals	Dinner £20-£25. Supper £15. Lunch £15. Packed lunch £5. Pub 2 miles.
closed	Rarely.
directions	From Banbury-Chipping Norton road, turn to 'the Barfords' from South Newington; on for 1 mile; house on right up avenue of limes.

Keith & Maggie Hainsworth
Mill House,
Shenington,
Banbury,
Oxfordshire OX15 6NH

tel   01295 670642

George & Victoria Irvine
Buttermilk Stud,
Barford St Michael,
Banbury,
Oxfordshire OX15 0PL

tel   01295 722929
e-mail   buttermilk@btconnect.com

Map 8   Entry 357

Map 8   Entry 358

Oxfordshire

The Old Post House

Great natural charm in the 17th-century Old Post House: shiny flagstones, rich dark wood, mullion windows combine with luxurious fabrics, papers, colours and fine furniture. Bedrooms are big, with antique wardrobes, oak headboards and swathes of fabric at the windows. The walled gardens are rich with espaliered fruit trees and there's a pool. Christine, a well-travelled ex-pat, has an innate sense of hospitality – as do her two Springer spaniels – and breakfasts are delicious. There's morning weekday traffic but your sleep should be sound, and the village of Deddington is delightful. *Children over 12 welcome.*

Home Farmhouse

The house is charming: low, wobbly ceilings, exposed beams, stone fireplaces and winding stairs; the bedrooms, perched above their own staircases like crows' nests, are decorated with extravagant swathes of rich, floral chintz. All rooms are unusual, full of character, old and luxurious; one bathroom may prove a little over the top for some. The family's history and travels are evident all over and the barn room has its own entrance. The Grove-Whites are super and run their B&B as a team. And there are two delightful dogs – Ulysses and Goliath… it's all so easy-going you'll find it hard to leave.

	The Old Post House	Home Farmhouse
rooms	3: 1 double with separate shower; 1 double with bath; 1 twin sharing bath (let to same party only).	3: 2 twins/doubles, both with bath/shower; 1 double with separate bath.
price	£70. Singles £45.	£74. Singles £47.
meals	Pubs & restaurants in village.	Dinner £26. Supper £18.
closed	Rarely.	Christmas.
directions	A4260 Oxford-Banbury. In Deddington, on right next to cream Georgian house. Park opposite.	From M40, junc. 10, A43 for Northampton. After 5 miles, left to Charlton. There, left & house on left, 100 yds past Rose & Crown.

	Christine Blenntoft	Col & Mrs Grove-White
	The Old Post House,	Home Farmhouse,
	New Street,	Charlton,
	Deddington,	Banbury,
	Oxfordshire OX15 0SP	Oxfordshire OX17 3DR
tel	01869 338978	01295 811683
fax	01869 337760	01295 811683
e-mail	kblenntoft@aol.com	grovewhite@lineone.net
web		www.homefarmhouse.co.uk

Map 8 Entry 359

Map 8 Entry 360

Oxfordshire

Lower Farm Bed & Breakfast

Lucy thought she was escaping the pressures of professional life when she changed tack and took on the conversion of this farmhouse's 18th-century outbuildings. (Little did she know!). Rising superbly to the challenge, she has created an engaging, rather luxurious place to stay – five miles from Oxford, deep in the country and overlooking Otmoor nature reserve. The rooms, opening off a corridor, have oak rafters, inviting beds and lovely fabrics. Murals add an unusual touch to The Owl and The Ivy, while The Old Dairy has a roll-top bath and a witty shower. Beckley is a pretty village, with a great pub.

Langsmeade House

Marianne has applied talent and her Dutch background to make her 1920s house irresistibly comfortable. There are two sitting rooms, velvet and tapestry sofas, wooden floors, panelling, excellent beds and some lovely Dutch furniture. Big-hearted Marianne imposes few rules, prepares terrific breakfasts and gives lifts in her London cab to Oxford's Park & Ride (so you don't have to worry about your car), the Ridgeway *and* to restaurants; she will collect you up until 1am! Traffic noise from the nearby M40 is constant – loud outside, audible inside – but we defy you not to be charmed.

rooms	3: 1 twin, 1 double, both with bath/shower; 1 double with shower.
price	£80-£95. Singles from £60.
meals	Pubs & restaurants nearby.
closed	Rarely.
directions	From Headington r'bout on Oxford ring road exit for Crematorium, Islip & Beckley. Follow Bayswater Rd; at T-junc. left then immed. right. Pass Abingdon Arms, keep left to Otmoor Lane. After 1 mile stone entrance.

rooms	4: 2 doubles both with separate bath/shower; 1 twin sharing bath/shower (same party only); 1 single with separate shower.
price	£40-£70. Singles £40.
meals	Dinner £17.50. Lunch £5. Packed lunch £3.50. Good pub 2 miles.
closed	Rarely.
directions	M40 from London, junc. 7 for Thame, left for Milton Common. Pass Belfry Hotel on right. House on left near end of road.

	Lucy Halliday
	Lower Farm Bed & Breakfast,
	Lower Farm,
	Otmoor Lane,
	Beckley,
	Oxfordshire OX3 9TD
tel	01865 358546
e-mail	lhalliday@tiscali.co.uk
web	www.lowerfarmbandb.com

	Mrs M Aben
	Langsmeade House,
	Milton Common,
	Thame,
	Oxfordshire OX9 2JY
tel	01844 278727
fax	01844 279256
e-mail	enquiries@langsmeadehouse.co.uk
web	www.langsmeadehouse.co.uk

Map 8 Entry 361

Map 8 Entry 362

Rutland

Old Hall Coach House

A rare and special setting on the edge of Rutland Water, with far-reaching lake and church views. Inside: high ceilings, stone archways, fine antiques and a conservatory overlooking a lovely garden and croquet lawn. Bedrooms are traditional with modern touches and very comfortable; the double has a super new bathroom. Rutland is a mini-Cotswolds of stone villages and gentle hills, the lake encourages you to sail, fish, walk or ride, and Georgian Stamford, Burghley House and Belvoir Castle are nearby. Hard to imagine anyone who would not love it here: Cecilie is charming and a terrific cook.

rooms	3: 1 double with bath/shower; 1 twin, 1 single, both with separate bath.
price	£80. Singles £40.
meals	Dinner £25.
closed	Occasionally.
directions	From A1 Stamford bypass A606 for Oakham for 3 miles. Fork left for Edith Weston; past village sign; 1st right, Church Lane; past church, right down hill; on right on left bend.

Cecilie Ingoldby
Old Hall Coach House,
Edith Weston,
Oakham,
Rutland LE15 8HQ
tel   01780 721504
e-mail   cecilieingoldby@aol.com
web   www.oldhallcoachhouse.co.uk

Map 9 Entry 363

Shropshire

Greenbanks

Here, deep in Shropshire, you won't be disturbed. Victorian, dignified and built of warm red brick, Greenbanks has an air of unruffled calm. The floral bedrooms are dainty and comfortable, the double with a vast bed, a sofa and a real feeling of privacy, the twin with big sash windows overlooking the pond and a side garden patrolled by pheasants. All parts of the attractive, rambling garden have been designed to entice birds, butterflies and other wildlife: there are woodland walks, shrubs and splendid borders that spill over onto the smooth lawns. Feast your eyes on the distant Welsh hills.

rooms	2: 1 twin/double, 1 twin, both with bath. Separate shower room.
price	£90. Singles £55.
meals	Dinner, 4 courses, £28.
closed	Christmas.
directions	In Ellesmere, at A528/A495 r'bout, A528 for Shrewsbury; 10 yds, left into Swan Hill; 1 mile, left onto 'No Through Road'; 0.5 mile, left over cattle grid.

Christopher & Tanda
Wilson-Clarke
Greenbanks ,
Coptiviney,
Ellesmere,
Shropshire SY12 0ND
tel   01691 623420
fax   01691 623420
e-mail   wilson.clarke@ukonline.co.uk

Map 7 Entry 364

Shropshire

Pinfold Cottage

Heart-warming B&B. Vintage toys and games add to the merry clutter, illustrations from children's books cover the walls, bedrooms are charming, simple and homely. But the biggest treat is Susan. Generous with her time, spirit and home cooking, she quickly engages you in lively conversation, her laughter echoed by Polly the parrot. Other natural sounds are provided by the well-fed birdlife, and the trickle of the stream that meanders through the enchanting garden. Take a glass of wine to the grassy bank and revel in the peace. Breakfasts are healthy and delicious, the value is superb.

Top Farmhouse

A house with a huge heart, to which the loyal return. The house is ancient, magpie-gabled and rambling, the church and pound are 800 years old and Pam is theatrical, gregarious and fun. Downstairs is attractive, warm and cosy, a lattice of beams dividing the dining room from the drawing room where wine and conversation flow. Upstairs, floors rise, fall and creak, beds are brass or varnished pine, trays are filled with treats and windows are double-glazed. Pam's breakfasts are as generous as her spirit.
Children over 11 welcome.

rooms	2: 1 double, 1 single, both with separate shower. Extra bath available.	rooms	3: 1 twin, 1 double, both with shower; 1 family with bath/shower.
price	£45. Singles £25.	price	£55–£65. Singles from £35.
meals	Dinner, 3 courses, from £10. Packed lunch £5. Excellent restaurant 0.5 miles.	meals	Packed lunch available. Good pub within walking distance.
closed	Rarely.	closed	Rarely.
directions	From Oswestry, A483 from A5 for Welshpool. 1st left to Maesbury; 3rd right at x-roads with school on corner; 1st house on right.	directions	From Shrewsbury, A5 north. Through Nesscliffe & after 2 miles, left to Knockin. Through Knockin, past Bradford Arms. House 150 yds on left.

	Mrs Sue Barr		Pam Morrissey
	Pinfold Cottage,		Top Farmhouse,
	Newbridge,		Knockin,
	Maesbury,		Oswestry,
	Oswestry,		Shropshire SY10 8HN
	Shropshire SY10 8AY	tel	01691 682582
tel	01691 661192	e-mail	p.a.m@knockin.freeserve.co.uk
e-mail	suebarr100@hotmail.com	web	www.topfarmknockin.co.uk

Map 7 Entry 365

Map 7 Entry 366

Shropshire

Brimford House

Tucked under the Breidden Hills, farm and Georgian farmhouse have been in David's family for four generations. Views stretch all the way to the Severn; the simple garden does not try to compete. Bedrooms are spotless and fresh: a half-tester with rope-twist columns and Sanderson fabrics, a twin with Victorian wrought-iron bedsteads, a double with a brass bed and huge bathroom with roll-top bath. Liz, friendly and helpful, serves you breakfast round the tulip-legged table: tuck into fresh farm eggs and homemade preserves. Farmhouse comfort, great value, and walks from the door.

Meole Brace Hall

The Hathaways take B&B to a new state of excellence and love having guests in their heavenly house: Georgian and listed, with manicured gardens. It is the quintessence of English period elegance. Joan is a terrific cook who radiates courtesy and charm; Charles cheerfully assumes the role of 'mine host'. Their sumptuous home is rich with antiques, polished mahogany and eye-catching wallpapers and fabrics, and the Blue Room has an elegant half-tester bed. Summer breakfasts are taken in the conservatory, as is afternoon tea. A 20-minute stroll from Abbey and town, but it feels a million miles away.

rooms	3: 1 double, 1 twin, both with shower; 1 double with bath.
price	£55-£60. Singles £30-£50.
meals	Packed lunch £4. Good pub 3-minute walk.
closed	Rarely.
directions	From Shrewsbury A458 Welshpool road. After Ford, right onto B4393. Just after Crew Green, left for Criggion. House 1st on left after Admiral Rodney pub.

rooms	3: 2 doubles with bath/shower; 1 twin with shower.
price	From £75. Singles from £59.
meals	Dinner from £35.
closed	Rarely.
directions	A5/A49 junc. (south of bypass) follow signs to centre. Over 1st mini r'bout, 2nd exit at next; 2nd left into Upper Rd; 150 yds on at bend, left & immed. right into Church Lane. Drive at bottom on left.

	Liz & David Dawson
	Brimford House,
	Criggion,
	Shrewsbury,
	Shropshire SY5 9AU
tel	01938 570235
fax	01938 570235
e-mail	info@brimford.co.uk
web	www.brimford.co.uk

	Joan Hathaway
	Meole Brace Hall,
	Shrewsbury,
	Shropshire SY3 9HF
tel	01743 235566
fax	01743 236886
e-mail	hathaway@meolebracehall.co.uk
web	www.meolebracehall.co.uk

Map 7 Entry 367

Map 7 Entry 368

Shropshire

Acton Pigot

Elegant surrounds yet a family farmhouse feel. The fine old house sits well on its ancient piece of ground, its sash windows looking across to the site of England's first parliament. Happy in their role of hosts, the Owens spoil you with afternoon tea before a log fire (and in the lovely garden in summer). Come for deep beds, soft lights, fine linen, hand-printed wallpaper and English oak in stair, beam and floor. Bedrooms are inviting and cosy. The two-acre garden hugs the house – a treat with rare plants, croquet lawn, shady spots and pool for summer. A restorative place run by lovely people.

Jinlye

Wuthering Heights in glorious Shropshire – and every room with a view. There's comfort too, in the raftered lounge with its huge open fire, the swish dining room for fun breakfasts, the conservatory scented in summer – and the spacious bedrooms with their deep-pile carpets, new mattresses and sumptuous touches… expect faux-marble reliefs, floral sinks, boudoir chairs and spotless *objets*. Sheltered Jinlye sits in lush landscaped gardens surrounded by hills, rare birds, wild ponies and windswept ridges. Kate, Jan and their Papillons look after you well.

rooms	3: 1 double, 1 twin/double, both with bath; 1 family with shower.
price	From £65. Singles £40.
meals	Dinner from £15. Good pub 2 miles.
closed	Christmas.
directions	From A5 & Shrewsbury, onto A458 for Bridgnorth; 200 yds on, right to Acton Burnell. Entering Acton Burnell, left to Kenley; 0.5 miles, left to Acton Pigot; house 1st on left.

rooms	7: 3 doubles, 2 twins/doubles, 2 twins, all with bath/shower.
price	£60-£80. Singles £45-£60.
meals	Packed lunch on request. Good pubs & restaurants nearby.
closed	Christmas Day.
directions	From Shrewsbury A49 to Church Stretton past Little Chef & right towards All Stretton. Right, immed. past phone box, up a winding road, up the hill to Jinlye.

John & Hildegard Owen
Acton Pigot,
Acton Burnell,
Shrewsbury,
Shropshire SY5 7PH

tel	01694 731209
fax	07850 124000
e-mail	acton@farmline.com
web	www.actonpigot.co.uk

Jan & Kate Tory
Jinlye,
Castle Hill, All Stretton,
Church Stretton,
Shropshire SY6 6JP

tel	01694 723243
fax	01694 723243
e-mail	info@jinlye.co.uk
web	www.jinlye.co.uk

Map 7 Entry 369

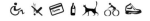

Map 7 Entry 370

Shropshire

Hannigans Farm

High on the hillside, a mile up the drive, the views roll out before you – stunning. Privacy and peace are yours in the converted dairy and barn across the flower-filled yard. Big, carpeted, ground-floor rooms have comfy beds and new sofas; one has views that roll towards the setting sun. In the morning Fiona and Alistair, delightful, easy-going and fun, serve you home eggs, fruit, honey and jam in the book-lined dining room of their farmhouse. Feel free to take tea in the garden with its little hedges and manicured lawns, feel restored in this quiet Shropshire corner.

The Birches Mill

Just as a mill should be, tucked in the nook of a postcard valley. It ended Gill and Andrew's search for a refuge from the city; you'll feel lucky to share its seclusion and natural beauty. The fresh, breezy rooms in the 17th-century part have dainty brass beds, goose down duvets and fine linen – one has an original roll-top bath. The new stone and oak extension blends beautifully and has become a large, attractive twin. Gill and Andrew are the most affable hosts, and have brought artistic and culinary flair to this stunning valley of meadowland and woods. *Children over eight welcome.*

rooms	2 twins, both with bath.
price	£55. Singles by arrangement.
meals	Pub 1.25 miles, restaurant 4 miles.
closed	Rarely.
directions	From Bridgnorth, A458 to Shrewsbury. 0.5 miles after Morville, right onto stone road & follow signs for 1 mile, to farm.

rooms	3: 1 double with bath; 1 double with separate bath; 1 twin with bath/shower.
price	£72-£76. Singles by arrangement.
meals	Dinner £25. Packed lunches £4. Pub 3 miles.
closed	November-February.
directions	From Clun A488 for Bishops Castle. 1st left, for Bicton. There, 2nd left for Mainstone. 1st right after Llananhedric Farm; house by river at bottom of hill.

Mrs Fiona Thompson
Hannigans Farm,
Morville,
Bridgnorth,
Shropshire WV16 4RN

tel   01746 714332
fax   01746 714092
e-mail hannigansfarm@btinternet.com
web   www.hannigans-farm.co.uk

Gill Della Casa & Andrew Farmer
The Birches Mill,
Clun,
Craven Arms,
Shropshire SY7 8NL

tel   01588 640409
fax   01588 640409
e-mail gill@birchesmill.fsnet.co.uk
web   www.virtual-shropshire.co.uk/birchesmill

Map 7 Entry 371

Map 7 Entry 372

Shropshire

Clun Farm House

These young owners make a good team: Susan the cook (award-winning marmalade at breakfast, seasonal produce at dinner), Anthony the guide, happy to show you the historic village and the heavenly hills beyond. Both are enthusiastic collectors of country artefacts and have filled their listed 16th-century farmhouse with eye-catching things; not every kitchen range has a cowboy's saddle above it and this one echoes Susan's roots. Old polished oak contrasts beautifully with chic florals and bold walls. Walk the Shropshire Way; return to a cosy woodburner, a warm smile and a delicious dinner.

Upper Buckton

Good-sized bedrooms with fine furniture, luxurious beds, excellent linen, bathrobes and bathroom treats — a generous place. Standing in lush gardens that slope down to a millstream and across meadows to the River Teme, this is a gracious Georgian house with lovely views. It has a millstream and a weir, a motte and bailey castle site, a heronry, a point-to-point course and a ha-ha. Yvonne's reputation for imaginative cooking using local produce is a great attraction for walkers returning from a day in the glorious Welsh Borders. There's an interesting wine list, too. *Children by arrangement.*

rooms	2: 1 double (with extra bunk-bed room) with shower; 1 twin/double with separate shower.
price	From £60. Singles by arrangement.
meals	Dinner from £20. Packed lunch £3.50. Good pubs/restaurants nearby.
closed	Occasionally.
directions	A49 from Ludlow & onto B4368 at Craven Arms, for Clun. In High St on left 0.5 miles from Clun sign.

rooms	3: 1 double with shower; 2 twins/doubles, both with separate bath.
price	£76–£84. Singles £48–£52.
meals	Dinner, 4 courses, £22.50.
closed	Rarely.
directions	From Ludlow, A49 to Shrewsbury. At Bromfield, A4113. Right in Walford for Buckton, on to 2nd farm on left. Large sign on building.

Anthony & Susan Whitfield
Clun Farm House,
High Street,
Clun,
Shropshire SY7 8JB
tel 01588 640432
fax 01588 640432
web www.clunfarmhouse.co.uk

Hayden & Yvonne Lloyd
Upper Buckton,
Leintwardine,
Craven Arms,
Ludlow,
Shropshire SY7 0JU
tel 01547 540634
fax 01547 540634

Map 7 Entry 373

Map 7 Entry 374

Shropshire

Bromley Court

A trio of Tudor cottages houses these generous two-storey suites. Prints, plates and old timbers on white walls, beds are deep, bathrooms pristine and each room comfortably traditional: a red sofa, pink toile de Jouy, new patchwork on an antique brass bed. Each has a sitting room, an enchanting river view and all you might expect for the price: your hosts are true pros. You'll probably most enjoy tucking into croissants and coffee at the breakfast bar in your suite but if you really want the works, head for the chintzy dining room. Ludlow – foodie hotspot of Britain – lies the other side of the town walls.

rooms	3 suites: 1 double with bath/shower & separate wc; 1 double, 1 family, both with bath/shower.
price	From £95. Singles from £80.
meals	Excellent restaurants nearby.
closed	Never.
directions	Broadgate Mews at top of Lower Broad Street, close to Broadgate and town walls.

Patricia & Philip Ross
Bromley Court,
Broadgate Mews,
73/74 Lower Broad Street,
Ludlow,
Shropshire SY8 1PH

tel   01584 876996
e-mail   phil@ludlowhotels.com
web   www.ludlowhotels.com

Map 7 Entry 375

Timberstone Bed & Breakfast

The house is young, engaging and fun – like its owners Tracey and Alex. She, once in catering, is a reflexologist and new generation B&Ber. Come for the Bowen Technique (gentle massage) in the garden studio, logs in winter, charming bedrooms under the eaves, a claw-foot bath painted chocolate brown. In the warm guest sitting room brimming with art are books and lovely things picked up on travels: a kilim on aged oak boards, a straw hat on a white wall. Eggs come from their happy hens, breakfasts are special and gastronomic Ludlow lies five miles down the road, filled with Michelin stars.

rooms	3: 1 double, 1 twin/double, 1 family, all with separate bathrooms.
price	£50-£70. Singles from £30.
meals	Excellent pubs/restaurants nearby.
closed	Rarely.
directions	B4364 Ludlow-Bridgnorth. After 3 miles, right to Clee Stanton; on for 1 mile; sharp bend to right, then 1st left; 1st house on left.

Tracey Baylis
Timberstone Bed & Breakfast,
Clee Stanton,
Ludlow,
Shropshire SY8 3EL

tel   01584 823519
mobile   07905 967263
e-mail   timberstone1@hotmail.com
web   www.virtual-shropshire.co.uk/timberstone

Map 7 Entry 376

Shropshire

Cleeton Court

A tiny lane leads to Cleeton Court, where Ros welcomes you with tea and homemade cake. With views over meadows and heathland, the part 14th-century renovated farmhouse feels immersed in countryside – rare peace. You have a private entrance to your rooms, and the use of the drawing room, prettily striped in yellow and cream, elegantly comfortable with sofas and log fire. Beamed bedrooms are delightfully furnished, one with a magnificent, chintzy four-poster and a vast bathroom; recline in the cast-iron bath, gaze on views from the west-facing window as you soak. *Children over 5 welcome.*

rooms	2: 1 twin/double, 1 four-poster, both with bath.
price	£60–£80. Singles £40.
meals	Excellent restaurants & pubs 4 miles.
closed	Christmas & New Year.
directions	From Ludlow, A4117 for Kidderminster for 1 mile; left on B4364 for Cleobury North; on for 5 miles. In Wheathill, right for Cleeton St Mary; on for 1.5 miles; house on left.

	Rosamond Woodward
	Cleeton Court,
	Cleeton St Mary,
	Ludlow,
	Shropshire DY14 0QZ
tel	01584 823379
fax	01584 823379
e-mail	kenmorecl@aol.com
web	www.cleetoncourt.co.uk

Map 7 Entry 377

Shortgrove

A unique, late 15th-century listed house on a gated common away from all roads. It's gloriously homely inside with buckled beams (some padded!) and creaky, carpeted floors; the two sitting rooms, one in the old cider mill end, have plump chairs and an inglenook fire for chilly nights. Bedrooms, cottagey not grand, sit cosily and comfortably under the eaves, their lovely leaded windows overlooking the two-acre garden and much of Shropshire beyond. All this, a super dog and kind, generous Beryl producing fine breakfasts – and marmalade – from her Aga.

rooms	2: 1 double with separate bath; 1 twin with bath.
price	From £70. Singles £46.
meals	Pub 5-minute drive.
closed	November–Easter.
directions	Off A49, 1 mile south of Woofferton into School Lane. Immed. left at 2nd School Lane sign. Through gate onto common. Fork left where track divides and continue to end of track.

	Beryl Maxwell
	Shortgrove,
	Brimfield Common,
	Ludlow,
	Shropshire SY8 4NZ
tel	01584 711418

Map 7 Entry 378

Somerset

Higher Orchard

A little lane tumbles down to the centre of lovely old Dunster (the village is a two minute-walk) yet here you have open views of fields, sheep and sea. Exmoor footpaths start behind the house and Janet encourages you to explore, by bike or on foot; ever helpful and kind, she can assist with luggage and transport. The 1860s house keeps its Victorian features, bedrooms are quiet and simple and the double has a view to Blue Anchor Bay, the castle and church. All is homely, with stripped pine, cream curtains, fresh flowers, garden fruit and home-laid eggs for breakfast. *Children & pets by arrangement.*

rooms	3: 1 double with bath/shower; 2 twins/doubles, both with shower.
price	£50. Singles £30.
meals	Packed lunch from £3.50. Excellent restaurants a short walk.
closed	Christmas.
directions	From Williton, A39 for Minehead for 8 miles. Left to Dunster. There, right fork into 'The Ball'. At T-junc. at end of road, right. House 75 yds on right.

Mrs Janet Lamacraft
Higher Orchard,
30 St George's Street,
Dunster,
Somerset TA24 6RS
tel   01643 821915
e-mail   lamacraft@higherorchard.fsnet.co.uk
web   www.higherorchard.fsnet.co.uk

Map 2 Entry 379

The Old Priory

The 12th-century priory leans against its church, has a rustic gate, a walled garden, a tumble of flowers. Both house and hostess are dignified, unpretentious and friendly. Here are old oak tables, flagstones, panelled doors, higgledy-piggledy corridors and a four-poster that stands on a sea of ancient oak boards. But a perfect English house in a sweet Somerset village needs a touch of pepper and relaxed, cosmopolitan Jane adds her own special flair with artistic touches here and there, and books and dogs for company. Dunster Castle towers above on the hill, walks start from the door.

rooms	3: 1 double with separate shower; 1 twin, 1 four-poster, both with bath.
price	£70-£75. Singles by arrangement.
meals	Good restaurants & pubs 5-minute walk.
closed	Christmas.
directions	From A39 into Dunster, right at blue sign 'unsuitable for goods vehicles'. Follow until church; house adjoined.

Jane Forshaw
The Old Priory,
Dunster,
Somerset TA24 6RY
tel   01643 821540

Map 2 Entry 380

Somerset

Wyndham House

The Vincents have made the house 'smile' again; charming and Georgian, it overlooks Watchet marina within sight and sound of the sea. Bedrooms are pleasantly traditional – the pale blue double with pretty curtains looks onto a mediterranean courtyard; the twin, with chintz valances and curtains, looks out to the Bristol Channel. Expect homemade cakes and generous breakfasts – Susan loves to cook. The garden has palm trees, ponds, burgeoning borders and a revolving summer house. The steam railway runs right by and takes you through the Quantock Hills, or to the coast. *Children & dogs by arrangement.*

rooms	2: 1 double with separate bath; 1 twin with shower.
price	From £60. Singles from £35.
meals	Pub/restaurants a short walk.
closed	Christmas.
directions	From railway station & footbridge in Watchet, up South Rd (for Doniford). After 50 yds, left into Beverly Drive. House 50 yds on left with gravel parking area.

Susan & Roger Vincent
Wyndham House,
4 Sea View Terrace,
Watchet,
Somerset TA23 0DF

tel 01984 631881
fax 01984 631881
e-mail rhv@dialstart.net

Map 2 Entry 381

Stowey Brooke House

Coleridge lived just round the corner – you can visit his house, now in National Trust hands. There's a captivating mix of buildings, from medieval on, in this Quantock village; Castle Street is part of the conservation area and is almost film-set perfect. The cottage is 17th century, with fresh, pretty, traditional rooms criss-crossed with beams. You get wrought-iron beds that are deeply comfortable, good sheets and towels and many thoughtful touches: handmade biscuits, spare toothbrushes, mints, chocolates... It's wonderfully quiet, too – just the murmuring of the brook to lull you to sleep.

rooms	3: 1 double with bath & shower; 1 double with bath; 1 twin with shower.
price	From £50. Singles £30.
meals	Pub/restaurant 50 yds.
closed	Rarely.
directions	A39 to Bridgwater. After 8 miles, left towards Nether Stowey. Left at clock tower into Castle Street; house 100 yds on left.

Mark Stacey & Jackie Jones
Stowey Brooke House,
18 Castle Street,
Nether Stowey,
Bridgwater,
Somerset TA5 1LN

tel 01278 733356
e-mail marka@stacey77.fsnet.co.uk
web www.stoweybrookehouse.co.uk

Map 2 Entry 382

Somerset

Parsonage Farm

Breakfast beside the open fire is a feast: homemade bread and jam, eggs from the hens, juices from the orchard, pancakes and porridge from the Aga. This is an organic smallholding and your enthusiastic hosts have added an easy comfort to their 17th-century rectory farmhouse – quarry floors, log fires, books, maps and piano in the cosy sitting room. Suki, from Vermont, has turned a stable into a studio, and her pots and paintings add charm to the décor. Big bedrooms have fresh flowers and tranquil views. Wonderful walking and cycling in the Quantock Hills, and the new 'Coleridge Way' starts from the door.

Friarn Cottage

Wildlife bounds, flits and creeps through the glorious garden that flows from the woods above; this happy, well-loved house deep in the Quantocks is a magical place to stay. Laze on your terrace and soak in the views to the fields where your wildlife-loving hosts' Exmoor ponies graze. You get your own, charming, self-contained wing – books and antiques, gentle colours, china, flowers and binoculars to help you twitch… these kind hosts are happy for you to stay all day. Breakfast alfresco, have supper by candlelight or eat at the local pub. A superb value place to stay – and 38 square miles of great walking.

rooms	3: 1 double with shower & sofabed; 1 twin/double with bath & pull-out bed; 1 double sharing bath.
price	£50–£64. Singles £32–£45.
meals	Dinner, 2-3 courses, £17–£21. Light supper £7.
closed	Christmas.
directions	A39 Bridgwater-Minehead. 7 miles on, left at Cottage Inn for Over Stowey; 1.8 miles; house on right after church.

rooms	1 twin/double with bath and sitting room.
price	£58. Singles £29.
meals	Dinner £12–£15. Light supper from £7. Pub 3-mile drive.
closed	Rarely.
directions	M5 exit 23 Bridgwater, A39 past Cannington. Branch left at Cottage Inn; over x-roads towards Over Stowey. Left signed Adscombe; right up hill at Adscombe Farm; cottage in front, gate on left.

Susan Lilienthal
Parsonage Farm,
Over Stowey,
Bridgwater,
Somerset TA5 1HA
tel   01278 733237
fax   01278 733511
e-mail   suki@parsonfarm.co.uk
web   www.parsonfarm.co.uk

Michael & Penny Taylor-Young
Friarn Cottage,
Over Stowey,
Quantock Hills,
Bridgwater,
Somerset TA5 1HW
tel   01278 732870
fax   01278 732870

Map 2 Entry 383

Map 2 Entry 384

Somerset

Tilbury Farm

The highest B&B in Somerset – up with the buzzards and the wind. Renovation is the Smiths' business and their conversion is exemplary. Reclaimed flags and seasoned oak enhance the natural beauty of the old farmhouse and barns; Pamela is a perfectionist, full of life and plans. Antiques on seagrass floors, dusky pink walls and crisp linen, a sitting room cosy with log fires in winter, a wonderfully monastic dining room for delicious breakfasts. And the setting is spectacular: 20 acres of fields and woodland, wildlife lake and spring. On a clear day can you see for 30 miles. *Children over 10 welcome.*

Saltmoor House

So much to delight the eye: elegant Georgian lines, beautiful pictures and Italianate murals, an 18th-century French mirror and Empire chairs, checks, stripes and toile de Jouy... all exist in perfect harmony. The house, 18th-century and listed, is one of the most stylish retreats we know. There's comfort too, in thick bathrobes, warm towels, fat pilllows. Elizabeth's cooking is sublime and imaginative and she uses plenty of home-grown produce. You are in the heart of the Somerset Moors and Levels, surrounded by mystical views and countryside of huge environmental significance: wonderful.

rooms	3: 2 doubles, 1 twin, all with bath/shower.	
price	£55-£60. Singles £35-£40.	
meals	Pubs 0.5 miles.	
closed	Rarely.	
directions	From Taunton, A358 north for Williton. Approx. 7 miles on, right for West Bagborough. Through village, up hill for 0.5 miles. Farm on left.	

rooms	3: 2 doubles, both with separate bath; 1 twin with shower.
price	From £100. Singles £50.
meals	Dinner, 3-4 courses, £20-£25. BYO.
closed	Rarely.
directions	From M5, junc. 24; 5 miles via Huntworth to Moorland; 2 miles after Moorland, house on right after sharp right-hand bend.

Mrs Pamela Smith
Tilbury Farm,
West Bagborough,
Taunton,
Somerset TA4 3DY
tel   01823 432391

Crispin & Elizabeth Deacon
Saltmoor House,
Saltmoor,
Burrowbridge,
Bridgwater,
Somerset TA7 0RL
tel   01823 698092
e-mail   saltmoorhouse@aol.com
web   www.saltmoorhouse.co.uk

Map 2 Entry 385

Map 2 Entry 386

Somerset

Bashfords Farmhouse

A feeling of warmth and happiness pervades the exquisite 17th-century farmhouse in the Quantock hills. The Ritchies have made a fine job of the renovation, and there's a homely feel with splashes of style — well-framed prints, good fabrics, comfortable sofas. Rooms are pretty, fresh and large and look over the cobbled courtyard or open fields; the sitting room has an inglenook, sofas and books. Charles and Jane couldn't be nicer, know about local walks and love to cook (local meat and game, tarte tatin, homemade bread and jams). A delightful garden rambles up the hill.

Causeway Cottage

Robert, an ex-restaurateur, is a South African and as easy-going as they so often are; Lesley's cooking (she has been published) gets heaps of praise from guests — and she runs cookery courses. This imaginative couple knocked through three labourers' houses to make a perfect Somerset cottage, with an apple orchard and views across fields to the lofty church. The bedrooms are light, restful and simple with their green check bedspreads, white walls and pine furniture. Elegance and simplicity, an unobtrusive and delightful family, and easy access to the M5. Very special. *Children over 10 welcome.*

rooms	3: 1 double with shower; 1 double with separate shower; 1 twin with separate bath.
price	£55–£60. Singles £32.50–£35.
meals	Dinner £25.
closed	Rarely.
directions	From M5 junc. 25. A358 for Minehead. Leave A358 at West Bagborough turning. Through village for 1.5 miles. Farmhouse 3rd on left past pub.

rooms	2: 1 double with shower; 1 twin with bath.
price	£60. Singles by arrangement.
meals	Supper from £18. Good pub/restaurant 0.75 miles.
closed	Christmas.
directions	From M5 junc. 26 West Buckland road for 0.75 miles. 1st left just before Stone building. Bear right; 3rd house at end of lane, below church.

	Charles & Jane Ritchie
	Bashfords Farmhouse,
	West Bagborough,
	Taunton,
	Somerset TA4 3EF
tel	01823 432015
e-mail	info@bashfordsfarmhouse.co.uk
web	www.bashfordsfarmhouse.co.uk

	Lesley & Robert Orr
	Causeway Cottage,
	West Buckland,
	Wellington,
	Somerset TA21 9JZ
tel	01823 663458
fax	01823 663458
e-mail	orrs@westbuckland.freeserve.co.uk
web	www.causewaycottage.co.uk

Map 2 Entry 387

Map 2 Entry 388

Somerset

Blackmore Farm

Come for atmosphere and architecture: the Grade I-listed manor-farmhouse is remarkable. Medieval stone walls, a ceiling open to a beamed roof, ecclesiastical windows, a fire blazing in the Great Hall. Ann and Ian look after guests and farm (900 acres plus dairy) with equal enthusiasm. Furnishings are comfortable not lavish, bedrooms are cavernous and the oak-panelled suite (with secret stairway intact) takes up an entire floor. Breakfast at a 20-foot polished table in the carpeted but baronial Great Hall, store your bikes in the chapel, book in for a wedding. A rare place.

The Old Rectory

With its thatched roof and Strawberry Hill gothic windows, The Old Rectory in this conservation hamlet is captivating. You won't find family bustle – the house is run faultlessly and professionally – but there is immense comfort, a hushed environment and a pretty garden which peace-seekers will find restorative. You have large sofas in the sitting room, thick carpeting, easy chairs in the bedrooms and excellent hotel-standard dinners with lots of local produce. Carved Tudor oak beams in the sitting room and panelled passages speak of the house's history; French windows in the dining room give onto sweeping lawns.

	Blackmore Farm		The Old Rectory
rooms	4: 1 double, 1 twin, 1 four-poster, 1 suite, all with bath or shower.	rooms	5 twins/doubles, all with bath/shower.
price	£60–£80. Singles £38–£45.	price	£85–£95. Singles £55.
meals	Pubs/restaurants 5-minute walk.	meals	Dinner, 4 courses, £30.
closed	Rarely.	closed	Christmas.
directions	From Bridgwater, A39 west around Cannington. After 2nd r'bout, follow signs to Minehead; 1st left after Yeo Valley creamery; 1st house on right.	directions	At Horton Cross r'bout (junc. A303/A358) A358 for Chard. After Donyatt, left for Ilminster. After 1 mile, right for Cricket Malherbie. House on left after 1 mile, 200 yds past church.

Ann Dyer
Blackmore Farm,
Cannington,
Bridgwater,
Somerset TA5 2NE

tel	01278 653442
fax	01278 653427
e-mail	dyerfarm@aol.com
web	www.dyerfarm.co.uk

Michael & Patricia Fry-Foley
The Old Rectory,
Cricket Malherbie,
Ilminster,
Somerset TA19 0PW

tel	01460 54364
fax	01460 57374
e-mail	info@malherbie.co.uk
web	www.malherbie.co.uk

Map 2 Entry 389

Map 2 Entry 390

Somerset

Gabriels

Charming Gabriels, once derelict, has transformed itself into a special B&B. It is all most comforting and welcoming: splendid breakfasts, an inviting sitting room with a garden view, plump duvets, new mattresses, white wicker chairs, goose down pillows, fruit and flowers. Bedrooms are airy, bathrooms delightfully kitted out. There are also washing and drying rooms for walkers, amazing value suppers and, best of all, hosts whose charm and generosity — they'll happily ferry you to walks and pubs — are invigorating but not overwhelming. All this, and a fruit-treed garden lovingly revived.

Chinnock House

Fiona's flair has revived the grand little flax merchant's house — Regency, listed and buried down a tangle of lanes. She is a charming ex-Londoner, happy in this haven of elegance and peace. It's a delightful set-up: in the house, a big light double, casually smart with a huge pillowed bed; in the coach house, two twins (one up, one down), a flagged Aga kitchen, a sitting room under the eaves. Breakfast is at your hosts' gleaming dining table. You are surrounded by a glorious garden — French formality meets English profusion — in a hamlet that could be in France. *Children over eight welcome.*

rooms	3: 1 double, 1 twin/double both with bath/shower; 1 double with shower.
price	£52–£58. Singles from £26.
meals	Supper, 3 courses, £14. BYO. Good bistro/pubs within 5 miles.
closed	Rarely.
directions	From Crewkerne, 2.5 miles westwards, lane signed Winsham. House at bottom of Fore St, close to High St & shop.

rooms	3: 1 double with bath. Coach house: 2 twins, sharing bath.
price	£60–£90. Singles from £35.
meals	Pubs/restaurants nearby.
closed	Christmas & New Year's Eve.
directions	Take either of two lanes off A30. Follow sign for West Chinnock but ignore left turn to West Chinnock itself. House on right about 100m after Middle Chinnock church on left.

	Mrs Sue Leighton
	Gabriels,
	Fore Street,
	Winsham, Chard,
	Somerset TA20 4DX
tel	01460 30936
fax	01460 30936
e-mail	info@staygabriels.co.uk
web	www.staygabriels.co.uk

	Mrs F Wynn-Williams
	Chinnock House,
	Middle Chinnock,
	Crewkerne,
	Somerset TA18 7PN
tel	01935 881229

Map 2 Entry 391

Map 3 Entry 392

Somerset

Estate Farmhouse

A warm, interesting, artistic house with owners to match. The Burnhams, one of whom worked in fashion, have an eye for colour, material and form; coir matting sits stylishly with well-loved antiques and bedrooms feel fresh and new. Floorboards bend and creak, ceilings dip and wave, there are plump white duvets, pictures, prints and lots of well-thumbed books. The twin is the bigger, its bathroom comfortable and close. Breakfasts (some produce from their daughter's organic deli) are served at a long table in a charming dining room, overseen by ancestors. *Children by arrangement.*

The Lynch Country House

Peace, seclusion and privacy at this immaculate Regency house in lush Somerset. First-floor bedrooms are traditionally grand, second-floor rooms cosier but as smart; those in the coach house have a more modern feel. Deep warm colours prevail, fabrics are flowery and carpets soft green. You'll feel as warm as toast and beautifully looked after. A stone stair goes right to the top where the observatory lets in a cascading light; the flagged hall, high ceilings, long windows and private tables at breakfast give a country-house hotel feel. The vast, lovely grounds are rich in trees and wildlife.

rooms	2: 1 double with shower; 1 twin with separate bath.
price	£60. Singles £45.
meals	Good pub 300 yds.
closed	Christmas.
directions	From Somerton Lake B3153 for Langport. Right after 2 miles for Pitney, just before Halfway Inn. Down to bottom of road; house last but one on right, with dark green railings.

rooms	9: 1 double, 1 twin, 2 four-posters, all with bath; 1 double (with extra single) with separate bath. Coach house: 1 twin, 3 doubles, all with shower.
price	£60-£95. Singles £50-£60.
meals	Restaurants 5-minute walk.
closed	Christmas.
directions	M3 junc. 8, A303. At Podimore r'bout A372 to Somerton. At junction of North St & Behind Berry.

Peter & Jane Burnham
Estate Farmhouse,
Pitney,
Langport,
Somerset TA10 9AL
tel 01458 250210

Mr Roy Copeland
The Lynch Country House,
4 Behind Berry,
Somerton,
Somerset TA11 7PD
tel 01458 272316
fax 01458 272590
e-mail the_lynch@talk21.com
web www.thelynchcountryhouse.co.uk

Map 3 Entry 393

Map 3 Entry 394

Somerset

Mill House

Two and a half hours from London, peace and serenity on the Somerset Levels. A stream flows under one end of the listed building into the Brue and you can fish without leaving the grounds. Rita and Michael took on the handsome mill house five years ago and gave it antique elegance and period colours. Bedrooms are carpeted and comfortable, mattresses new, bathrooms pristine; views sail over the mill stream to fields. Aga-fresh breakfasts are brought to a smart dining table, the marmalades are Rita's and the attention to detail is wonderful. *Children over 10 welcome.*

Brue House

Breakfast off cheerful Spode china as you gaze onto the well-loved garden. Brue House is tucked away at the end of a lane, with just the church and river beyond: it is blissfully quiet. The house (Victorian in style, built in 1930) dances with light and creativity. Delightful Carole-Anne and Stuart have settled happily in this little Saxon town after years abroad, and work from their studio from home. They have converted a pottery opposite into two ground-floor rooms for guests; slopey ceilings, painted furniture and fresh flowers make them a delight to return to after the rigours of sightseeing.

rooms	3: 1 twin/double, 1 double both with bath; 1 single with shower.
price	£56-£72. Singles from £30.
meals	Excellent pub 1 mile.
closed	January.
directions	A303; A37 towards Bristol; onto B3153 at Lydford. Right at Keinton Mandeville, down Coombe Hill; right at T-junc, bottom of hill. House 1st on right.

rooms	2 twins with shower.
price	£55.
meals	Pubs/restaurants 3-5 minute-walk.
closed	Christmas.
directions	From A303, Bruton signs; join town one-way circuit. At end of high street, right to bridge; before crossing, left into Patwell Lane. At end on right.

Michael & Rita Knight
Mill House,
Mill Road,
Barton St. David,
Somerset TA 11 6DF

tel 01458 851215
fax 01458 851372
e-mail b&b@millhousebarton.co.uk
web www.millhousebarton.co.uk

Stuart & Carole-Anne Adlington
Brue House,
Patwell Lane,
Bruton,
Somerset BA10 0EG

tel 01749 813524
fax 01749 813163
e-mail sadlington@compuserve.com

Map 3 Entry 395

Map 3 Entry 396

Somerset

The Dairy House

A captivating place, tucked under Cadbury Hill. What were once 17th-century stables have been transformed by perfectionist Emma. Step through a smoky-blue stable door into a self-contained little cottage – all yours. The living room has a grey slate floor, pale walls, an old French dresser and painted wooden stairs winding up to an airy, sloping-ceilinged bedroom. It is subtle, understated and beautifully restful. The cottage stands in its own pretty orchard but you're also welcome to explore Emma's gorgeous walled garden. Breakfast is served in the Dairy House. *Children over 10 welcome.*

Yarlington House

A mellow Georgian manor surrounded by impressive parkland, formal gardens, rose garden, apple tree pergola and laburnum walk. Your hosts are friendly and kind, artists with an eye for detail; her embroideries are everywhere. Something to astound at every turn: fine copies of 18th-century wallpapers, 18th-century fabric around the canopied bed and a bedroom whose Regency striped wallpaper extends across the entire ceiling creating the effect of a Napoleonic tent. There are elegant antiques, 50s bathrooms, a heated pool (summer only). Surprising, unique. *Children by arrangement.*

rooms	1 twin/double with bath; sofabed in sitting room (for same party only); shower.
price	£80. Singles £50.
meals	Pub/restaurant 1.5 miles.
closed	Occasionally.
directions	From Wincanton A303 west, exit Chapel Cross for Sparkford. Right for Sparkford, left for Little Weston. House 0.25 mile on left.

rooms	2: 1 double, 1 twin, both with bath.
price	£80–£100. Singles £50.
meals	Pubs/restaurants nearby.
closed	August.
directions	From Wincanton, 2nd left on A371, after Holbrook r'bout. Then 3rd right; 1st gateposts on left.

Emma & Graham Barnett
The Dairy House,
Little Weston,
Sparkford,
Somerset BA22 7HP
tel   01963 440987
fax   01963 441200
e-mail   grahambarnett@lineone.net

Countess Charles de Salis
Yarlington House,
Wincanton,
Somerset BA9 8DY
tel   01963 440344
fax   01963 440335

Map 3 Entry 397

Map 3 Entry 398

Somerset

Bratton Farmhouse

This is a place full of delicious paradoxes – a gorgeous old (1690) house which is at the same time calm and full of life: cosy and fresh, ancient yet modern. Quietly amusing Australian host Suellen has created an airy, vital effect throughout and the bedrooms are a joy. One, in the main house, has wood-panelled walls and a vast bed with old French embroidered linen. The other, in a newly converted studio across the courtyard, has its own attractive living room. There's stabling for your horse and the pretty garden spills over into open countryside, promising walks and rides galore.

Lower Farm

The Good Life in the depths of Somerset: organic vegetables on an organic farm, homemade apple juice, cereal, and jams, own eggs... and a delightful family. The Dowdings used to have a Special Place in France, and have converted an old stone barn into a self-contained apartment with lime-washed walls and toile de Jouy. Do your own thing, or have Susie cook breakfast for you. The place has a charmingly French feel, with hens in the orchard and a woodburner in the oak-floored sitting room; Charles grinds their own wheat for daily bread-making. Wonderful Hadspen Garden is a mile away.

rooms	2: 1 double/twin with shower and separate wc; 1 double with separate bath/shower.
price	From £55. Singles from £30.
meals	Dinner, 3 courses, £25. Lunch £10. Packed lunch £5. Pub 2 miles.
closed	Rarely.
directions	A303 then A371 signed Wincanton & Castle Cary. Follow signs to Castle Cary. After approx. 3 miles, right to Bratton Seymour. House 0.4 miles on right.

rooms	2: 1 double, 1 twin, both with bath; 2 extra beds in sitting room; shower.
price	From £70.
meals	Pub 0.5 miles.
closed	Rarely.
directions	From A303 at Wincanton, A371 for Castle Cary. Before C. Cary, right on A359 for Bruton. 2nd right for S. Montague. Over x-roads by inn. Round sharp bend, church on left. House on right; right into yard.

	Suellen Dainty			Charles & Susie Dowding
	Bratton Farmhouse,			Lower Farm,
	Bratton Seymour,			Shepton Montague,
	Wincanton,			Wincanton,
	Somerset BA9 8BY			Somerset BA9 8JG
tel	01963 32458		tel	01749 812253
mobile	07796 462551		e-mail	lowerfarm@clara.co.uk
e-mail	brattonfarmhouse@yahoo.co.uk		web	www.lowerfarm.org.uk
web	www.brattonfarmhouse.co.uk			

Map 3   Entry 399

Map 3   Entry 400

Somerset

Pennard House

Grand, yes, but without a hint of stuffiness and a splendid place to stay. Pennard has been in Susie's family since the 17th century – the cellars date from then and the superstructure is stately, lofty and Georgian. You have the run of the library, drawing room, magnificent billiard room, 60-acre orchard, meadows, woods, grass tennis court and six acres of garden with a spring-fed pool (swim with the newts). Bedrooms are large and have good views; one is circular with a corner bath in the room. Multi-lingual Martin runs an antiques business from here and he and Susie delight in sharing their home.

The Manor House

Tucked into a hamlet, the house oozes tranquillity. Late medieval, owned by Glastonbury monks, an architectural flourish at every turn: plasterwork ceiling, Jacobean staircase, Tudor fireplace. English country-house furnishings are gorgeously mixed with Indian textiles and antiques. Three bedrooms in a private wing – share a boldly stylish bathroom and are prettily feminine with hand-crafted bedheads, antiques and rich fabrics. The garden delights with rose pergola, knot garden and fish pond. Local bread and organic meats for breakfast, and Harriet and Bryan cultured and engaging.

rooms	3: 1 twin/double with separate bath/shower; 1 double, 1 twin, both with bath/shower.
price	From £70. Singles by arrangement.
meals	Good pub 2 miles.
closed	Rarely.
directions	From Shepton Mallet south on A37, through Pylle, over hill & next right to East Pennard. After 500 yds, right & follow lane past church to T-junc. at very top. House on left.

rooms	3: 1 double with separate bath; 1 double, 1 single (single let to same party).
price	£70. Singles from £30.
meals	Good pub 2 miles.
closed	15 December-15 January, otherwise rarely.
directions	A361 Shepton Mallet-Glastonbury. At Pilton, turn between village stores and Crown Inn onto Totterdown Lane; 1 mile; at T-junc. in W. Compton turn right; next right 100 yds onto lane. On left.

	Martin & Susie Dearden		Harriet Ray
	Pennard House,		The Manor House,
	East Pennard,		West Compton,
	Shepton Mallet,		Shepton Mallet,
	Somerset BA4 6TP		Somerset BA4 4PB
tel	01749 860266	tel	01749 890582
fax	01749 860730	fax	01749 890582
e-mail	susie.d@ukonline.co.uk	e-mail	jbr-halr.westcompton@virgin.net

Map 3 Entry 401   Map 3 Entry 402

Somerset

Broadgrove House

In lushest Somerset, at the end of a long lane, utter tranquillity: a 17th-century stone house, a walled cottage garden, fruit trees and horses. Inside is just as special. Beams, flagstones and inglenook fireplaces have been sensitively restored; rugs, pictures, comfy sofas and polished antiques add warmth and serenity. The twin has its own sitting room; the large, light double has two views. Breakfast on homemade and farmers' market produce before exploring Longleat, Stourhead, Wells. Sarah, engaging, well-travelled and a great cook, looks after guests and horses with equal enthusiasm. *Shooting available.*

Claveys Farm

For the artistic seeker of inspiration and the adventurous, not those who thrill to standardised luxury. Fleur was recently asked to replicate parts of the Sistine Chapel ceiling for an arts programme; Francis works for English Heritage. With their passion for art, real food and lively conversation, the Kellys promise you a rich stay. Rugs are time-worn, panelling and walls are distempered with natural pigment, bedrooms are simple. In the flagged kitchen of this 18th-century house, delicious home-grown meals, eggs from the free-range hens, bottles warmed on the Aga for an orphaned lamb. Mells is a dream.

rooms	2: 1 twin with shower; 1 double with separate bath.
price	From £80. Singles £50.
meals	Dinner, 3 courses, from £25. Pub/restaurant 3 miles.
closed	Rarely. Christmas & New Year
directions	Directions given when booking.

rooms	3: 1 double/family, 1 twin sharing bathroom; 1 single; separate wc.
price	£55. Singles £30.
meals	Dinner, 3 courses, £15. BYO. Lunch occasionally; packed lunch £4. Good pub/restaurant 0.5 mile.
closed	Rarely.
directions	From A361 Shepton Mallet, left for Mells; 2 miles, left at T-junc; 0.25 miles, left at small x-roads, for Leigh-on-Mendip; on right.

Sarah Voller
Broadgrove House,
Leighton,
Frome,
Somerset BA11 4PP

tel	01373 836296
mobile	07775 918388
e-mail	svoller@supanet.com

Fleur & Francis Kelly
Claveys Farm,
Mells,
Frome,
Somerset BA11 3QP

tel	01373 814651
e-mail	info@fleurkelly.com
web	www.fleurkelly.com/bandb

Map 3 Entry 403

Map 3 Entry 404

Somerset

Hillview Cottage

Don't tell too many of your friends about this place. It's an unpretentious ex-quarryman's cottage, presided over by Catherine – a warm-spirited and cultured host who'll make fresh coffee, chat about the area, even show you around Wells Cathedral (she's an official guide). This is a comfy, tea-and-cakes family home with rugs on wooden floors, antique patchwork quilts and an old Welsh dresser in the kitchen.
The bedrooms have a French feel, and there's a sitting room with books and magazines. Walks from the door, lawn tennis and croquet. Wonderful – and great value, too.

rooms	2: 1 twin/double with bath/shower. Further twin available for members of same party.
price	£50. Singles £30.
meals	Good pubs 0.25 miles.
closed	Christmas & New Year.
directions	From Wells A371 to middle of Croscombe. Right at red phone box & then immed. right into lane. House up on left after 0.25 miles. Straight ahead into signed drive.

Michael & Catherine Hay
Hillview Cottage,
Paradise Lane,
Croscombe,
Wells,
Somerset BA5 3RL

tel	01749 343526
fax	01749 676134
e-mail	cathyhay@yahoo.co.uk

Map 3 Entry 405

Manor Farm

Such a happy place. Rosalind's enthusiasm for welcoming guests is unstinting; she loves bringing people together and, as a geologist and walking enthusiast, can shed new light on the area – the house is stuffed with books and maps. Pet sheep, chickens, ducks and friendly cats, too. The large Garden Suite has been adapted for wheelchair users; accessible from its pretty and secluded walled garden and with an inglenook fireplace in its own sitting room, it has 17th-century charm.
The other rooms in this loved retreat are homely with new pine and white units. Breakfasts are generous, views lovely.

rooms	4: 1 double with bath; 1 twin/double with separate bath, shower & wc; 1 suite (twin/double plus extra bed), 1 double, both with shower;
price	£60-£80. Singles from £40.
meals	Packed lunches & light snacks. Good pub 1 mile.
closed	Rarely.
directions	From Wells, A371 for Shepton Mallet for 1 mile; left onto B3139. In Dulcote, left at fountain. House 4th on right after Manor Barn.

Rosalind Bufton
Manor Farm,
Dulcote,
Wells,
Somerset BA5 3PZ

tel	01749 672125
mobile	07732 600694
e-mail	manorfarm@wells-accommodation.co.uk
web	www.wells-accommodation.co.uk

Map 3 Entry 406

Somerset

Stoneleigh House

The 18th-century farmhouse, with old beams, flagstone floors, pine panelling and country antiques, is sunny and attractively furnished. It lies on the southern slopes of the Mendips with glorious walks to be walked – unless you are tempted to doze under the old apple tree in the garden. Wander among the fine old barns and you'll come across an ancient forge, a cider press, a threshing floor... and Tony's collection of classic cars. Cosy, cottagey rooms have hospitality trays, a fresh, cared-for feel and long views to Glastonbury Tor. *Children over 10 welcome.*

Harptree Court

One condition of Linda's moving to her husband's family home was that she should be warm! She is – and you will be, too. Linda has softened the 1790 house and imbued the rambling rooms with a bouncy youthfulness – they're sunny and sparkling and beds and windows are dressed in delicate florals, in perfect contrast to solid antique pieces. On one side of the soaring Georgian windows, 17 acres of parkland with ponds, an ancient bridge and carpets of spring flowers; on the other, your log-fired sitting room and extravagant bedrooms. You can have dinner with the family, or alone. Easy.

rooms	3: 1 double with shower; 1 twin/double with bath; 1 double with separate bath.
price	£70. Singles £45.
meals	Good pub 100 yds.
closed	Christmas Day.
directions	From Wells towards Cheddar on A371. At Westbury-sub-Mendip pass Westbury Inn & Post Office Stores on right. House 200 yds on, on left.

rooms	3: 1 double with bath; 1 double with separate bath; 1 twin with separate shower.
price	£60-£80. Singles from £60.
meals	Dinner, 2 courses, from £15; 3 courses, £20. Excellent pub 400 yds.
closed	Rarely.
directions	Turn off A368 on to B3114 towards Chewton Mendip. After approx 0.5 miles right into drive entrance, straight after first crossroads. Left at top of drive.

	Tony & Wendy Thompson Stoneleigh House, Westbury-sub-Mendip, Wells, Somerset BA5 1HF
tel	01749 870668
fax	01749 870668
e-mail	stoneleigh@dial.pipex.com
web	www.stoneleigh.dial.pipex.com

	Linda Hill Harptree Court, East Harptree, Bristol, Somerset BS40 6AA
tel	01761 221729
e-mail	location.harptree@tiscali.co.uk
web	www.harptreecourt.co.uk

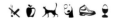

Map 3 Entry 407

Map 3 Entry 408

Somerset

Rolstone Court Barn

A converted Victorian grainstore, full of light, good family furniture, portraits and interesting finds. It's down a narrow lane on the Somerset Levels and has a big, Mendip-view garden. They have young grandsons and a black labrador, so are very child- and dog-friendly. Kathlyn is also impressively practical – she took a china restoration diploma to repair the Meissen bird figures they inherited. Two prettily decorated rooms under the eaves and one on the first floor; there is also a lovely sitting room with open fire and a smart dining room. The next-door farm is organically run – which the rabbits seem to appreciate!

rooms	3: 1 double with bath/shower; 1 double, 1 family room sharing bath/shower.
price	£60. Singles £35.
meals	Pubs nearby.
closed	Rarely.
directions	M5 junc. 21; north onto A370 towards Bristol. Take 2nd right to Rolstone, then 1st left (unmarked lane). House 3rd & last.

Kathlyn Read
Rolstone Court Barn,
Rolstone,
Hewish,
Weston-super-Mare,
Somerset BS24 6UP
tel   01934 820129
e-mail   read@rolstone-court.co.uk
web   www.rolstone-court.co.uk

Map 3 Entry 409

Church House

Eggs from the hens, organic sausages, homemade preserves served at a long table on Villeroy & Boch china – great attention to detail at this Georgian rectory. All is pristine, sparkling, light and fresh; walls are cream, goose down duvets as soft as a cloud, bathrooms stylish and sumptuous and each bedroom has a harmonious blend of new furniture – rattan, Provençal or classic. There is the odd caravan visible but this is a world away from Weston, with sweeping views across Bristol Channel. Close to airport and roads, the perfect gathering point for friends – warm, inviting, professional B&B.

rooms	5: 2 doubles, 1 twin, all with bath/shower; 2 doubles, both with shower.
price	From £70. Singles £50.
meals	Good pubs 400 yds.
closed	Rarely.
directions	M5 junc. 21, follow signs for Kewstoke. After Old Manor Inn on right, left up Anson Rd. At T-junc. right into Kewstoke Rd. Follow road for 1 mile; church on right; drive between church & church hall.

Jane & Tony Chapman
Church House,
27 Kewstoke Road,
Kewstoke,
Weston-super-Mare,
Somerset BS22 9YD
tel   01934 633185
fax   01934 633185
e-mail   churchhouse@kewstoke.net

Map 2 Entry 410

Staffordshire

Martinslow Farm

You are inside the Peak District National Park: not a sound intrudes and the views stretch into the long, long distance. It is a treat to find such a clean, neat and cosy place to stay in such an area, and your hosts – new to B&B – are immensely affable. The bedrooms are in the stable block, unfrilly, comfortable with new mattresses and in neutral tones; they look over the driveway and the bathrooms have the stupendous views. For bad weather there is a small, modest sitting room with a good fireplace. The food is local and Diana and Richard love dogs, country pursuits and good company.

rooms	2: 1 double with shower; 1 twin with bath/shower.
price	£70. Singles from £30.
meals	Supper from £15. Good pub 15-minute walk.
closed	Rarely.
directions	A523 Leek-Ashbourne. At Winkhill, signs to Grindon. Over x-roads, left at T-junction; 300 yds; house on right below lane.

Richard & Diana Bloor
Martinslow Farm,
Winkhill,
Leek,
Staffordshire ST13 7PZ
tel   01538 304500
fax   01538 304141
e-mail   richard.bloor@btclick.com

Map 8 Entry 411

Slab Bridge Cottage

A 19th-century cottage in a quiet, idyllic setting beside the Shropshire Union Canal – one of England's prettiest. Bedrooms have floral curtains and all is spotless and cosy, with open fires, stripped pine floors, old oak furniture, pretty bathrooms, fresh flowers. Eat outside on the terrace overlooking the canal, or on the narrowboat on an evening cruise – but do book! Diana, who was awarded an MBE for her work with deaf children, makes her own bread, biscuits, cakes and jams; David cuts fresh vegetables and salads from the garden. On a good day for the hens there are home-laid eggs, too.

rooms	2: 1 double with separate bath; 1 double with separate shower.
price	£55. Singles £40.
meals	Dinner £17.50. Packed lunch £5. Pub 2 miles.
closed	Christmas & New Year.
directions	M6 junc. 12; A5 west to r'bout; straight on. 1 mile to Stretton x-roads, right then 1st left (Lapley Lane); 3 miles to small x-roads at white house; left. Cottage 0.5 miles, on right.

Diana Walkerdine
Slab Bridge Cottage,
Little Onn,
Church Eaton,
Staffordshire ST20 0AU
tel   01785 840220
fax   01785 840220
e-mail   ddwalkerdine@btinternet.com

Map 8 Entry 412

Staffordshire

Chartley Manor

The rare Tudor manor has beams, warm colours, fun touches and fresh flowers. Jeremy was born here and deals in antiques (the rooms are filled with polished oak and pewter), Sarah is great at breakfasts; both are generous and enthusiastic hosts. In the Sudbury Yellow drawing room are family portraits and delicious sofas, while bedrooms are cosily carpeted and heavily beamed. One has oak panelling, buttery damask hangings and a secret door to the shower. There's a nature trail in the woodland and masses of history: Mary Queen of Scots was incarcerated in the castle opposite.

rooms	2 doubles with separate bath/shower.
price	£60-£80. Singles £35.
meals	Good restaurants/pubs 1 mile.
closed	Christmas & New Year.
directions	Halfway between Stafford & Uttoxeter on A518, just past Chartley Castle ruin on left & at top of hill, on right.

Jeremy & Sarah Allen
Chartley Manor,
Chartley,
Stafford,
Staffordshire ST18 0LN
tel   01889 270891
mobile   07958 304836
e-mail   jeremy.allen4@btopenworld.com
web   www.chartleymanor.co.uk

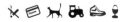

Map 8 Entry 413

Manor House

An enchanting, rambling, Jacobean farmhouse, the kind of time capsule you can't re-invent. Mullioned windows, aged oak, floors that slope… curios, small lamps, pewter, pictures and books galore: magic on a winter's night with the fire roaring. There are gorgeous grounds full of birdsong, tennis and croquet and a summer house that sports a turret from Sheffield Infirmary. Rooms have majestic four-posters with good mattresses and great views; bathrooms flaunt lace, drapes and tassels. Chris and Margaret are busy, informal hosts; the attitude here is very much 'make yourselves at home'.

rooms	3: 1 four-poster with shower; 2 four-posters both with bath.
price	£52-£58. Singles from £32.
meals	Good places to eat within 4 miles.
closed	Christmas.
directions	From Uttoxeter, B5030 for Rocester. Beyond JCB factory, left onto B5031. At T-junc. after church, right onto B5032. 1st left for Prestwood. Farm 0.75 miles on right over crest of hill, through arch.

Chris & Margaret Ball
Manor House,
Prestwood,
Denstone, Uttoxeter,
Staffordshire ST14 5DD
tel   01889 590415
fax   01335 342198
e-mail   cm_ball@yahoo.co.uk
web   www.4posteraccom.com

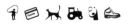

Map 8 Entry 414

Suffolk

Murray Lodge

The 1905 house has racing connections and the famous course is a trot up the road. The whole fabulous place overlooks Newmarket and sits in two-acre grounds behind electric white gates. Christine runs an immaculate ship... bedrooms vary from big to huge, one has a balcony, another a dressing room, all have soft carpets and big beds with fine linen and bathrooms are stocked with goodies. There's a comfortably clubby feel to the panelled public rooms, a log fire in winter, local sausages for breakfast and croquet in the grounds. In short, an ultra-swish B&B. *Children over eight welcome.*

rooms	4: 2 doubles, 1 twin/double all with bath & shower; 1 double with separate bath & shower.
price	£75-£130.
meals	Dinner, 4 courses, £35 (min. 4 people). Good pub/restaurant 5-minute walk.
closed	Christmas.
directions	M11 exit 9 onto A11; at Six Mile Bottom onto A1304 for Newmarket. After Racecourse, pass Total garage on left, right after 100 yds into unmade road to gates.

Martyn & Christine Knight
Murray Lodge,
Queensberry Road,
Newmarket,
Suffolk CB8 9AU

tel	01638 664162
mobile	07796 493541
e-mail	knight@murray-lodge.co.uk
web	www.murray-lodge.co.uk

Map 9 Entry 415

Northgate House

In spite of the grandness, a warm, engaging home. The Grade I-listed house is a paean to architecture – Tudor, Queen Anne, Georgian, Edwardian – and rich with illustrious touches: Corinthian columns on fireplaces, glowing wooden floors, antique Doulton loos. Joy, gracious and kind, has added delicious colours and textures. Large bedrooms – the quietest at the back – have cream panelling and impeccable towels; breakfasts include fine compotes and you overlook the walled garden. The house fronts onto the road that is a minute's walk from the Abbey; the rear is glorious country house.

rooms	3: 1 double, 1 twin/double, 1 four-poster, all with bath/shower.
price	£90-£110. Singles £55-£65.
meals	Good pubs/restaurants within walking distance.
closed	Christmas & New Year.
directions	From A14, Bury Central exit & follow brown signs for Historic Centre. At r'bout, 1st left into Northgate St. House on right, shortly after lights. Courtyard parking at far end.

Joy Fiennes
Northgate House,
Northgate Street,
Bury St Edmunds,
Suffolk IP33 1HQ

tel	01284 760469
fax	01284 724008
e-mail	northgate_hse@hotmail.com
web	www.northgatehouse.com

Map 10 Entry 416

Suffolk

The Old Vicarage

Just what you'd expect from an old vicarage: a fine Pembroke table in the flagstoned hall, a large open log fire in the sitting/dining room, a refectory table covered in magazines like *The Field*… an inviting sofa, a piano, family photos, hunting scenes and silver pheasants. And a quiet and stillness that helps stressed souls unwind. Bedrooms are large, chintzy and handsomely furnished, and the double has hill views. Weave your way through the branches of the huge copper beech to the garden that Jane loves. She grows her own vegetables, and keeps hens and house with equal talent. *Children over seven welcome.*

rooms	2: 1 double, 1 twin, both with separate bath; 1 single off the twin.
price	From £64. Singles £40.
meals	Dinner £20. BYO. Packed lunch £6. Good pub/restaurant 2 miles.
closed	Christmas Day.
directions	From Cambridge, A1307 for Haverhill. Left to Withersfield. At T-junc., left. Almost 3 miles on, high yew hedge; at 'Concealed Entrance' sign on left, sharp turn into drive.

Ms Jane Sheppard
The Old Vicarage,
Great Thurlow,
Newmarket,
Suffolk CB9 7LE

tel	01440 783209
fax	01638 667270

𝕏 🕯 🐕 👞 🍷

Map 9 Entry 417

Haughley House

A timber-framed, medieval manor in three acres of garden overlooking 30 acres of farmland. The attractive village is in a conservation area, and your hosts, the Lord of the Manor and his wife. They also happen to be accomplished cooks and use the finest ingredients, including their own beef, game and eggs, and vegetables and soft fruits from the kitchen garden. You'll find genuine country house style here, flowery wallpapers, much charm, and, surprisingly, spanking new shower rooms, even a stairlift. Ask Jeffrey to show you the manorial records and the priest hole. Aga-cooked breakfasts are a feast.

rooms	3: 2 doubles, both with shower; 1 twin/double with bath.
price	From £60. Singles by arrangement.
meals	Dinner, 4 courses, £25.
closed	Rarely.
directions	From A14 exit 48, after 0.5 mile take right hand fork; house 100 yds on right.

Jeffrey & Caroline Bowden
Haughley House,
Haughley,
Suffolk IP14 3NS

tel	01449 673398
fax	01449 673170
e-mail	bowden@keme.co.uk
web	www.haughleyhouse.co.uk

🧍 𝕏 🕯 🍶 🚜 🚲 👞 🍷

Map 10 Entry 418

Suffolk

The Old Vicarage

Englishness at its very best. Angela and Tim couldn't be kinder and the house has the patina of a gracious, beloved family home. Built in the early 1800s, it has a proper country kitchen and welcoming, elegant bedrooms. Sitting and dining rooms meld grace with comfort; the walls are rich with paintings and long windows look onto the glorious garden. "It's a tree garden," says Angela – one of the most stunning is a great magnolia. But there are fruit trees, too, and fruit and veg on the menu. You may breakfast under the cedar on the lawn in summer. *Minimum stay two nights at weekends.*

The Red House

An exceptional town in a special region, and you are in the heart of it (and near the Harwich ferries, too). The little house tumbles with books, photos, plants and flowers; Diana was once a stage manager in the theatre and has a quiet sense of style. The sitting room is terracotta, a comfy place to be, bedrooms are simple and comfortable, with pale walls and furniture in pine, pretty duvets and a cafetière, and you have a garden full of roses – enjoy a sunny Sunday breakfast, a glass of wine or a pot of tea while the cats bask in the sun. There's a fishpond too, so keep a close eye on small children.

	The Old Vicarage
rooms	2: 1 double with bath; 1 twin/double with bath/shower.
price	£72. Singles £40.
meals	Dinner with wine, 2 courses, £15, 3 courses, £18-£20.
closed	Rarely.
directions	From Clare, B1069 for Newmarket; 1st right to Poslingford & Stansfield. After 1 mile & 30mph sign, right; first white gate on left.

	The Red House
rooms	3: 2 doubles, 1 twin, all with bath/shower.
price	From £65. Singles from £45 (Mon-Thur only).
meals	Pubs/restaurants a short walk.
closed	Christmas & January; open New Year.
directions	From Sudbury, B1115 to Lavenham. Pass Swan Hotel on right, next right into Market Lane, cross Market Place, right, then left. House on right next to school.

Angela Hudson-Evans
The Old Vicarage,
New House Lane,
Poslingford,
Clare,
Suffolk CO10 8QX
tel   01787 277289
e-mail   hudsonevans@aol.com
web   www.poslingford.com

Diana Schofield
The Red House,
29 Bolton Street,
Lavenham,
Suffolk CO10 9RG
tel   01787 248074
e-mail   redhouse-lavenham@amserve.com
web   www.lavenham.co.uk/redhouse

Map 10 Entry 419

Map 10 Entry 420

Suffolk

Guinea House

A 16th-century wool merchant's house on a quiet street close to the centre of medieval Lavenham. Gillian has made it a most delightful and unusual place to stay. The bedrooms are enchanting – white-painted and beamed, with eccentric windows, pretty fabrics, fresh flowers and thoughtful touches. All rooms have super bathrooms. Behind the house, unguessed-at from the front, is a secret garden. Breakfast out here in the summer on delicious local sausages, potato cakes and fresh fruit; on cooler mornings, you breakfast snugly in front of the dining room's inglenook.

Wood Hall

Susan greets you with the warmest of welcomes. Janus-like, her house looks both ways, Georgian to the front, and beamed-Tudor behind. Breakfast on summer mornings on the terrace in the walled garden on homemade marmalade, jams and fruit compotes; in winter, settle beside the fire with a warm drink. The bedrooms, one delicately floral, the other with pink sponged walls, are elegant and quintessentially English: padded bedheads, plump duvets, thick curtains, armchairs, writing desks, candles, standard lamp, books and tea trays brimming with goodies.

rooms	3: 2 doubles, 1 twin, all with bath/shower.
price	£75-£80. Singles £45.
meals	Packed lunches £5. Excellent pubs/restaurants a short walk.
closed	Rarely.
directions	From Swan Hotel in High Street, turn into Water Street. 3rd left into Shilling Street; long pink house on left.

rooms	2: 1 double with shower; 1 twin/double with bath & separate wc.
price	£70. Singles £40 (not Saturdays).
meals	Dinner £20 (Sun & Mon only, if staying more than one night). BYO. Good pub 150 yds.
closed	Christmas/New Year.
directions	B1115 for Lavenham from Sudbury 3.5 miles; right to Little Waldingfield; house on left, 200 yds beyond The Swan. Parking at rear of house.

Bill & Gillian de Lucy
Guinea House,
21 Shilling Street,
Lavenham,
Suffolk CO10 9RH

tel	01787 249046
fax	01787 249619
e-mail	gdelucy@aol.com
web	www.guineahouse.co.uk

Mrs Susan T Del C-Nisbett
Wood Hall,
Little Waldingfield,
Lavenham,
Suffolk CO10 0SY

tel	01787 247362
fax	01787 248326
e-mail	susan@woodhallbnb.fsnet.co.uk
web	www.thewoodhall.co.uk

Map 10 Entry 421

Map 10 Entry 422

The Hall

Milden, Lavenham, Suffolk CO10 9NY

When you find somewhere so alive with familial love, you've struck gold. Over five generations of Hawkins have filled this seemingly grand 16th-century hall farmhouse with splendid period furniture and odds and ends that weave together in 'country' style. Some of the rooms are vast, all are old-fashioned and spared from the sometimes homogenising hand of interior design. Juliet is a passionate conservationist, full of ideas for making the most of the surrounding countryside, on foot or by bicycle. Expect delicious home-grown bacon, sausages, bantam eggs or fruit compotes for breakfast.

Christopher farms and Juliet is a conservation advisor and they manage their land as sustainably as possible. Chemical use is kept to an absolute minimum. Families can enjoy wildlife activities – scavenger hunts and pond dipping – or venture out on planned, car-free trips from Milden by boat, bus, bicycle or on foot. Heating is by woodburner, the wood is coppiced from the hedgerows, much of the waste is imaginatively recycled and local produce is promoted.

rooms	3: 1 family room, 2 twins, all sharing bath.
price	£60–£80. Singles from £40.
meals	Dinner, 2 courses, £20. Supper £13. BYO. Excellent pubs/restaurants 2-3 miles.
closed	Rarely.
directions	From Lavenham, A1141 for Monks Eleigh. After 2 miles, right to Milden. At x-roads, right to Sudbury on B1115. Hall's long drive 0.25 miles on left.

	Juliet & Christopher Hawkins
tel	01787 247235
fax	01787 247235
email	hawkins@thehall-milden.co.uk
web	www.thehall-milden.co.uk

SPECIAL GREEN ENTRY see page 12

Map 10 Entry 423

Suffolk

Nether Hall

Gaze from the comfort of your bed onto a garden that cascades with roses in summer. This is a charming 16th-century home in a valley made famous by John Constable; make the most of this delightful area. The River Box meanders through the garden, the house, barn and stables are old, the tennis court new and inside is warmly enticing. Uneven floors and ancient doors, little windows and wonky beams, woodsmoke from the inglenook, chintz and checks on the chairs. And there's a downstairs bedroom with its own entrance. Jennie immediately puts you at ease and is renowned for her breakfasts.

Hill House

The handsome red-brick house was once the home of children's author Paul Jennings, and sits in an enchanting, part-walled secret garden with views to Dedham Vale. Artist Anne, and Gerald, give you an elegant welcome and bedrooms with crisp linen, harmonious colours and painted brass beds. One bedroom overlooks the garden with a beautiful Japanese maple and ponds. Though the children have flown, three middle-aged cats remain – visitors find it a calm, comforting, welcoming home. Fine breakfasts, delightful people, a special bathroom – and John Constable's village right outside the door.

rooms	3: 1 double, 1 twin/double, both with bath; 1 single with separate bath.
price	£80. Single from £50.
meals	Good pubs 1 mile.
closed	Rarely.
directions	3 miles from A12, on B1068 between Higham & Stoke-by-Nayland. On south side of road, 300 yds east of Thorington Street.

rooms	3: 1 double with separate bath/shower; 1 double, 1 single sharing 1st bathroom (let to same party only).
price	£70. Singles by arrangement.
meals	Good pubs & restaurants nearby.
closed	Rarely.
directions	From A12, B1070 to East Bergholt; there, 1st right (Hadleigh Rd), left at T-junc., right at next T-junc.; through village; pass church on left & down hill. House on left, behind yew hedge.

Patrick & Jennie Jackson
Nether Hall,
Thorington Street,
Stoke-by-Nayland,
Suffolk CO6 4ST

tel   01206 337373
fax   01206 337496
e-mail patrick.jackson7@btopenworld.com

Gerald & Anne Becker
Hill House,
Rectory Hill,
East Bergholt,
Suffolk CO7 6TH

tel   01206 299554
fax   01206 299621
e-mail geraldannebecker@hotmail.com

Map 10 Entry 424

Map 10 Entry 425

Suffolk

Mulberry Hall

Your luggage will be carried up the uneven tread in this handsome hall house of 1523; it was owned by Cardinal Wolsey and has Henry VIII's coat of arms above the fire. It rambles round corners, is rich in beams and beloved family pieces, and has two winding stairs. Penny, gentle and well-travelled, gives you tea and cakes in the drawing room and lights a log fire on chillier days. In the garden: old roses, pear pergola and mulberry tree; in the bedrooms: leaded windows, beamed walls, good beds. Homemade jam on home-baked bread when you wake, soft robes for the bath before bed.

rooms	2: 1 double with separate shower; 1 twin with bath.
price	From £60. Singles from £35.
meals	Supper £8–£12. Good pub/restaurant 5-8 miles.
closed	Rarely.
directions	5 miles west of Ipswich (off A1071). 200 yds after village Post Office Stores, left; next to farmyard.

	Penny Debenham
	Mulberry Hall,
	Burstall,
	Ipswich,
	Suffolk IP8 3DP
tel	01473 652348
fax	01473 652110
e-mail	pennydebenham@hotmail.com

Map 10 Entry 426

Melton Hall

There's more than a touch of theatre to this beautiful listed house. The dining room is opulent red; the drawing room, with its delicately carved mantelpiece and comfortable George Smith sofas, has French doors to the terrace. There's a four-poster in one bedroom, an antique French bed in another and masses of fresh flowers and books. The seven acres of garden include an orchid and wildflower meadow designated a County Wildlife Site. River walks, the coast and Sutton Hoo – the Saxon burial site – are close by. Cindy, her delightful children and their little dog, Snowball, give a great welcome.

rooms	3: 1 double with bath; 1 double, 1 single, sharing bath.
price	£77–£97. Singles from £52.
meals	Dinner, 1/ 2/ 3 courses, £12/ £22/ £29. BYO.
closed	Rarely.
directions	From A12 Woodbridge bypass, exit at r'bout for Melton. Follow for 1 mile to lights; there, right. Immediately on right.

	Mrs Lucinda de la Rue
	Melton Hall,
	Woodbridge,
	Suffolk IP12 1PF
tel	01394 388138
mobile	07775 797075
e-mail	delarue@meltonh.fsnet.co.uk

Map 10 Entry 427

Suffolk

Butley Priory

Wild marshes, deserted beaches –
silence, but for the call of the birds. The
Augustinian monastery has been brought
to life by Frances, artist and musician.
Decorative stonework clasps the
windows and the vaulted dining room
soars heavenwards; it is breathtaking…
and bohemian. Forty-seven steps lead to
three bedrooms, one with its own log
fire – goose down duvets, white linen,
cascades of damask, a 'secret' shower –
and outside are seven acres of gardens
full of unusual and idiosyncratic features,
and riverside and woodland walks.
Come, too, for sea food in Aldeburgh
and wild beaches, both a short drive.

rooms	3: 2 doubles with shower; 1 small double with bath/shower.
price	£65–£140. Singles by arrangement.
meals	Pub 15-minute walk.
closed	Rarely.
directions	From A12 at Woodbridge, B1084 for Orford for 6 miles. Directly after sign to Rendlesham Forest, right at Butley High & Low Corner; on for 1 mile; at bottom of hill, drive to right, signed.

Frances Cavendish
Butley Priory,
Butley,
Woodbridge,
Suffolk IP12 3NR

tel	01394 450046
fax	01394 450482
e-mail	cavendish@butleypriory.co.uk
web	www.butleypriory.co.uk

Map 10 Entry 428

Dunan House

You may get wild mushrooms for
breakfast, and new-laid eggs from the
chickens. This is an unusual, invigorating
place to stay, with a bright, bold décor.
Ann is a potter and her artistry is
apparent everywhere: even the hens live
in hand-painted houses. Bedrooms are
upbeat and attractive, with woven rugs,
crisp linen and imaginative, decorative
touches, and the double at the top is a
wonderful eyrie, with its own little
sitting room and long views. Ann and
Simon, an illustrator, are entertaining
company. This is excellent value and
close to town and sea. *Minimum stay two
nights at weekends.*

rooms	2: 1 twin/double, 1 double with simple sofabed, both with bath/shower.
price	£60–£80. Singles from £40.
meals	Pubs & restaurants nearby.
closed	Christmas & New Year
directions	From A1094 drive towards town from r'bout. First right towards hospital, thro' 'Private Road' gate. House 100 yds on left, opp. tennis courts.

Mr Simon Farr & Ms Ann Lee
Dunan House,
41 Park Rd,
Aldeburgh,
Suffolk IP15 5EN

tel	01728 452486
fax	01728 452486
e-mail	info@dunanhouse.co.uk
web	www.dunanhouse.co.uk

Map 10 Entry 429

Suffolk

Ocean House

Wrap-around sea views – you are almost on the beach. Phil, from Zimbabwe, and Juliet are easy-going hosts happy to share this special place. The furniture is Victorian, some mahogany, some walnut; the colours are soft; the bed linen the kind you long to have at home. White cotton crocheted bedspreads come from the market at Victoria Falls; here are old things, good taste, books and magazines galore, rugs on wooden floors, a special light from every window, and fresh milk and biscuits on the bedside coffee/tea tray. You can borrow bikes, play table tennis in the cellar, and sail. Perfect.

Arch House

The plaster hedgehog over the lintel confirms that this is the work of Edwardian architect Cecil Lay. Arch House stands in three acres of garden, meadow and woodland by the River Hundred. Hugh is a good shot and fisherman; there could be trout, salmon or game for dinner. Home-grown vegetables too – The atmosphere is friendly and fun, and Araminta is a qualified aromatherapist. Bedrooms are colourful, with plenty of books, and the casually elegant drawing/dining room has a boudoir grand piano you're welcome to play. *Holistic therapy weekends availble.*

rooms	2: 1 double with bath; 1 twin with shower.
price	£70-£75. Singles £60-£65.
meals	Dinner £12.50-£15. Restaurant 25 yds.
closed	Rarely.
directions	From Ipswich A12 north. Right onto A1094 after 20 miles. House in centre of Aldeburgh seafront, between two lookout towers, with parking outside.

rooms	2: 1 double, 1 twin sharing separate bath.
price	£50-£60. Singles £25.
meals	Dinner from £15. BYO. Excellent pub nearby.
closed	Rarely.
directions	From A12 take A1094 into Aldeburgh. Left at r'bout onto B1122 for 2.5 miles into Aldringham. House on left.

Juliet & Phil Brereton
Ocean House,
25 Crag Path,
Aldeburgh,
Suffolk IP15 5BS
tel   01728 452094

Araminta Stewart
& Hugh Peacock
Arch House,
Aldeburgh Road,
Aldringham,
Suffolk IP16 4QF
tel   01728 832615
e-mail amintys@aol.com
web   www.archhouse-aldeburgh.com

Map 10 Entry 430

Map 10 Entry 431

Suffolk

The Old Methodist Chapel

Atmosphere and architecture – it's easy to see what seduced Jackum and David into converting this Grade II-listed Victorian chapel into a home. Your bedrooms are charming – the Stable Room, with access to a conservatory and courtyard garden, has cream walls, oak floors, wooden beams; the flag-floored Retreat Room sports bright rugs and bedcovers from far-flung places. The chapel is comfortably, cosily cluttered and the Browns are easy-going, friendly people. Potions and lotions by your bath, videos and music in your rooms, books and flowers in every corner, and famous bacon from Peasenhall.

Ferry House

The village is enchanting; artists have congregated here for over a century. Ferry House was built in the 1930s for a playwright, using a butterfly design to catch the light – it has Art Deco touches, hand-painted fireplace tiles and books and flowers everywhere. Bedrooms are simple but smart, bath and shower rooms luxurious and new. There's a warm cloakroom for wet birdwatchers' clothes and a welcoming glass of sherry; for summer, a garden room with sofa, TV and small snooker table. You are only 200 yards from the River Blyth and the sea, and Cathryn and John are delightful. *Children over 10 welcome.*

rooms	2: 1 double with separate bath & garden access; 1 twin with shower.
price	£65-£80. Singles £45-£55.
meals	Good pubs/restaurants within walking distance.
closed	Rarely.
directions	From A12 in Yoxford, A1120 signed Peasenhall & Stowmarket. Chapel 200 yds on right.

rooms	3: 1 double with shower; 2 singles sharing bath.
price	From £60. Singles from £30.
meals	Packed lunch £3.50. Pub/restaurant 150 yds.
closed	Christmas.
directions	From A12, B1387 to Walberswick. House on left at far end of village, near river. Three miles from A12.

Jackum & David Brown
The Old Methodist Chapel,
High Street,
Yoxford,
Suffolk IP17 3EU

tel   01728 668333
mobile 07810 432470
e-mail browns@chapelsuffolk.co.uk
web   www.chapelsuffolk.co.uk

Mrs Cathryn Simpson
Ferry House,
Walberswick,
Southwold,
Suffolk IP18 6TH

tel   01502 723384
fax   01502 723384
e-mail ferryhouse.walberswick@virgin.net
web   www.ferryhouse-walberswick.com

Map 10 Entry 432

Map 10 Entry 433

Suffolk

Rowan House

Pat has turned an unusual, modern house into a charming B&B. A plucky lady with years of experience, she's filled the house with plants, antiques, attractive watercolours and old books. Pastel bedrooms are light and comfortable; one has its own shower room, the other is a skip across the corridor. Peace and quiet, fresh food (much locally produced), a lovely hostess and much Suffolk charm; the heritage coast, medieval churches and Southwold are the icing on the cake. Woottens Nursery is nearby too, popular among serious plant collectors. A grand old house in a modern shell.

rooms	2: 1 twin with shower; 1 twin/double with separate shower.
price	£40-£60. Singles £22-£30.
meals	Dinner on request. Good pubs close by.
closed	Rarely.
directions	From A12, 3.3 miles north of Darsham level crossing, left at x-roads for Wenhaston. Left below Star Inn & immed. right into lane. House 2nd on left.

Patricia Kemsley
Rowan House,
Hall Road,
Wenhaston,
Southwold,
Suffolk IP19 9HF
tel   01502 478407
e-mail   rowanhouse@freeuk.com

Map 10 Entry 434

Church Farmhouse

A very quiet hamlet with a 12th-century thatched church opposite the lovely listed Elizabethan farmhouse with Georgian additions. It has been meticulously restored with ancient and modern character. Sarah, well-travelled and entertaining, has created a relaxed atmosphere in which you feel entirely at home. She's a terrific cook too, so let her prepare dinner from the best local ingredients. The bedrooms have gorgeous fabrics, fresh flowers and laundered bed linen; all are peaceful and overlook the garden and rolling fields. An oft-tinkled Bechstein is there for you to play.

rooms	3: 1 double, 1 twin, both with bath; 1 single (double bed) with separate bath.
price	From £70. Singles from £40.
meals	Dinner from £25. Restaurants 4 miles.
closed	Christmas.
directions	A12 for Wangford; left signed Uggeshall; house 1 mile on left before church.

Sarah Jupp
Church Farmhouse,
Uggeshall,
Southwold,
Suffolk NR34 8BD
tel   01502 578532
fax   01953 888306
e-mail   sarah-jupp@lineone.net
web   www.uggeshall.fsnet.co.uk

Map 10 Entry 435

Suffolk

The Old Vicarage

You'll love this Georgian vicarage in its tranquil corner with easy access to the heritage coast – and the enchanting Suffolk brick façade hints at the elegance within. Well-proportioned rooms are grand but not too grand – fine old furniture, family portraits in gilded frames, photographs, books – and bedrooms are a treat: a four-poster bed, towelling robes, garden views. There is a delightful guest sitting room, too. Paula is good company, loves cooking and keeps the flowers fresh. For breakfast expect the best – local bacon and sausages, homemade marmalade, linen napkins in silver rings.

Valley Farm Vineyards

Start the day with a Wissett Sparkler, bubbly from the vineyard that yields a startling variety of wines, all produced by sustainable viticultural methods. The Crafts ran a B&B in the States and though there's a touch of US-style luxury – big beds, good American sheets, excellent bathrooms – the charm is rooted in Elizabethan England. The Tudor bedroom has five tiny windows and exposed beams; the exterior has timber, stucco and pantiles. In the Victorian extension, two lofty bedrooms and a sumptuous drawing room where you breakfast and dine overlooking a very pretty garden.

	The Old Vicarage		Valley Farm Vineyards
rooms	3: 1 four-poster, 1 double, 1 twin sharing two bathrooms.	rooms	3: 2 doubles, both with shower; 1 double/twin with separate bath/shower.
price	£50–£70. Singles £35.	price	£65–£75. Singles from £45.
meals	Packed lunch £5. Good pub 15-minute walk.	meals	Dinner, 3 courses, £25 with wine.
closed	Rarely.	closed	Christmas.
directions	From A12, 4 miles north of Yoxford, left for Wenhaston. Pass Star Inn & school on left. After 400 yds, on left, red brick wall around churchyard; drive at far end.	directions	From Halesworth, Wissett road. Through Wissett, towards Rumburgh. Pass church on left & after 0.5 miles turning for Valley Farm on left.

	Mrs P Heycock		Janet Craft
	The Old Vicarage,		Valley Farm Vineyards,
	Church Corner,		Wissett,
	Wenhaston,		Halesworth,
	Southwold,		Suffolk IP19 0JJ
	Suffolk IP19 9EG	tel	01986 785535
tel	01502 478339	web	www.valleyfarmvineyards.com
fax	01502 478068		
e-mail	theycock@aol.com		

Map 10 Entry 436

Map 10 Entry 437

Suffolk

Priory House

An enchanting, soft, 16th-century Suffolk combination of bricks and beams; enjoy the peace of house and garden throughout the day, if you wish. It is friendly and handsome, with antique furniture and William Morris-style floral sofas and chairs. The fascinating dining room was once a cheese room where 'Suffolk Bang' was made; from here you can wander into the kitchen for a chat with Rosemary. You get your own wing, and one of the bedrooms is delightfully half-timbered with a sloping ceiling. The Southwold coast is just half an hour away. *Children over 10 welcome.*

rooms	3: 1 double with bath/shower; 1 double, 1 twin, both with separate bath.
price	From £60. Singles £35.
meals	Good pubs/restaurants 8-minute walk.
closed	Christmas week.
directions	From Scole, A140, right onto A143 for Gt Yarmouth. After 7 miles, right at Harleston. B1116 to Fressingfield. Pass church & Fox & Goose on left. At top of hill, right, then left into Priory Rd.

Stephen & Rosemary Willis
Priory House,
Priory Road, Fressingfield, Eye,
Suffolk IP21 5PH

| tel | 01379 586254 |
| fax | 01379 586254 |

Map 10 Entry 438

Grange Farm

The tennis court and garden are surrounded by a 12th-century listed moat – this is a glorious old place. Ancient stairs rise and fall all over the 13th-century house, there are sloping floors and raw beams and a dining room that was once the dairy. The family room has a billiard table and toy cupboard; the sitting room is cosy with baby grand, open fire, fresh flowers and lots of books. Elizabeth is delightful and generous, and gives you homemade cake on arrival, and local honey and own bread and marmalade for breakfast. *Children over 10 welcome.*

rooms	3: 1 double, 2 twins, sharing bath. Extra wc available.
price	£50. Singles £25. Ask for children's rates.
meals	Good pub 2-mile walk.
closed	December-February.
directions	A1120 (Yoxford to Stowmarket) to Dennington. B1116 north for approx. 3 miles. Farm on right 0.9 miles north of Owl's Green & red phone box.

Elizabeth Hickson
Grange Farm,
Dennington, Woodbridge,
Suffolk IP13 8BT

tel	01986 798388
mobile	07774 182835
e-mail	scotthickson@tiscali.co.uk
web	www.grangefarm.biz

Map 10 Entry 439

Suffolk

Tannington Hall

Set off in a horse-drawn carriage for lunch at a local inn, return to Tannington Hall for a delicious dinner. Tony and Lydia's Tudor farmhouse has beams, inglenook fireplace and an intricate ceiling from 1620; bedrooms, soft and serene, have antique furniture and quilts. South-facing windows look onto scented gardens, orchards and orangery; bridges cross moats to grazing horses and sheep. Relax on a sun-bathed window seat with a good book – or play a tune on the grand piano. The log-fired sitting room is cosy in winter and the dining room has a great table and candelabra. Fun, civilised, peaceful.

Sandpit Farm

Idyllic views of the wide Alde valley from this deeply comfortable, listed farmhouse. The river borders their 20 acres of meadows, orchard, gardens, tennis court, ponds and remains of brick-lined moat, and they encourage wildflowers and wildlife; Susie's flock of hens and guinea fowl strut freely. Family antiques and portraits, easy colour schemes, some beams and open fires, home-laid eggs and local produce for breakfast and every cosseting thing in the pretty bedrooms. Ten miles from the coast, five from Snape Maltings and wonderfully relaxing. *Painting classes possible.*

rooms	3: 2 doubles, both with shower; 1 twin with separate bath.
price	£90.
meals	Dinner from £20. BYO. Hampers £5–£15. Good pub/restaurant 4 miles.
closed	Christmas Day.
directions	From A1120 Earl Soham to Saxtead. Left after Windmill, signed Tannington. On for 3 miles. Hall signed on left.

rooms	2: 1 double with shower; 1 twin with separate bath.
price	From £55–£60. Singles from £40.
meals	Good pub/restaurant 1.5 miles.
closed	Rarely.
directions	From A1120, Yoxford to Stowmarket, east to Dennington; take B1120, Framlingham. First left; house 1.5 miles on left.

Lydia & Tony Harvey
Tannington Hall, Framlingham,
Woodbridge,
Suffolk IP13 7NH

tel	01728 627999
mobile	07880 707566
e-mail	enquiries@tanningtonhall.com
web	www.tanningtonhall.com

Mark & Susie Marshall
Sandpit Farm,
Bruisyard, Framlingham,
Saxmundham,
Suffolk IP17 2EB

tel	01728 663445
e-mail	susannemarshall@suffolkonline.net
web	www.aldevalleybreaks.co.uk

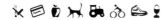

Map 10 Entry 440

Map 10 Entry 441

Surrey

Hunters

Impossible to believe London is 45 minutes away. Surrounded by lawns, woodland and a palm-dotted terrace, the house feels buried deep in sunny countryside. Large and relaxed, it makes the most of the natural light: rugs on polished wood, flagstones, creamy colours, elegant furniture. Bedrooms (one with balcony) have a smooth, luscious, contemporary feel with bold shots of colour, Ros's vibrant paintings, perhaps an ethnic touch or a modern sculpture. Bathrooms are chic spaces of stone and natural wood. Take walks, play golf, relax over those woodland views, return to a delicious dinner. Great value.

Greenaway

An enchanting cottage. People return time and again – for the house, the dovecote, the garden, the countryside, and Sheila and John. In a vast sitting room, low-slung beams and striking colours jostle for your attention. A sturdy, turning oak staircase leads to the sweet bedrooms that sit above; a peek at them all will only confuse you: each one is gorgeous. There's an ornate bedstead in the Chinese room and, in another, an oak bedstead and beams. A further room has a hint of French decadence: golds, magentas and silk-lined bed covers. An exceptional place.

rooms	3: 2 doubles with shared shower; 1 double with balcony & separate bath.
price	From £65. Singles from £40.
meals	Dinner, 3 courses, from £20. Excellent pub 4 miles.
closed	Christmas.
directions	From A3 onto B3002 for Bordon; 1 mile; through Grayshott; church on right, drive to house on left.

rooms	3: 1 double with bath; 1 twin, 1 double, sharing bath.
price	£70-£85. Singles from £55.
meals	Hotel restaurant 0.25 miles.
closed	Rarely.
directions	A3 to Milford, then A283 for Petworth. At Chiddingfold, Pickhurst Road off green. 3rd on left, with large black dovecote.

Mrs Ros Richards
Hunters,
Grayshott,
Surrey GU26 6DL
tel   01428 606623
mobile   07788 420439
e-mail   rosrichards@hotmail.com

Sheila & John Marsh
Greenaway,
Pickhurst Road,
Chiddingfold,
Surrey GU8 4TS
tel   01428 682920
fax   01428 685078
e-mail   jfmarsh@nildram.co.uk
web   www.greenaway.nildram.co.uk

Map 4 Entry 442

Map 4 Entry 443

Surrey

High Edser

Ancient wattle and daub, aged timbers and bags of character – it really does ramble. Built in 1532, it sits in two and a half acres of smooth lawns beyond which lie the village and the Surrey hills. Unlike many houses with beams and low ceilings, this one is light and inviting and has the sort of family clutter that makes you feel at home. Patrick is enthusiastic and dynamic, Carol gives you homemade marmalade at breakfast; both leave you plenty of space to unfurl at your own pace. The carved wooden fireplace in the stone-flagged dining room is spectacular, and there's a snug study just for guests.

Lower Eashing Farmhouse

A homely place with a lovely walled garden and super hosts; Gillian, who speaks French, German and Spanish, enjoys welcoming people from all over the world. The house, 16th to 19th century, has exposed timbers, books and bold colours. The dining room is red; the guest sitting room, decorated with artefacts from around the world, is big enough for a small company meeting – or a wedding group. Your hosts, who are great fun, run an efficient and caring ship. In the walled garden the distant rumble of the A3 reminds you how well placed you are for Gatwick and Heathrow.

rooms	3: 2 doubles, 1 twin, all sharing bath.
price	£55-£60. Singles £25-£35.
meals	Good pubs/restaurants 300 yds-3 miles.
closed	Christmas.
directions	From A3, 1st exit after M25, for Ripley. Through Ripley & West Clandon, over dual c'way (A246) onto A25. 3rd right to Shere. There, right to Cranleigh. House 5 miles on left, 1 mile past Windmill pub.

rooms	4: 1 twin/double with bath/shower; 1 twin/double with separate bath/shower; 2 singles sharing shower.
price	£60-£75. Singles £40-£55.
meals	Good pub 300 yds.
closed	Occasionally.
directions	A3 south. 5 miles after Guildford, Eashing signed left at service station. House 150 yds on left behind white fence.

Patrick & Carol Franklin Adams
High Edser,
Shere Road,
Ewhurst, Cranleigh,
Surrey GU6 7PQ

tel   01483 278214
fax   01483 278200
e-mail   beds@highedser.co.uk
web   www.highedser.co.uk

David & Gillian Swinburn
Lower Eashing Farmhouse,
Lower Eashing,
Godalming,
Surrey GU7 2QF

tel   01483 421436
fax   01483 421436
e-mail   davidswinburn@hotmail.com

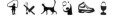

Map 4 Entry 444

Map 4 Entry 445

Surrey

Old Great Halfpenny

The quintessence of pastoral England, yet perfectly placed for airports and easy access to London. The gorgeous, 16th-century, listed farmhouse sits on a country lane beneath the Pilgrim's Way. Beyond the pretty garden – Michael's passion – roll the North Downs and wooded hills with hardly a house in sight. Bedrooms are beautifully furnished by Alison, an interior designer, with lovely fabrics and antique French beds. You will be treated to breakfast on the terrrace in the summer and large log fires in winter. It feels as rural as Devon, yet you are almost within walking distance of Guildford. Special.

rooms	2 doubles, both with separate bath.
price	£70–£80. Singles from £50.
meals	Good pubs/restaurants 2 miles.
closed	Christmas & New Year.
directions	From London, exit A3 before Guildford, signed Burpham. Ring for detailed directions - 2 miles.

Michael & Alison Bennett
Old Great Halfpenny,
Halfpenny Lane,
St Martha,
Guildford,
Surrey GU4 8PY
tel   01483 567835
mobile   07768 745765
e-mail   bennettbird@btopenworld.com

Map 4   Entry 446

Littlefield Manor

Such a surprise to bump along a farm track and find 400 acres of arable land so close to London... The glorious old manor – Jacobean at the front, Tudor at the back – has all the features you'd expect. John, who runs a livery next door, feels at home with the higgle and piggle of the place: all wooden floors and worn rugs, wonky ceilings, window seats and church panel doors. Bedrooms and bathrooms are big but not smart, with timbered walls and a mish-mash of furniture. The twin overlooks an immaculate rose garden tended by John's charming mother: scents waft in through the window in summer.

rooms	2: 1 twin/double, 1 double, both with bath.
price	£70. Singles £50.
meals	Good pub 1 mile.
closed	Rarely.
directions	From M25, A3; exit at Guildford, follow signs A323 Aldershot for 2 miles to big black & white r'bout. House 400 yds on left.

John & Pooh Tangye
Littlefield Manor,
Littlefield Common,
Guildford,
Surrey GU3 3HJ
tel   01483 233068
fax   01483 233686
e-mail   john.tangye@virgin.net
web   www.littlefieldmanor.co.uk

Map 4   Entry 447

Surrey

Swallow Barn

A squash court and stables, once belonging to the next-door manor, have become a happy, homely house. Full of family memories and run by interesting and helpful people, it has a mature charm – and lovely trees in the garden, a paddock and a summer pool. Given the hushed tranquillity you are surprisingly close to the airports and the M25. The bedrooms are small but one has its own entrance, another the use of a sunny sitting room, the third a balcony; beds are firm, garden views pretty and breakfasts generous and scrumptious. *Children over eight welcome.*

rooms	3: 1 double with bath & sitting room; 1 twin with shower; 1 twin with separate shower.
price	£80. Singles £50.
meals	Pub/restaurant 0.75 miles.
closed	Rarely.
directions	From M25, exit 11, A319 into Chobham. Left at T-junc.; left at mini-r'about onto A3046. After 0.7 miles, right between street light & postbox. House 2nd on left.

Joan & David Carey
Swallow Barn,
Milford Green,
Chobham, Woking,
Surrey GU24 8AU

tel   01276 856030
fax   01276 856030
e-mail   swallowbarn@web-hq.com
web   www.swallow-barn.co.uk

Map 4 Entry 448

Sussex

Little Orchard House

House and owner have a vibrancy that is unique. Sara has created a special atmosphere in her truly welcoming, rule-free townhouse in history-laden Rye. You'll be enchanted by original art, fine antiques and attention to detail, but masses of books and personal touches herald the fact that this is a real home. Super, luxurious bedrooms have views of either a quiet cobbled street or the large, quiet garden, complete with a smuggler's watchtower. There is a bookroom for rainy days and a sitting room with open fire. Breakfasts are generous, delicious and organic/free-range. *Private parking nearby.*

rooms	2: 1 four-poster with shower; 1 four-poster with bath & shower.
price	£80-£100. Singles £50-£70.
meals	Pubs/restaurants nearby.
closed	Rarely.
directions	In Rye, follow signs to town centre & enter Old Town through Landgate Arch into High St. West St 3rd on left. House halfway up on left.

Sara Brinkhurst
Little Orchard House,
West Street,
Rye,
Sussex TN31 7ES

tel   01797 223831
mobile   07790 363950
e-mail   info@littleorchardhouse.com
web   www.littleorchardhouse.com

Map 5 Entry 449

Sussex

Wellington House

The house is a warm marriage of Victorian red-brick front and 16th-century coach house rear. Inside, the friendly Brogdens have worked an informal magic, and comfort rules, from the cosy sitting room just for guests to the big, peaceful bedrooms above. These are creamy-walled, carpeted, comfortable: new mattresses, antique bed linen, pristine shower rooms and good toiletries. Breakfast is a joy – homemade yogurts and fresh fruits as well as full English. You can visit Bodiam by river boat, comb Camber Sands – or walk to Christopher Lloyd's wonderful gardens at Great Dixter.

Farthings Farm

You are on a dairy farm in deepest Sussex but far from Cold Comfort! The pretty Edwardian farmhouse is refreshingly light and agreeable, its owners enlightened and good company. The contemporary sitting/dining room has a happy mix of family furniture, books, music, a basket of games, a real fire and views to lake and woods. French windows open to a terrace with lavender, roses and herbs – bliss for fine-weather breakfasts; bedrooms are country-style and serene. Battle is a 20-minute walk on the 1066 footpath; return to one of Penny's delicious dinners and home-grown produce.

rooms	2 doubles, both with shower.
price	£65. Singles from £40.
meals	Supper, 3 courses, from £18 (min. 4 people). Good pub 0.75 miles.
closed	Christmas & New Year.
directions	Follow brown tourist signs in Northiam village for Great Dixter House & Gardens to Dixter Rd. House at main road end, next to opticians.

rooms	3 twins/doubles, all with shower.
price	£60. Family rooms £50. Singles £35.
meals	Dinner £18. Good pub/restaurant 1 mile.
closed	Christmas & New Year.
directions	A271 from Battle, left onto B2204 for 1 mile. Left after nursery; 0.5 miles down farm track, left at sign.

Fanny & Vivian Brogden
Wellington House,
Dixter Road,
Northiam,
Rye,
Sussex TN31 6LB

tel   01797 253449
mobile   07989 928236
e-mail   fanny@frances14.freeserve.co.uk

Penny & John Rodgers
Farthings Farm,
Catsfield,
Battle,
Sussex TN33 9BA

tel   01424 773107
e-mail   penny.rodgers@btopenworld.com
web   www.farthingsfarm.co.uk

Map 5 Entry 450

Map 5 Entry 451

Sussex

Fox Hole Farm

Whitewashed, carpeted and beamed, a woodburner twinkling in its inglenook, the pretty tile-hung farmhouse is as cosy as can be. Come for stacks of woody character, a rolling hillside setting and lovely hosts whose kindness goes beyond the call of duty. There are woodpeckers outside the window, nightingales in the wood and low-beamed bedrooms with latch cupboards, mellow boards and latticed windows that reveal sheep and hill views. A fine breakfast (eggs straight from the hens) will set you up for a two-mile woodland walk to the small historic town of Battle.

Globe Place

A listed 17th-century house beside the church in a tiny village, 10 minutes from Glyndebourne. Alison is a great cook and gives you not only a delicious and generous hamper, but tables and chairs too. Willie is a former world rackets champion who gives tennis coaching; there's a court in the large, pretty garden, and a swimming pool. Relax by the inglenook fire in the drawing room after a walk on the Cuckoo Trail or the South Downs, then settle down to a great supper – local fish, maybe, with home-grown vegetables. An easy-going, fun and informal household. *Children over 12 welcome.*

rooms	3 doubles, all with bath.
price	From £59. Singles from £33.
meals	Pubs/restaurants 1 mile.
closed	December-January.
directions	From Battle on A271, 1st right to Heathfield. After 0.75 miles, right into drive.

rooms	4: 1 double, 1 single sharing bath (single for same party); 1 double, 1 single sharing bath (single for same party).
price	£65-£70. Singles £30-£35.
meals	Dinner £22.50. Picnic £28-£30. Good pub 12 minute-walk.
closed	Christmas.
directions	From Boship r'bout on A22, A267. 1st right to Horsebridge & immed. left to Hellingly. House next to church, in Mill Lane.

Paul & Pauline Collins
Fox Hole Farm,
Kane Hythe Road,
Battle,
Sussex TN33 9QU
tel   01424 772053
fax   01424 772053
e-mail   foxholefarm@amserve.com

Alison & Willie Boone
Globe Place,
Hellingly,
Sussex BN27 4EY
tel   01323 844276
e-mail   aliboone@globeplace.plus.com

Map 5 Entry 452

Map 5 Entry 453

Old Whyly

How fitting that Old Whyly was the home of one of King Charles's Cavaliers; now it is a haven for modern-day sybarites. Rich colours, lush fabrics, deep sofas, fine oils – there's an effortless elegance to this fabulous home. And the treats continue outside: a lake with black swans, a heated pool, a tennis court and a garden annually replenished with thousands of tulip bulbs. Dine under the pergola in summer – food is a passion and Sarah's menus adventurous with a modern slant. Glyndebourne's close by: make a party of it and be treated to a divine 'pink' hamper with blankets included.

Park Cottage

A thoroughly charming, small country house, with a courtyard at the front and a walled garden at the back, each a riot of colour in spring and summer. When you arrive you are offered tea and homemade cake – a lovely start. Bedrooms are bright and fresh, with sumptuous linen on big beds, good furniture and homemade biscuits on the tea tray. Lucy fills the house with flowers and tells you all you need to know – you'll feel beautifully looked after. Wander from the garden to parkland behind; only birdsong disturbs the peace. Handy for opera lovers, with Glyndebourne so close.

rooms	3: 1 twin/double with bath; 1 twin/double with shower; 1 twin with separate bath.
price	£90–£120. Singles by arrangement.
meals	Dinner, 3 courses, £25. Lunch from £16. Hampers £35.
closed	Rarely.
directions	0.5 miles past Halland on A22, south from Uckfield; 1st left off Shaw r'bout towards E. Hoathly; on for 0.5 miles. Drive on left with postbox; central gravel drive.

rooms	2: 1 double, 1 twin/double, both with bath.
price	£80. Singles from £65.
meals	Packed lunch £10. Good pub 1 mile.
closed	Christmas & New Year.
directions	A26 for Uckfield; straight at Little Horsted r'bout for Ridgewood. 1st right down New Road; at phone box right down concealed drive. House 2nd on left.

Sarah Burgoyne
Old Whyly,
East Hoathly,
Sussex BN8 6EL
tel   01825 840216
fax   01825 840738
e-mail   stay@oldwhyly.co.uk
web   www.oldwhyly.co.uk

Mrs Lucy Ann
Park Cottage,
Ridgewood,
Uckfield,
Sussex TN22 5TG
tel   01825 767104
e-mail   l.ann@btinternet.com
web   www.parkcottage-sussex.co.uk

Map 5 Entry 454

Map 4 Entry 455

Sussex

South Paddock

A real one off, with hosts who cater to your every whim. Jennifer enjoys helping you plan your day and books tables at the village pub; Graham makes his own jams and marmalades and, ex-Army, has created a regimental 'museum' in the downstairs loo. Visitors from 59 nations have enjoyed the comforts of this unspoilt, wisteria-clad 1930s bastion of old-Englishness. Bedrooms are Seventies' comfy, log fires crackle in winter and the garden is a treat, its fruit and veg plot big enough to feed an army.
Children over 10 welcome.

rooms	3: 1 double, 1 twin, both with separate bath; second twin available.
price	From £72. Singles from £45.
meals	Pub in village.
closed	Rarely.
directions	From M25, A22 to Maresfield. At mini-r'bout in centre of village, under stone arch opp. church & pub, & over 5 speed bumps. House 1st on left.

Graham & Jennifer Allt
South Paddock,
Maresfield Park,
Uckfield,
Sussex TN22 2HA
tel   01825 762335

Map 4 Entry 456

The Faulkners

A charming 1425 Wealden hall house of low ceilings, buckling beams, Georgian windows and quirky corners. Every space has character, enhanced by Celia's collections of hand-carved breadboards, shaving brushes and straw hats. Cosy, carpeted bedrooms have country furnishings and natural colours and the double overlooks the garden; spend a happy hour wandering among the colours and scents. Outdoors has received the same lavish attention as in, there are homemade breads and compotes for breakfast, beautiful gardens nearby and the Lavender Line railway steams through the village.

rooms	3: 1 double with separate bath; 2 singles sharing bath.
price	From £70. Singles from £40.
meals	Good pub 5-minute drive.
closed	Christmas & New Year.
directions	From Uckfield, A26 Lewes road. Right for Isfield & on for 1 mile. Right over level crossing & house on sharp left bend with high fence & gate, approx. 0.5 miles on.

Celia Rigby
The Faulkners,
Isfield,
Sussex TN22 5XG
tel   01825 750344
fax   01825 750577
e-mail   celia.rigby@imagenius.co.uk

Map 4 Entry 457

Sussex

Hope Court

Feel nurtured in this large, late-Victorian suburban house. Norma, an intrepid traveller, fills the most English of bedrooms with flowers; the bathrooms have fine soaps and shampoos. The twin is cosy with matching chintz-skirted dressing-table and curtains, the king-size double comes with tea trays, dressing gown and slippers. All doors lead to the garden, it seems: wisteria and roses scent the air and you can play croquet amid the beauty. The guest sitting room and the dining room have patios, too, and the views to Ashdown Forest are exceptional. *Children over eight welcome.*

The Grange

There's a time-worn feel to this dreamy family home. Books are stuffed into shelves, walls are decorated with years of children's paintings, wooden African hippos guard the stair. An old rectory in a secluded spot that sits in a lovely garden beside the church, it is beautifully old-fashioned with its oak stairs and display of antique swords and ancient tapestry in the hall. Yet there's nothing austere: you are in the easiest of family homes. Your carpeted bedroom with iron bedstead overlooks the paddock and is plain but comfortable, and has a single room that lies off it.

rooms	3: 1 double with bath/shower; 1 twin with shower; 1 double with separate bath.
price	From £58. Singles from £33.
meals	Pubs/restaurants 800 yds.
closed	Occasionally.
directions	A26 from Tunbridge Wells for Uckfield. At Crowborough Cross, take Beacon Rd; 4th right into Warren Rd; bottom of hill to Rannoch Rd; right. House on left after 200 yds.

rooms	1 double with bath.
price	From £55. Singles £30.
meals	Pubs 200 yds.
closed	Occasionally.
directions	In the centre of Hartfield, take road (Church Street) between The Haywaggon & The Anchor pubs. Past church on left; house beyond church, on left.

	Norma Backhouse
	Hope Court,
	Rannoch Road,
	Crowborough,
	Sussex TN6 1RA
tel	01892 654017
fax	01892 654017

	Bunny & James Murray Willis
	The Grange,
	Hartfield,
	Sussex TN7 4AG
tel	01892 770259
fax	01892 771110

Map 5 Entry 458

Map 5 Entry 459

Sussex

Tiltwood House

The luscious Tiltwood began life in the 1840s. The style, grace and proportion are reminiscent of a grand hotel yet Valerie has turned the main portion into a superbly comfortable home and managed not to go over the top. In your room: white throws across armchairs, a vast luxurious bed, light streaming through sash windows, fresh grapes and bowls of Kettle chips. Lavish bathrooms have oodles of towels – in one there's enough space for a maharaja. Linger over coffee and sumptuous breakfasts. And if you are flying to somewhere even more exotic, Gatwick is only seven minutes away and lifts can be arranged.

rooms	2 doubles with bath/shower.
price	£87. Singles £55.
meals	Dinner £15-£25. Packed lunch £10. Pubs/restaurants 2.5 miles.
closed	Christmas.
directions	M23 exit 10; A264 for East Grinstead. 2nd r'bout, take 3rd exit Turners Hill Road B2028 1st left into Sandy Lane. Left at T-junc. Continue through village past 40mph signs - 2nd drive on right.

Valerie Johns
Tiltwood House,
Hophurst Lane,
Crawley Down,
Sussex RH10 4LL
tel   01342 712942
e-mail   vjohnstiltwood@aol.com
web   www.tiltwood-bedandbreakfast.co.uk

Map 4 Entry 460

Little Lywood

At the opposite end of the house from the owners you feel nicely private; the bathroom is a couple of steps from your door. The softly-lit, unfussy room has a pine dressing table, rattan chairs, matching curtains and duvet covers, and fresh flowers. The Sussex Archaeological Society says this old forester's cottage, once on the Borde Hill Estate, has Elizabethan origins: the small mullioned windows and ancient timbers bear this out. Jeannie and Nick are delightful company, but will leave you to come and go as you please. Within easy reach of Sussex's great gardens – and the one here is lovely, too.

rooms	1 double with separate bath.
price	£60. Singles £40.
meals	Pubs 2.5 miles.
closed	Rarely.
directions	From Haywards Heath, B2028 to Lindfield. House on left, 1.5 miles after passing church at north end of Lindfield.

Jeannie & Nick Leadsom
Little Lywood,
Ardingly Road,
Lindfield,
Sussex RH16 2QX
tel   01444 892571
e-mail   nick@littlelywood.freeserve.co.uk

Map 4 Entry 461

Sussex

Copyhold Hollow

It hides in a hollow behind a 1,000-year-old box hedge, this sweet 16th-century farm turned ale house. Enter a quirky jumble of small stairs, wonky walls, mind-your-head ceilings and exposed timbers. Bedrooms have goose down duvets and wonderful views, crooked floors are carpeted-cosy, windows hung with floral curtains, ancient doors latched… and there's a fabulous inglenook for chilly nights. Frances did the renovation herself, and coaxed her one joyful acre of garden and woodland back to life. She cheerfully gives you the best ingredients for breakfast, and stacks of walking advice.

Knole House

Down leafy Clappers Lane to this special place. Nick and Jill, he an artist, she a professional cook, are born to hospitality. You get a roaring log fire in the sitting room in winter, a cottage kitchen that's colourful and warm and a double with a shower room that hides behind trompe l'oeil – ingenious. The place is alive with fun touches and Nick's art, there are two delightful pointers and Toby the cat. The two-acre garden, with pool, is enchanting. Breakfast by the waterfall in summer – you'll eat well as Jill loves to cook. Who'd guess Gatwick was a 25-minute drive, and Brighton only 10 miles?

rooms	4: 2 doubles, 1 twin, all with shower; 1 single with bath.
price	From £70. Singles from £50. Additional bed £25.
meals	Pubs/restaurants 2-3 miles. Packed lunch available.
closed	Rarely.
directions	M23, exit junc.10a; B2036 for Cuckfield. There, over mini r'bout. At 2nd r'bout, left into Ardingly Rd; right at 3rd r'bout into Hanlye Lane; left at T-junc., 1st right for Ardingly; 0.5 miles on right.

rooms	3: 1 double with extra bed, 1 single, both with shower; 1 single with separate bath.
price	£60-£80. Singles £30-£40.
meals	Dinner by arrangement. Good pubs 0.5 miles.
closed	Rarely.
directions	Clappers Lane runs south from A281 towards Fulking village. Knole House 1st on left, approx. 0.75 miles.

	Frances Druce
	Copyhold Hollow,
	Copyhold Lane,
	Borde Hill,
	Haywards Heath,
	Sussex RH16 1XU
tel	01444 413265
e-mail	sp@copyholdhollow.co.uk
web	www.copyholdhollow.co.uk

	Nick & Jill Bremer
	Knole House,
	Clappers Lane,
	Fulking,
	Henfield,
	Sussex BN5 9NH
tel	01273 857387
e-mail	art@nickbremer.com
web	www.knolehouse.co.uk

Map 4 Entry 462

Map 4 Entry 463

Sussex

Stream Cottage

Their Cumbrian house was in Special Places; now Mike and Janet have moved to one of Sussex's prettiest villages. Built in 1587, the thatched cottage is so endearing that you wish there were more bedrooms. Narrow stairs lead to your very own little sitting room; the bedroom is beyond. Dramatic beams bisect primrose walls, the ceiling slopes to floor-level windows and an exquisite quilt covers the big white bed. Robes are provided for the trip to the bathroom downstairs. The Wrights really know how to look after people: aromatherapy is on offer, and the breakfast menu is out of this world.

rooms	1 double with separate bath/shower.
price	From £70. Singles £50.
meals	Excellent pub in village.
closed	Christmas & occasionally.
directions	Off A24 onto A283 for Storrington. There, B2139, then right into village; house on left opp. phone box.

Mike & Janet Wright
Stream Cottage,
The Square,
Amberley, Arundel,
Sussex BN18 9SR

tel	01798 831266
fax	01798 831266
e-mail	enquiries@streamcottage.co.uk
web	www.streamcottage.co.uk

Map 4 Entry 464

Blakehurst Farm

Immerse yourself in the warmth of family and farming life. Alex and Claire, a hardworking and friendly couple with four young children, are the third generation of Locks to farm here and have created a delightful place to stay. Inside the late 18th-century house all is natural, unpretentious and attractive. Fine wildlife photographs taken by a local gamekeeper decorate the dining room, while bedrooms are immaculate and restful, with crisp white linen and views over the orchard or across the fields to Arundel Castle. You can walk or cycle straight onto the South Downs, and the sea is five miles away.

rooms	3: 1 double, 1 twin/double, both with shower; 1 double with separate bath.
price	£70. Singles from £35.
meals	Pubs/restaurants 2-3 miles.
closed	Rarely.
directions	From Arundel east; first left-hand turning off dual carriageway A27, signed Blakehurst. Farm 0.5 miles on left.

Claire Lock
Blakehurst Farm,
Arundel,
Sussex BN18 9QG

tel	01903 889562
fax	01903 889562
web	www.blakehurstfarm.co.uk

Map 4 Entry 465

Sussex

The Well House

A delightful hideaway – your Normandy-styled annexe leads into its own large walled garden and has a private entrance. In the 17th century it was a humble shelter but the thatch and beams are immaculate now. Marilyn's style reflects her warm personality – you have white bedding on a big brass bed, a rich rug on dark boards, small armchairs and a wood-burning stove, a hat stand for clothes and a fine chest of drawers. It's luxurious but cosy, with a shower room to match; even your own small dining room. Pub and unspoilt beach, with dunes, are a seven-minute walk. Perfect. *Minimum stay two nights.*

Castle Cottage

However beautiful the countryside and the walks, you will be most enchanted by what your hosts have achieved. In birdsung woodland, a small house with a separate weather-boarded family barn and a cobbled conservatory. The barn's A-frame roof draws in the light and the front views, and there are perfect decorative touches: Persian carpets, dashing blue paints, a wrought-iron staircase, sculptures, handmade paper, superb lighting. The double in the house has the same magic. But the tree house upstages all, high in a giant chestnut, with vast bed, veranda, sauna and shower room. Beautifully built – and ineffable.

rooms	1 double with shower.
price	From £65.
meals	Pub & restaurants 2 & 10 minute walk.
closed	Rarely.
directions	A259 Littlehampton/Bognor. Left towards sea signed Climping Street & Beach. House 4th on right with private lay-by opposite.

rooms	3: 1 double, 1 family both with separate bath/shower; 1 double treehouse with shower.
price	£75–£120.
meals	Pubs/restaurants 1.5 miles.
closed	Rarely.
directions	From Fittleworth, south on B2138. Right onto Coates Lane; 1 mile, then right onto 'private drive'. Right at castle, right again & immed. left.

Marilyn Craine
The Well House,
Climping Street,
Climping, Littlehampton,
Sussex BN17 5RQ

tel 01903 713314
fax 01903 713540
e-mail info@baronshall.co.uk
web www.baronshall.co.uk

Alison Wyatt
Castle Cottage,
Coates Castle,
Fittleworth,
Sussex RH20 1EU

tel 01798 865001
fax 01798 865032
e-mail alison@castlecottage.info
web www.castlecottage.info

Map 4 Entry 466

Map 4 Entry 467

Sussex

Fitzlea Farmhouse

A wooded track leads to the beautiful, mellow, 17th-century farmhouse with tall chimneys and a cluster of overgrown outbuildings. Wood-panelled walls and ancient oak beams, a vast open fireplace, mullioned windows and welcoming sofas create an atmosphere of relaxed, country-house charm. You breakfast in the Aga-warmed kitchen; in spring, the scent of bluebells wafts through open doors. The large, comfortable, timbered bedrooms — one canopied bed incorporates original oak panelling — overlook fields, rolling lawns and woodland where you can stroll in peace. Heavenly. *Children by arrangement.*

Amberfold

Deer come to your window and miles of unspoiled woodland walks start from the door. Not really a B&B, more a peaceful bolthole for independent nature lovers — welcoming hosts live in the neighbouring listed cottage and lavishly replenish your fridges daily with a choice of bread, hams, cheeses, yogurts, coffee and more. There are a kettle and a toaster and all mod cons for self-serve, continental-style breakfast. The annexes are 'country' simple, but Annabelle has lavished thought upon them. You have your own front door and terrace and can come and go as you please — or stay all day.

rooms	3: 1 double, 1 twin, sharing bath; 1 family with bath.
price	£50-£70. Singles by arrangement.
meals	Excellent pubs/restaurants 2-5 miles. Packed lunches by arrangement.
closed	Christmas.
directions	Given on booking.

rooms	2 double studios for 2, both with shower.
price	From £65. Singles from £45.
meals	Pubs 20-minute walk.
closed	Rarely.
directions	From Midhurst, A286 for Chichester. After Royal Oak pub on left, Greyhound on right, on for 0.5 miles, left to Heyshott. On for 2 miles, do not turn off, look for white posts & house sign on left.

	Maggie Paterson Fitzlea Farmhouse, Selham, Petworth, Sussex GU28 0PS
tel	01798 861429

	Alex & Annabelle Costaras Amberfold, Heyshott, Midhurst, Sussex GU29 0DA
tel	01730 812385

Map 4 Entry 468

Map 4 Entry 469

Sussex

The Quag

Buried in a birchwood, The Quag feels remote, yet Midhurst – "the second most attractive town in England" – is only two miles away. Feel private in your own quarters with bedroom, striking bathroom with chequerboard floor, pine-floored sitting room (big enough for a child's bed) and separate stairs to the garden. You breakfast in the main house at a long wooden table with antique wheatsheaf-back chairs. Views are to the lawns that run down to Winterbourne stream, then across to the South Downs. Mark works for Christie's; Loveday looks after you. A happy, relaxed atmosphere and good value.

Redford Cottage

In a tiny village, an enchanting house – home to much-loved books and very kind hosts. The immense inglenook dates back to 1510 and the guest rooms are exceptionally private. The room in the main house, cosy, old-worldly and floral, has a book-lined sitting room with a woodburner and access to undulating lawns; the barn has the woody spaciousness of a ski chalet and is perfect for friends... old rugs, new pine, games, views and (up open stairs) beds tucked under a slopey ceiling. The silence is filled with birdsong and you are surrounded by wildlife and the rolling South Downs. Breakfasts are a treat.

rooms	1 twin with bath/shower & sitting room.
price	From £60. Singles £40.
meals	Excellent pubs/restaurants nearby.
closed	Christmas & occasionally.
directions	A272 Midhurst to Petersfield. 2 miles from Midhurst, left signed Minsted. Count seven telegraph poles, then 1st left. White house 1st on right.

rooms	3: 1 suite with shower. Barn: 2 twins/doubles, one with shower, one with bath & shower.
price	£85. Singles £50.
meals	Good pubs/restaurants nearby.
closed	Christmas.
directions	On old A3, north from Petersfield, at hill brow right for Rogate, left after 300 yds to Milland. Follow lane through woods for 6 miles; right for Midhurst & Redford. On right 150 yds beyond Redford sign.

Loveday & Mark Wrey
The Quag,
Minsted,
Midhurst,
Sussex GU29 0JH
tel   01730 813623
fax   01730 817844
e-mail beds@wrey.co.uk

Caroline & David Angela
Redford Cottage,
Redford,
Midhurst,
Sussex GU29 0QF
tel   01428 741242

Map 4 Entry 470

Map 4 Entry 471

Sussex

Severals House

In a sunny clearing deep in the woods stands a mellow house in a garden full of lavender. The Fairlies first happened upon it 20 years ago and fell in love with it. Originally two woodcutters' cottages – an old brick path still leads to the well – it was built in the year of Trafalgar. Jock, who weaves rugs using authentic 18th-century colours, has a fine collection of books: his father was a friend of P G Wodehouse and co-authored the Bulldog Drummond series. Jock is a star and he and Serena are the nicest of hosts. Bedrooms are large and comfy and breakfasts include Midhurst Royal sausages.

The Barnhouse

We've seen some impressive barn conversions but this one is something! It's just outside the town where Lord Tennyson lived, at the foot of Blackdown; from the garden you can hear the river Wey. Look through the big windows and you see straight into the main 'hall'; with its complex pattern of golden beams and rafters against stark white walls, it's a stunning space. Guests have their own wing: a little sitting room opening onto a pretty paved area and stylish bedrooms overlooking the garden and woods. Alan and Susie are a great couple who've migrated from London in pursuit of peace and a garden.

rooms	2: 1 double with separate bath; 1 single with bath.
price	£70. Singles £40.
meals	Pubs/restaurants 1-2 miles.
closed	Rarely.
directions	From centre of Midhurst, A272 to Petersfield. 1 mile on, see Woolbeding on right; go past. Carry on A272; 300 yds on, left into wood. Blue 'single track road' sign. House 300 yds on right.

rooms	2: 1 double with bath; 1 double with separate bath.
price	From £65.
meals	Good pubs & restaurants 3 miles.
closed	Christmas & New Year.
directions	A286 out of Haslemere; after 1.5 miles, Bell Vale Lane to left; after 200 yds, 1st turn to left; house immed. on right.

	Serena & Jock Fairlie
	Severals House,
	Severals Wood,
	Midhurst,
	Sussex GU29 0LX
tel	01730 812771

	Susie & Alan Mackay
	The Barnhouse,
	Bell Vale Lane,
	Haslemere,
	Sussex GU27 3DJ
tel	01428 643921
fax	01428 643921
e-mail	info@barnhousebandb.co.uk
web	www.barnhousebandb.co.uk

Map 4 Entry 472

Map 4 Entry 473

Sussex

The Flint House

Calm, kind Vivien feeds the birds from the stable door, then turns breakfasts into an early-morning house party. Be spoiled by kippers and porridge and, later, delicious cakes for tea. The garden has a tennis court and lovely views; the house, built by Napoleonic prisoners of war, was once part of the Goodwood estate. Sunny, ground-floor bedrooms in the converted cattle byre (with a reading room and pool table between them) have white bedspreads, chintz curtains bathrooms have huge hot towel rails and spoiling treats. You are close to Goodwood, and husband Tim manages a thoroughbred stud.

rooms	2: 1 double, 1 twin, both with bath/shower.
price	£65-£85. Singles £40-£50.
meals	Excellent pubs in village, 1 mile.
closed	Christmas.
directions	A272 to Midhurst, A286 to Singleton. Left for Goodwood; over downs, past racecourse, next right for Lavant; 0.5 miles, 1st on right.

Tim & Vivien Read
The Flint House,
Pook Lane,
East Lavant,
Chichester,
Sussex PO18 0AS

tel 01243 773482
mobile 07860 244396
e-mail theflinthouse@ukonline.co.uk

Map 4 Entry 474

Easton House

Mary, relaxed and comfortable in her 16th-century former farmhouse, has lived here for 30 years. Flagstoned floors, beams, a cosily cluttered drawing room filled with Bechstein piano, cello, double bass… And cats and more cats: some real, others framed or created from wood, metal or stone. The bedrooms (the twin being the smallest) have bathrooms with views of Bosham and the place has the feel of a lived-in home. Wide Sussex skies overhead, a short stroll to the water's edge – the Chidham Peninsula is a paradise for birdwatchers – and it's 20 minutes' walk to an excellent pub.

rooms	3: 1 double, 1 twin, sharing bath; 1 double with separate bath.
price	From £50. Singles £35.
meals	Good pub 1 mile.
closed	Christmas.
directions	From Chichester for Portsmouth; pass Tesco on right; 3rd exit off r'bout, to Bosham & Fishbourne. A259 for 4 miles, pass Saab garage on right; next left into Chidham Lane. House last on left, 1 mile.

Mary Hartley
Easton House,
Chidham Lane,
Chidham,
Chichester,
Sussex PO18 8TF

tel 01243 572514
fax 01243 573084
e-mail eastonhouse@chidham.fsnet.co.uk

Map 4 Entry 475

Sussex

Lordington House

On a sunny slope of the Ems valley, life ticks by peacefully as it has always done… apart from a touch of turbulence in the 16th century. The house is vast and impressive, with majestic views past clipped yew, box and walled garden to the AONB beyond. Inside is engagingly old-fashioned: Edwardian beds with firm mattresses and floral bedspreads, carpeted Sixties-style bathrooms, shepherdess wallpapers up and over wardrobe doors. Expect tea cosies and homemade marmalade at breakfast, great old paintings and a magnificently panelled drawing room. *Children over five welcome.*

Crede Farmhouse

Lesley, once a dancer, is vivacious and kind; Peter helps cook delicious Aga-breakfasts. This fine flint house (1810) is a cottagey haven inside: all is fresh, peaceful and beautifully maintained. The double room is primrose and white with green views, the sweet 'single' has a wrought-iron double bed and overlooks a barn. Crackling fires and ticking clocks in winter, a pool and garden in summer, your hosts' easy generosity and delectable Bosham (history, harbour, sailing boats) make this special. Chichester Theatre is up the road.

rooms	4: 1 double with bath/shower; 1 double/twin with separate bath/shower; 1 double, 1 single sharing bath/shower.
price	From £65. Singles from £35.
meals	Dinner £20. Packed lunch from £5. Pub 1 mile; restaurants 4-8 miles.
closed	Rarely.
directions	Lordington (marked on AA road maps) west of B2146, 6 miles south of South Harting. Enter through white railings by letterbox; fork right after bridge.

rooms	2: 1 double with bath; 1 single (let to same party only).
price	£65-£80. Singles £45-£55.
meals	Good pubs/restaurants 5-minute walk.
closed	Christmas.
directions	From Chichester, A259 west for Bosham; through Fishbourne, past garden centre, left into Walton Lane. After sharp bend, right into Crede Lane; 200 yds to end of drive. On left, with white garage.

Mr & Mrs John Hamilton
Lordington House,
Lordington,
Chichester,
Sussex PO18 9DX

tel 01243 375862
fax 01243 375862
e-mail audreyhamilton@onetel.com

Mrs Lesley Hankey
Crede Farmhouse,
Crede Lane,
Bosham,
Sussex PO18 8NX

tel 01243 574929
e-mail lesley@credefarmhouse.fsnet.co.uk

Map 4 Entry 476

Map 4 Entry 477

Warwickshire

Abbey Farm

Views sweep lakewards and upwards to Merevale Hall... there are abbey ruins in the back garden. Tim, Ali and family arrived three years ago, drawn to this ethereal place and its many acres. Hospitable and generous, they whip up great meals and Aga-cooked breakfasts: Old Spot bacon, black pudding, vine tomatoes, home eggs. Everywhere is charmingly uncluttered with plain Georgian mantles, mullioned and arched windows, fat sofas, scrubbed pine tables; two of the bedrooms and bathrooms are huge. This is family-friendly B&B: cots if you need them, coots on the lake, happy hosts and acres of space.

rooms	3: 1 double with bath & shower; 1 double with shower; 1 double with separate bath/shower.
price	£59–£79. Singles from £45.
meals	Dinner, 3 courses, from £18.
closed	Rarely.
directions	M42 exit J10. Head east on A5 towards Atherstone Nuneaton Hinckley. At 3rd r'bout, right into Merevale Lane (B4116). House 1st on left about 0.3 miles, just after 50mph signs.

Tim & Alison Jones
Abbey Farm,
Merevale Lane,
Atherstone,
Warwickshire CV9 2LA
tel   01827 715091
fax   01827 715091
e-mail   tim@abbeyfarmbandb.co.uk
web   www.abbeyfarmbandb.co.uk

Map 8 Entry 478

Hardingwood House

Near Shakespeare's town, a theatrical home with an extravagantly Tudor feel. Denise, warm and delightful, spoils guests with big bedrooms, private dressing rooms and deep gold-tapped baths. There are books, flowers, antique clocks and plush sofas; tapestry and velvet curtains frame small leaded windows; dark timbers and reds and pinks abound. The conversion of the 1737 barn is immaculate inside and out: the kitchen gives onto a stunning patio and there are two conservatories for breakfast. Much rural charm, yet close to Birmingham and the NEC. *Advance booking essential.*

rooms	3: 1 double, 2 twins, all with bath.
price	£70. Singles £45.
meals	Pub 1 mile.
closed	Rarely.
directions	At M6 junc. 4, A446 for Lichfield. Get in right lane & 1st exit towards Coleshill. From High St, turn into Maxstoke Lane. After 4 miles, 4th right. 1st drive on left.

Mrs Denise Owen
Hardingwood House,
Hardingwood Lane,
Fillongley,
Coventry,
Warwickshire CV7 8EL
tel   01676 542579
fax   01676 541336
e-mail   denise@hardingwoodhouse.fsnet.co.uk

Map 8 Entry 479

Warwickshire

Park Farm House

Fronted by a circular drive, the warm red-brick farmhouse is listed and old – it dates from 1655. Linda is friendly and welcoming, a genuine B&B pro. There's a stylish, spotless guest sitting room with oriental touches and three bedrooms in apple pie order: new mattresses on mahogany and brass beds, fine fabrics, duvets or blankets on request, heaps of towels. No decorative excesses, just a smart country feel, and breakfasts and dinners that spoil you with the best local produce. A haven of rest from the motorway (morning hum only), and close to Birmingham, Warwick and Stratford.

rooms	3: 2 doubles with bath/shower; 1 twin with shower.
price	£70-£72. Singles from £39.
meals	Dinner, 3 courses, from £20. Supper £16.
closed	Rarely.
directions	M6/M69 exit 2; B4065 thro' Ansty to Shilton; left at lights then next left. Over m'way; after telephone box, right to Barnacle; thro' village, left into Spring Road, house at end.

Linda Grindal
Park Farm House,
Barnacle,
Shilton,
Coventry,
Warwickshire CV7 9LG

tel 0247 6612628
fax 0247 6616010
web www.parkfarmguesthouse.co.uk

Map 8 Entry 480

Shrewley Pools Farm

A charming, eccentric home – and fabulous for families, with so much room to play and so much to see: sheep, turkeys, geese, Saddleback pigs. A fragrant, romantic garden, too, and a fascinating house (1640), all low ceilings, aged floors and steep stairs. Timbered passages lead to large, pretty, sunny bedrooms with leaded windows and polished wooden floors. (The family room has everything needed for a baby.) There's a proper farmhouse dining room where Cathy serves sausages, bacon, pork, game and lamb from the farm. Next door is Big Pool where you may fish with a day ticket.

rooms	2: 1 twin with separate bath; 1 family (double, single & cot) with bath.
price	From £50. Singles from £32.50.
meals	Dinner from £15. Packed lunch £3. Children's high tea £3. Good pub/restaurant 1.5 miles.
closed	Christmas & New Year.
directions	From M40 junc. 15, A46 for Coventry. Left onto A4177. 4.5 miles to Five Ways r'bout. 1st left, on for 0.75 miles; signed opp. Farm Gate Poultry: track on left.

Cathy Dodd
Shrewley Pools Farm,
Haseley,
Warwick,
Warwickshire CV35 7HB

tel 01926 484315
web www.shrewleypoolsfarm.co.uk

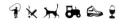

Map 8 Entry 481

Warwickshire

Mows Hill Farm

From the flagstoned kitchen, peep through the stable door at the cattle munching in their stalls. The place has been in the family for generations and the late-Victorian farmhouse is a homely, friendly place to stay. Lynda and Edward have completely redecorated: the sitting and dining rooms are elegant and comfortable, the family room is a symphony of lavender and white, the double room dramatic cream and navy. You get a proper farmhouse breakfast in the new conservatory – homemade bread and jams, home-reared bacon, just-laid eggs – and green field views reach out from every window.

rooms	2: 1 family with shower; 1 double with separate bath.
price	£70. Singles from £35.
meals	Pub/restaurant 3 miles.
closed	Rarely.
directions	A3400 Hockley Heath; B4101 (Spring Lane); left into Umberslade Rd. At 2nd triangle, keep right & onto Mows Hill Rd; 0.25 miles on right.

Mrs Lynda Muntz
Mows Hill Farm,
Mows Hill Road, Kemps Green,
Tanworth in Arden,
Warwickshire B94 5PP
tel   01564 784312
fax   01564 783378
e-mail mowshill@farmline.com
web   www.b-and-bmowshill.co.uk

Map 8 Entry 482

Salford Farm House

Beautiful within, solidly handsome without. A flagstoned hallway and an old rocking horse, ticking clocks and the smell of beeswax. Jane has a flair for interior decoration and, thanks to subtle colours, oak beams and beautiful old furniture, has achieved a seductive combination of comfort and style. She and Richard are friendly, easy hosts; she was a ballet dancer, he has green fingers and runs his own fruit farm nearby. (The freshly-picked produce appears in pretty bowls on the breakfast table.) Look out across the attractive garden to glorious views of neighbouring farmland.

rooms	2: 1 twin/double with bath/shower; 1 twin/double with shower.
price	£80. Singles £50.
meals	Dinner £24.
closed	Rarely.
directions	A46 from Evesham or Stratford; exit for Salford Priors. On entering village, right opp. church, for Dunnington. House on right, approx. 1 mile on, after 2nd sign on right for Dunnington.

Jane Gibson & Richard Beach
Salford Farm House,
Salford Priors,
Evesham,
Warwickshire WR11 8XN
tel   01386 870000
e-mail salfordfarmhouse@aol.com
web   www.salfordfarmhouse.co.uk

Map 8 Entry 483

Warwickshire

Cross o' th' Hill Farm

From the veranda you can see the church where Shakespeare is buried. (A footpath across the fields gets you there – and to Stratford – in 12 minutes!). There's been a farm on this rural spot since before Shakespeare's time but part of the house is Victorian. Built around 1860, it's full of light, with wall-to-ceiling sash windows, glass panelling in the roof and elegant, gracious rooms. The lovely garden, visited by pheasants and woodpeckers, dates from the same period – there's even a sunken croquet lawn. Decima grew up here; she and David are lovely hosts, and passionate about art and architecture.

rooms	3 doubles: 1 with bath, 1 with shower, 1 with separate bath.
price	£64–£74. Singles £45–£55.
meals	Pubs/restaurants 20-minute walk.
closed	20 December–February.
directions	From Stratford south on A3400 for 0.5 miles, 2nd right on B4632 for Broadway Rd for 500 yds. 2nd drive on right for Farm.

Decima Noble
Cross o' th' Hill Farm,
Stratford upon Avon,
Warwickshire CV37 8HP

tel	01789 204738
e-mail	decimanoble@hotmail.com

Map 8 Entry 484

Winton House

An 1856 Victorian farmhouse with log fires, old pine and wonderful views to folklore-rich Meon Hill; stories of witchcraft and other spookery abound. The bedrooms are imaginative: a pine box bed and a medieval frieze of flying angels (pure fairy tale), four-posters, lace and antique quilts. Delicious breakfast menus, including vegetarian, make imaginative use of home-grown orchard fruits. A great start for a day's walking on the Heart of England Way, or a ride on one of the many cycle tracks. Bikes are available and there's a disused railway line which takes you straight into Stratford-upon-Avon.

rooms	3: 2 four-posters, both with shower; 1 family room with separate bath.
price	From £70.
meals	Pub 0.5 miles.
closed	Rarely.
directions	From Stratford, A3400 south, then B4632 (for Broadway & Mickleton) for 6 miles. Left for Upper Quinton. 400 yds on left.

Mrs Gail Lyon
Winton House,
The Green, Upper Quinton,
Stratford-upon-Avon,
Warwickshire CV37 8SX

tel	01789 720500
fax	07831 485483
e-mail	gail@wintonhouse.com
web	www.wintonhouse.com

Map 8 Entry 485

Warwickshire

The Old Manor House

You can fish or play tennis to your heart's content, from beautiful, landscaped, rose-strewn gardens that slope gently down to the River Stour. Jane, a Cordon Bleu cook, runs her 16th- and 17th-century house with huge energy and friendliness. The A-shaped double in the main part of the house has ancient beams, oak furniture and a lovely bathroom, while a pretty blue twin and a single are in the other wing: private and self-contained, with a large and elegant drawing and dining room for all visitors to share. It's seductively easy to relax here; breakfasts are carefully prepared.

Blackwell Grange

Sheep-dotted views entice you from mullioned windows, Wyandotte bantams strut the summer lawns, and the peace is profound. The mellow stone farmhouse surrounded by fields is a homely and unstuffy place to stay; there are flagstones, beams and floorboards that creak, and a guest sitting room that invites you with books, magazines, comfy sofas and open fire. Generous-sized bedrooms have well-loved furniture and touches of chintz, bathrooms are well-equipped and the room on the ground floor is perfect for wheelchairs. Footpaths, bridleways and lanes radiate from the door.

rooms	3: 1 twin with bath; 1 double with separate bath. 1 single available.
price	From £75. Singles from £40.
meals	Dinner from £20. Excellent local restaurants.
closed	Rarely.
directions	From Stratford, A422 for 4 miles for Banbury. After 4 miles, right at r'bout onto A429 for Halford. There, 1st right. House with black & white timbers straight ahead.

rooms	4: 3 twins/doubles, all with bath & shower; 1 single with shower.
price	From £68-£75. Single from £35.
meals	Excellent pubs 1-1.5 miles.
closed	Rarely.
directions	From Stratford-upon-Avon, A3400 for Oxford. After 5 miles, right by church in Newbold-on-Stour & follow signs to Blackwell. Fork right on entering Blackwell. Entrance beyond thatched barn.

Jane Pusey
The Old Manor House,
Halford,
Shipston-on-Stour,
Warwickshire CV36 5BT

tel   01789 740264
fax   01789 740609
e-mail info@oldmanor-halford.fsnet.co.uk
web   www.oldmanor-halford.co.uk

Liz Vernon Miller
Blackwell Grange,
Blackwell,
Shipston-on-Stour,
Warwickshire CV36 4PF

tel   01608 682357
fax   01608 682357
e-mail sawdays@blackwellgrange.co.uk
web   www.blackwellgrange.co.uk

Map 8 Entry 486

Map 8 Entry 487

Warwickshire

Idlicote House

From the upper bedrooms you look onto never-ending green – oaks, fields and meadows… you could imagine Mr Darcy riding out for dinner. Inside is just as stately, ideal for a house-party weekend. There's a finely panelled twin but the vast suite is the jewel in the crown with its East meets West collaboration of furniture, fabrics and colours. There's a grand dining room for breakfast and a library/sitting room as big as a church. Outside, big terraces, ancient trees, an 800-acre farm and the only sound that of garrulous pheasants. Kari runs it all without fuss.

Oxbourne House

Hard to believe the house is new, with its beamed ceilings, fireplaces and antiques. Bedrooms are fresh, crisp, cosy and cared for, the triple with an 'up in the attic' feel; lighting is soft, beds excellent, bathrooms top of the range and views far-reaching. In the garden are tennis, sculpture – Posy helps organise exhibitions – and Graeme's beautiful handmade pergola. Wake to birdsong and fresh eggs from home ducks and hens; on peaceful summer nights, watch the dipping sun. Posy and Graeme are hugely likeable and welcoming: a most comforting place to stay.

rooms	3: 1 suite, 1 single sharing bath (single let to same party); 1 twin with separate bath.	rooms	3: 1 double with shower; 1 twin/double, 1 triple, both with bath.
price	£90. Singles from £45.	price	£60-£70. Singles from £40.
meals	Supper by arrangement. Pubs/restaurants within 3.5 miles.	meals	Dinner from £15. Good pub 2-minute walk.
closed	Christmas & New Year.	closed	Rarely.
directions	From Shipston-on-Stour, turn off A3400 north to Honington. In Idlicote, left at pond & through stone gateposts. House on left, after church.	directions	A422 from Stratford-on-Avon for Banbury. After 8 miles, right to Oxhill. Last house on right on Whatcote Road.

	Kari Dill		Graeme & Posy McDonald
	Idlicote House,		Oxbourne House,
	Idlicote,		Oxhill,
	Shipston-on-Stour,		Warwick,
	Warwickshire CV36 5DT		Warwickshire CV35 0RA
tel	01608 661473	tel	01295 688202
fax	01608 661381	mobile	07753 661353
e-mail	dill@idlicote.freeserve.co.uk	e-mail	graememcdonald@msn.com
		web	www.oxbournehouse.co.uk

Map 8 Entry 488

Map 8 Entry 489

Warwickshire

Dockers Barn Farm

Wonderful to leave the busy world behind and head down the track that leads – eventually – to the barn. Bedrooms have been carefully decorated, with star-painted ceilings and colourwashed walls, wooden-latched doors open to sunny, sky-lit bathrooms and the annexe room has its own entrance and a wrought-iron four-poster. Carolyn and John keep horses and hens, have set 10 acres aside for nature conservation, have nesting barn owls and couldn't be nicer. And there's a garden hot tub with hydrotherapy jets – you can use for a small charge – magic under the stars! *Children over eight welcome.*

Loxley Farm

You can get from your bath to your seat in the Stratford theatre in 10 minutes, if you hurry. This is a Grade II-listed thatched house, dated 1501 and set in an extremely pretty garden. Even the barn where you sleep – also thatched, beamed and listed – is 17th century. The Garden Suite has its own gorgeous conservatory – great for watching the wildlife – while the Hayloft has a little sitting room and kitchenette. Both have splendid corner baths. The rooms don't get a great deal of natural light but are comfortably equipped. Breakfast is in the main house and is the time to be sociable with the delightful Anne.

rooms	2: 1 four-poster (with extra single), 1 double, both with bath/shower.
price	£52–£58. Singles from £35.
meals	Pubs/restaurants 3 miles.
closed	Christmas.
directions	From Stratford, A422 to Pillerton Priors, then on to Pillerton Hersey. There, at bottom of hill, 1st right onto Oxhill Bridle Rd. House at very end (1 mile). Or M40 junc. 12, 6 miles on B4451.

rooms	2 doubles, both with bath/shower.
price	£70. Singles £45.
meals	Pub 3-minute walk.
closed	1 December-7 January.
directions	From Stratford, A422 Banbury road for 4 miles; turn for Loxley; through village, left at bottom of hill; 3rd house on right.

	Carolyn & John Howard
	Dockers Barn Farm,
	Oxhill Bridle Road,
	Pillerton Hersey, Warwick,
	Warwickshire CV35 0QB
tel	01926 640475
fax	01926 641747
e-mail	jwhoward@onetel.com
web	www.dockersbarnfarm.co.uk

	Mrs Anne Horton
	Loxley Farm,
	Loxley,
	Warwick,
	Warwickshire CV35 9JN
tel	01789 840265
fax	01789 840645
e-mail	loxleyfarm@hotmail.com

Map 8 Entry 490

Map 8 Entry 491

Warwickshire

Marston House

A generous feel pervades this lovely family home; Kim's kitchen is the hub of the house. She and John fizz with good humour and take pride in those times when family and guests come together. Tea on arrival, delicious scrambled eggs and homemade jams for breakfast, perhaps a guided walk around the village. The house is big and sunny; old rugs cover parquet floors, soft sofas tumble with cushions and sash windows look onto the garden, peaceful with croquet lawn. Bedrooms are light, roomy and supremely comfortable. A special place with a big heart.

rooms	2: 1 double, 1 twin/double, both with separate bath.
price	From £70. Singles from £40.
meals	Dinner £25 (min. 4 people). Kitchen supper £18. Good pub 5-minute walk.
closed	Rarely.
directions	M40 exit 11. From Banbury, A361 north for 7 miles; at Byfield village sign, left into Twistle Lane; on to Priors Marston; 5th on left with cattle grid, after S-bend.

Kim & John Mahon
Marston House,
Priors Marston,
Southam,
Warwickshire CV47 7RP

tel	01327 260297
fax	01327 262846
e-mail	kim@mahonand.co.uk
web	www.ivabestbandb.co.uk

Map 8 Entry 492

Wiltshire

85 Exeter Street

The dreaming spire of the cathedral is a two-minute walk away but, tantalisingly, the bedrooms look over a quiet tiny courtyard. You are so central here that you can wander on foot (having parked by the house or walked from the station). Susan is refreshingly enthusiastic about her new 'career' and determined to keep any weary professionalism at bay. Bedrooms are simple, traditional and attractive: William Morris curtains, a five-foot bed and a shower cabinet in one; a single bed with spare roll-out bed in the other. The breakfast room has one big table plus sofas, and encourages conviviality.

rooms	2: 1 double with shower; 1 single/twin with separate bath/shower.
price	£60-£70. Singles from £50.
meals	Pubs & restaurants an easy walk.
closed	Rarely.
directions	Ring road around Salisbury to south of city; past r'bout to Southampton; at next r'bout, 3rd exit onto Exeter Road (signed Blandford/Hospital). No. 85 near city centre. Park opp. house; ask for permit on arrival.

Susan Orr-Ewing
85 Exeter Street,
Salisbury,
Wiltshire SP1 2SE

tel	01722 417944
mobile	07904 814408
e-mail	susan.orr-ewing@virgin.net

Map 3 Entry 493

Wiltshire

Ebblesway Courtyard

Toast your toes on warm stone flags in this cloister-like conversion – the underfloor heating system helped Ebblesway win its conservation award. The farm's Victorian agricultural outbuildings have been sympathetically converted into a studio (Peter makes harpsichords) and a B&B. Bedrooms feed off a corridor; walls are simple white or bare brick, ceilings high and beamy, lighting perfect. You'll want for nothing with Gail in charge (her blueberry pancakes are wonderful); Peter is charming too. Ebblesway lies in the Cranbourne Chase AONB – ideal for country walks.

The Duck Yard

Your own terrace, your own entrance, your own sitting room, your own wing – a treat. All is as fresh as a daisy, brand new and beautifully thought through. Peaceful too, at the end of the lane, with a colourful cottage garden, a summerhouse and roaming bantams. Unflappable Harriet is a professional cook and cheerfully rustles up fine meals at short notice; breakfasts, too, are delicious, with eggs from those happy hens. Your carpeted bedroom and pristine bathroom are tucked under the eaves, the sitting room is bright and cheerful. Warm, generous, good value B&B. *Children over 10 welcome.*

rooms	4: 1 double, 1 twin/double, 2 singles, all with shower.
price	£70-£78. Singles £48.
meals	Good pubs 1 mile.
closed	December-January.
directions	A354 from Salisbury to Blandford. In Coombe Bissett, right to Broadchalke. House signed 1 mile after White Hart on right behind Stoke Manor.

rooms	1 twin/double with bath/shower.
price	£60. Singles £40.
meals	Dinner, 3 courses, £20. Packed lunch £7. Good pub 2 miles.
closed	Christmas & New Year.
directions	A303 to Wylye, then for Dinton. After approx. 4 miles left at x-roads, for Wilton & Salisbury. On for 1 mile, down hill, round sharp bend, signed Sandhills Rd. 1st low red brick building on left.

	Gail & Peter Smalley
	Ebblesway Courtyard,
	High Road,
	Broadchalke,
	Salisbury,
	Wiltshire SP5 5EF
tel	01722 780182
e-mail	enquiries@ebblleswaycourtyard.co.uk
web	www.ebblleswaycourtyard.co.uk

	Harriet & Peter Combes
	The Duck Yard,
	Sandhills Road,
	Dinton,
	Salisbury,
	Wiltshire SP3 5ER
tel	01722 716495
fax	01722 716163
e-mail	harrietcombes_1@hotmail.com

Map 3 Entry 494

Map 3 Entry 495

Wiltshire

Baverstock Manor

Instantly gracious – the 15th-century honey stone that lights up in sunlight, the Jacobean 'extension', the wisteria, the solidity... Inside it is creaky, friendly, engagingly chaotic, full of well-worn antiques and faded rugs in glorious colours. If you're travelling with family, choose the roomy twin that connects with the little single, its small, florally dressed windows overlooking gardens and pheasants. The twin/double has a pretty bed and an ancient stone fireplace. Come for history not luxury, oodles of character and a pool and a tennis court nearby. *Children over eight welcome.*

Little Langford Farmhouse

A rare treat to have your milk fresh from the cow – the Helyers have a pedigree herd of Holstein Friesians. The bedrooms of this rather grand Victorian-gothic farmhouse are large and pretty with period furniture and crisp linen; there are impressive countryside views, a baby grand and a billiard room. Everything is elegant and polished yet cosy at the same time, and the Helyers are immensely friendly and welcoming. Terrace doors are thrown open for delicious alfresco breakfasts in summer. The estate is 1,450 acres and an SSSI, treasured for its wild flowers and butterflies. *Children by arrangement.*

rooms	3: 1 twin/double with separate bath; 1 twin/double, 1 single sharing bath.
price	£70-£80. Singles £35-£45.
meals	Packed lunch £6. Excellent pubs within 4 miles.
closed	December-January.
directions	From Salisbury, A36 to Wilton, then A30 (to Shaftesbury). After 3 miles, in Barford St Martin, right onto B3089; after 2 miles, right to Baverstock; after 0.75 miles stone gateway on right, on S-bend.

rooms	3: 1 twin/double, 1 double, both with shower; 1 twin with separate shower.
price	£60-£65. Singles £45-£55.
meals	Pub/restaurant 1.75 miles.
closed	Christmas & New Year.
directions	Exit A303 at A36 junc; follow signs for Salisbury. 2 miles; right for The Langfords. In Steeple L., right for Hanging L. At T-junc. opp. village hall, left for Little Langford. House 0.75 miles on left.

Tim & Belinda Hextall
Baverstock Manor,
Dinton,
Salisbury,
Wiltshire SP3 5EN
tel 01722 716206
fax 01722 716510
e-mail hextallbavers@hotmail.com

Patricia Helyer
Little Langford Farmhouse,
Little Langford,
Salisbury,
Wiltshire SP3 4NR
tel 01722 790205
fax 01722 790086
e-mail bandb@littlelangford.co.uk
web www.littlelangford.co.uk

Map 3 Entry 496

Map 3 Entry 497

Wiltshire

Perrior House

Folded into stunning countryside, this listed, one-time butcher's shop has been in Darea's family for years. Stylishly cluttered, sparkingly clean, there are beautiful objects and lovely pieces at every turn. Darea's enthusiasm for books and travel is infectious: she can identify every rich and rare specimen in her garden, keeps detailed diaries and albums of her many travels and has thrown nothing away. Your chintzy bedrooms are seductively cosy; one looks over the well-tended, walled garden and a playground. A fascinating corner of England; Stonehenge, Longleat and Stourhead beckon.

The Manor

Isabel is a delight and a great cook (she used to run a chalet in the Swiss Alps), happy to chat by the Aga as she chops and stirs. She has decorated her beautifully converted home in style: the drawing room is elegantly English, with a cosy fire and a touch of the orient, bedrooms are prettily papered in pale pink and blue, mattresses are of the finest quality. Breakfast is eaten at a polished oak table, glazed doors thrown open to the garden in summer. This is a treat of a 17th-century brick-and-flint manor in a beguiling spot by the river Avon; fishermen, bring your gear.

rooms	2: 1 twin with bath; 1 twin/double with separate bath.
price	£60-£65. Singles £35-£40.
meals	Excellent pub 50 yds.
closed	Rarely.
directions	Exit A303 at junc. with A36 for Wylye. In village, cross river & round sharp left-hand bend. House 25 yds on right.

rooms	2 twins/doubles, both with bath/shower.
price	£60-£65. Singles £35- £40
meals	Dinner, 3 courses, £25. Good pub/restaurant 2-minute walk.
closed	Rarely.
directions	From Upavon towards Andover on A342. Manor 3rd house on right & last before bridge.

	Mrs Darea Browne Perrior House, Wylye, Warminster, Wiltshire BA12 0QU
tel	01985 248228
e-mail	dareabrowne@aol.com

	Isabel Green The Manor, Upavon, Pewsey, Wiltshire SN9 6EB
tel	01980 635115
mobile	07919 278334
e-mail	isabelbgreen@hotmail.com
web	www.themanorupavon.co.uk

Map 3 Entry 498

Map 3 Entry 499

Wiltshire

Puckshipton House

An intriguing name, Puckshipton: it means Goblin's Barn. The house is deep in the lush countryside of the Vale of Pewsey, reached by a long tree-lined drive. You stay in the Georgian end, with a private entrance that leads to a Regency-blue hall. Rooms are stylish and uncluttered, an attractive mix of old and new. One bedroom has a splendid four-poster, the other has oak beds made by James, forester and fine furniture-maker. He and Juliette are a charming young couple with four small children. The dining room has a woodburner and the sitting room an open fire: a relaxed and lovely place to stay.

St Cross

Everything is small-scale, pretty and very English. Serena's 17th-century thatched cottage is at the end of a russet-brick terrace on a tranquil country road. Guests have their own sunny sitting room (and log fire if it's chilly) overlooking a garden full of wisteria and lavender. The bedrooms are sloping-ceilinged and cosy: the double is chintzy and bright, with a bay window, the twin dramatically criss-crossed with beams. Serena is an artist and you'll enjoy her company. She has a nice sense of humour and knows masses about the area, crop circles included – 'croppies' from many nations meet at an inn nearby.

rooms	2: 1 twin/double with separate bath/shower; 1 four-poster with bath & shower.
price	£70-£75. Singles £50.
meals	Good pubs & restaurant 5-minute drive.
closed	Christmas.
directions	Devizes A342 towards Rushall; left to Chirton, right to Marden & through village. On for 0.25 miles; right into private drive.

rooms	2: 1 double, 1 twin sharing bath.
price	£55-£60. Singles £40-£45.
meals	Dinner £15-£25, by arrangement. Good pub 0.5 mile.
closed	Rarely.
directions	From Marlborough A345 to Pewsey. After station right to Woodborough. Follow road through village. Manor House on right. St Cross next door, up lane on left.

Juliette & James Noble
Puckshipton House,
Beechingstoke,
Pewsey,
Wiltshire SN9 6HG
tel   01672 851336
e-mail   noble.jj@gmail.com
web   www.puckshipton.co.uk

Mrs Serena Gore
St Cross,
Woodborough,
Pewsey,
Wiltshire SN9 5PL
tel   01672 851346
fax   01672 851346

Map 3 Entry 500

Map 3 Entry 501

Wiltshire

Hilcott Farm House

A charming Georgian farmhouse and a fresh, stylish B&B – Val and David moved out of London in search of peace and found it in these rolling downs. Val is an interior decorator specialising in paint finishes and has stamped her subtle mark on every room: a restful terracotta-linen in the guest sitting room, bold yellow checks in the bathroom. It's comforting too: old rugs on wooden floors, log fires, tranquil bedrooms, crisp cotton, plump pillows, a happy dog. Organic lamb and salmon for dinner, fresh vegetables from the pretty walled garden, Marlborough, Avebury and Stonehenge a short drive away.

Westcourt Farm

Rozzie and Jonny left London four years ago to restore a medieval cruck truss hall house (beautifully) and create wildflower meadows, hedgerows and ponds. They are delightful people, newish to B&B and eager to welcome you. Rooms are freshly decorated, crisp yet traditional; the country furniture is charming, the crucks and trusses a carpenter's delight. Bedrooms have new beds and fine linen, bathrooms are spot-on, and there's a lovely dining room. Encircled by footpaths and fields, Westcourt is the oldest house in a perfect village, two minutes from an excellent pub.

rooms	3: 1 double with bath; 1 twin, 1 single, both with separate bath.	rooms	2: 1 twin with separate bath; 1 double with separate shower.
price	From £65. Singles from £35.	price	£65. Singles £35.
meals	Dinner, 3 courses, £25. Pubs 1 mile.	meals	Good pub/restaurant in village.
closed	Rarely.	closed	Christmas & New Year.
directions	From Marlborough, A345 thro' Pewsey; 3 miles on, at Woodbridge Inn r'bout, right to Hilcott; house 2nd on left over cattle grid. From M3 & A303, 11 miles from Amesbury r'bout via Upavon & Woodbridge r'bout.	directions	A338 Hungerford-Salisbury; after 4 miles signed Shalbourne; through village & fork left at pub; 150 yds, 2nd drive on right.

Val Maclay
Hilcott Farm House,
Hilcott,
Marlborough,
Wiltshire SN9 6LE
tel   01672 851372
fax   01672 851192
e-mail   beds@hilcott.com
web   www.hilcott.com

Jonny & Rozzie Buxton
Westcourt Farm,
Shalbourne,
Marlborough,
Wiltshire SN8 3QE
tel   01672 871399
e-mail   info@westcourtfarm.com
web   www.westcourtfarm.com

Map 3 Entry 502

Map 3 Entry 503

Wiltshire

Fisherman's House

Dangle your toes in the Kennet River; it flows briskly past the clipped lawn of this exquisitely decorated home. It looks every inch a doll's house, but Jeremy and Heather add a deft human touch. The elegance of excellent breakfasts taken in the conservatory is balanced by the comforting hubbub emanating from the family kitchen. There's a sitting room for guests with an open fire and, upstairs, the thickly curtained, valanced and, in places, ornate bedrooms are ingeniously clustered around the chimney breast. Time slips by effortlessly here, and many people come to visit the crop circles.

Upper Westcourt

Long views down Pewsey Vale, a stroll to the pub, tennis for energetic moments, garden corners for dozing with a book. This a relaxed, comfortable house that suits every mood, while the polished old furniture, rich curtains, photographs and paintings give it a family feel. Bedrooms and bathrooms are sunny with florals, watercolours and books, there are drawing room sofas to sink into before a winter log fire, and breakfasts may include fresh raspberries and tomatoes from the garden. Traditional good taste and charming, welcoming, well-organised hosts.

rooms	4: 1 double with bath & additional double (let to same party only); 1 twin, 1 single sharing bath.
price	£70. Singles £35.
meals	Lunch/packed lunch from £3. Pub 500 yds. Restaurant 2 miles.
closed	Christmas.
directions	From Hungerford, A4 for Marlborough. After 7 miles, right for Stitchcombe, down hill (bear left at barn) & left at T-junc. On entering village, house 2nd on left.

rooms	2: 1 double/twin, 1 twin with bath/shower; 1 single let to same party only.
price	£60-£70. Singles £30-£40.
meals	Pubs within walking distance.
closed	Christmas & Easter
directions	A346 to Burbage. In High St, turn west to Westcourt, over bypass. At T-junc., right; 300 yds on left.

Jeremy & Heather Coulter
Fisherman's House,
Mildenhall,
Marlborough,
Wiltshire SN8 2LZ

tel	01672 515390
fax	01672 519009
e-mail	jjs.coulter@virgin.net
web	freespace.virgin.net/jjs.coulter

Mrs Carolyn Hill
Upper Westcourt,
Burbage,
Malborough,
Wiltshire SN8 3BW

tel	01672 810 307
fax	01672 810 307
e-mail	prhill@onetel.com
web	www.upperwestcourt.co.uk

Map 3 Entry 504

Map 3 Entry 505

Wiltshire

Westcourt Bottom

Swim in the pool, shelter under the loggia, book an art class with Bill. A delightful place with hosts to match and Bill, sculptor and painter, has applied his considerable flair to the renovation and decoration of this large 17th-century thatched cottage. Beams criss-cross the sitting room, bedrooms are colourful and charming, there are antique rugs on walls and floors and art everywhere. The garden has sculpted hedges, clouds of lavender, a carp-filled pond and a roaming pig. There's marvellous walking nearby. *Children by arrangement. Minimum stay two nights on bank holiday & summer weekends.*

rooms	3: 1 double with bath; 1 double, 1 twin, sharing bath.
price	£60-£65. Singles £30-£35.
meals	Dinner, 4 courses, £25. Good pubs/restaurants 1.5 miles.
closed	Rarely.
directions	A346 Marlborough-Salisbury. At r'bout ending Burbage bypass, B3087 Pewsey road. Right at x-roads 0.3 miles on; 1st on right.

Felicity & Bill Mather
Westcourt Bottom,
165 Westcourt,
Burbage, Malborough,
Wiltshire SN8 3BW

tel   01672 810924
fax   01672 810924
e-mail   westcourt.b-and-b@virgin.net
web   www.westcourtbottom.co.uk

Map 3   Entry 506

Glebe House

A generous and attractive restoration of a 19th-century cottage, with landscaped garden and views to Spye Park. You are in a peaceful hamlet yet near Lacock and other national treasures. Ginny radiates charm and spoils you with thoughtful touches: homemade biscuits by the bed, homemade soaps by the bath. The drawing room is vastly comfortable with log fires, coral sofas, choice pieces. Bedrooms are elegant; wind up the stair past the family portraits to soft eiderdowns and toile de Jouy. Birds trill in the garden, the parrot chats by the Aga and there are three guest-loving dogs. *Children over six welcome.*

rooms	2: 1 double, 1 twin both with separate bath.
price	£55-£60. Singles £30-£35.
meals	Dinner, 3 courses, from £18.
closed	Christmas & New Year.
directions	From Devizes-Chippenham A342. Follow Chittoe & Spye Park. On over cross roads onto narrow lane. House 2nd on left.

Mrs G Scrope
Glebe House,
Chittoe,
Chippenham,
Wiltshire SN15 2EL

tel   01380 850864
mobile   07767 608841
e-mail   gscrope@aol.com
web   www.glebehouse-chittoe.co.uk

Map 3   Entry 507

Wiltshire

Burghope Manor

An impressively handsome medieval manor house. Arched, mullioned windows, jutting gables, tall chimneys and a porticoed entrance raise expectations of an interior that are not disappointed. There's a vast Tudor fireplace with Elizabethan graffiti, a whole gallery of ancestral oil paintings and some fascinating old furniture and artefacts. You dine in spring with the scent of wisteria and lilac wafting through the dining room windows. Bedrooms are plush with big beds and some modern touches, views sail over the grounds.

Alcombe Manor

Down a maze of magical lanes discover this hamlet and its 17th-century manor house: a deeply romantic place. Panelling, wooden floors, a couple of medieval windows, scattered sofas, great log fires — it is intimate, inviting, warm. A fine oak staircase leads to light and charming bedrooms, all a good size; carpeted floors creak companionably and every ancient leaded window has a dreamy garden view... five acres of English perfection, no less, with topiary and a stream dashing through. Your hosts are delightful, the peace is palpable, and you are just five miles from Bath and all its treasures.

rooms	3: 2 doubles, 1 twin, all with bath/shower.
price	£95-£110.
meals	Dinner for groups only.
closed	Rarely.
directions	From Bath A36 Warminster road for 5 miles, left onto B3108, under railway bridge & up hill. 1st right, turn off Winsley bypass into old village, then 1st left, into lane marked 'except for access'.

rooms	3: 2 twins both with separate bath/shower; 1 single sharing bath.
price	From £70. Singles by arrangement.
meals	Pubs nearby. Dinner by arrangement.
closed	Rarely.
directions	M4 junc. 17; A4 to Bath through Box; right for Middle Hill & Ditteridge; 200 yds, left signed Alcombe. Up hill for 0.5 miles, fork right; 200 yds on left.

John & Elizabeth Denning
Burghope Manor,
Winsley,
Bradford-on-Avon,
Wiltshire BA15 2LA

tel   01225 723557
fax   01225 723113
e-mail   info@burghope.co.uk
web   www.burghope.co.uk

Simon & Victoria Morley
Alcombe Manor,
Box,
Corsham,
Wiltshire SN13 8QQ

tel   01225 743850
mobile   07887 855634
e-mail   morley@alcombebox.fsnet.co.uk

Map 3 Entry 508

Map 3 Entry 509

Wiltshire

The Labyrinth

A mere suggestion of entrance, a hint of accessibility, the doorway entices all but the least curious (and a bit nervous). The interior is a study in the social impact of prolonged darkness, for there is no other light but that from the door. In extremis, which is where most people find themselves, you may use a torch to guide you along the labyrinth of tunnels. Some use the Minotaur's Cave trick: a piece of string unravelled as you go. Some guests, despite every caution, have never emerged. But that's part of the fun. Our first inspector there has not returned, so we must assume she is enjoying herself.

The Coach House

In an ancient hamlet a few miles north of Bath, an impeccable conversion of an early 19th-century barn. Bedrooms are fresh and cosy with sloping ceilings; the drawing room is elegant with porcelain and chintz, its pale walls the ideal background for striking displays of fresh flowers. Sliding glass doors lead to a south-facing patio... then to a well-groomed croquet lawn bordered by flowers, with vegetable garden, tennis court, woodland and paddock beyond. Helga and David, generous and kind, tell you all you need to know about the region, from the splendours of Bath just south to the golf courses so nearby.

rooms	Who knows? If you should return, please call and let us know.
price	Your sanity.
meals	Fresh root vegetables available.
closed	Never.
directions	Knowing a girl called Ariadne seems to help; otherwise a ball of garden string is recommended.

rooms	2: 1 double, 1 twin/double, sharing bath (2nd room for same party).
price	£60–£70. Singles £35.
meals	Dinner £16. Also excellent local pubs.
closed	Rarely.
directions	From M4 junc. 17, A429 for Chippenham. A420 to Bristol (East) & Castle Combe. After 6.3 miles, right into Upper Wraxall. Sharp left opp. village green; at end of drive.

King Minos of Crete
The Labyrinth,
Ominous Door,
Shady Woods,
Wiltshire 1ML 0ST

e-mail minos&minotaur@labyrinth.co.uk

Helga & David Venables
The Coach House,
Upper Wraxall,
Bath,
Wiltshire SN14 7AG

tel 01225 891026
e-mail david@dvenables6.wanadoo.co.uk
web www.upperwraxallcoachhouse.co.uk

Map 3 Entry 511

Wiltshire

Manor Farm

Farmyard heaven in the Cotswolds. A 17th-century manor farmhouse in 550 arable acres; horses in the paddock, dozing dogs in the yard, tumbling blooms outside the door and a perfectly tended village, with duck pond, a short walk away. What beautiful bedrooms – softly lit, with muted colours, plump goose down pillows and the crispest linen. Breakfast in front of the fire or in the garden is a banquet of delights, thanks to Victoria. This is the postcard England that we all dream of, with Castle Combe and Lacock nearby – and there's a tot of whisky before bed. *Children over 12 welcome.*

Manor Farm

You know at once that to stay here is a treat! The road through the sleepy Wiltshire village brings you to a delectable Queen Anne house with smooth, stripey lawns. Generous windows give the creamy front a wide-eyed look; tall, elegant chimneys top the mossy grey roof. Clare spoils her guests. Multi-talented, an artist too, she takes everything in her stride in the most relaxed and charming manner. Breakfast is served in the big yellow kitchen. The pretty drawing room has an endearingly lived-in feel and the bedrooms are friendly and fresh, with creaky floors and original painted panelling.

rooms	3: 2 doubles, both with bath; 1 twin with separate bath.
price	£64. Singles £35.
meals	Excellent pub 1 mile. Wild venison suppers by special arrangement.
closed	Christmas.
directions	From M4 A429 to Cirencester (junc. 17). After 200 yds, 1st left for Grittleton; there, follow signs to Alderton. Farmhouse near church.

rooms	2: 1 double, 1 twin with bath (let to members of same party). Further bathroom available.
price	£60-£80. Singles from £40.
meals	Good pub/restaurant 200 yds.
closed	Christmas & New Year.
directions	M4 exit 17. North on A429 for Malmesbury, right on B4042. Right after 3 miles to Little Somerford. Past pub, right at crossroads, 50 yds on, house behind tall wall.

Victoria Lippiatt-Onslow
Manor Farm,
Alderton,
Chippenham,
Wiltshire SN14 6NL
tel   01666 840271
fax   07721 415824
e-mail   victoria.lippiatt@btinternet.com
web   www.themanorfarm.co.uk

Clare Inskip
Manor Farm,
Little Somerford,
Malmesbury,
Wiltshire SN15 5JW
tel   01666 822140
mobile   07970 892344
e-mail   clareinskip@hotmail.com

Map 3 Entry 512

Map 3 Entry 513

Wiltshire

Winkworth Farm

Tony's farmer's handshake and beaming smile disarm you instantly; Doi is friendly, professional and loves doing B&B. The vine-hung, thyme-carpeted arbour and gazebo are magical in summer, and there is much in the deliciously walled garden to hold your attention. The interior is inviting, too. Gently decorated bedrooms have space, views, flowers and old photographs; all are hugely comfortable. The dark blue dining room has wooden floors and a solid oak table with tapestry chairs while the drawing room has French windows overlooking the garden, and an open fire. A happy, easy-going place.

Bullocks Horn Cottage

An exceptional house that the Legges have turned into a haven of peace and seclusion. Large sofas devour you and fires warm you; in summer, you eat in the cool shade of the arbour, draped in wisteria and climbing roses. The garden, featured in various magazines, is exceptional, and the conservatory with its huge oak table explodes with flowers and colour and lovely views. Garden veg and herbs are used at dinner to magnificent effect. Bedrooms are quiet with lovely views, Liz and Colin are easy and young at heart; within minutes you'll feel like a visiting friend.
Minimum stay two nights July-August.

rooms	3: 2 doubles, both with bath; 1 triple with separate bath/shower.
price	£50-£60. Singles from £35.
meals	Good pubs 1-5 miles.
closed	Christmas.
directions	From Malmesbury B4042 for Wootton Bassett. Left to Lea. In Lea, right opp. school. House along drive through fields, 1 mile from road.

rooms	2: 1 twin with bath; 1 twin with separate bath.
price	£65-£70. Singles £40.
meals	Dinner, 2 courses, £18. BYO.
closed	Christmas & Easter.
directions	From A429, B4040 thro' Charlton, past Horse & Groom. 0.5 miles, left signed 'Bullocks Horn No Through Road'. On to end of lane. Right; 1st on left.

Tony & Doi Newman
Winkworth Farm,
Lea,
Malmesbury,
Wiltshire SN16 9NH
tel   01666 823267
e-mail   doinewman@winkworth89.freeserve.co.uk
web   www.winkworthfarm.com

Colin & Liz Legge
Bullocks Horn Cottage,
Charlton,
Malmesbury,
Wiltshire SN16 9DZ
tel   01666 577600
e-mail   legge@bullockshorn.clara.co.uk
web   www.bullockshorn.co.uk

Map 3 Entry 514

Map 3 Entry 515

Wiltshire

Manor Farmhouse

On a fine oak "antique of the future", Helen serves you breakfasts that will have you hoping to stay just one more day… and her delicious dinners are matched by Philip's wines. Lovely flagstoned floors, little window seats, a carved lintel that dates the house as 1703, a sweeping open garden with a high wall that abuts the church and so many thoughtful touches: lavender bags, roses and scrummy shortbread, newspapers at breakfast, cosy chairs in the guest sitting room, a winter fire. It is a deeply relaxing place, unpretentious yet expertly run. *Children over eight welcome.*

1 Cove House

Dotted around the Threlfalls' half of the manor house are fashion prints, vintage clothes, hatboxes and dressmakers' dummies – Valerie, kind and outgoing, lectures on fashion history. Expect William Morris fabrics and muslin at sash windows, a baby grand in the swagged ballroom, a gabled guest sitting room in the attic. The good-sized Chinese bedroom has curios brought back from travels; the twin room is smaller. A conservatory looks onto a huge lawn; seek out the small Victorian vegetable garden with gravel walkways and the illuminated Wendy house tucked away beneath giant yews.

rooms	2: 1 double with shower; 1 family room with separate bath/shower.	rooms	2: 1 double with bath; 1 twin with separate shower.
price	£65-£70. Singles £45.	price	£58-£60. Singles £37.
meals	Dinner from £18.50. Village pub 0.5 miles.	meals	Good pubs 3-minute walk; excellent restaurants a short drive.
closed	Christmas & New Year.	closed	Christmas & New Year.
directions	A429 Malmesbury to Cirencester. In Crudwell, at Plough, right for Minety & Oaksey. Straight on; left between church & tithe barn pillars.	directions	From Cirencester, A419 for Swindon for 4 miles. Turn off dual carriageway for Ashton Keynes. Left immed. after White Hart, 100 yds on, left through stone pillars, house on right.

Helen & Philip Carter
Manor Farmhouse,
Crudwell,
Malmesbury,
Wiltshire SN16 9ER
tel   01666 577375
e-mail user785566@aol.com

Valerie & Roger Threlfall
1 Cove House,
Ashton Keynes,
Wiltshire SN6 6NS
tel   01285 861226
fax   01285 861226
e-mail roger@covehouse.co.uk

Map 3 Entry 516

Map 3 Entry 517

Worcestershire

Old Country Farm

Ella's passion for this remote, tranquil place – and the environment in general – is infectious. She believes the house was once home to a Saxon chief. Certainly, it has beams dating from 1400; since then it has evolved into the rambling mix of russet stone and colour-washed brick you see today. The kitchen is warm and delightful, with a big, gleaming gateleg table and a pleasingly overcrowded dresser. Friendly, low-ceilinged bedrooms are simple and rustic. Ella's parents collected rare plants and the garden is full of hellebores and snowdrops; roe deer and barn owls flit about in the surrounding woods.

Home Farm

A half-moated house in a magical spot: the timbered part — 14th century and listed — peeps through the trees as you approach. Gorgeous in summer (terrace, gardens, ducks), relaxing all year round, a special B&B. Antiques, soft colours and an open fire in the guest sitting room, fresh fabrics and uncluttered comfort in the bedrooms and peaceful views to the Abberley Hills and beyond. Roger and Anne are generous hosts and give you local bacon at breakfast, stewed fruits and jam from their plums. Make time for Great Witley, the finest baroque church in England. *Children over 10 welcome.*

rooms	3: 1 double with bath; 1 double with separate shower; 1 double with separate bath.
price	£60–£90. Singles £35–£55.
meals	Good pubs/restaurants 3 miles.
closed	Rarely.
directions	From Worcester A4103 for 11 miles; B4220 for Ledbury. After leaving Cradley, left at top of hill for Mathon, right for Coddington; house 0.25 miles on right.

rooms	3: 1 twin with bath; 1 twin with separate bath/shower; 1 single with shower.
price	£65–£70. Singles £35–£40.
meals	Good pubs 1-5 miles.
closed	Christmas & New Year.
directions	On entering Great Witley from Worcester on A443, left onto B4197 to Martley; after 0.25 miles 1st right on sharp left-hand bend by grass triangle/chevrons; up hill 1st house on right.

	Ella Quincy
	Old Country Farm,
	Mathon,
	Malvern,
	Worcestershire WR13 5PS
tel	01886 880867
e-mail	ella@oldcountryhouse.co.uk
web	www.oldcountryhouse.co.uk

	Roger & Anne Kendrick
	Home Farm,
	Great Witley,
	Worcester,
	Worcestershire WR6 6JJ
tel	01299 896825
fax	01299 896176
e-mail	anniekendrick@hotmail.com
web	www.homefarmbandb.com

Map 8 Entry 518

Map 8 Entry 519

Yorkshire

Cliffe Hall

What remains is the Victorian section of an earlier mansion, embellished by Richard's family in 1858. Inside, a beautifully proportioned and charming family home: huge reception rooms, plasterwork ceilings, acres of sofas, family portraits, cases of books. Bedrooms are traditional and uncontrived, bathrooms carpeted, twin beds super-comfy; large windows look onto the glorious grounds (tennis? croquet?) and a lawn that runs down to the Tees where you fish for trout. Soft, timeless grandeur, visiting thesps, two sweet dogs and a hostess who is as special as her house.

rooms	2 twins, both with separate bath.
price	£70. Singles £35.
meals	Good pub 1 mile.
closed	10 December–1 January.
directions	From A1, exit onto B6275. north for 4.2 miles. Into drive (on left before Piercebridge); 1st right fork.

Caroline & Richard Wilson
Cliffe Hall,
Piercebridge,
Darlington,
Yorkshire DL2 3SR
tel   01325 374322
fax   01325 374947

Map 12 Entry 520

Dunsa Manor

Come when there are drifts of snowdrops up the drive. A ha-ha divides the lawns and terraces from the farm; the house is framed by trees. Built by Ignatius Bonomi in 1841, it has been in the family for 140 years. Striking reception rooms (Shaheen had to promise her mother-in-law not to strip off the old Coles wallpaper) face south to the hills. Generous bedrooms are furnished with antiques and you can bathe in a candelabra-lit tub or under an ultra-modern shower. Shaheen is warm and witty and an accomplished cook. Great country for walks and rides: hire a horse or bring your own.

rooms	2: 1 double with separate shower; 1 twin/triple with separate bath.
price	£70–£75.
meals	Dinner, 4 courses, £30.
closed	Rarely.
directions	Off A66 west of Scotch corner. Left for Dalton 1.75 miles. After 200 yds look for stone wall & black iron gates on left. 1st drive on left.

Shaheen Burnett
Dunsa Manor,
Dalton,
Richmond,
Yorkshire DL11 7HE
tel   01325 718251
mobile   07817 028237
e-mail   shaheendunsa@aol.com
web   www.dunsamanor.com

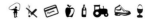

Map 12 Entry 521

Yorkshire

Hill Top

Books, magazines, bath essences, biscuits by the bed – Christina is lovely and spoils you as she would a friend. Her pretty, listed, limestone farmhouse dates from 1820 and is deceptively big. Ivory walls are a perfect foil for some good furniture and paintings. Bedrooms are light and airy; the main bedroom is part of a suite separated from the house by a latch door and nicely self-contained. Newsham is an AONB and the panoramic views over rolling countryside are superb. Waterfalls, moorland, castles beckon – and this is a handy stopover to and from Scotland. *Babes in arms and children over seven welcome.*

rooms	2: 1 twin with bath & shower; 1 twin sharing bath (let to same party only).
price	£60. Singles £30.
meals	Dinner, 2-3 courses, £12.50-£15.50. Good pub/restaurant 1.5 miles.
closed	Christmas & New Year.
directions	From Scotch Corner west on A66. Approx. 7 miles on, down hill. Left to Newsham. Through village; 2nd left for Helwith. House on right at top, name on gate.

Christina Farmer
Hill Top,
Newsham,
Richmond,
Yorkshire DL11 7QX

| tel | 01833 621513 |
| e-mail | plow67@tiscali.co.uk |

Map 12   Entry 522

The Old Rectory

The views are over glorious Teesdale, the village – solid in stone and 'twixt two borders – is perfect, and the cricket club bowls from one county to another! Across the pretty cobbled yard, up a steep stone stair, is an enchanting bedroom in the coach house: a lofty, cross-beamed ceiling, fresh fabrics at little windows, a country bathroom, coir and crisp linen, a big bed. Angela's watercolours add to the artistic mood and, outside, her green fingers have crafted a lovely walled garden. Inside the rectory, antiques and oils (mostly of horses). James and Angela are great hosts and you'll eat well.

rooms	3: 1 twin with separate bath; 1 single (let to same party). Coach house: 1 double with bath/shower.
price	£80. Singles £45.
meals	Dinner, 4 courses, £27.50. Supper £17.50. Pubs & restaurants 3-10 miles.
closed	Christmas & New Year.
directions	South off A66 for Barningham, 10 miles west of Scotch Corner. Immed. left for Barningham; 2 miles; left into courtyard 100 yds from T-junc. in village.

James & Angie Delahooke
The Old Rectory,
Barningham,
Richmond,
Yorkshire DL11 7DW

tel	01833 621122
mobile	07770 674651
e-mail	jdelahooke@aol.com

Map 12   Entry 523

Yorkshire

Millgate House

This will take your breath away. One moment you are on a town pavement facing a sober Georgian front; the next, in a lofty room, elegant with Adam fireplace, fine mouldings, period furniture and myriad prints and paintings. Bedrooms and bathrooms are similarly splendid, with sumptuous fabrics, cast-iron baths and exquisite Swale valley views; breakfasts are superb. As if this were not enough, there is the most enchanting award-wining walled garden adorned with hostas, clematis, old roses – a feast for the senses in summer. Tim and Austin are engaging hosts.

Brandymires

The Wensleydale hills lie framed through the windows of the time-warp bedrooms; no TV, no fuss, just utter calm. In the middle of the Yorkshire Dales National Park, this is a glorious spot for walkers. Gail and Ann bake their own bread and make jams and marmalade, and their delicious, well-priced dinners are prepared with fresh, local produce and served at your own table. Two bedrooms, not in their first flush of youth, have four-posters; all have the views. If you're arriving by car, take the 'over-the-top' road from Buckden to Hawes for the most stunning countryside. *Minimum stay two nights.*

rooms	3: 1 double, 1 twin, both with bath/shower; 1 double with separate bath/shower & sitting room.
price	£85. Singles £60.
meals	Pub/restaurant 250 yds.
closed	Never.
directions	Next door to Halifax Building Society, opposite side of Barclays at bottom of Market Place. Green front door with small brass plaque.

rooms	3: 1 twin, 2 four-posters, sharing two bath/shower rooms.
price	£44. Singles £27.
meals	Dinner, 4 courses, £16 (not Thursday); good value wine list. Good restaurant 5-minute walk.
closed	November-mid-February.
directions	300 yds off A684, on road north out of Hawes, signed Muker & Hardraw.

Austin Lynch & Tim Culkin
Millgate House,
Richmond,
Yorkshire DL10 4JN

tel   01748 823571
mobile   07951 940939
e-mail   oztim@millgatehouse.demon.co.uk
web   www.millgatehouse.com

Gail Ainley & Ann Macdonald
Brandymires,
Muker Road,
Hawes,
Yorkshire DL8 3PR

tel   01969 667482

Map 12   Entry 524

Map 12   Entry 525

Yorkshire

Rookery Cottage

Before you, the perfect English country village with close-clipped verges; beyond the fruit-treed garden, the glorious Fell. Four 17th-century almshouses have become this sweet retreat run by kind Ursula: a Mrs Tiggy Winkle house in which one low-panelled room leads to another. Waxed oak and shining silver, frilled flounces, a generous bath, Floris soaps, decorative flowers on the basin and wc... it is warm, cottagey, feminine. Breakfast brings homemade jams and marmalades, perhaps kedgeree made from Ronnie's catch of the day. Dine at the old pub opposite, one of the north country's finest.

Lovesome Hill Farm

Who could resist home-grown beef casserole followed by sticky toffee pudding? This is a working farm and the Pearsons the most genuine farming folk imaginable; even in the mayhem of the lambing season they greet you with homemade biscuits and tea. Their farmhouse is as unpretentious as they are, and bedrooms (four in converted outbuildings) are plain and old-fashioned, with garden and hill views. The A167 traffic hum mingles with the odd sheepdog bark; you are brilliantly placed for the dales. Good for walkers, families, and business people.

rooms	2: 1 twin, 1 double, sharing bath.
price	£65. Singles from £45.
meals	Packed lunch £5. Pub 20 yds.
closed	Rarely.
directions	From Masham, A6108. Leyburn 8 miles on. House on left, opp. Blue Lion Country Inn.

rooms	5: 1 twin, 1 double, 1 single, 1 family, all with shower. Gate Cottage: 1 double with bath.
price	£56. Singles £30-£40. Gate Cottage: £72.
meals	Dinner 2-3 courses, £15-£20. BYO. Packed lunch for walkers. Good pub/restaurant 4 miles.
closed	December-February.
directions	From Northallerton, A167 north for Darlington for 4 miles. House on right, signed.

Mrs Ursula Bussey
Rookery Cottage,
East Witton,
Leyburn,
Yorkshire DL8 4SN

tel	01969 622918
fax	01969 622918
e-mail	b&tb@rookerycottage.co.uk
web	www.rookerycottage.co.uk

John & Mary Pearson
Lovesome Hill Farm,
Lovesome Hill,
Northallerton,
Yorkshire DL6 2PB

tel	01609 772311
fax	01609 772311
e-mail	pearsonlhf@care4free.net
web	www.lovesomehill.co.uk

Map 12 Entry 526

Map 12 Entry 527

Yorkshire

Busby House

A peaceful spirit, warmth and friendliness pervades this elegant farmhouse which incorporates the former cottage and dairy buildings. Anne goes to great lengths to make you comfortable, giving you deliciously traditional dinners and fresh cakes for tea. The kitchen has a New England feel; the good-sized bedrooms are pale and pretty, and look south over the large garden and the glorious hills beyond. You will be drawn to explore the gentle, rolling dales, the moors and the coastline. York, Durham and other fascinating historic places are nearby.

Stonebeck Gate Farm

Over the glorious moors to Little Fryup and this farm. Free-range dogs and boys scramble and amble in an atmosphere of happy chaos and your hosts are the nicest people: warm, hard-working Jill and unflappable Andrew, who farms. The listed flagged yard was filmed by the BBC for posterity but don't expect anything fancy inside: utilitarian furniture and flowery carpets welcome dripping Barbours and hiking boots. Bedrooms have space and dreamy views; bathrooms are internal but snug. There may be homemade muffins at breakfast and own beef and lamb at dinner; Jill's a super cook.

rooms	2: 1 twin, 1 double, both with separate bath.
price	£85-£90. Singles £55.
meals	Dinner from £25. BYO. Good pubs/restaurants 7 miles.
closed	December-January.
directions	North on A19; A172 for Stokesley. Pass sign on right to Carlton & Busby. House 0.5 miles further on left, with 2 red triangular reflectors each side of tree-lined drive.

rooms	2: 1 double, 1 family, both with separate bath.
price	£55. Singles £35.
meals	Dinner, 3 courses, £17.50. Packed lunch available.
closed	Rarely.
directions	From Malton, A170 Pickering road to Cropton. Thro' Rosedale Abbey, up onto moor & over cattle grid; 1.5 miles on, right for Fryup; 2 miles, right at T-junc. Farm 1st on left, signed Castleton.

Anne Gloag
Busby House,
Stokesley,
Yorkshire TS9 5LB
tel   01642 710425
fax   01642 713838

Jill Kelly
Stonebeck Gate Farm,
Little Fryup,
Danby, Whitby,
Yorkshire YO21 2NS
tel   01287 660363
fax   01287 669363
e-mail   jill@stonebeckgatefarm.co.uk
web   www.stonebeckgatefarm.com

Map 12 Entry 528

Map 13 Entry 529

Yorkshire

Holly Croft

Huge kindness and thoughtful touches (hot water bottles, lifts to the pub, cake and tea on arrival) make this home special. The décor is Edwardian plush – wallpapers striped and floral, curtains lavish – the comfort indisputable. The double has an elaborate floral-and-rose headboard with matching drapes, there are bathrobes in fitted wardrobes, big showers and generous breakfasts – own jams, Yorkshire teas, kippers if you choose – are served in the conservatory or round the polished mahogany table. After a bracing clifftop walk return to a homely sitting room and a log fire.

Rectory Farmhouse

Walk from the front door straight onto the North Yorkshire Moors and leave your car behind – it's only a 30-minute stride down the fields to the train station and Steam Railway. Michael, Heather and their son David have been here since 1997; along with dogs, cats, horses, rabbit … and fresh eggs from the hens. The bright guest sitting room has a roaring log fire, there are separate tables in the dining room, comfy bedrooms and country florals. Enjoy proper Yorkshire dinner (organic and locally-sourced). Breakfasts are just as good. Good value, superb walking and great riding, too. *Children over eight welcome.*

	Holly Croft
rooms	2: 1 twin with shower; 1 double with separate bath & shower.
price	£65. Singles from £40.
meals	Pub 600 yds; more within 2 miles.
closed	Rarely.
directions	A171 from Scarborough to Whitby; at Scalby x-roads, by tennis courts, take road on right. Signed 500 yds on right.

	Rectory Farmhouse
rooms	3: 1 double, 1 twin/double, both with shower; 1 twin/double with bath and shower.
price	£48-£60. Singles £30.
meals	Dinner, 2 courses, £12. Packed lunch £3-£5. Good pub in village.
closed	Christmas.
directions	From A169 take Lockton/Levisham road. Once through Lockton, look for house sign after 0.75 miles on right, in Levisham.

John & Christine Goodall
Holly Croft,
28 Station Road,
Scalby,
Scarborough,
Yorkshire YO13 0QA
tel   01723 375376
fax   01723 360563
web   www.holly-croft.co.uk

Michael & Heather Holt
Rectory Farmhouse,
Levisham,
Pickering,
Yorkshire YO18 7NL
tel   01751 460491
e-mail   stay@levisham.com
web   www.levisham.com

Map 13 Entry 530

Map 13 Entry 531

Yorkshire

Hunters Hill

The moors lie behind this solid, stone farmhouse, five yards from the National Park, in farmland and woodland with fine views… marvellous walking country. The house is full of light and flowers; bedrooms are pretty but not overly grand. The attractive sitting room has deeply comfortable old sofas, armchairs and fine furniture, while rich colours, hunting prints and candles at dinner give a warm and cosy feel. The Orr family has poured a good deal of affection into this house and the result is a home that's happy and remarkably easy to relax in… Wonderful.

rooms	2: 1 twin/double with shower; 1 twin/double with separate bath.
price	£70. Singles from £45.
meals	Dinner, 3 courses, £30. Pub/restaurant 500 yds.
closed	Rarely.
directions	From A170 Kirkbymoorside & Pickering road, to Sinnington. On village green, keep river on left & fork right between cottages. Up lane, bearing right up hill. House past church beyond farm buildings.

The Orr Family
Hunters Hill,
Sinnington,
York,
Yorkshire YO62 6SF
tel   01751 431196
e-mail   ejorr@tiscali.co.uk

Map 13 Entry 532

Barugh House

In a friendly village, a listed Georgian house that is a joy for sybarites. The well-travelled Woods look after you immaculately – plump pillows and towelling robes, fresh flowers and magazines, treats for your dog and superb breakfasts for you. Dinners may be of roast rack of Brawby lamb and almond cake with homemade ice cream. Bedrooms are strikingly elegant, views sweep over the garden to the moors and the sitting room has an open fire. Colourful lupins stand proud in the garden that is Janie's delight; massed roses and dreamy sunsets vie for your attention. Special.

rooms	2: 1 twin, 1 double, sharing bath.
price	£70. Singles £35.
meals	Dinner, 4 courses, £20. Packed lunch £6.
closed	Rarely.
directions	From Malton, B1257 for Helmsley. Through Amotherby then right to Kirkbymoorside. On for 3.25 miles. At Great Barugh, left at T-junc. House on right, 50 yds past pub.

Janie Wood
Barugh House,
Great Barugh,
Malton,
Yorkshire YO17 6UZ
tel   01653 668615
e-mail   barughhouse@aol.com

Map 13 Entry 533

Yorkshire

Manor Farm

Pass the stables into the scullery and the sweet smell of saddles and tack; enter a warm kitchen where muslin-wrapped hams hang to dry. This is special: a thriving and immaculate working farm with a relaxed, artistic owner. Low-ceilinged bedrooms are stuffed with colour, old armchairs and thick rugs, books and rose china. There's a garden room for summer breakfasts – home-baked bread from a neighbour, eggs and bacon home-grown – and a charming garden tucked deep in the wedge of Thixendale. Wonderful for those seeking a remote escape. *Ask about upholstery courses.*

Low Penhowe

With the Turners at the helm, you are on a safe ship. They see to everything so perfectly – the crispness of the breakfast bacon, the freshness of the home eggs and bread, the positioning of the bowls of flowers, the stoking of the fire in your drawing room. Bedrooms fresh, pretty and polished; bathrooms dazzling. The house faces north, with its back tucked under a protective hill, and has views that go on for miles – Castle Howard and the North York Moors to the front and, dotted all around, abbeys, castles, rivers, ruins and woods. The next-door farm runs a conservation scheme and the place hums with wildlife.

rooms	2: 1 twin with sitting room & bath; 1 double sharing bath (let to same party only).
price	£60. Singles £30.
meals	Packed lunches £5. Good village pub.
closed	Rarely.
directions	Left at top of Garrowby Hill A166; 4 miles to Thixendale. Thro' village, farm on left. 10 miles from Malton, thro' Birdsall on unclassified roads.

rooms	2: 1 double with bath; 1 twin/double with separate bath.
price	£60. Singles from £35.
meals	Good pubs within 2 miles. Packed lunches £6.
closed	Christmas.
directions	A64 at Whitwell on the Hill, right for Kirkham. Over the crossing & Derwent, pass Kirkham Priory & Stone Trough Inn. Right at T-junc, left for Burythorpe, straight over x-roads, 700 yds; right up drive.

	Gilda & Charles Brader
	Manor Farm,
	Thixendale,
	Malton,
	Yorkshire YO17 9TG
tel	01377 288315
fax	01377 288315
e-mail	info@manorfarmthixendale.co.uk
web	www.manorfarmthixendale.co.uk

	Christopher & Philippa Turner
	Low Penhowe,
	Burythorpe,
	Malton,
	Yorkshire YO17 9LU
tel	01653 658336
mobile	07900 227000
e-mail	lowpenhowebandb@aol.com
web	www.bedandbreakfastyorkshire.co.uk

Map 13 Entry 534

Map 13 Entry 535

Yorkshire

No 54

The welcome tea and homemade cakes sets the tone for your stay; this is a happy place. No. 54 was once two cottages on the Duncombe estate; now it's a single house and Lizzie has made the most of the space. Buttermilk walls, be-rugged flagged floors, country furniture, open fires and a stylish lack of clutter. A single-storey extension has been fashioned into three extra bedrooms around a secluded courtyard. Thoughtful extras – magazines, cafetiere, an umbrella – make you feel cherished, and the breakfasts will fuel the most serious of walks. Make a house party and bring your friends!

rooms	4: 1 double with bath/shower; 1 double, 1 twin both with shower; 1 single with separate shower.
price	£74. Singles from £29.50.
meals	Dinner, 2-3 courses, £20-£22. Good restaurants 10-minute walk.
closed	Christmas & New Year
directions	A170 to Helmsley; right at mini r'bout in centre, facing The Crown; house 500 yds along A170, on right.

Lizzie Would
No 54,
Bondgate,
Helmsley,
Yorkshire YO62 5EZ

tel	01439 771533
fax	01439 771533
e-mail	lizzie@no54.co.uk
web	www.no54.co.uk

Map 13 Entry 536

Sproxton Hall

Drive through a stone archway into an old courtyard; the 17th-century beamed farmhouse, once attached to Rievaulx Abbey, is still very much part of a working farm. Inside, a magnificent grandfather clock and a genuine Yorkshire farming welcome from Andrew and Margaret. The guests' sitting and dining rooms are full of 18th-century antiques and the bedrooms are frilled, flowery and comfortable, with lovely views; the double has a half-tester bedstead with a soaring canopy. A great place to stay, run with graceful efficiency by Margaret. *Children over 10 welcome.*

rooms	3: 1 twin, 1 double, both with shower; 1 twin with separate bath & shower.
price	£64-£72. Singles £45.
meals	Excellent pubs & restaurants 1-3 miles.
closed	Christmas & New Year.
directions	From Thirsk A170 for 12 miles. Right onto B1257 (1 mile before Helmsley); 50 yds on, left by church. House at end of 'No Through Road'.

Margaret & Andrew Wainwright
Sproxton Hall,
Sproxton,
Helmsley,
Yorkshire YO62 5EQ

tel	01439 770225
fax	01439 771373
e-mail	info@sproxtonhall.demon.co.uk
web	www.sproxtonhall.co.uk

Map 13 Entry 537

Yorkshire

Shallowdale House

Wide windows frame an outstanding view. This spot, on the edge of the North York Moors National Park, was chosen for its outlook and the house designed to make the most of the scenery... views stretch from the Pennines to the Wolds. Big, stylish, modern, the house is set in two acres of hillside garden. Light floods the uncluttered, elegant rooms; the drawing room has an open fire in winter; generous bedrooms and bathrooms are attractive and comfortable. Phillip and Anton love this work, so you will be treated like angels and served freshly cooked dinners of outstanding quality. *Children over 12 welcome.*

The Old Rectory

The house was a rectory first, then the residence of the Bishops of Whitby. Both Turner and Ruskin stayed here as guests of Reverend William Kingsley, cousin of author Charles. Built of warm brick it's surrounded on three sides by rambling gardens, rare old trees, a tennis court, orchard and croquet lawn. The elegant, deep pink dining room looks south over the garden and you have use of the superb drawing room with its fine Venetian window and a particularly enticing window-seat. A gracious, comfortable house with big, beautiful rooms and approachable, charming owners. *Children over 10 welcome.*

rooms	3: 2 twins/doubles, both with bath/shower; 1 double with separate bath/shower.
price	£82-£99. Singles £65-£75.
meals	Dinner, 4 courses, £30.
closed	Rarely.
directions	From Thirsk, A19 south, then 'caravan route' via Coxwold & Byland Abbey. 1st house on left, just before Ampleforth.

rooms	2: 1 twin with wc & separate bath & shower; 1 double with separate bath & dressing room.
price	From £60. Singles from £35.
meals	Good pub opposite.
closed	Rarely.
directions	Take A168 (Northallerton road) off A19; over r'bout; left into village; house opposite pub, next to church.

Anton van der Horst & Phillip Gill
Shallowdale House,
West End,
Ampleforth,
Yorkshire YO62 4DY

tel	01439 788325
fax	01439 788885
e-mail	stay@shallowdalehouse.co.uk
web	www.shallowdalehouse.co.uk

Tim & Caroline O'Connor-Fenton
The Old Rectory,
South Kilvington,
Thirsk,
Yorkshire YO7 2NL

tel	01845 526153
fax	01845 523849
e-mail	ocfenton@freenet.co.uk

Map 12 Entry 538

Map 12 Entry 539

Yorkshire

Thorpe Lodge

Bring together a designer and an avid gardener, give them a Grade II-listed Georgian house in the gateway to the Dales and you have an classic English family home. Visitors use the South Wing with a separate entrance via the mediterranean-style courtyard, and dine, deliciously, in the green-painted winter dining room by an open fire... or, in summer, in the cool white dining room overlooking the courtyard. Bedrooms are traditional and vast – big enough to lounge in – both have long garden views. The Jowitts are impressive hosts who do everything with massive care and attention to detail.

Lawrence House

A perfectly proper house run with faultless precision by John and Harriet – former wine importer and interior decorator respectively. The walk to Fountains Abbey and Studley Royal – the most complete remains of a Cistercian abbey in Britain – is a treat: you are spoiled for things to do and can consider your options in the manicured garden. Magnificent countryside, with views and deer all around. Two generously decorated bedrooms and bathrooms have thoughtful touches such as bathrobes and toiletries, and you can dine before an open fire. *Golf, riding and clay pigeon shooting can be arranged.*

rooms	2 twins/doubles, both with bath & shower.
price	From £80.
meals	Dinner, £25. Good pubs/restaurants nearby.
closed	Rarely.
directions	Near southern end of Ripon bypass, turn to Bishop Monkton. After 0.75 miles, gateway on left turning into wood; signed.

rooms	2: 1 twin/double, 1 twin, both with bath.
price	£110. Singles £70.
meals	Dinner £28.
closed	Christmas & New Year.
directions	A1 to Ripon. B6265/Pateley Bridge road for 2 miles. Left into Studley Roger. House last on right.

Tommy & Juliet Jowitt
Thorpe Lodge,
Ripon,
Yorkshire HG4 3LU
tel 01765 602088
fax 01765 602835
e-mail jowitt@btinternet.com
web www.thorpelodge.co.uk

John & Harriet Highley
Lawrence House,
Studley Roger,
Ripon,
Yorkshire HG4 3AY
tel 01765 600947
fax 01765 609297
e-mail john@lawrence-house.co.uk
web www.lawrence-house.co.uk

Map 12 Entry 540

Map 12 Entry 541

Yorkshire

Mallard Grange

Hens, cats, sheepdogs wander the garden, an ancient apple tree leans against the wall, the boys play cricket on the lawn and guests unwind. Enter the rambling, deep-shuttered 16th-century farmhouse, cosy with well-loved family pieces, and feel at peace with the world. From the white Spode on the tea trays to the generous breakfasts: perfect farmhouse B&B. A winding steep stair leads to big, friendly bedrooms, two cheerful others await in the outhouses and Maggie's enthusiasm for this glorious area is as genuine as her love of doing B&B. *Minimum stay two nights at weekends.*

Laverton Hall

Rachel and Christopher have swapped their Fulham B&B for the 'big house' of Laverton with it's space, beauty, history (it's 400 years old), three walled gardens and comfort in great measure: feather pillows, thick white towels, sumptuous breakfast and dinner. The sunny guest sitting room is elegant and charming, the cream and white twin and the snug little single share a country-house bathroom and long views to the river, and for families the rooms interconnect. The area is rich with abbeys and great houses, Harrogate is a half-hour drive and then there are the glorious Dales to be explore.

rooms	4: 1 double with bath; 3 twins/doubles, all with shower.
price	£70–£85. Singles from £60.
meals	Good pubs & restaurants 10-15 minute drive.
closed	Christmas & New Year.
directions	B6265 from Ripon for Pateley Bridge. Past entrance to Fountains Abbey. House on right, 2.5 miles from Ripon.

rooms	2: 1 twin/double, 1 single, sharing bath; separate wc.
price	£90. Single £50.
meals	Supper, 3 courses, £20. Good pubs & restaurants 1 mile.
closed	Christmas.
directions	Leave Ripon on Pateley Bridge Rd. 0.25 miles, right at Garden Centre to Galphay. Thro' Galphay, 0.5 miles, right at T-junc. to Kirkby Malzeard; 0.5 miles, left to Laverton; 0.5 miles, last on right.

	Maggie Johnson
	Mallard Grange,
	Aldfield,
	Ripon,
	Yorkshire HG4 3BE
tel	01765 620242
mobile	07720 295918
e-mail	maggie@mallardgrange.co.uk
web	www.mallardgrange.co.uk

	Rachel Wilson
	Laverton Hall,
	Laverton,
	Ripon,
	Yorkshire HG4 3SX
tel	01765 650274
e-mail	cwracewear@hotmail.com

Map 12 Entry 542

Map 12 Entry 543

Yorkshire

Scar Lodge

An air of quiet decency surrounds 17th-century Scar Lodge, tucked into a quiet corner of cobbled Grassington. Reputed to have been a brew house for monks at Fountains Abbey, it still feels like an unworldly retreat. Edwardian beds on wooden floors, comforting touches (fresh fruit, bathrobes), patchwork and stitched linen. There's a sitting room you may share and a sunny spot upstairs for reading and making tea. Valerie, thoughtful and kind, is an accomplished artist; note the artwork inside and out. Inspirational walks start from the door. *Children by arrangement.*

Knowles Lodge

Chris's father loved Canada and built his timber-framed house in the style of a log cabin. No pioneer austerity here, you'll be glad to hear, but a comfortable and comforting place to stay. Honey walls and polished floors give the sitting room a light, airy feel, cheerful throws on squishy sofas make it cosy, and there are fine views of the River Wharfe and Dales Way. Bedrooms are attractive with chintz cushions and fresh flowers; bathrooms are charming. You're superbly well looked after: Pam loves cooking and Chris buys his wines from a friend with a French vineyard. Great walking and trout fishing, and the solitude a balm.

rooms	2: 1 double with shower; 1 double with separate bath & shower.
price	£55–£65. Singles £32.50–£37.50.
meals	Packed lunch £3.50. Pubs & restaurants in Grassington.
closed	Rarely.
directions	B6265 Skipton-Grassington; enter 'main street' Grassington & right-hand fork past Grassington House Hotel; right after Folk Museum into Gillsfold; narrow road into Grange; 1st left, on right.

rooms	3: 2 doubles, 1 twin, all with bath & shower.
price	£70. Singles £40.
meals	Dinner £22.50. Packed lunch £5. Pubs/restaurants within 3 miles.
closed	January-February.
directions	From Skipton A59 to Bolton Abbey. At r'bout, B6160 for Burnsall. 3 miles after Devonshire Arms, right immed. after Barden Tower for Appletreewick. Down hill, over bridge, up hill & on for 0.5 miles. Cross bridge; immed. on left.

	Valerie Emmerson
	Scar Lodge,
	Hardy Grange,
	Grassington, Skipton,
	Yorkshire BD23 5AJ
tel	01756 753388
fax	01756 753388
e-mail	val@grassington.plus.com
web	www.scarlodge.co.uk

	Pam & Chris Knowles-Fitton
	Knowles Lodge,
	Appletreewick,
	Skipton,
	Yorkshire BD23 6DQ
tel	01756 720228
fax	01756 720381
e-mail	pam@knowleslodge.com
web	www.knowleslodge.com

Map 12 Entry 544

Map 12 Entry 545

Yorkshire

The Old Vicarage

Judi and Steve have restored vicarage and garden to their former glory. You get glowing pine floors, country furniture, old china, a fine collection of gardening books… it's inviting and friendly. Chat in the Aga-warm kitchen, curl up on a comfy sofa, enjoy the delicious home cooking; later soak in a roll-top slipper bath and drift off in a cosy wrought-iron bed. In the garden, over 100 varieties of clematis and rose to be discovered down cobbled paths past lily pond and willows. Garden and village have won awards – and the hill-walking is unsurpassed in this Nidderdale AONB.

Knox Mill House

Peter and Marion are quiet hosts, concerned for your rest and well-being. Their cottage, part of a 200-year-old mill, looks out over garden and mill stream to open fields. Although just a mile from the centre of Harrogate, it feels exceptionally rural and there's masses of wildlife. The guest sitting room with coal-effect fire has a tiny breakfast alcove with a vaulted stone ceiling and bookshelves leading off. Bedrooms and bathrooms are similarly modest and cosy. Peter was a professional golfer for 20 years and can arrange for you to play nearby. *Children over 12 welcome.*

rooms	3: 1 double with shower; 1 double, 1 twin, sharing bath (let to same party).
price	£60. Singles £40.
meals	Dinner, 3 courses, £20. BYO.
closed	Rarely.
directions	From Harrogate, A59 (west). Right B6451. Right at Wellington pub. House on right, next to Christ Church.

rooms	3: 1 double, 1 twin, both with shower; 1 twin with separate bath.
price	£55–£60. Singles by arrangement.
meals	Good restaurants 1 mile; pub 0.5 miles.
closed	Rarely.
directions	From Harrogate, A61 towards Killinghall. Knox Mill Lane on right after approx. 0.5 miles.

Judi Smith
The Old Vicarage,
Darley,
Harrogate,
Yorkshire HG3 2QF
tel   01423 780526
mobile   07989 538597
e-mail   judiandsteve@theoldvicaragedarley.co.uk
web   www.theoldvicaragedarley.co.uk

Peter & Marion Thomson
Knox Mill House,
Knox Mill Lane,
Harrogate,
Yorkshire HG3 2AE
tel   01423 560650
fax   01423 560650

Map 12 Entry 546

Map 12 Entry 547

Yorkshire

Britannia Lodge

A splendid house in a splendid town – prepare to be thoroughly spoiled. A pot of tall orchids in the hall sets the tone of this stylish, generous place; your hosts are perfectionists, and give you good mattresses on large beds, pretty fabrics, thick towels, deep baths and powerful showers. Wake to a feast of free-range eggs, homemade bread, specially smoked bacon and cafetières of steaming fresh coffee cheerfully served. All this in Harrogate's most elegant corner – the Duchy is comfortable walking distance from fine antique shops, restaurants and the Pump Room Museum.

Braythorne Barn

The naked bones of the mid 18th-century barn are beautiful; the fine furniture, paintings, colourful fabrics and rugs are the gilding on the lily. Beams and floors are light oak, windows and doors hand-crafted and sunlight dances around the rooms. Trina has given the bedroom a Scandinavian, stripes-and-gingham feel. The bathroom is spotless, the sitting room – all yours – generously furnished. Walk the Priests Way, from Bolton Abbey to Knaresborough. Buttercup the donkey, lots of chickens and Trina's porridge, dry-cured bacon and eggs... a rural idyll. *Children over 12 welcome. Minimum stay two nights.*

rooms	3: 1 double with bath & shower: 1 double with bath/shower; 1 twin with shower.
price	£82.50.
meals	Restaurants 50 yds.
closed	Christmas.
directions	A61 Ripon Road from town centre. Swan Road first left. House 150 yds ahead.

rooms	1 twin with bath & sitting room.
price	£70. Singles from £40.
meals	Packed lunches £6. Pubs/restaurants 2-4 miles.
closed	Rarely.
directions	From Pool-in-Wharfedale, A658 over bridge towards Harrogate. 1st left to Leathley; right opp. church to Stainburn (1.5 miles). Bear left at fork; house next on left.

	Nigel & Julia Macdonald
	Britannia Lodge,
	16 Swan Road,
	Harrogate,
	Yorkshire HG1 2SA
tel	01423 508482
fax	01423 526840
e-mail	info@britlodge.co.uk
web	www.britlodge.co.uk

	Trina Knockton
	Braythorne Barn,
	Stainburn,
	Otley,
	Yorkshire LS21 2LW
tel	0113 284 3160
fax	0113 284 2297
e-mail	enquiries@braythornebarn.co.uk
web	www.braythornebarn.co.uk

Map 12 Entry 548

Map 12 Entry 549

Yorkshire

Ponden House

Brenda's sturdy new house of reclaimed stone sits high on the wild Pennine Way. The spring water makes wonderful tea and the house hums with interest and artistic touches. Comfy old sofas are enlivened with throws, there are homespun rugs and hangings, paintings, plants and a piano. Feed the hens, plonk your boots by the Aga, chat with your lovely leisurely hostesss as she turns out a fish pie or a vegetarian treat; food is a passion. Bedrooms are exuberant but cosy, bathrooms are fresh and there's a hot tub under the stars (bookable by groups in advance). Brilliant value.

rooms	3: 2 doubles with shower; 1 twin sharing bath.
price	£48-£52. Singles £25.
meals	Dinner, 3 courses, £15. Packed lunches £4.
closed	Rarely.
directions	From B6142 for Colne. Pass through Stanbury village, on past Old Silent Inn. Access is either via Ponden Mill or Ponden reservoir.

Brenda Taylor
Ponden House,
Stanbury,
Haworth,
Yorkshire BD22 0HR
tel   01535 644154
e-mail   brenda.taylor@pondenhouse.co.uk
web   www.pondenhouse.co.uk

Map 12 Entry 550

Thurst House Farm

English to the core, this solid former farmhouse in fine Pennine scenery, its stone mullion windows denoting 17th-century origins. Your gentle, gracious hosts give guests a private, good-sized sitting room — carpeted and cosy, with flowery curtains, good antiques and, on chilly evenings, an open fire. Bedrooms are generous, and cottagey, with old brass beds and fresh flowers. Homemade bread, marmalade and jams at breakfast, eggs from their hens, and good, traditional English dinners, too — just the thing for walkers who've trekked the Calderdale or the Pennine Way. *Children over eight welcome.*

rooms	2: 1 family suite, 1 double, both with shower.
price	£70. Singles by arrangement.
meals	Dinner £25. Packed lunch £4. Good restaurants within 6 miles.
closed	Christmas & New Year.
directions	Ripponden on A58. Right up Royd Lane 100 yds before lights; right at T-junc. opp. Beehive Inn; on for 1 mile. House on right, gateway on blind bend, reverse in.

David & Judith Marriott
Thurst House Farm,
Soyland,
Ripponden,
Sowerby Bridge,
Yorkshire HX6 4NN
tel   01422 822820
mobile   07759 619043
e-mail   thursthousefarm@bushinternet.com

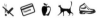

Map 12 Entry 551

Yorkshire

Field House

You drive over bridge and beck to this listed, 1713 farmhouse – expect comfort, homeliness and open fires. Pat and Geoff are genuine folk who enjoy sharing their knowledge of walks and local history, and ramblers will be in heaven – step out of the front door, past the walled garden, through the field with horses and Jacob sheep straight into open countryside. A roll-top bath sits in the new oak-floored bathroom – the other bathroom is a 70s-blue suite – and rooms are big and plain, in farmhouse-style with floral-print linen and curtains. Geoff's breakfasts and welcome are generous in the finest Yorkshire manner.

St Lawrence House

Step through a bright red door into a yellow hall, cross a tiny courtyard and slip into a one-up, one-down hideaway. The former stable lad's cottage, tucked behind the main house, has a snug sitting room – flagged floor, modern rugs, books – and stairs to a breezy, cream and blue bedroom overlooking the garden. Breakfast on fruit smoothies, pancakes, organic bacon in a jolly dining room, comfortable with mismatched chairs and vintage pieces. Richard and Carol are bright, warm and welcoming and about to open a deli next door. Close to York, a peaceful, stylish refuge in a quiet but surprising backwater.

	Field House		St Lawrence House
rooms	3: 1 double with bath/shower; 1 twin with shower; 1 twin with separate bath/shower.	rooms	1 suite with double, sofabed and shower.
price	£52–£60. Singles £28–£40.	price	From £55. Singles £40.
meals	Dinner from £10. Packed lunch available. Pub/restaurant 200 yds.	meals	Supper, 2 courses, £12. Packed lunch £5. Good pubs in village.
closed	Rarely.	closed	Rarely.
directions	1 mile from Halifax on A58 Leeds road. Turn between Stump Cross Inn car park & Clarence Smith's carpet shop. 100 yds to gates.	directions	From A1041 in Snaith, turn into Market Place; house opposite church, beside library.

Pat & Geoff Horrocks-Taylor
Field House,
Staups Lane,
Stump Cross,
Halifax,
Yorkshire HX3 6XW
tel   01422 355457
e-mail   stayatfieldhouse@yahoo.co.uk
web   www.fieldhouse-bb.co.uk

Richard Bridge & Carol Dunk
St Lawrence House,
31 Market Place,
Snaith,
Yorkshire DN14 9HE
tel   01405 869629
mobile   07854 007452
e-mail   richard.bridge@ntlworld.com
web   www.stlawrencehouse.com

Map 12 Entry 552

Map 13 Entry 553

Scotland

Scottish Counties

The powers that be have changed the names of some Scottish counties. To help you find the right county at the top of our pages, we've listed the changes below:-

Scottish Counties

- Aberdeenshire includes Aberdeen city
- Angus
- Ayrshire includes East Ayrshire, North Ayrshire & South Ayrshire
- Argyll & Bute includes Argyll, Isle of Mull, Isle of Gigha
- Dumfries & Galloway includes Wigtownshire
- Dunbartonshire includes East and West Dunbartonshire
- Edinburgh & the Lothians includes East Lothian, Midlothian, West Lothian & Edinburgh
- Fife includes Clackmannanshire
- Highland includes Caithness, Inverness-shire, Isle of Skye, Sutherland
- Lanarkshire
- Moray includes Banffshire
- Perth & Kinross includes Ross-shire
- Renfrewshire includes East Renferwshire
- Scottish Borders includes Berwickshire, Peeblesshire, Roxburghshire, Selkirkshire
- Stirling includes Stirlingshire
- Western Isles includes Uist & Harris

Photo Achamore House, entry 560

Map

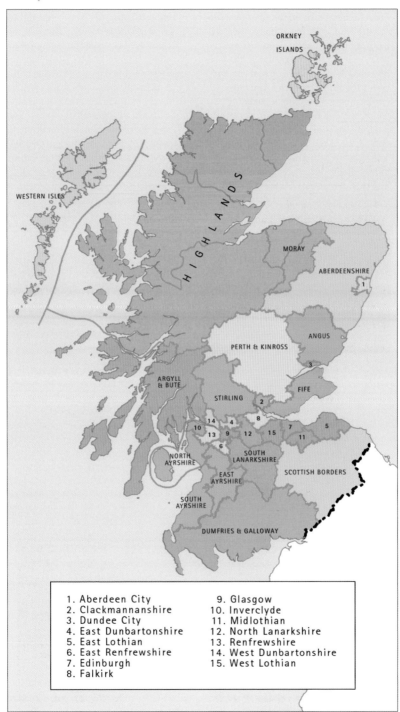

ORKNEY ISLANDS

WESTERN ISLES

H I G H L A N D S

MORAY

ABERDEENSHIRE

1

PERTH & KINROSS

ANGUS

3

ARGYLL & BUTE

FIFE

STIRLING

2

14 4

8

10

13 9

12 15

7

5

6

11

NORTH AYRSHIRE

SOUTH LANARKSHIRE

SCOTTISH BORDERS

EAST AYRSHIRE

SOUTH AYRSHIRE

DUMFRIES & GALLOWAY

1. Aberdeen City
2. Clackmannanshire
3. Dundee City
4. East Dunbartonshire
5. East Lothian
6. East Renfrewshire
7. Edinburgh
8. Falkirk
9. Glasgow
10. Inverclyde
11. Midlothian
12. North Lanarkshire
13. Renfrewshire
14. West Dunbartonshire
15. West Lothian

Aberdeenshire

Lynturk Home Farm

You're treated very much as friends and your hosts are delightfully easy-going. It's peaceful here, too, on the Aberdeenshire 'Castle Trail'. The handsome farmhouse has been in the family since 1762 and you can roam the surrounding 300 acres of rolling hills. Inside, good fabrics and paints, hunting prints and some lovely family pieces. The stunning drawing room, with pier glass mirror, ancestral portraits and enveloping sofas, is reason enough to come, and the food is great – Veronica is Cordon Bleu trained. Eat in the candlelit, deep sage dining room.
Fishing, shooting & golf breaks available.

Frog Marsh

The Victorian granite property was once the village post office, then the Mossat Shop & Tearoom – renowned throughout Scotland. Now lovingly restored, the tea room is once again the dining room – at whose cheerful tables Louise serves delicious breakfasts and dinners. A light-filled staircase leads up to two lovely bedrooms – classic-contemporary with ultra-modern bathrooms – and then there's the super suite in the loft with its seven windows and sweeping views. If you can tear yourself away, there is much to see and do, with castles, gardens and walking right on your doorstep.

rooms	3: 1 twin/double with bath/shower; 1 twin/double with bath; 1 double with separate bath.
price	From £70. Singles £35.
meals	Dinner, 4 courses, £25. Pub 1 mile.
closed	Rarely.
directions	20 miles from Aberdeen on A944 (towards Alford); through Tillyfourie, then left for Muir of Fowlis & Tough; after Tough, 2nd farm drive on left, signed.

rooms	3: 1 double with shower; 1 twin with separate shower; 1 suite with bath/shower.
price	£60-£90. Singles £55.
meals	Dinner, 3 courses, £22.50. Packed lunches £8.
closed	Rarely.
directions	North West from Aberdeen, A944 26 miles to Alford. After 0.25 miles right for Mossat. After 6 miles left towards Strathdon, 3rd house on right

John & Veronica Evans-Freke
Lynturk Home Farm,
Alford,
Aberdeenshire AB33 8DU
tel   01975 562504
fax   01975 563517
e-mail   lynturk@hotmail.com

Louise Barker
Frog Marsh,
Mossat,
Alford,
Aberdeenshire AB33 8PL
tel   01975 571355
fax   01975 571366
e-mail   stay@frogmarsh.com
web   www.frogmarsh.com

Map 19 Entry 554

Map 19 Entry 555

Aberdeenshire

Auld Cummerton

Glen Nochty, 'the lost valley', is on the doorstep, which says it all. Views stretch over wild, beautiful Deeside mountains; hard to find a more remote spot. Startling to discover the house was a ruin three years ago: now it cossets with country-house furnishings. Bedrooms have understated opulence – an oak four-poster, rich fabrics, elegant antiques – shower rooms are immaculate and Carol welcomes you with tea and scones or a tot of whisky. The big outdoors, castles and gardens beckon; return to a garden enveloped by buzzards, deer, squirrels. Enthusiastic, engaging owners; a magical, exhilarating place.

rooms	2: 1 four-poster, 1 double/twin both with shower.
price	£80. Singles from £40.
meals	Good pub 1 mile.
closed	November to Easter.
directions	At Bellabeg village shop on A944, take road to 'Lost Gallery'. After 0.25 miles, right up track to house in woodland.

Mrs C Luffman
Auld Cummerton,
Glen Nochty,
Strathdon,
Aberdeenshire AB36 8UP
tel   01975 651337
fax   01975 651349
e-mail   bluffman.cu@aberdeenshire.gov.uk
web   www.b-and-b-scotland.co.uk/cummerton.htm

Map 19 Entry 556

No. 3 Candacraig Square

If the address suggests a metropolis, note that there is no sign of Nos. 1 or 2 and that the only noise comes from the River Don. Candacraig, the erstwhile laundry for this 1520 estate, is a Highland retreat for those who like to mix style with gentle eccentricity. Iain and Mary run an easy-going ship – breakfast times are negotiated and the art of conversation is practised with an easy flair. There's much comfort, too: claw-foot baths, wall-hangings, old pine dressers, cut velvet curtains. Don't miss Iain's traditional Scottish cooking, or Nelson the one-eyed deer. Balmoral is down the road.

rooms	3: 1 double with shower; 1 double with bath & shower; 1 double with separate bath & shower.
price	£70. Singles from £42.50.
meals	Dinner, 3 courses, £25.
closed	Rarely.
directions	East on A944 towards Strathdon. House signed on right through pillared entrance gates.

Iain & Mary Edgar
No. 3 Candacraig Square,
Strathdon,
Aberdeenshire AB36 8XT
tel   01975 651472
fax   020 7681 1218
e-mail   no3@buchanan.co.uk
web   www.candacraig.com

Map 19 Entry 557

Aberdeenshire

Lys-na-Greyne House

Peaceful, calm, unhurried elegance and a natural welcome – a superb place. Expect a sweeping stair, sun-streamed rooms, a warm country-house hotel feel and the most comfortable beds in Scotland. Your room may be huge – two are – and one comes with a dressing room and a balcony. All have choice antiques, bathrobes, fine linen and views of river, field, forest and hill where osprey and lapwing glide. Meg picks flowers and organic veg from the garden and her food is delicious; David will happily whisk you off into the hills. Nearby, golf, fishing and castles by the hatful.

Angus

Ethie Castle

Amazing. A listed Peel tower that dates to 1300 and which once was home to the Abbot of Arbroath, murdered in St Andrews on Henry VIII's orders. His private chapel remains, as does his secret stair. As for the rest of the house: turret staircases, beautiful bedrooms, a 1500s ceiling in the Great Hall, a Tudor kitchen with a walk-in fireplace that burns night and day. Kirstin and Adrian are experts at breathing new life into old houses and have already started to reclaim the garden. Lunan Bay, one of Scotland's most glorious beaches, is at the end of the road. There's a loch too.

rooms	3: 1 twin/double with bath/shower; 1 twin/double with separate bath; 1 twin/double with separate bath/shower. Extra shower.
price	£70–£90. Singles from £35.
meals	Dinner £25. Supper £20. Pub/bistro 15-minute walk.
closed	Rarely.
directions	From Aboyne, A93 west for Braemar. Just after 50mph sign, left down Rhu-na-Haven Rd. House 400 yds on, 4th gateway on right.

rooms	2: 1 twin/double, 1 four-poster, both with separate bath/shower.
price	From £75. Singles from £55.
meals	Dinner, 4 courses with wine, £28. Packed lunch up to £10. Good pub/restaurant 3 miles.
closed	Rarely.
directions	North from Arbroath on A92; right after Shell garage for Auchmithie; left at T-junc.; on for 2 miles; at 90° bend, private road to Ethie Barns; on right.

David & Meg White
Lys-na-Greyne House,
Rhu-na-Haven Road,
Aboyne,
Aberdeenshire AB34 5JD

tel	01339 887397
fax	01339 886441
e-mail	meg.white@virgin.net

Adrian & Kirstin de Morgan
Ethie Castle,
Inverkeilor,
Arbroath,
Angus DD11 5SP

tel	01241 830434
fax	01241 830432
e-mail	kmydemorgan@aol.com
web	www.ethiecastle.com

Map 19 Entry 558

Map 16/19 Entry 559

Argyll & Bute

Achamore House

A shop, pub, restaurant, 120 people. No traffic jams here on this island, tucked between the mainland and Islay. Despite its grandeur – turrets, Arts & Crafts doors, plasterwork ceilings – Achamore is homely, with warm wood panelling and light-washed rooms. Bedrooms are huge with shuttered windows, oversize beds, heavy antiques. Owner Don, a genial American, offers guests the run of the house – billiard room, library, TV room (great for kids). With 50 acres of gardens and a quiet beach it's ideal for gatherings. Organic breakfasts, occasional dinners.

The Old Manse

Within seconds of arrival you know you've made a wise choice. Yes, there's Loch Fyne at the end of the drive, the pleasing proportions of a 19th-century manse and the pretty sloping garden, but the Macphersons make a bigger impact… They are ambassadors for all that we are hoping to achieve, and great fun. Bedrooms are naturally stylish with striking wallpapers, antique pieces and fine beds and views; the drawing room with log fire and the deep green book-lined dining room, sparkling with silver and crystal, are perfect. The food's excellent, too – exceptionally fresh and most of it local.

rooms	8: 1 double, 1 family both with bath; 2 twins/doubles sharing bath; 2 doubles sharing bath; 2 singles sharing bath.
price	£70–£120. Singles from £35.
meals	Dinner, 4 courses, £32. Pub/restaurant 1 mile.
closed	Rarely.
directions	Uphill from ferry landing, turn left at T-junc.; 1 mile, stone gates on right, signed; house at end of drive.

rooms	3: 1 twin with shower; 1 twin, 1 double, sharing bath.
price	£65. Singles £40.
meals	Dinner, 2-3 courses, £20-£25. BYO. Packed lunch £5. Pub 1 mile.
closed	Rarely.
directions	From Tarbet, A83 for Cairndow. Before village, left, A815, to Strachur. There, bear left away from loch. Immed. see sign on right to Strachur Free Church. House at top.

Don Dennis
Achamore House,
Isle of Gigha,
Argyll & Bute PA41 7AD
tel   01583 505 400
fax   01583 505 387
e-mail   gigha@atlas.co.uk
web   www.achamorehouse.com

Sheila & Rob Macpherson
The Old Manse,
Strachur,
Argyll & Bute PA27 8DF
tel   01369 860247
e-mail   sheilamacpherson@
         strachur247.freeserve.co.uk

Map 14 Entry 560

Map 14 Entry 561

Argyll & Bute

Corranmor House

An exceptional setting on the magical Ardfern peninsula. And Barbara and Hew are generous, kind and as committed to their guests as they are to the 400-acre farm. The drawing room is the original 16th-century bothy, the elegant red dining room sparkles with silver and candles; they enjoy dining with guests and the food is memorable: home goose or lamb, perhaps, or local fish. Bedrooms are exceptionally private – the double across the courtyard, the suite with its snug log-fired sitting room. Wander and admire; the eye always comes to rest on the water and boats of Loch Craignish and the Sound of Jura.

rooms	2: 1 double with bath & sitting room; 1 suite (1 double, 2 singles, sitting room & bath, for same party).
price	£70. Suite £70-£125. Singles £35.
meals	Dinner from £23. With lobster, £40. Lunch from £10. Good pubs & restaurants 0.75 miles.
closed	22 December-3 January; 4th week of August.
directions	A816, B8002 to Ardfern, & through village; 0.75 miles past church, long white house high on right. Right by Heron's Cottage, up drive.

Hew & Barbara Service
Corranmor House,
Ardfern,
Lochgilphead,
Argyll & Bute PA31 8QN

tel	01852 500609
fax	01852 500609
e-mail	corranmorhouse@aol.com

Map 14 Entry 562

Glenmore

A pleasing buzz of family life and no need to stand on ceremony. Built in 1854, it's the later 30s additions to the house that set the style: carved doorways, red-pine panelling, Art Deco pieces, oak floors, elaborate cornicing and a curvy stone fireplace. Alasdair's family has been here for 140 years and much family furniture remains. One of the huge doubles is arranged as a suite with a single room and a sofabed; bath and basins are chunky 30s style with chrome plumbing. Beyond the organic garden boats bob on Loch Melfort: fancy a boat trip to Crinan? The local Scottish dancing teacher is your man.

rooms	2: 1 double with separate bath/shower; 1 family suite with bath/shower & single (let to same party only).
price	£60-£80. Singles £35.
meals	Pubs/restaurants nearby.
closed	Christmas & New Year.
directions	From A816 0.5 miles south of Kilmelford; a private tree lined avenue leads to Glenmore. House signed from both directions.

Melissa & Alasdair Oatts
Glenmore,
Kilmelford,
Oban,
Argyll & Bute PA34 4XA

tel	01852 200314
e-mail	oatts@glenmore22.fsnet.co.uk
web	www.glenmorecountryhouse.co.uk

Map 17 Entry 563

Argyll & Bute

Sithe Mor House

Terrific views from this lovely house on the shores of Loch Awe; its own bay and jetty below, acres of sky above and a winning pair at the helm. Patsy ensures all runs smoothly and John, a former oarsman of repute and the first man to row each way across Scotland, sweeps you along with joie de vivre. With 20-foot-high domed ceilings in the bedrooms, loch views, ornate plasterwork, antlers and oils, this 1880s house oozes a baronial feel and there's massive luxury in bathrooms, beds and fabrics. Stay for dinner, borrow a kilt, marvel at the Oxford and Cambridge boat race memorabilia.

Bridge of Awe Lodge

Mr Knight is of the old school, carries your bag upstairs and offers you tea from a silver pot. The Awe roars past the foot of the tumbling grounds; your host, a keen fisherman, can show you where the salmon leap. The 1960s lodge conceals a fading rococo interior stuffed with vast paintings and furniture; a quick tour will net you six busts in the conservatory and an eccentric collection of bric-a-brac. Tasty dinner cooked by the housekeeper is served by a fire on cold nights. Bedrooms are floral and airy, bathrooms are a decent size and outside the windows are two munros.

rooms	3: 1 double, 1 twin/double, both with bath; 1 double with separate shower.
price	£70-£110. Singles £45-£65.
meals	Dinner, 2-4 courses, £22-£33. Restaurants & pub 0.5-3 miles.
closed	Rarely.
directions	A82 from Glasgow; A85 from Tyndrum. At Taynuilt left onto B845 to Kilchrenan Village. After 1 mile take single track 'No Through Road ' to Taychreggan. House is last house on left.

rooms	3: 2 twins/doubles, 1 twin, all with bath.
price	£80-£90. Singles by arrangement.
meals	Dinner £25. Good pub 3 miles.
closed	Christmas & New Year.
directions	A85 from Crainlarich 23 miles; 1.5 miles after Awe Barrage, right at 'Inverawe Fisheries' just before bridge; 1st entrance left after main road, in tall hedge. If you reach Taynuilt you've gone too far!

Patsy & John Cugley
Sithe Mor House,
Kilchrenan,
Loch Awe,
Argyll & Bute PA35 1HF
tel 01866 833234
e-mail patsycugley@tiscali.co.uk
web www.sithemor.com

Robert Knight
Bridge of Awe Lodge,
Taynuilt,
Argyll & Bute PA35 1HT
tel 01866 822642
fax 01866 822510
e-mail bridgeofawelodge@amserve.com

Map 17 Entry 564

Map 17 Entry 565

Argyll & Bute

Dun Na Mara

Twenty paces from the door, past the standing stone, and you're on your own beach with views across Ardmucknish Bay to the Isle of Mull – a staggering Hebridean landscape. The 1911 house, built by a Glasgow shipping magnate, has been given a 21st-century makeover by these two ex-Edinburgh architects. The result is a cool, calm, minimalist interior: low-slung beds, velvet throws, piles of cushions, luxury bathrooms, DVDs… this is B&B for the next generation. Breakfast on banana and walnut porridge, eggs en cocotte, the full Scottish works.
Children over 12 welcome.

Lochside Cottage

The road runs out in a mile, the hills of Glen Creran cradle you, a private loch laps at the end of the garden. Bedrooms, spotless in 1970s-style, have pretty floral curtains; the spacious drawing room has comfy sofas and a Bluthner Grand piano. Stella and Earle are unrestrained in their pampering: tea when you arrive, maybe in the garden; delicious food beautifully presented; beds turned down and bedlights on, Roberts radios, books, flowers and a mini fridge in one of the rooms. Otters, deer, swans, geese and peace surround you, the walks are stunning and Beinn Sguilard is a three-hour climb.

rooms	7: 4 doubles, 2 twins, all with bath & shower; 1 single with bath/shower.
price	£74–£92. Singles from £45.
meals	Pubs 3 miles.
closed	Rarely.
directions	North from Oban on A828; over Connel Bridge; north for two miles; house signed left just after lay-by, before Benderloch village.

rooms	3: 1 double, 1 twin, both with bath; 1 twin with separate shower.
price	£60–£70. Singles £30–£35.
meals	Dinner, 5 courses, £25. BYO.
closed	Rarely.
directions	14 miles north of Connel Bridge, 20 miles south of Ballachulish on A828. At north r'bout of new bridge follow Invercreran signs for 2 miles, then straight up glen for 1.5 miles. Cottage on right.

Mark McPhillips & Suzanne Pole
Dun Na Mara,
Benderloch, Oban,
Argyll & Bute PA37
tel   01631 720233
e-mail   stay@dunnamara.com
web   www.dunnamara.com

Earle & Stella Broadbent
Lochside Cottage,
Fasnacloich,
Appin,
Argyll & Bute PA38 4BJ
tel   01631 730216
fax   01631 730216
e-mail   broadbent@lochsidecottage.fsnet.co.uk
web   www.lochsidecottage.fsnet.co.uk

Map 17 Entry 566

Map 17 Entry 567

Ayrshire

The Carriage House

An avenue of limes, 250 acres of parkland, rhododendrons, wellingtonia – what a view to wake to! Luke's family have owned the estate and castle for 900 years. Their stylishly converted carriage house, with its ochre walls and cobbled courtyard, is full of light and comfortable good taste; polished floors, handsome antiques, family photographs. Bedrooms mix contemporary fabrics with fine furniture, and Aga-cooked breakfasts are taken in a huge kitchen with hand-crafted fittings. Tennis court, swimming pool, country walks: this is an elegant place to unwind. The Borwicks are confident and keen hosts.

Nether Underwood

You have all the comforts of a country-house hotel yet are treated as friends. Antique furniture, rich, thick drapes, family photos and everything just so in the Thomsons' unusual and elegant 1930s-style house. The yellow drawing room with its Adam fireplace is smart and large; the beds are comfy, the bedrooms cosy. Felicity, who specialises in Scottish dishes, serves delicious breakfasts at the refectory table in the dark red dining room. A stream runs through the very pretty garden towards 13 acres of woodland, its banks home to squabbling ducks.

	The Carriage House		Nether Underwood
rooms	3: 1 double, 1 twin/double, both with bath/shower; 1 double with shower.	rooms	4: 3 doubles, all with bath/shower; 1 twin with separate bath.
price	£80. Singles £45.	price	£99. Singles £55.
meals	Pubs & excellent restaurants nearby.	meals	Excellent pub 10-minute drive; restaurants 15-minute drive.
closed	Rarely.	closed	Occasionally.
directions	From Beith enter Dalry on A737. First left (signed Bridgend Ind Est); uphill thro' houses, past farm on right at top of hill. First right into Blair Estate.	directions	B730 off A77 southbound; to junction marked 'Nether Underwood 2 miles'. Right at next Nether Underwood sign; at end of lane on left.

	Luke & Caroline Borwick		Felicity & Austin Thomson
	The Carriage House,		Nether Underwood,
	Blair,		Symington,
	Dalry,		Kilmarnock,
	Ayrshire KA24 4ER		Ayrshire KA1 5NG
tel	01294 833100	tel	01563 830666
fax	01294 834422	fax	01563 830777
e-mail	blairenterprises@btconnect.com	e-mail	mail.netherunderwood@virgin.net
web	www.blairestate.com	web	www.netherunderwood.co.uk

Map 14 Entry 568

Map 14 Entry 569

Dumfries & Galloway

Chipperkyle

Sink into the sofas without worrying about creasing them; this beautiful, 18th-century, Scottish-Georgian family home has not a hint of formality, and the sociable Dicksons put you at your ease. Sitting and dining rooms connect through a large arch; there are family pictures, rugs on wooden floors and flowers everywhere. Upstairs: a cast-iron bed dressed in good linen, striped walls, flowered curtains, lots of books and windows with views – this wonderful house gets better and better. There are 200 acres, a dog, cat, donkeys and hens, and you can walk, play golf, sail or cycle in magnificent countryside.

Chlenry Farmhouse

A wonderful approach: you could be in a Walter Scott novel. Beyond the romantic old buildings in the glen and the rushing burn, the handsome house comes into view. It is a big traditional farmhouse full of old-fashioned comfort and fresh flowers, with charming owners and friendly dogs. In peaceful bedrooms, solid antiques jostle with tasselled lampshades, silk flowers and magazines on country matters; there are proper big bath tubs and suppers for walkers. Meals can be simple or elaborate, often with game or fresh salmon; gardens and golf courses wait to be discovered.

rooms	2: 1 twin with separate bath/shower; 1 double with bath/shower. Cot etc. available.
price	£80.
meals	Supper occasionally available. Good pub 3 miles, restaurant 5 miles.
closed	Christmas.
directions	A75 Dumfries ring road for Stranraer. Approx. 15 miles to Springholm & right to Kirkpatrick Durham. Left at x-roads, after 0.8 miles, up drive on right by white lodge.

rooms	3: 1 twin with separate bath; 1 double, 1 twin sharing bath.
price	£60. Singles from £36.
meals	Dinner, 4 courses, £26. Supper, £12.50. Packed lunch £5. Good pub 1.5 miles.
closed	Christmas & New Year.
directions	A75 for Stranraer. In Castle Kennedy, right opp. Esso station. Approx. 1.25 miles on, after right bend, right signed Chlenry. Down hill, 300 yds on left.

	Willie & Catriona Dickson Chipperkyle, Kirkpatrick Durham, Castle Douglas, Dumfries & Galloway DG7 3EY
tel	01556 650223
e-mail	special_place@chipperkyle.co.uk
web	www.chipperkyle.co.uk

	David & Ginny Wolseley Brinton Chlenry Farmhouse, Castle Kennedy, Stranraer, Dumfries & Galloway DG9 8SL
tel	01776 705316
mobile	07704 205003
e-mail	wolseleybrinton@aol.com
web	www.chlenryfarmhouse.com

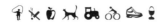

Map 11 Entry 570

Map 14 Entry 571

Dumfries & Galloway

Craigadam

A 1703 farmhouse set in 700 acres, where pheasants strut proudly up the drive. The farmhouse becomes a 'country house' inside: walking sticks and fishing rods by the door, polished floors and panelling in a dining room whose table seats 26. There's a fountain in the courtyard and an honesty bar in the snooker room, while themed bedrooms (India, China, Scotland, Africa) might have a brass bed or a free-standing bath. The Pickups farm and provide a lot of what you eat (organic lamb, venison, partridge, duck). Spot buzzards and sparrowhawks, fish, play golf, cycle, sail or ride nearby.

Applegarth House

An old peaceful manse at the top of the hill, right next door to the church, with a 12th-century motte. Views from the pretty garden stretch for miles around. The house is a good size and airy, with original pine floors, now varnished, and sweeping stairs. Off the large and light landing are spotless bedrooms with shuttered windows and garden and country views. Jane cooks well: stewed fruits for breakfast, fine porridge; guinea fowl with fennel for dinner, or salmon fishcakes with lemon sauce. After which the tawny owls should lull you to sleep.

rooms	10: 6 twins, 1 double, all with bath & shower; 1 twin, 1 twin/double, both with bath; 1 twin/double with shower.
price	£76. Singles from £50.
meals	Dinner £20. Good pub 5 miles.
closed	Christmas & New Year.
directions	A75, then north on A712 towards Corsock. After 2 miles, Craigadam signed on right.

rooms	3: 1 double with separate bath; 2 twins, both with bath/shower.
price	£76-£80. Singles from £48.
meals	Dinner £25. BYO. Hotel restaurant 1.5 miles.
closed	Rarely.
directions	M74 junc. 17 to Lockerbie. B7076 for Johnstonebridge. 1st right after 1.5 miles; after 100 yds left over m'way bridge. After 1 mile, right at T-junc., then 2nd left to church. Next to church.

	Mrs Celia Pickup
	Craigadam,
	Castle Douglas,
	Dumfries & Galloway DG7 3HU
tel	01556 650100
fax	01556 650100
e-mail	inquiry@craigadam.com
web	www.craigadam.com

	Frank & Jane Pearson
	Applegarth House,
	Lockerbie,
	Dumfries & Galloway DG11 1SX
tel	01387 810270
fax	01387 811701
e-mail	jane@applegarthtown.demon.co.uk

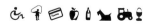

Map 15 Entry 572

Map 15 Entry 573

Dumfries & Galloway

Knockhill

Fabulous Knockhill: stunning place, stunning position, a country house full of busts and screens, oils and mirrors, chests and clocks, rugs and fires. In the intimate drawing room stuffed with treasures, floor-to-ceiling windows look down the wooded hill. Fine stone stairs lead to country-house bedrooms that are smart yet homely: bedheads of carved oak or padded chintz, books and views. A grand farming feel and delicious Scottish meals; the Morgans are the most unpretentious and charming of hosts. Mellow, authentic, welcoming – an enduring favourite.

Kirklands

Light and airy, the 1800 manse has big classic rooms looking south to England. Friendly Elisabeth runs an immaculate ship, Archie is a gifted gardener full of plans. Drawing room windows frame country views; there are log fires, polished floors, charming watercolours, fresh flowers. Generous bedrooms come with crisp linen, patchwork quilts, window seats, maybe a chaise longue; bathrooms are big and old-fashioned. The village is on one side, one of the best trout streams in Scotland is across the lane and a three-mile circular walk starts from the door. *Children over eight welcome.*

rooms	2: 1 twin with bath/shower; 1 twin with separate bath.
price	£70–£75. Singles £37.50.
meals	Dinner £25. Good pub 5 miles.
closed	Rarely.
directions	From M74 junc. 19, B725 for Dalton for 1.2 miles. Look out for signpost by church in Ecclefechan. Right at next x-roads to Lockerbie, 1 mile on, right at stone lodge. House at top of long drive.

rooms	3: 1 double with bath; 1 twin with bath/shower; 1 twin/double with separate bath & shower room.
price	£70–£80. Singles £35–£40.
meals	Good restaurant 2 miles.
closed	February & March.
directions	M6, junc. 44, then A7 12 miles into Canonbie. Over bridge, signed 'Churchyard', immed. right; immed. left into yard.

Yda & Rupert Morgan
Knockhill,
Lockerbie,
Dumfries & Galloway DG11 1AW
tel   01576 300232
fax   01576 300818
e-mail   info@morganbellows.co.uk

Elisabeth & Archie Findlay
Kirklands,
Church Road,
Canonbie,
Dumfries & Galloway DG14 0RA
tel   01387 371769
fax   01387 371784
e-mail   irvineho@aol.com

Map 15 Entry 574

Map 15 Entry 575

Dunbartonshire

Blairbeich Plantation

Blairbeich is magnificent – a wonderland in the woods. It is a fusion of Californian and Scandinavian styles with a mini-loch lapping three feet from its walls. There are light stone floors and cathedral ceilings and delightful ground-floor bedrooms that look onto the loch – an enclave of wilderness that universities come to study. Despite all this it is the interior that knocks you flat: Malla has covered every square inch with something spectacular and the sitting room is a private art gallery. Mosaic showers, Grecian urns, rare orchids and woodpeckers... and curling on the loch in winter. Fantastic.

Edinburgh & the Lothians

20 Blackford Road

From your cushioned window seat you gaze onto a wildlife-filled walled garden – a special spot for breakfast on a warm day. Come for unexpected tranquillity and old-world luxury in the centre of the city. Your quietly friendly, dog- and garden-loving hosts give you two comfortable bedrooms, charming with white-painted Victorian shutters. The double, slightly smaller than the twin, has a serene toile de Jouy canopied bed and matching drapes. And there's an elegant drawing room to retire to, private and cosy with cream sofas, soft lights, drinks tray and beautiful books.

rooms	2: 1 double with bath & shower; 1 double with shower.
price	£60–£90. Singles from £50.
meals	Dinner, 4 courses, £30. Lunch £10–£15. Packed lunch £7.50–£10. Good pub/restaurant 1.5 miles.
closed	Rarely.
directions	From west, A811 into Gartocharn; 1st right (School Road); 1 mile up to T-junction, then left; house on right, signed.

rooms	2: 1 double/twin, 1 twin, both with separate bath.
price	£60–£75. Singles £40–£45.
meals	Good restaurants 500 yds.
closed	Rarely.
directions	A720 city bypass, take Lothianburn exit to city centre. Continue for 2.5 miles on Morningside Rd; right into Newbattle Terrace; 2nd left into Whitehouse Lane. Immed. right into Blackford Road. On right.

Malla Macdonald
Blairbeich Plantation,
Gartocharn,
Loch Lomond,
Dunbartonshire G83 8RR

tel   01389 830257
fax   01389 830752
e-mail   macdonald@blairbeich.com
web   www.blairbeich.com

John & Tricia Wood
20 Blackford Road,
Edinburgh EH9 2DS

tel   0131 447 4233
fax   0131 447 1248
e-mail   jwood@dsl.pipex.com

Map 14 Entry 576

Map 15 Entry 577

7 Gloucester Place

A cantilevered staircase, a soaring cupola: the classic Georgian townhouse is five minutes from Princes Street. Rooms are cosy yet immaculate, sprinkled with paintings and *objets* from far-flung travels. Bedrooms on the second floor (one shower room is on the first) are comfy, traditional and well-stocked with books and radio (and there are Z-beds for children). Bag the south-facing double with its stunning Art Deco bathroom and garden views. Late breakfasts are fine by Naomi, who is happy to chat to you or to leave you in peace. An interesting and hospitable place to unwind.

rooms	3: 1 double with shower; 1 double with separate bath; 1 double with separate shower.
price	£80–£90. Singles from £40.
meals	Excellent pubs/restaurants nearby.
closed	Christmas & Rarely.
directions	From George St (city centre), down Hanover St, across Queen St at lights. Left into Heriot Row, right onto India St, then left.

Naomi Jennings
7 Gloucester Place,
Edinburgh EH3 6EE
tel	0131 225 2974
mobile	07803 168106
e-mail	naomijennings@hotmail.com
web	www.stayinginscotland.com

Map 15 Entry 578

13 Lansdowne Crescent

In a hushed crescent a short stroll from museums, galleries, shops and restaurants, a warm, friendly, elegant house with a communal garden over the road (you are given a key). Design junkies will get their fix inside: a cool grey dining room with stripped floors, modern paintings and beautiful objects made by Susan. The bedroom is large, light and airy with an Italian black leather bed, dimmer side lights, a red leather armchair, good books and a sparkling little shower room with thick white towels. Breakfast is presented so perfectly on modern ceramics that it is almost a shame to eat it.

rooms	1 double with shower.
price	From £60.
meals	Restaurants within walking distance.
closed	Christmas, New Year & occasionally.
directions	Directions given when booking. Free parking outside 6.30pm-8.30am. Haymarket Station car park £6 per day.

Susan Chaplin
13 Lansdowne Crescent,
Edinburgh EH12 5EH
tel	0131 467 2983
fax	0131 467 2983
e-mail	mnschaplin@blueyonder.co.uk

Map 15 Entry 579

44 Inverleith Row

Buzzing with life, the house – 1830s Georgian – is homely and cluttered in the communal bits, yet your rooms are pristine: comfortable chairs, garden views, striking colours. Sarah is friendly and laid-back and mixes B&B and a busy family life with humour; she treats you like a friend, too. Lots of the decoration is extraordinary, some of it inherited from the previous Italian owner – gold cornicing, murals… Unusual, stunning. A cupola lights the stairwell; one bedroom has an enormous bathroom, one a sitting area. No sitting room, but this is Edinburgh and it doesn't matter.

16 Lynedoch Place

The house has kept its fine features: a cantilever staircase and cupola, a bow-walled dining room, spiral stairs down to the basement where there are a twin and a double bedroom. The twin/double at the very top is our favourite with lovely views from the window seat, light yellow walls and a pretty fireplace and watercolours. A rare find, too – an entire Georgian house (1821) so close to the city centre. Susie and Andrew (and Gertie the yellow lab) are welcoming, congenial hosts; they can also give you inside knowledge of this most beautiful of Scottish cities. *Children & dogs welcome.*

rooms	2: 1 double, 1 twin/double, sharing bath (2nd room let to same party).
price	£80–£100. Singles £40–£55.
meals	Restaurants nearby.
closed	Rarely.
directions	In Edinburgh, 500 yds north of Botanic Gardens.

rooms	3: 1 double, 1 twin, 1 twin/double all with shower.
price	£70–£110.
meals	Many restaurants close by.
closed	Christmas.
directions	From Haymarket train station towards Princes Street, turn left down Palmerston Place; travel 500 yds and turn right up Belford Rd for 500 yds; Belford Rd becomes Lynedoch Place.

Sarah Nicholson
44 Inverleith Row,
Edinburgh EH3 5PY
tel   0131 552 8595
fax   0131 551 6675
e-mail   inverleithbandb@yahoo.com

Andrew & Susie Hamilton
16 Lynedoch Place,
Edinburgh EH3 7PY
tel   0131 225 5507
fax   0131 226 4185
e-mail   susie.lynedoch@btinternet.com
web   www.16lynedochplace.co.uk

Map 15 Entry 580

Map 15 Entry 581

7 Danube Street

Impressive architectural features — cantilevered staircase, marble fireplaces, double-barrelled cupola, soaring ceilings — coupled with Fiona's professional interior design talents make for a stunning city base. It is sumptuous: generous curtains, thick bedspreads, fluffy towels and Molton Brown goodies in boutique hotel-style bathrooms. The chandelier has real candles and the beds are four-poster or canopied. Fiona and Colin are lovely, their breakfasts are superb, and you have a fascinating 10-minute stroll through some of Europe's finest classical architecture to the very heart of the city.

rooms	3: 1 double, 1 single, 1 four-poster, all with bath.
price	£100–£130. Single £60.
meals	Good restaurants 5-minute walk.
closed	Christmas Day.
directions	From Edinburgh, Queensferry Rd for Forth Rd Bridge. 3rd right after Dean Bridge into Dean Park Crescent; 2nd right into Danube St.

	Fiona Mitchell-Rose
	7 Danube Street,
	Edinburgh EH4 1NN
tel	0131 332 2755
e-mail	seven.danubestreet@virgin.net
web	www.sevendanubestreet.com

Map 15 Entry 582

2 Fingal Place

The delights of the city will come alive with your multi-lingual hostess — Gillian is a Blue Badge Guide. Bedrooms below stairs are attractively decorated in muted pinks, greens and cream; one has a lovely carved wooden bedhead and looks onto the patio garden. Scottish shortbread and books in the bedrooms, local artists' paintings on the walls and, from your breakfast table, a springtime view of crocuses, daffodils and blossom. A seductive city launch-pad, with the Meadows park opposite (look upwards to Arthur's Seat) and a short walk from the university, concerts, theatres, shops and museums.

rooms	2: 1 twin with bath/shower; 1 twin (with single room attached) with bath/shower.
price	£70–£80 (£85–£95 during Festival). Singles from £55.
meals	Pubs/restaurants 100 yds.
closed	22–27 December.
directions	From centre of Edinburgh (West End), Lothian Rd to Tollcross (clock) & Melville Drive. At 2nd major lights, right into Argyle Place; immed. left into Fingal Place.

	Gillian Charlton-Meyrick
	2 Fingal Place,
	The Meadows,
	Edinburgh EH9 1JX
tel	0131 667 4436
e-mail	gcmeyrick@blueyonder.co.uk

Map 15 Entry 583

Edinburgh & the Lothians

Craigbrae

The Westmacotts are wonderfully easy-going and the stone farmhouse is typically Scottish, with huge windows. In the green and coral drawing room expect family paintings, excellent china, loads of books; in the large, prettily decorated bedrooms are comfy sofas, thick towels and striped linen. All face west for a sunny afternoon arrival. You are a 12-minute drive from Edinburgh airport but there are green rolling hills, a cobbled farmyard and a working cooperage opposite. From Dalmeny village trains run to the city every half hour and Louise is happy to meet you at the station.

rooms	3: 1 double with bath/shower; 2 twins/doubles sharing 2 bath/shower rooms; separate wc. Basins in all rooms.
price	£60-£80. Singles from £30.
meals	Good pubs/restaurants 2 miles.
closed	Christmas.
directions	From lights in centre of Kirkliston, follow sign for Forth Rd Bridge (A8000) & on at r'bout. Approx. 0.5 miles on, 1st right after Milton Farm. Down lane, over small bridge & right before cottages.

Louise & Michael Westmacott
Craigbrae,
Kirkliston,
Edinburgh EH29 9EL

tel	0131 331 1205
fax	0131 319 1476
e-mail	louise@craigbrae.com
web	www.craigbrae.com

Map 15 Entry 584

60 Braid Road

Good solid Victorian architecture in a good solid Morningside street. But the house is light and airy, and the sun pours in through wide windows. Nice quiet bedrooms come with books and magazines, garden flowers, good linen, pretty china; the twin is on the ground floor. Breakfast is the full McMonty, much of it organic; Iola, who is charming, is also a good cook, and makes her own breads and jams. There's a peaceful garden with a patio that catches the evening sun: perfect for relaxation after a day of city exploration. The centre of Edinburgh is a long walk or a short bus ride away.

rooms	2: 1 double with separate shower; 1 twin with separate bath.
price	£60-£72. Singles by arrangement.
meals	Pub 200 yds; restaurant 800 yds.
closed	23-28 December.
directions	Enter Edinburgh on A702. 0.5 miles from bypass, fork right down Braid Rd, after pedestrian crossing. House 0.5 miles on left after mini-r'bout. Free on-street parking.

Iola & Michael Fass
60 Braid Road,
Morningside,
Edinburgh EH10 6AL

tel	0131 446 9356
fax	0131 447 7367
e-mail	iolafass@blueyonder.co.uk
web	www.braidroad.com

Map 15 Entry 585

Edinburgh & the Lothians

1 Albert Terrace

A warm-hearted home with a lovely garden, an American hostess and two gorgeous Siamese cats. You are 20 minutes by bus from Princes Street yet the guests' snug sitting room overlooks pear trees and clematis and the rolling Pentland Hills. Cosy up in the winter next to the log fire; in summer, take your morning paper onto the terrace above the sunny garden. Books, fresh flowers, interesting art and ceramics and – you are on an old, quiet street – utter, surprising peace. One bedroom has a fine antique American four-poster. Clarissa is arty, easy, generous and loves her Sawday guests.

rooms	3: 1 four-poster with bath; 1 double, 1 single with shared bath.
price	£65-£85. Singles £35-£42.50.
meals	Good pubs/restaurants nearby.
closed	23-28 December.
directions	From centre of Edinburgh, A702 south, for Peebles. Pass Churchill Theatre (on left), to lights. Albert Terrace 1st right after theatre.

	Clarissa Notley
	1 Albert Terrace,
	Edinburgh EH10 5EA
tel	0131 447 4491
e-mail	canotley@aol.com

Map 15 Entry 586

Lochmill House

Susan is delightful and kind and spoils you rotten. Her home-baking is wicked (expect a feast for breakfast), her green fingers produce fresh flowers from a pretty, peaceful garden all year round, and she's hot on Scottish history so can help you make the best of your stay. The house is modern and on the edge of town, a mile or so from the M8 and very easy for Edinburgh and Glasgow. Big lovely rooms swim with light, there's a smart mult-windowed sitting room to relax in and spotless country-cosy bedrooms with wicker chairs and crisp linen. *Children over 12 welcome.*

rooms	2: 1 twin with shower; 1 twin with separate bath/shower.
price	£64. Singles £32.
meals	Supper/dinner by arrangement. Packed lunch £6. Pub & restaurants 0.5 miles.
closed	Christmas & occasionally.
directions	From west M9, junc 4. From east M9 junc. 3, then A803 into Linlithgow. There, north onto A706 for Bo'ness & 0.2 miles on left. Follow to very end of road.

	Mr & Mrs W Denholm
	Lochmill House,
	3 Lade Court,
	Linlithgow,
	West Lothian EH49 7QF
tel	01506 846682
mobile	07759 959414
e-mail	susanedenholm@hotmail.com

Map 15 Entry 587

Edinburgh & the Lothians

Inveresk House

All the big villas around here are built on land that once belonged to Inveresk House, hence the enormous trees that shade the house. Alice has chosen to cover every wall with paintings (much is her own vibrant work) and fill every room with ornate antiques, squashy sofas in bright pinks and chintzes, flowers, gilt, mirrors and some seriously gorgeous rugs. Bedrooms and bathrooms are large, comfortable and spotlessly clean with an old-fashioned feel. The house was built on a Roman site and guards a 16th-century secret tunnel; Cromwell plotted his siege of Edinburgh Castle from here.

Glebe House

Gwen has lavished a huge amount of time and love on her 1780s manse. The perfect Georgian family house with all the well-proportioned elegance you'd expect, it is resplendent with original features – fireplaces, arched glass, long windows – that have appeared more than once in interiors magazines. Bedrooms are light, airy and hung with generous swathes of fabric. The sea is a stone's throw away and golfers have 21 courses to choose from. There's also a fascinating sea bird centre close by – yet you are 30 minutes from Edinburgh. Regular trains take you to the foot of the castle.

rooms	3: 1 double, 1 twin, 1 family, all with bath.
price	£90. Singles £50.
meals	Pubs/restaurants nearby.
closed	Rarely.
directions	From Edinburgh, A199 (A1) to Musselburgh. There, follow signs to Inveresk. At top of Inveresk Brae, sharp right into cul-de-sac. 2nd opening on right, opp. gates with GM on them, bear right past cottages to house.

rooms	3: 1 double with shower; 1 twin, 1 four-poster, both with bath/shower.
price	£60–£90. Singles by arrangement.
meals	Restaurants 2-minute walk.
closed	Christmas.
directions	From Edinburgh, A1 for Berwick. Left onto A198, follow signs into North Berwick. Right into Station Rd signed 'The Law', to 1st x-roads; left into town centre; house on left behind wall.

Alice & John Chute
Inveresk House,
3 Inveresk Village,
Musselburgh,
East Lothian EH21 7UA

tel	0131 665 5855
fax	0131 665 0578
e-mail	chute.inveresk@btinternet.com
web	www.invereskhouse.com

Gwen & Jake Scott
Glebe House,
Law Road,
North Berwick,
East Lothian EH39 4PL

tel	01620 892608
mobile	07973 965814
e-mail	gwenscott@glebehouse-nb.co.uk
web	www.glebehouse-nb.co.uk

Map 15 Entry 588

Map 16 Entry 589

Edinburgh & the Lothians

Markle House

A relaxed southern Scottish idyll. Carina and Jim have poured energy, affection and an artistic streak into their lovely 18th-century family home. Expect multi-levelled spaciousness and a drawing room overflowing with faded rugs and tapestry cushions, books and warm colours. A comforting hubbub emanates from the kitchen – Carina produces magic from the Aga and early breakfasts for golfers. Bedrooms come with lush curtains and perfect beds, there are dogs for the children, luxuries in the bathrooms and your hosts are the nicest people. Edinburgh, golf courses and beaches are no distance.

rooms	2: 1 double, 1 twin, both with bath/shower.
price	£70. Singles £55.
meals	Dinner with wine, £25. Lunch from £20.
closed	20 December-6 January.
directions	From Edinburgh A1 for Berwick-upon-Tweed. Left for East Linton, left under r'way bridge & thro' village; 0.5 miles , left for Markle. 1st white house on right.

Carina & Jim McGuinness
Markle House,
East Linton,
East Lothian EH40 3EB
tel   01620 860570
fax   01620 860937
e-mail   mcguinness@marklehouse.fsnet.co.uk

Map 16 Entry 590

Eaglescairnie Mains

Surrounded by 350 acres of undulating countryside yet so close to Edinburgh! The Georgian farmhouse sits in lovely gardens, its peace interrupted by the odd strutting pheasant. On sunny days breakfast in the conservatory, heady with jasmine and trailing geraniums. Smart bedrooms have inspired fabrics and colours, great views and space; the drawing room is delectable, with deep coral walls and a log fire. Barbara is warm and charming. Play tennis or explore the farm – it's won awards for conservation. Michael's commitment to the countryside is wide-ranging and deep.

rooms	4: 2 doubles, both with bath/shower; 1 twin with shower; 1 single with separate bath.
price	£55-£70. Singles from £35.
meals	Two excellent pubs 1 mile.
closed	Christmas.
directions	From A1 at Haddington B6368 south for Bolton & Humbie. 2.5 miles on through Bolton; at top of hill, fork left for Eaglescairnie. Entrance 0.5 miles on left.

Barbara Williams
Eaglescairnie Mains,
Gifford,
Haddington,
East Lothian EH41 4HN
tel   01620 810491
fax   01620 810491
e-mail   williams.eagles@btinternet.com
web   www.eaglescairnie.com

Map 16 Entry 591

Fife

Woodmill

Staying at Woodmill is all about a good day out in the country – and a warm, welcoming return home. Lots of space, lashings of hot water, crackling fires, a whisky from the honesty bar, an elegant supper (game in season), a good bottle of wine and a big feather sofa to retire into. Bedrooms, one with its own seating area, are smart with a contemporary twist, bathrooms have fresh hand-made soaps and the countryside stretches in every direction. Steven arranges country pursuits; the perfect place for walkers, stalkers and fishermen. And golfers: St Andrews is a 25-minute drive.

Fincraigs

Tubs of bright flowers in a cobbled yard welcome you to Fincraigs. In the hall, lit by a Georgian fanlight, a pretty stone staircase leads to delightful bedrooms. This 18th-century farmhouse, once the factor's house, has an air of great comfort and warmth, and Felicity, Tom and the dogs make you feel instantly at home. There's a sunny drawing room with open fire and old family pieces, and a guest sitting area upstairs. Fincraigs' 10 acres, presided over by ducks and geese, include an orchard and walled garden. Fishing villages, the Tay estuary and St Andrews, home of golf, are close by. The views are a joy.

rooms	2: 1 double with shower; 1 double with separate bath.
price	£70–£85.
meals	Dinner with wine, from £28. Restaurant 6 miles.
closed	Christmas & New Year.
directions	On B937 between Lindores and Collessie. 1 mile from Collessie, look for a big white stone at the road end. Up drive to house.

rooms	2: 1 double with shower; 1 twin with bath.
price	From £70. Singles from £35.
meals	Dinner, 3 courses, £20. Pubs 3–5 miles.
closed	Christmas & New Year.
directions	From A92 heading north, left after Rathillet, at Balmerino Gauldry sign. Fincraigs 1 mile from main road on left.

	Clare Wade
	Woodmill,
	Lindores,
	Fife KY14 6JA
tel	01337 830088
fax	01337 810469
e-mail	stay@woodmillhouse.co.uk
web	www.woodmillhouse.co.uk

	Felicity & Tom Gilbey
	Fincraigs,
	Kilmany,
	Cupar,
	Fife KY15 4QQ
tel	01382 330256
fax	01382 330256
e-mail	anyone@fincraigs.freeserve.co.uk

Fife

18 Queen's Terrace

Sitting on the sunny terrace overlooking a water garden that's filled with birdsong, it's hard to imagine that you are in the heart of St Andrews and a mere 10-minute walk from the Royal & Ancient golf club. Jill's stylish and traditional home shows off her artistic flair; the light, restful drawing room and elegant dining room are full of character, sunlight and flowers. Large bedrooms have especially comfortable beds, crisp linens and antique throws. An enchanting place – and Jill, friendly and generous, is a mine of information on art, gardens and walks. *Children over 12 welcome.*

rooms	4: 2 doubles, 1 twin, all with shower; 1 double with bath/shower.
price	From £75. Singles £50.
meals	Dinner, 3 courses with wine, £35.
closed	Rarely.
directions	Into St Andrews on A917; pass Old Course Hotel. Right at 2nd mini r'bout, left through arch at 2nd mini r'bout. 250 yds, right into Queens Gardens. Right at T-junc. On left opp. church.

Jill Hardie
18 Queen's Terrace,
St Andrews,
Fife KY16 9QF

tel	01334 478849
fax	01334 470283
e-mail	jill_hardie@hotmail.com

Map 15/19 Entry 594

Kinkell

An avenue of beech trees patrolled by guinea fowl leads to the house. If the sea views and the salty smack of St Andrews Bay air don't get you, step inside and have your senses tickled. The elegant drawing room has two open fires, a grand piano, fine windows with working shutters upstairs and original pine floor – gorgeous. Bedrooms and bathrooms are spotless, sunny and warm. There's great cooking too, with maybe crab or pheasant served in the dining room; Sandy and Frippy excel in the kitchen. From the front door head down to the beach, walk the wild coast or jump on a quad bike in the back field.

rooms	3: 1 twin/double with bath; 1 twin/double with shower; 1 twin with bath & shower.
price	£70-£80. Singles from £45.
meals	Dinner £25. Many restaurants 2-3 miles.
closed	Rarely.
directions	From St Andrews, A917 for 2 miles for Crail. Driveway in 1st line of trees on left after St Andrews.

Sandy & Frippy Fyfe
Kinkell,
St Andrews,
Fife KY16 8PN

tel	01334 472003
fax	01334 475248
e-mail	fyfe@kinkell.com
web	www.kinkell.com

Map 16/19 Entry 595

Fife

Falside Smiddy

A 1744 smithy – the last horse walked out in the early 1980s – renovated by Keith and Rosie, who built the house around Keith's pipe organ. A simple place, rich in spirit, and good value. There are home eggs and garden veg; Rosie cooks soups and casseroles and turns berries into jams. The sitting/breakfast room is roomy, the wood-burning stove makes winters cosy, bedrooms are smallish, with comfy beds and pretty florals. Both rooms are double-glazed and the traffic passes quietly at night. Golf, beach walks, and the fishing villages of Crail and Pittenweem to explore.

rooms	2: 1 twin with shower; 1 twin with bath/shower.
price	£50–£60. Singles £35.
meals	Dinner from £20. Pub 2 miles.
closed	Occasionally.
directions	From St Andrews, A917 for Crail. After 4 miles, ignore turning for Boarhills, & continue to small river. Over bridge; house 2nd on left.

Rosie & Keith Birkinshaw
Falside Smiddy,
Boarhills,
St Andrews,
Fife KY16 8PT
tel   01334 880479
e-mail   rosiebirk@btinternet.com

Map 16/19 Entry 596

Ladywell House

Frances Shand Kydd once owned this large stone manse near the (surprisingly) English-looking conservation village of Falkland. Duncan and Camilla are now happily settled here and, apart from Diana's Room, whose décor remains unchanged, they have thrown out the florals and whistled in the new. Bedrooms are smart: cool neutral colours, crisp white linen hugs squishy goose down, shutters open to wide views and bathrooms twinkle. Downstairs is easy-going and fun, the atmosphere calm. The 10-minute stroll to the village may be trickier after Duncan's huge, locally-sourced breakfasts.

rooms	3: 1 double, 1 twin both with shower; 1 twin with separate bath.
price	£70. Singles from £45.
meals	Excellent pub 15-minute walk.
closed	Christmas & New Year
directions	A92 north; 1st exit at 'New Inn' r'bout, signed Falkland. 2.5 miles just before village, farm road on left signed Ladywell House. Then 1st right through black gates.

Duncan & Camilla
Heaton Armstrong
Ladywell House,
Falkland,
Fife KY15 7DE
tel   01337 858414
mobile   07931 304436
e-mail   duncan@tullochscott.co.uk
web   www.ladywellhousefife.co.uk

Map 15 Entry 597

Fife

Blair Adam

If staying in a place with genuine Adam features is special, how much more so in the Adams' own family home! They've been in this corner of Fife since 1733: John laid out the walled garden, son William was a prominent politician, Sir Walter Scott used to come and stay. The house stands in a swathe of parkland and forest overlooking the hills and Loch Leven, with big, friendly, light-flooded rooms filled with intriguing contents. The pretty bedroom is on the ground floor and you eat either in the splendid dining room or with the family in the kitchen — you choose.

Kennels Cottage

A fresh, stylish gamekeeper's cottage. It's perfect. Step inside to white walls, white sofas, beiges and creams and the odd flash of gold, a buddha in a fireplace, books, modern paintings and a contemporary lack of clutter. Bedrooms and bathrooms are spotless, bright and designed for comfort; huge towels, gorgeous linen on brand new beds, absolute peace. Tanya and Sandy, fresh from Hong Kong, spoil you at breakfast — served in a bright white dining room and locally-sourced. Explore the garden or take a picnic and wander through what was the Dollarbeg estate, alive with pheasant and deer.

rooms	1 twin with bath.
price	£80. Singles £50.
meals	Dinner, 2 courses £15. BYO. Packed lunch £5. Good restaurant 5 miles.
closed	Christmas.
directions	From M90 exit 5, B996 south for Kelty. Right for Maryburgh, through village, right through pillars onto drive, under motorway via tunnel, then up to house.

rooms	3: 2 doubles with shower; 1 family with bath/shower.
price	£60-£70. Singles £45.
meals	Packed lunches £10. Good pub 2 miles.
closed	January & February.
directions	From Dollar take B913 towards Blairingone. House 2 miles from Dollar just before Blairingone.

	Keith & Elizabeth Adam Blair Adam, Kelty, Fife KY4 0JF
tel	01383 831221
mobile	07986 711099

	Tanya Worsfold & Sandy Stewart Kennels Cottage, Dollarbeg, Dollar, Clackmannanshire FK14 7PA
tel	01259 742476
fax	01259 743716
e-mail	tanya.worsfold@btinternet.com
web	www.guesthousescotland.co.uk

Map 15 Entry 598

Map 15 Entry 599

Glasgow

Finglen House

The Campsie Hills rise behind (climb them and you can see Loch Lomond), the Fin Burn takes a two-mile tumble down the hill into the garden and herons and wagtails can be spotted from the breakfast table. All this 40 minutes from Glasgow! Sabrina's designer flair has permeated the whole house: good beds in stylish rooms, proper linen, French touches, eclectic art, cast-iron baths and cream-painted wooden floors. A fresh, elegant drawing room with log fire is yours to share. Douglas, a documentary film maker, knows the Highlands and Islands well; he and Sabrina are fun and good company.

Highland

Thrumster House

Log fires burn at both ends of the galleried hall; stimulating conversation embraces history, nature and countryside pursuits. The atmosphere of this Victorian's laird's house has been described by an American guest as "Steamboat gothic"; the curtains date back to 1863 and the vaulted wooden ceiling has an ecclesiastical feel. Thrumster was designed for parties, music and fine cooking (produce from the estate, seafood from Wick). Islay's trail reveals some fascinating landscapes on these stunning 10,000 acres — you are in the heart of the neolithic Yarrows — and trout fishing is free to guests.

rooms	2: 1 double with bath; 1 double with separate bath.
price	£70. Singles £40.
meals	Pub 5 minute drive..
closed	Christmas and New Year.
directions	A81 from Glasgow right on A891 at Strathblane. Three miles on, in Haughhead, look for a wall & trees on left, & turn in entrance signed Schoenstatt. Immed. left to house.

rooms	2: 1 double with shower; 1 twin with separate bath.
price	£65. Singles £35.
meals	Dinner, 3 courses, £25 with wine.
closed	Rarely.
directions	A99 north through Ulbster. After 2 miles, pass church & 'Yarrow Archaeological Trail' sign, then 1st left (200 yds) & up drive to house.

	Sabrina & Douglas Campbell Finglen House, Campsie Glen, Glasgow G66 7AZ
tel	01360 310279
mobile	07774 820454
e-mail	sabrina4@supanet.com
web	www.finglenhouse.com

	Islay MacLeod Thrumster House, Thrumster, Caithness KW1 5TX
tel	01955 651387
fax	01955 651733
e-mail	islay.macleod@btinternet.com
web	www.thrumster.co.uk

Map 15 Entry 600

Map 21 Entry 601

The Factor's House

Robert is the Factor of a traditional sporting estate and he has a fascinating remit: to supervise thousands of acres of private land and livestock. Day, an enthusiastic gardener, runs a super family home; both are the sort of folk you'd be happy to meet at the end of a trip. It's spectacular here with striking views and you tower 300 feet above the North Sea. Seascapes from the double and dining and drawing rooms; the ground-floor twin, pretty in gingham and embroidered linen, has French doors to the garden. Excellent food – maybe estate venison – a charming walled garden and a sense of escape.

St Callan's Manse

Caroline was up to her eyes in it the day we visited, but still found time to rustle up venison sausages for lunch while keeping an eye on her new arrivals – six lambs that had been born that morning, one of which was asleep in front of the Aga. Outside, 21 hens and eight ducks roam the garden; you eat their eggs at breakfast – in the kitchen with Caroline or in the dining room with the view. Bedrooms are snug: library steps for bedside tables, electric blankets, old armoires, tartan blankets. There's a hammock for the views, and Rogart's hills await your feet. *2.5% credit card charge. Dogs by arrangement.*

rooms	3: 1 double, 1 twin, both with separate bath; 1 twin with separate shower.
price	£80. Singles £50.
meals	Dinner, £25.
closed	Christmas & Easter.
directions	A9 north of Helmsdale, before bottom of Berriedale Braes, left into drive of Langwell House. Right at mirror, up to white gates; left & left again to house.

rooms	2 doubles, both with separate bath.
price	£80. Singles £65.
meals	Dinner, 2-4 courses, £14.50-£25. BYO. Good pub/restaurant in village, 1.5 miles.
closed	Occasionally.
directions	From Inverness, A9 north. Cross Dornoch bridge. 14 miles on, A839 to Lairg. Cross small bridge in Rogart & sharp right uphill, for St Callan's church. House 1.5 miles on, on right, next to church.

Davina & Robert Howden
The Factor's House,
Berriedale,
Caithness,
Highland KW7 6HD

tel   01593 751280
fax   01593 751251
e-mail robert@welbeck2.freeserve.co.uk

Robert & Caroline Mills
St Callan's Manse,
Rogart,
Sutherland,
Highland IV28 3XE

tel   01408 641363
fax   01408 641313
e-mail saintcallan@aol.com
web   www.miltonbankcottages.co.uk

Map 21 Entry 602

Map 21 Entry 603

Highland

Craigiewood

You're in the middle of nowhere: if you follow the paths you may see wild goats or red kites. Head for the Moray Firth and look back across the water to Inverness, or walk down to Munlochy Bay in search of dolphins. Climbing roses and a remarkable 'Californian Glory' flourish outside; inside are bedrooms decorated in country style and a sitting room with hand-painted floors. There are bowls of fruit, maps and walking sticks, and a garden reclaimed from recalcitrant Black Isle gorse. Gavin runs garden tours and can take you off to Inverewe, Attadale, Cawdor and Dunrobin Castle.

rooms	2: 1 twin with bath; 1 twin with shower.
price	£56-£64. Singles £35.
meals	2 miles to local pub.
closed	Christmas & New Year.
directions	A9 north over Kessock Bridge. At N. Kessock junc. filter left to r'bout, follow signs to Kilmuir. After 0.25 miles, right to Kilmuir; follow road uphill, left at top, then straight on. Ignore 'No through road' sign, pass Drynie Farm, follow road to right; house 1st left.

Araminta & Gavin Dallmeyer
Craigiewood,
North Kessock,
Inverness,
Highland IV1 3XG

tel	01463 731628
mobile	07831 733699
e-mail	2minty@high-lights.co.uk
web	www.craigiewood.co.uk

Map 18 Entry 604

Geddes House

A stupendous, moated house, in the family since 1780. You get columns, a grand piano, big fireplaces, trophies, a snooker table, gilt mirrors, silver candelabras and Elizabeth, who welcomes you in the friendliest way. Beautifully Georgian, the house sits in its own estate; 2.5 lochs to fish, wonderful walks, a boat and 1,000 acres of organically reared cattle. The manor – from the antler-bedecked billiard room to the Italian hand-painted and panelled drawing room to the huge four-poster room with its bearskin – sparkles with traditional life lived to the full. Superb.

rooms	3: 2 twin/doubles, both with bath/shower; 1 four-poster with shower & separate bath.
price	£80. Singles £40.
meals	Dinner, 3 courses, £24. Good pub/restaurant 3 miles.
closed	Rarely.
directions	From Inverness, A96 for Nairn. After 9.5 miles right on B9090 through Cawdor. 3 miles, B9090 turns left for Nairn, but cont. onto B9101. At Geddes sign, turn right, up drive.

Elizabeth & Jamie
Mackintosh-Walker
Geddes House,
Nairn,
Inverness-shire IV12 5QX

tel	01667 452241
fax	01667 456707
e-mail	elizabeth@geddesonline.co.uk
web	www.elizabeth@geddesonline.co.uk

Map 18 Entry 605

Highland

Farr Mains

This much loved home, in epic Highland countryside, has been in the Murray family for three generations. The house is comfortable without being imposing, an 1850 original with later add-ons, mostly clad in gleaming white wood. Christina is lively, down-to-earth, a great hostess. Wholesome, whole-hearted hospitality is guaranteed – along with home-produced honey and fruit and veg from the garden (pretty, and awash with daffodils in spring). The position is perfect for exploring the Highlands in every direction; return to a cosy drawing room with a peat fire. Three llamas add an unexpected, exotic touch.

The Old Ferryman's House

You get plants, baskets, flowers in every conceivable container. This former ferryman's house is small, homely, delightful, yards from the River Spey with its spectacular mountain views. Explore the countryside or relax in the garden with a tray of tea and homemade treats. The sitting room is cosy with a woodburning stove and lots of books (no TV). Generous Elizabeth, who lived in the Sudan and is a keen traveller, cooks delicious meals: heathery honeycomb, homemade bread and preserves, herbs from the garden, wild salmon. An unmatched spot for explorers, and very good value.

rooms	2: 1 family room with bath/shower; 1 twin with shower.
price	£60. Singles £35.
meals	Dinner £15. Lunch £5. Good pub/restaurant 20-minute drive.
closed	Christmas & New Year.
directions	North of Aviemore for 26 miles, left onto B851 for Fort Augustus. Over bridge, through Inverarnie to Farr. House 2nd gate on left, past playground.

rooms	4: 1 double, 1 twin, 2 singles, sharing 1 bath & 2 wcs.
price	£49. Singles £24.50.
meals	Packed lunches £5.50. Dinner £18. BYO.
closed	Occasionally in winter.
directions	From A9, follow main road markings through village, pass golf club & cross river. From B970 to Boat of Garten; house on left, just before river.

James & Christina Murray
Farr Mains,
Farr,
Inverness,
Inverness-shire IV2 6XB
tel   01808 521205
fax   01808 521466
e-mail farrmains@hotmail.com

Elizabeth Matthews
The Old Ferryman's House,
Boat of Garten,
Inverness-shire PH24 3BY
tel   01479 831370
fax   01479 831370

Map 18 Entry 606

Map 18 Entry 607

Highland

Invergloy House

A peaceful, no-smoking home run by Margaret, a professional musician and James, a retired chemical engineer. It is a converted coach house with stables in the beautiful Great Glen that sits among 50 wild lochside acres of rhododendron, woodland and wonderful trees – and free fishing. Bedrooms are traditional, and the views of Loch Lochy and the surrounding mountains from the big picture window in the guest drawing room are spectacular. Walk to the private shingle beach on the loch, spot the wild roe deer in the grounds and savour the secluded peace.
Children over eight welcome.

The Grange

A Victorian townhouse with its toes in the country: the mountain hovers above, the loch shimmers below and whales have been sighted from the breakfast table. Bedrooms, one in a turret, another with a terrace, are large, luscious, warm and inviting – all crushed velvet, beautiful blankets and immaculate linen. Bathrooms are breathtaking and ooze panache. Expect neutral colours, decanters of sherry, a carved wooden fireplace, a Louis XV bed. Thoughtful breakfasts are served at glass-topped tables with flowers and white china; Joan's warm vivacity and love of B&B makes her a wonderful hostess.

rooms	2: 1 twin with small shower; 1 double with bath/shower.
price	From £60. Singles £30-£35.
meals	Good restaurants/bistro 2-5 miles.
closed	Rarely.
directions	From Spean Bridge north on A82. After 5 miles, house signed on left.

rooms	4 doubles, all with bath/shower.
price	£98-£110. Singles 10% off room rate.
meals	Seafood restaurants 12-minute walk.
closed	Mid-November-Easter.
directions	A82 Glasgow-Fort William; there, right up Ashburn Lane, next to Ashburn guesthouse. On left at top.

Margaret & James Cairns
Invergloy House,
Spean Bridge,
Highland PH34 4DY

tel 01397 712681
fax 01397 712681
e-mail cairns@invergloy-house.co.uk
web www.invergloy-house.co.uk

Joan & John Campbell
The Grange,
Grange Road,
Fort William,
Inverness-shire PH33 6JF

tel 01397 705516
fax 01397 701595
e-mail info@thegrange-scotland.co.uk
web www.thegrange-scotland.co.uk

Map 18 Entry 608

Map 17 Entry 609

Lyndale House

Edinbane, Isle of Skye IV51 9PX

The sky envelops you, sea, lochs and views surround you and Linda has created a quiet, delightful retreat. The 300-year-old tacksman's house is hidden down a private drive – and with what energy and enthusiasm it has been renovated. Marcus is restoring the walled garden, too, which produces certified organic fruit and veg. Lovely views from your bedroom and the drawing room, both bathed in an explosion of golden light at sunset; fresh flowers, bathrobes, peace and seclusion. Wander down to the shore through an avenue of trees, explore the island by pony from the local stables.

Delicious wholesome breakfasts are prepared using fresh produce from Lyndale's 1.5 acre, Soil Association-certified, walled garden. So, no pesticides are involved in the growing of fruit, free-range chickens or veg; they are also members of the Slow Food movement. Rare breeds, indigenous to the islands – Hebridean sheep and a Highland pony – also live here. Inside the house chemicals are avoided, eco-friendly cleaning products are used and organic soaps are yours to enjoy in the bathrooms.

rooms	3: 1 double with shower; 1 double with separate bath; 1 twin sharing bath (let to same party only).
price	From £80. Singles £50.
meals	Restaurant 3 miles.
closed	Christmas & New Year.
directions	Cross Skye Bridge; A87 north, through Broadford & Portree. At Borve, A850 (left fork) for Dunvegan; pass Treaslane river; 2.4 miles onb, gates & Gate Lodge. House 0.5 miles along drive.

		Marcus & Linda Ridsdill Smith
tel		01470 582329
email		linda@lyndale.net
web		www.lyndale.net

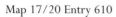

SPECIAL
GREEN ENTRY
see page 12

Map 17/20 Entry 610

Highland

Kinlochfollart

The pretty white house faces the loch, surrounded by sheep and wild Skye terrain. This is Clan MacLeod territory and the isle is steeped in inter-clan rivalries stretching back 800 years. Donald tends the garden, Rosemary cooks and bakes her own bread and the family home is a delightful place to stay. Much loved antiques, old-fashioned bathrooms, comfortable beds, books and a glorious crackling fire – it's warmly inviting. Dine convivially and well at a mahogany table set to perfection; make the most of your hosts' keen knowledge of this fascinating, mesmerising landscape and its history.

rooms	4: 2 twins/doubles, both with bath/shower; 2 singles with separate bath/shower.
price	From £80. Singles from £40.
meals	Dinner, 4 courses with wine, £28. Pub/restaurant in village.
closed	Christmas, New Year & occasionally.
directions	From Skye Bridge, signs for UIG on A87 to Sligachan Hotel. Left fork on A863 to Dunvegan (22 miles). There, left on A87 (just after Health Centre) for Glendale; 0.75 miles, white house in trees.

Donald & Rosemary MacLeod
Kinlochfollart,
Dunvegan,
Isle of Skye IV55 8WQ

tel	01470 521470
fax	01470 521740
e-mail	klfskye@tiscali.co.uk
web	www.klfskye.co.uk

Map 17/20 Entry 611

Moray

Blervie

The Meiklejohn coat of arms flies from the flagpole, an apple's throw from the orchard in which King Malcolm met his death. Blervie is a small 1776 mansion, "a restoration in progress", its finely proportioned rooms crammed with fresh flowers and splendid things to catch the eye. A large dresser swamped in china, a piano in the hall, books everywhere and the sweet smell of burnt beech from grand marble fireplaces. Big bedrooms have comfy old sofas at the feet of four-posters; bathrooms are eccentrically old-fashioned. Fiona and Paddy both enjoy country pursuits and looking after their guests.

rooms	2: 1 four-poster with single bed & separate bath; 1 four-poster with bath.
price	£70.
meals	Dinner, 4 courses, £25.
closed	Christmas & New Year.
directions	From A96 to Forres. South at clocktower, straight across r'bout onto B9010. Pass hospital; 1 mile on, left at Mains of Blervie sign. Right at farm.

Paddy & Fiona Meiklejohn
Blervie,
Forres,
Moray IV36 2RH

| tel | 01309 672358 |
| e-mail | meiklejohn@btinternet.com |

Map 18 Entry 612

Moray

Westfield House

This is the grand home of an illustrious family: Macleans have lived here since 1862. The carpet in the hall is clan tartan; the oak stair is hung with oils, standards and the odd ceremonial sword. John farms 500 acres while Veronica runs a play school and cooks sublimely; dinner is served at a long candelabra-ed table on a rich red carpet. A winter fire crackles in the cosy guest sitting room, old-fashioned bedrooms are warm and inviting – plump pillows, fine linen, books, lovely views – and the peace is interrupted only by the call of the guinea fowl. Lots of good eating places are nearby.

Grange House

Exceptional Scottish hospitality from people who know how to spoil. Nothing is too much trouble for Doreen and Bill: a delicious meal, delightful conversation, much laughter and a drawing room with a fire for coffee. Bill tends the tranquil grounds (woodland, lawns, wildlife, flowers) and produces the vegetables; Doreen keeps the house immaculate. Bedrooms have cosy carpets, big comfy beds, matching duvets and walls, pretty toiletries, fluffy towels and fresh flowers. An hour from Aberdeen airport yet so near the little fishing villages of the Moray coast. *Children by arrangement.*

	Westfield House	Grange House
rooms	3: 1 twin with bath; 1 twin with separate bath & shower; 1 single with separate bath.	2: 1 double with shower; 1 twin with bath/shower.
price	£80. Singles from £35.	£70. Singles from £35.
meals	Dinner, 3 courses, £20. Good pub 3 miles.	Dinner, 3 courses with wine, £25. Pub 3.5 miles.
closed	Rarely.	Occasionally.
directions	From Elgin, A96 west for Forres & Inverness; after 2.5 miles, right onto B9013 for Burghead; after 1 mile, signed right at x-roads. Cont. to 'Westfield House & Office'.	From Keith, A95 for Banff. After 3.5 miles, left signed Grange Church. Left again opp. church.

John & Veronica Maclean
Westfield House,
Elgin,
Moray IV30 8XL
tel   01343 547308
fax   01343 551340
e-mail veronicamaclean@hotmail.com

Doreen & Bill Blanche
Grange House,
Grange,
Keith,
Banffshire AB55 6RY
tel   01542 870206
fax   01542 870206
e-mail wd.blanche@zetnet.co.uk

Map 18 Entry 613

Map 19 Entry 614

Moray

Balwarren Croft

This is the good life – 30 acres at the end of the track, a field of Highland cattle, a loch that attracts so much bird life a hide is to be added, and a burn by which you can walk, that tumbles down the hill and through the wood. Hazel and James came here to croft 25 years ago. They renovated crumbling walls, licking them into good shape – James is a dry-stone waller (though he did use cement on the house) – and the whole place is a delight. A cathedral roof, shiny wooden floors, cashmere blankets, sparkling bathrooms, log fires, delicious food and lovely people – a special retreat.

Perth & Kinross

Finnart Lodge

In ancient times Rannoch was cattle-rustling country and a hint of Wild West lingers. You can, nevertheless, arrive in some style – from Euston on the overnight sleeper; your hosts will pick you up. But any elegance you may experience on board is beaten in spades at the lodge: the house and its position are beyond reproach. Ceiling-to-floor windows in the drawing room look straight down the loch (it starts 30 paces from the fire), tropical ferns flourish in the conservatory and one of the bedrooms has an 1880s bathroom. Walk through ancient Caledonian pine forest, fish and sail. A perfect place.

rooms	2 twins, both with shower.
price	£60. Singles £38.
meals	Dinner, 3 courses, £20. Good pub/restaurant 10 miles.
closed	December-February.
directions	North from Aberchirder on B9023. Right at Lootcherbrae (still B9023); 2nd left for Ordiquhill. After 1.7 miles, right at farm track opp. Aulton Farm; last croft up track.

rooms	3: 1 double with bath; 2 twins with bath/shower.
price	£80. Singles £40.
meals	Dinner, 3 courses, £25. Packed lunch £10. Good meals in nearby hotel.
closed	Christmas & occasionally.
directions	Take Calvine turn from A9. After 10 miles right towards Kinloch Rannoch. In main square, left over bridge. First right on South Loch Road. House 10 miles on right, signed.

Hazel & James Watt
Balwarren Croft,
Ordiquhill,
Cornhill,
Banffshire AB45 2HR

tel	01466 751688
fax	01466 751688
e-mail	balwarren@tiscali.co.uk
web	www.balwarren.com

Archie & Anne Boyd
Finnart Lodge,
Rannoch,
Perth & Kinross PH17 2QF

tel	01882 633366
fax	01882 633232
e-mail	aandaboyd@aol.com
web	www.finnart-lodge.co.uk

Map 19 Entry 615

Map 15/18 Entry 616

Perth & Kinross

Grenich Steading

Perched above silvery Loch Tummel is Lindsay's award-winning renovation of a once derelict barn. Inside, blue-and-white Portuguese tiles, seagrass matting and a woodburning stove, and two bedrooms with patchwork bedspreads. You get a kitchen, dining and sitting room so you can self-cater too (minimum one week). Gaze upon mountain-to-loch views from the patio, homemade fruitcake in hand; Lindsay is charming and loves nurturing both garden and guests. The sunsets and walks are fabulous, and there's so much to do, you'll barely be inside. *Children over eight welcome. Minimum stay two nights weekends May-September.*

rooms	2: 1 double, 1 twin sharing bath & sitting room (let to same party only).
price	£65. Singles £48.
meals	Dinner (May-Sept), 3 courses, £26 with wine. Inn 0.75 miles.
closed	Christmas & New Year.
directions	From A9 north of Pitlochry, take Killiecrankie turning. Left onto B8019 for Tummel Bridge & Kinloch Rannoch for 8 miles to Loch Tummel Inn. House 0.75 miles up forestry track, on right.

	Lindsay Morison Grenich Steading, Strathtummel, Pitlochry, Perth & Kinross PH16 5RT
tel	01882 634332

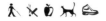

Map 15/18 Entry 617

Beinn Bhracaigh

A door in a wall leads to a secret garden and a handsomely gabled period villa; like the grand house in a fairytale. Guests have free run of the main rooms – all high ceilings, creamy walls, wooden floors, huge windows – comfortably spread with antiques and period features. Huge, restful bedrooms, with views to hills, are cool in cream and blue. There are power showers and luxury soaps, breakfast is a feast of local produce – with some surprises. After a day's walking, fishing and historical site-seeing, relax with a malt whisky – a choice of dozens – on the veranda. Ann and Alf are great hosts.

rooms	3: 1 twin/double, 1 double both with shower; 1 twin/double with bath/shower.
price	£55-£65. Singles from £37.50.
meals	Dinner, 2-3 courses, £15.95-18.95. BYO.
closed	Christmas
directions	From A9, turn for Pitlochry. In town centre, A924 to Moulin & Braemar; 700 yds, then right at brown sign for Hydro Hotel; this leads into Knockard Rd. House near entrance.

	Ann & Alf Berry Beinn Bhracaigh, Knockard Road, Pitlochry, Perth, Perth & Kinross PH16 5HJ
tel	01796 470355
mobile	07708 668436
e-mail	info@beinnbhracaigh.com
web	www.beinnbhracaigh.com

Map 15/18 Entry 618

Perth & Kinross

Craighall Castle

The view from the balcony that circles the drawing room is simply stunning, and the deep gorge provides the fabulous walks. Nicky and Lachie battle to keep up with the demands of the vast, impressive home that has been in the family for 500 years. You will forgive it any mustiness or dustiness, as staying here is a memorable experience. Nothing is contrived, sterile or luxurious, but there's so much drama and intrigue it could be the setting for a film. Breakfast is served in the 18th-century library, and you have the use of the Regency drawing room, too.

Over Kinfauns

Anne and David have the magic touch and their traditional Scottish farmhouse is the warmest of B&Bs. Inside is a rainbow of colour and light: pale wooden floors and heaps of flowers, happy dogs by the Aga, a conservatory/dining room that overlooks a delightful garden, a gate leading to the hills. Big bedrooms have antiques and crisp linen, pale carpets, coral walls and windows framing country views; bathrooms are large but cosy with luxurious towels. Don't miss Anne's food: another delight. The A90 can be busy by day but quietens down at night… readers are full of praise.

rooms	2: 1 four-poster with bath; 1 twin with extra single & separate bath.
price	£70. Singles £40.
meals	Restaurant 3 miles, pub 6 miles.
closed	Christmas & New Year.
directions	From Blairgowrie, A93 for Braemar for 2 miles. Just before end of 30mph limit, sharp right-hand bend, with drive on right. Follow drive for 1 mile.

rooms	2: 1 double with bath/shower; 1 twin with bath.
price	£70-£80. Singles from £45.
meals	Dinner £25. Good pub/restaurant 3 miles.
closed	Rarely.
directions	From A90 Perth to Dundee road, Kinfauns exit. Drive up hill for 0.25 miles, left, & straight up hill to gates on left.

Nicky & Lachie Rattray
Craighall Castle,
Blairgowrie,
Perth & Kinross PH10 7JB
tel   01250 874749
fax   01250 874749
e-mail   lrattray@calinet.co.uk

Anne & David MacLehose
Over Kinfauns,
Perth,
Perth & Kinross PH2 7LD
tel   01738 860538
mobile   07834 631200
e-mail   b&b@overkinfauns.co.uk
web   www.overkinfauns.co.uk

Map 15/18 Entry 619

Map 15/18 Entry 620

Perth & Kinross

Cairnies Cottage

A slice of heaven half a mile down the track. Eight acres and three wee lochs cradle these converted cottages. Inside, warmth, fresh colours, a tidy home; the bedroom is excellent, with white bathrobes and good linen. Other bounties include free-range organic eggs, an Aga-cooked breakfast, a huge sitting room with an open fire, lovely views towards the Grampians – and Norman, the smiling farmer, who had been playfully banished from his home the afternoon we visited so as not to make the place look 'untidy'. Down-to-earth people with a gentle sense of humour; good value, too.

Mains of Drummond

Once the farmhouse for Drummond Castle, now a B&B for those who wish to visit the castle gardens. The old dairy is now a cosy bolthole, with toile de Jouy fabrics, a sparkling white bathroom with lovely red towels, and wicker chairs on your own terrace. You breakfast in the main house, in an elegant conservatory. The parterre gardens date from 1630; they're considered to be among the finest in Europe. The castle, too, is magical, and has connections with Robert the Bruce, Mary Queen of Scots, James IV, Bonnie Prince Charlie and Cromwell. Robert speaks fluent French and Spanish.

rooms	1 twin with bath.
price	£50-£55. Singles from £28.
meals	Pub/restaurant 3 miles.
closed	Christmas & New Year.
directions	A85 west from Perth. After 6 miles, right for Glenalmond, Harrietfield; after 4 miles, left for Glenalmond; pass G. College, then right, for Mains of Cairnies. Sharp right at white gate; on right.

rooms	1 twin with bath/shower.
price	£70. Singles £45.
meals	Excellent restaurants/pubs nearby.
closed	Rarely.
directions	Off A9 on A822; left after Muthill marked golf course. After 2 miles, Y-junc., bear right past cottage The Allans; 1st left at farm x-roads.

Claire Milne
Cairnies Cottage,
Glenalmond,
Perth & Kinross PH1 3SE

tel   01738 880381
fax   01738 880381
e-mail   milne@cairniescottage.fsnet.co.uk
web   www.cairniescottage.co.uk

Carola & Robert Philippi
Mains of Drummond,
Crieff,
Perth & Kinross PH7 4JA

tel   01764 681285
fax   01764 681285

Perth & Kinross

Mackeanston House

A 1690 farmhouse full of beautiful pieces: ancient armoires, mahogany dressers, creaking floorboards and the biggest beds. Bedrooms have great style, pretty floral fabrics and lots of books; one has a bath in which you can lie and look out on the fields. Outside, a one-acre walled garden and new all-weather tennis court. In a conservatory, overlooking the garden with views to distant Stirling Castle and the Wallace Monument, you dine on salmon from the Teith or game from the hills. Colin is a Blue Badge guide. *Ask about personal tours & wine & whisky weekends.*

Old Kippenross

Pink since 1715 (a signal to Jacobites that the house was a safe haven), Old Kippenross rests in a wooded valley overlooking the River Allan — you may snare the odd commuting salmon. The Georgian part was built above the 500-year-old Tower House, and its rustic white-vaulted basement embraces dining room and sitting room, strewn with soft sofas and Persian rugs. Up the elegant spiral stair to sash-windowed bedrooms and bathrooms stuffed with towels. Chopin dedicated two nocturnes to a former daughter of the house and once strolled in the walled garden. *Children over 12 welcome. Dogs by arrangement.*

	Mackeanston House	Old Kippenross
rooms	2: 1 double, 1 twin/double, both with bath/shower.	2: 1 double, 1 twin, both with bath & shower.
price	£76-£80. Singles £53-£55.	£80. Singles from £50.
meals	Dinner £26. Good pub 1 mile.	Dinner £26. BYO. Pub 1.5 miles.
closed	Christmas.	Rarely.
directions	From M9, north, junc. 10 onto A84 for Doune. After 5 miles, left on B826 for Thornhill. Drive on left after 2.2 miles, right off farm drive.	Exit 11 of M9, B8033 for Dunblane. 500 yds, right over dual c'way, through entrance by stone gatehouse. Down drive, take 1st fork right after bridge. House along gravelled drive.

Fiona & Colin Graham
Mackeanston House,
Doune,
Stirling,
Perth & Kinross FK16 6AX
tel 01786 850213
mobile 07921 143018
e-mail enquiries@mackeanstonhouse.co.uk
web www.mackeanstonhouse.co.uk

Sue & Patrick Stirling-Aird
Old Kippenross,
Dunblane,
Perth & Kinross FK15 0LQ
tel 01786 824048
fax 01786 824482
e-mail kippenross@hotmail.com

Map 15 Entry 623

Map 15 Entry 624

Perth & Kinross

Braelangwell House

Braelangwell is a jaw-dropper: a 1790 Georgian mansion set in 77 acres, much of it ancient woodland. Three cows mow the lawn while Himalayan musk roses climb up one side of the house. Walk through the pillared entrance and you find a hall with an 1840-painted ceiling, a ballroom in Wedgewood blue, a stone-flagged billiard room and a dining room with painted floorboards and floor-to-ceiling windows. In the bedrooms you may find a brass bed, a slipper bath, toile de Jouy fabrics, Farrow & Ball paints; the four-poster Garden Room is well worth the out-splash.

Wemyss House

The setting overlooking the Cromarty Firth is stunning. Take an early morning stroll and spot buzzards, pheasants, rabbits and roe deer; the peace is palpable. The modern house with sweeping maple floors is flooded with light and fabulous views, big bedrooms are warmly decorated with Highland rugs and tweeds, there's Christine's grand piano in the living room and Stuart's handcrafted furniture at every turn. Aga breakfasts include homemade bread, preserves and eggs from a dozen happy hens; dinners sound delicious. Friendly and enthusiastic, Christine and Stuart love welcoming their guests.

rooms	3: 1 double with separate bath; 1 twin with bath & shower; 1 four-poster with bath.
price	£80-£120. Singles from £60.
meals	Pubs/restaurants 5 miles.
closed	January-February.
directions	Through Munlochy; leave A832 for B9160; on for three miles; ignore right turn for Mount High & phone box; on till house signed left, through gates.

rooms	2: 1 double, 1 twin both with bath/shower.
price	£60. Singles from £40.
meals	Supper from £25. Restaurants 15-minute drive.
closed	Rarely.
directions	From Inverness, A9 north. At Nigg r'bout, right onto B9175. Thro' Arabella; left at sign to Hilton/Shandwick; right towards Nigg; past church; 0.5 miles, right onto private road. House on right.

Laura & Ronnie Strange
Braelangwell House,
Balblair,
Black Isle,
Ross-shire IV7 8LT

tel	01381 610353
fax	01381 610467
e-mail	braelangwell@btinternet.com
web	www.braelangwell.co.uk

Christine Asher & Stuart Clifford
Wemyss House,
Bayfield,
Tain,
Perth & Kinross IV19 1QW

tel	01862 851212
e-mail	stay@wemysshouse.com
web	www.wemysshouse.com

Map 18 Entry 625

Map 18 Entry 626

Perth & Kinross

Loch Eye House

A delightful house, 15th century at the back, 1870 at the front, with lawns that tumble towards the loch. The interior is equally impressive, with the original tiled floor in the hall, an open fire in the drawing room and Nina Campbell fabric on the dining room wall. Lucinda has redecorated with flair, bringing a bright and breezy county-house elegance to her home. One of the bedrooms is done in lilacs and purples and one of the bathrooms has loch views; spot rare birdlife while you soak. There's a moor, a brand new tennis court and fishing on the loch. The views are sublime.

Tanglewood House

Windows for walls in this modern, curved, lochside house: a panorama of inspirational views unfolds as you move from room to room. The sitting room welcomes with its grand piano, open fire, books, CDs, games and telescope; bedrooms, one with a balcony, have comfortable beds, wicker chairs, crisp duvets and every little luxury. Anne, good company, gives you a perfect breakfast in a dining room with French windows (just-squeezed orange juice, Loch Fyne kippers). Explore the wild garden, then stroll to your rocky private beach and swim in the loch — the waters are warmed by the Gulf Stream.

	Loch Eye House	
rooms	3: 1 double with bath & shower; 1 double, 1 twin, sharing bath.	
price	£80. Singles £40.	
meals	Dinner, 3 courses, £25.	
closed	Occasionally.	
directions	A9 for Tain, then B9165 for Fearn. First left for Loandhu, then 1.5 miles & on left.	

	Tanglewood House
rooms	3: 1 double, 2 twins, all with bath/shower.
price	£76-£90. Singles £58-£65.
meals	Pubs in village 0.5 miles.
closed	Christmas & New Year.
directions	On outskirts of Ullapool from Inverness on A835, left immed. after 4th 40mph sign. Take cattle grid on right & left fork down to house.

Lucinda Poole
Loch Eye House,
Fearn,
Perth & Kinross IV20 1RS
tel   01862 832297
fax   01862 832914
e-mail   loofy@ndirect.co.uk

Anne Holloway
Tanglewood House,
Ullapool,
Perth & Kinross IV26 2TB
tel   01854 612059
e-mail   tanglewoodhouse@ecosse.net
web   www.tanglewoodhouse.co.uk

Map 18   Entry 627

Map 18   Entry 628

East Lochhead

Largs Road, Lochwinnoch, Renfrewshire PA12 4DX

Sailors, walkers and eco-warriors will love it here – in this solid, comfortable farmhouse where the welcome is genuine and the owners come showered with plaudits for their work with green tourism and Slow Food. Large, light bedrooms have traditional furniture and floral covers, the guests' sitting room is warmly cheerful with armchairs, paintings, grand piano and log burner, and amazing views stretch over garden, hills and loch beyond. Make the most of impeccably sourced breakfasts, delectable home-grown beef or lamb at dinner, and veg from an immaculate garden.

Ross and Janet are strong supporters of the Slow Food movement, raise highland cattle and Jacob sheep and avoid the use of pesticides on their land. They have also planted hedges, dug a new pond and manage meadows to encourage bird and animal life. Building materials and other produce are sourced locally, thus cutting down on carbon emissions and food miles; their energy and conservation initiatives are constantly evolving. A National Cycle route passes right by the house and you can hire bikes.

rooms	3: 1 double/family, 1 twin, both with bath/shower; 1 double with shower.
price	£70–£80. Singles from £45.
meals	Dinner £25. Packed lunch £7.
closed	Rarely.
directions	From Glasgow, M8 west to junc. 28a. A737 to Irvine. 7 miles, right on A760 to Largs. 2 miles past Lochwinnoch under r'way bridge, 600 yds on left. Brown tourist signs.

SPECIAL GREEN ENTRY
see page 12

		Ross & Janet Anderson
tel		01505 842610
fax		01505 842610
email		admin@eastlochhead.co.uk
web		www.eastlochhead.co.uk

Map 14 Entry 629

Scottish Borders

Skirling House

An intriguing house with 1908 additions, impeccably maintained. The whole lovely place is imbued with the spirit of Scottish Arts & Crafts, and augmented with Italianite flourishes. Mexican blankets embellish chairs, runners soften flagged floors and the carvings, wrought-ironwork and rare Florentine ceiling are sheer delight. Upstairs a more English comfort holds sway: carpets and rugs, window seats and wicker, gentle colours, fruit and flowers. Bob cooks the finest Scottish produce, Isobel shares a love of Scottish contemporary art. Outside, 25,000 newly planted trees and stunning views.

Lyne Farmhouse

A hearty Scottish breakfast will set you up for a day on the hills: whether you choose ponies, bikes or hiking boots, these 1,000 acres demand to be explored. At the end of the rough track is a proper working farm and rural getaway, in the family for years. There's a sitting room for guests (squishy black leather sofas, pale laminate floors) and fabulous views; bedrooms (flowery wallpaper and bed covers) have a bathroom up and a shower room down. Arran is passionate about all things horsey, wildlife and sheep surround you and there's a colourful garden for summer.

rooms	5: 2 doubles, 1 twin/double with bath/shower; 1 double, 1 twin with bath & shower.
price	£90. Singles £55.
meals	Dinner £27.50.
closed	Christmas; January-February.
directions	From Biggar, A702 for Edinburgh. Just outside Biggar, right on A72 for Skirling. Big wooden house on right opp. village green.

rooms	3: 2 doubles, 1 twin, sharing bath & shower room.
price	£48-£50. Singles £30.
meals	Dinner, 4 courses, £24. Supper £12. BYO. Packed lunch £3-£5.
closed	Christmas Day.
directions	4 miles west of Peebles on A72, signed on right-hand side of main road.

Bob & Isobel Hunter
Skirling House,
Skirling,
Biggar,
Scottish Borders ML12 6HD
tel   01899 860274
fax   01899 860255
e-mail enquiry@skirlinghouse.com
web   www.skirlinghouse.com

Arran & John Waddell
Lyne Farmhouse,
Lyne Farm,
Peebles,
Scottish Borders EH45 8NR
tel   01721 740255
fax   01721 740255
e-mail lynefarmhouse@btinternet.com
web   www.lynefarm.co.uk

Map 15 Entry 630

Map 15 Entry 631

Scottish Borders

Over Langshaw Farm

A peaceful, special place in the rolling hills of the Scottish Borders, with an inspiring commitment to organic food and good husbandry. The energy here goes into Friesians and ewes, family and guests, not fluffy towels and deep sofas! So, a delightful place for families and walkers, with simple bedrooms in farmhouse style and a guest sitting room with a log fire and white shutters. Plus all the nooks and crannies you'd expect to find in a 1700s house, and a sweet smiling welcome from Sheila. She and Martyn have detailed walking maps and could not be more helpful. Authentic and brilliant value.

rooms	2: 1 double with shower; 1 family with separate bath.
price	£50. Family room £60. Singles £28.
meals	Dinner from £15. Packed lunch from £4. Pubs/restaurants 4 miles.
closed	Never.
directions	North from Galashiels, A7 past Torwoodlea golf course & right to Langshaw. After 2 miles, right at T-junc., then left at Earlston sign in Langshaw. White house, in trees, signed at farm road.

Sheila & Martyn Bergius
Over Langshaw Farm,
Galashiels,
Scottish Borders TD1 2PE

tel	01896 860244
fax	01896 860668
e-mail	bergius@overlangshaw.fsnet.co.uk
web	www.overlangshaw.com

Map 15 Entry 632

Lessudden

A 16th-century Tweed valley tower house with a magnificent 17th-century staircase; Sir Walter Scott often visited his uncle and aunt who lived here. It is an attractive family home with a relaxed atmosphere, assorted animals and a sitting room you may share. Bedrooms are comfortable, big and homely, one overlooking the Cheviots, the other the Eildons. Although a visiting child was heard to exclaim that she loved this house because "there isn't a modern thing in it!" there are the vital nods to modernity: central heating and, for Angie's excellent cooking, a sparkling new kitchen.

rooms	2: 1 double with bath; 1 twin with separate bath.
price	From £60. Singles from £45.
meals	Dinner, 3 courses, £25. Pub in village, good restaurants 3 miles.
closed	Rarely.
directions	North on A68 to St Boswells. Right opp. Buccleuch Arms Hotel, on thro' village; left up drive immed. beyond turning to golf course.

Alasdair & Angela
Douglas-Hamilton
Lessudden,
St Boswells,
Scottish Borders TD6 0BH

tel	01835 823244
e-mail	alasdaird@lineone.net
web	www.lessudden.com

Map 16 Entry 633

Scottish Borders

New Belses Farm

Once lost by Lord Lothian in a game of backgammon, this Georgian farmhouse is safe in current hands. Delightful Helen divides her time between cooking – her passion – and caring for sundry pets, fan-tail doves, hens (fox permitting), family, farm and guests. Bedrooms glow in a harmony of old paintings, lush chintzes and beautiful antiques; beds are extra long, towels snowy white. It's like home, only better. Discover the Border villages by bike (they have electric ones), then back to a wholesome dinner around the farmhouse table, and coffee on plump sofas by the log fire. Heaven.

Hobsburn

An early 18th-century laird's house of personality and charm. It is surrounded by lawn, gardens and Scottish Border hills upon which woolly Highland cattle graze; Christopher can take you on a safari. He and Jacqui generously usher you in to a home rich with much-loved pieces, kilims and bold colours, pictures, posies, good books and laughter. There's a warmly elegant drawing room for guests and two super bedrooms, one Quaker-contemporary, the other traditional with French beds. Outside, 140 species of wild flowers in 60 acres, blissful peace and a gorgeous black lab. *Stabling available.*

	New Belses Farm		Hobsburn
rooms	2: 1 double, 1 twin, both with bath/shower.	rooms	2: 1 twin, 1 double (with extra bed), both with separate bath or shower.
price	£60-£70.	price	£80. Singles from £50.
meals	Dinner, 2-4 courses, from £20. Supper £12. Lunch by arrangement. Packed lunch £3-£5. Good pubs/restaurants 3.5-5 miles.	meals	Dinner with drinks, £30 Pub 500 yds.
closed	Rarely.	closed	Rarely.
directions	From Jedburgh, A68 for Edinburgh. Left after 3.5 miles to Ancrum; B6400 Ancrum to Lilliesleaf road; right after 4 miles, down drive (signed).	directions	A68 over Border & 1st left onto B6088 for Chesters. Thro' Chesters; enter Bonchester down hill towards large bridge. Pass Horse & Hounds; over small bridge; drive on left.

	Peter & Helen Wilson		Christopher & Jacqui
	New Belses Farm,		McLean May
	Ancrum,		Hobsburn,
	Jedburgh,		Bonchester Bridge, Hawick,
	Scottish Borders TD8 6UR		Scottish Borders TD9 8JW
tel	01835 870472	tel	01450 860720
fax	01835 870482	fax	01450 860330
e-mail	wilson699@totalise.co.uk	e-mail	b+b@mcleanmay.com
		web	www.hobsburn.com

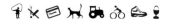

Map 16 Entry 634

Map 16 Entry 635

Stirling

Cardross

Dodge the lazy sheep on the long, slightly bumpy drive to arrive (eventually!) at a sweep of gravel and lovely old (1598) Cardross with its 14th-century tower. Bang on the enormous old door and either Archie or Nicola (plus labradors and Jack Russells) will usher you in. And what a delight it is; light and space, exquisite furniture, wooden shutters, marble fireplaces, fresh flowers, crisp linen, a cast-iron period bath – and that's just the bedroom. It all feels warm, kind and generous, the drawing room is vast, the food is excellent and the lovely Orr Ewings can tell you all the history.

The Moss

Rozie loves fishing and Jamie keeps bees; they live in a charming listed house full of lovely things and are great hosts. Outside are 28 acres where deer prune the roses, pheasants roam and a garden seat sits with its toes in the water. Generous, carpeted bedrooms are in a private wing and have big beds with feather pillows, books, flowers and cosy windows that overlook the garden. Expect walking sticks and the bell of HMS Tempest in the porch, rugs in the hall and smart sofas in the log-fired drawing room. Breakfast comes fresh from the Aga and is delivered to a big oak table with lovely long views.

	Cardross		The Moss
rooms	2: 1 twin with bath; 1 twin with separate bath.	rooms	3: 1 twin with bath; 2 doubles, sharing bath (2nd room let to same party).
price	£80-£90. Singles £50-£55.	price	£80. Singles £40.
meals	Dinner by arrangement. Good pubs/restaurants 2.5-6 miles.	meals	Good pubs/restaurants within 2 miles.
closed	January-March	closed	Rarely.
directions	A811 Stirling-Dumbarton to Arnprior; then B8034 towards Port of Menteith; 3 miles, then cross the Forth over humpback bridge. Drive with yellow lodge 150 yds from bridge on right.	directions	4 miles west of Blanefield. Left off A81 opp. Cairn Conservatories. After 300 yds, over bridge; 1st entrance on left.

Sir Archie & Lady Orr Ewing
Cardross,
Port of Menteith,
Kippen,
Stirling FK8 3JY
tel   01877 385223
fax   01877 385223
e-mail   adoewing@cardrossestate.demon.co.uk
web   www.cardrossholidayhomes.com

Jamie & Rozie Parker
The Moss,
Killearn,
Stirling G63 9LJ
tel   01360 550053
mobile   07787 123599
e-mail   themoss@freeuk.com

Map 15 Entry 636

Map 15 Entry 637

Western Isles

Airdabhaigh

A rare 'undiscovered' corner of Britain… moody hills, lochs and acres of treeless blowy shores are wildly atmospheric and there are miles of white sandy beaches, too. Weather systems chase each other over the vast skies throwing up ever-changing landscapes of brilliant blues, mossy greens and calamitous greys. Flora is inspirational; she's involved in Community Arts and runs dyeing and weaving workshops – a unique island experience. Wood panelling, thick walls and a peat fire – it's 100% authentic. You'll sleep soundly and cosily in pretty, simple bedrooms.

No 6

On Harris, you can reach up and touch the sky. Moorland walks start from the garden, seabirds swoop overhead. The house is built for practicality not beauty but once inside the warmth and views enchant. Bedrooms are unpretentious with pretty wallpapers and cushions; the shared primrose bathroom is clean and functional. Guests gather in the bright, cluttered sitting room to enjoy fantastic cooking – fresh seafood, home bakes – and share their days. Walk, fish, cycle, paint – Margaret is wonderful and offers transport, maps, beach towels; return to a warming tot by the fire. Real value.

rooms	2: 1 double, 1 twin, sharing shower.
price	£50. Singles £20-£25.
meals	Pub close by.
closed	Rarely.
directions	From Lochmaddy ferry, left on A867 for 8.6 miles to T-junc. Left on A865 for 2.4 miles (ignore signs to Carinish), then right at church. Up track. House 1st on left.

rooms	3: 1 double, 2 singles all sharing bathroom.
price	£40. Singles £20.
meals	Dinner from £16.50. Good pubs nearby.
closed	Rarely.
directions	A859 Tarbert to Leverburgh. In village, follow this road; left just before 30mph sign at Barraid Lever sign. 1st left at end of cul-de-sac; look for red gate.

Flora Macdonald
Airdabhaigh,
Uppertown,
Carinish,
North Uist,
Western Isles HS6 5HL
tel   01876 580611
mobile   07748 935204
e-mail   floraidh1@aol.com

Margaret Cowie
No 6,
Lever Terrace,
Leverburgh,
Isle of Harris HS5 3TU
tel   01859 520430
mobile   07733157273
e-mail   m_cowie@lineone.net
web   www.6leverterrace.co.uk

Map 20 Entry 638

Map 20 Entry 639

Wales

Cardiff

Rock House

Minutes from the beach, the limestone house with veranda and pretty terraced cottage garden has a thoroughly relaxing feel. Breakfast outside on fine days and watch the boats on the Bristol Channel as you tuck into Glamorgan sausages (leek and Caerphilly cheese) and home-grown tomatoes. Bedrooms are fresh and light with mahogany furniture, unusual paintings, comfy beds, goose down duvets and lovely patterned and crocheted antique bedspreads. Jane and David are easy-going, generous hosts – there's even a small bottle of wine in your room. It's a short hop to Cardiff centre and airport.

rooms	3: 1 double with bath & shower; 2 doubles sharing bath (2nd room let to same party).
price	£40-£60. Singles £35.
meals	Packed lunch £4. Good restaurants an easy walk.
closed	Occasionally.
directions	At r'bout with clock in Penarth centre, go straight on; 1st left (Church Rd), 1st right (Bradford Pl) & 1st right onto Beach Lane. Walk down passage & enter through back garden.

Jane & David Maw Cornish
Rock House,
9 Beach Road,
Penarth,
Cardiff CF64 1JX
tel   02920 704314
fax   02920 704314
e-mail   rockhouse-penarth@supanet.com
web   www.rockhouse-penarth.co.uk

Map 2 Entry 640

Carmarthenshire

Mandinam

On a heavenly bluff on the edge of the Beacons, beneath wheeling kites and moody Welsh skies, lies Mandinam, the 'untouched holy place'. Daniella and Marcus, an artist, are its guardians, the farm is now mostly conservation land and they look after you as friends. Expect bold rugs on wooden floors, weathered antiques, lofty ceilings, shutters, fires and scrumptious meals in a bright red dining room. The coach house studio, with hillside terrace and woodburning stove, is for dreamers; the new four-poster room has underfloor heating. Watch the sun go down before dinner, soak up the magic.

rooms	3: 1 double with separate bath; 1 four-poster with bath & shower off courtyard. 1 twin/double with shower.
price	£70. Singles by arrangement.
meals	Dinner with wine, £25. Lunch or picnic from £7.50. Pub 2.5 miles.
closed	Christmas.
directions	A40 Llandeilo-Llandovery, exit for Llangadog. Left at Mace shop; 50 yds; right for Myddfai. Pass cemetery, 1st right for Llanddeusant; 1.5 miles, track through woods on left.

Daniella & Marcus Lampard
Mandinam,
Llangadog,
Carmarthenshire SA19 9LA
tel   01550 777368
e-mail   info@mandinam.co.uk
web   www.mandinam.co.uk

Map 7 Entry 641

Carmarthenshire

Mount Pleasant Farm

Sheep bleat, red kites fly overhead and the views to the Black Mountain are breathtaking: your bedroom view must be one of the best in this book. Sue are her daughter are warm and delightful and Sue is a brilliant cook. Only the best local lamb and beef will do, the veg is organic and the eggs (bright orange!) are their own; vegetarians are spoiled too. After dinner there's snooker, a log fire, a cosy sofa; then a seriously comfortable bed in a room with a lovely country-house feel. Aberglasney and the National Botanic Garden are nearby, beautiful coastal walks less than an hour away.

Plas Alltyferin

From the highest point on these 270 acres you look down the valley to the rushing salmon river, long lawns, woodland, bluebell woods, a Norman hill fort and the Towy Valley. The house is Georgian, and keeps its period charm; the dining room has the original panelling. The drawing room is grand and smart, the two bedrooms less so, replete with the plumbing eccentricities and patina that you may expect of an aged house, but they are large and the beds are comfortable. The views are lovely and the welcome heartfelt – Gerard and Charlotte are the easiest and kindest of hosts. *Children over 10 welcome.*

rooms	3: 1 twin/double with bath; 1 twin/double, 1 single, sharing bath (let to same party).
price	£58. Singles £30-£35.
meals	Dinner, 3 courses, £17.50 with wine. Packed lunch £7.50.
closed	Christmas.
directions	A40 Llandovery-Llandeilo. At Llanwrda, right for Lampeter (A482). Out of village, 1st right after mounted pillar box in lay-by on left. Over bridge & up hill; 1st left. House 1st on right.

rooms	2: 1 twin with shower; 1 twin with bath/shower.
price	From £50. Singles from £30.
meals	Excellent pubs/restaurants within 2 miles.
closed	Rarely.
directions	From Carmarthen A40 east to Pont-ar-gothi. Left before bridge & follow small lane for approx. 2 miles keeping to right-hand hedge. House on right. Call for precise details.

	Sue, Nick & Alice Thompson
	Mount Pleasant Farm,
	Llanwrda,
	Carmarthenshire SA19 8AN
tel	01550 777537
fax	01550 777537
e-mail	rivarevivaluk@aol.com

	Charlotte & Gerard Dent
	Plas Alltyferin,
	Pont-ar-gothi,
	Nantgaredig,
	Carmarthenshire SA32 7PF
tel	01267 290662
fax	01267 290662
e-mail	dent@alltyferin.fsnet.co.uk
web	www.alltyferin.co.uk

Map 7 Entry 642

Map 6 Entry 643

Carmarthenshire

Capel Dewi Uchaf Country House

New life has been brought to what was a neglected, 14th-century chapel. Pilgrims used to stay here and you'll find the peace restorative; there's even fishing on a private stretch of water. Brass beds and beams, patchwork and chintz, objects galore, vases overflowing with flowers and bowls with fruit, beautifully laid tables for breakfast. There are dried flowers, trinkets, cafetières and good linen in the bedrooms, a teak-tabled terrace for summer teas and plants for sale. Wander at will in a garden that brims with colour, then move on to the National Botanic Garden of Wales. *Stabling for horses.*

Sarnau Mansion

Listed and Georgian, the house has its own water supply. Play tennis and revel in 16 acres of beautiful grounds complete with pond and woodland. Bedrooms are simply furnished, in heritage colours; bathrooms are big. The oak-floored sitting room with chesterfields has French windows onto the walled garden, the dining room is simpler with separate tables and there's good, fresh home cooking from Cynthia. One mile from the A40, you can hear a slight hum of traffic if the wind is in that direction. You are 15 minutes from the National Botanic Garden of Wales. *Children over 5 welcome.*

	Capel Dewi Uchaf		Sarnau Mansion
rooms	3: 1 double with bath/shower; 1 double with shower; 1 twin with separate bath.	rooms	3: 2 doubles, 1 twin, all with bath/shower.
price	£66. Singles £45.	price	£50-£60. Singles £30-£40.
meals	Dinner, 5 courses, £45 (min. 6 people). Restaurant 0.75 miles.	meals	Dinner, 3 courses, around £20. BYO. Good pub 1 mile.
closed	Christmas.	closed	Rarely.
directions	B4300 from Carmarthen to Capel Dewi. Leaving village follow sign on left & down drive off main road.	directions	From Carmarthen A40 west for 4 miles. Right for Bancyfelin. After 0.5 miles, right into drive on brow of hill.

Fredena Burns
Capel Dewi Uchaf Country House,
Capel Dewi Road,
Capel Dewi,
Carmarthenshire SA32 8AY

tel	01267 290799	tel	01267 211404
fax	01267 290003	fax	01267 211404
e-mail	uchaffarm@aol.com	e-mail	fernihough@so1405.force9.co.uk
web	www.walescottageholidays.uk.com	web	www.sarnaumansion.co.uk

Cynthia & David Fernihough
Sarnau Mansion,
Llysonnen Road,
Bancyfelin,
Carmarthenshire SA33 5DZ

Map 6 Entry 644

Map 6 Entry 645

Ceredigion

Broniwan

Carole and Allen have created a model organic farm, and it shows. They are happy, the cows are happy and the kitchen garden is the neatest in Wales. With huge warmth and a tray of Welsh cakes they invite you into their cosy, ivy-clad house of natural browns, reds and the odd vibrant flourish of local art. Another passion is literature; call to arrange a literary weekend. Plentiful birdlife in the wonderful garden with views to the Preseli hills adds an audible welcome from tree-creepers, redstarts and wrens. The National Botanic Garden of Wales and Aberglasney are nearby, the coastal paths a quick drive.

rooms	2: 1 double with shower; 1 double with separate bath.
price	£58-£60. Singles £30.
meals	Dinner £20. Light supper £14.50.
closed	Rarely.
directions	From Aberaeron, A487 for 6 miles for Brynhoffnant. Left at B4334 to Rhydlewis; left at Post Office & shop, 1st lane on right, then 1st track on right.

Carole & Allen Jacobs
Broniwan,
Rhydlewis,
Llandysul,
Ceredigion SA44 5PF
tel   01239 851261
fax   01239 851261
e-mail   broniwan@beeb.net

Map 6 Entry 646

Conwy

Rhiw y goch

The 1650 longhouse, once a gathering place for drovers, overlooks the lush Lledr valley. Old-fashioned armchairs stuffed with cushions pull up around the woodburner, a rug covers the black slate floor and there's a piano you may play; small concerts are sometimes held for charity. Blow the cobwebs away on the Lleyn peninsula, visit the gardens of Bodnant, return to 35 hillside acres where rhododendrons and azaleas merge seductively into wilder woodland – the garden is Abigail's passion. Big bedrooms are comfortable not luxurious – and you may bring your own wine. *Minimun stay two nights.*

rooms	2: 1 double, 1 family, sharing bath.
price	£54. Singles from £27.
meals	Packed lunch £5. Good pub 5-minute drive.
closed	Christmas & New Year.
directions	A470 Betws y Coed-Dollgelleau for 3 miles; right, 200 yds after sign for Ponty Pant railway station; follow lane to top of hill. On round to right, past green shed to house beyond.

Abigail King
Rhiw y goch,
Pont y pant,
Dolwyddelan,
Conwy LL25 0PQ
tel   01690 750231

Map 7 Entry 647

Denbighshire

Rhagatt Hall

Amble down through bluebell woods and parkland to the river, with pheasants and lambs for company. This large, stone-built Georgian house on the upper reaches of the river Dee is a peaceful place. Wholly modernised inside, it dates in part from the 14th century and is one of the oldest sites on the river. Fresh, immaculate rooms include a deep red drawing room with French windows that open to the terrace, and floral bedrooms looking towards the river or the Berwyn hills. A sunny walled garden hides a tennis court – and you can swim in the indoor pool under the painted gaze of an Egyptian god.

rooms	2: 1 twin, 1 double with extra bed, both with bath.
price	£80. Singles £50. Children's rates on request.
meals	Dinner, 3 courses, £22. Supper £12. Good pub/restaurant 2 miles.
closed	Christmas & New Year.
directions	From A5, right onto B5437. Over river, left; through Carrog village after 0.25 miles; keep left. House on right after 300 yds.

Frances Bradshaw
Rhagatt Hall,
Carrog,
Corwen,
Denbighshire LL21 9HY

| tel | 01490 412308 |
| e-mail | fjcb@btopenworld.com |

Map 7 Entry 648

Flintshire

Tower

Such a sense of adventure as you climb the steps to the tower bedrooms: the age and history of the place make the heart soar. Bedrooms have latticed mullioned windows, dark traditional furniture and, big beds. This is the only remaining fortified house on the border and it was built over 500 years ago, by the family who occupy it now. The medieval dining hall in the tower displays the coat of arms and the family motto, 'Without God there is Nothing'. A full Welsh breakfast is served by delightful hosts at the library end of the drawing room. Outside, four lovely acres of formal gardens.

rooms	3: 1 double with bath; 1 double, 1 twin/double, both with separate bath.
price	£80. Singles £50.
meals	Pubs & restaurants within 2 miles.
closed	22 December-3 January.
directions	To traffic lights in the centre of Mold, onto Wrexham St (B5444). After 0.7 miles, fork right to Nercwys. After 0.4 miles; entrance on right, through large black gates.

Charles & Mairi Wynne-Eyton
Tower,
Nercwys,
Mold,
Flintshire CH7 4EW

tel	01352 700220
e-mail	bookings@towerwales.co.uk
web	www.towerwales.co.uk

Map 7 Entry 649

Flintshire

Pentre Cerrig Mawr

Church records show that the house was built in Elizabethan times with some Victorian additions. Surrounded by bluebell woods, it is wonderfully remote and peaceful, and a two-acre terraced garden adds to the magic. Inside are beams, open fires and enchanting valley views from every window. Cosy bedrooms are full of comfort – goose down duvets, cushion-bedecked sofas, soft carpets; gold-tapped bathrooms have big towels and 'green' bathtime goodies. Much of the food is organic and local, and Charmian and Ted are super hosts. Handy for Chester. *Children over eight welcome.*

Plas Penucha

Polished parquet, tidy beams and a huge Elizabethan panelled lounge; Plas Penucha – 'the big house on the highest point in the parish' – has been in the family for 500 years. There's a little sitting room for guests with an open fire, and two bright and airy bedrooms with hill views to Offa's Dyke. You breakfast – deliciously – in the big L-shaped dining room: a genuine Arts & Crafts interior. Outside, rhododendrons, a rock garden and croquet; beyond, Caerwys, birthplace of the National Eisteddfod, and St Asaph, with the smallest medieval cathedral in the country.

rooms	2: 1 twin/double, 1 double, both with bath/shower.
price	£90-£100.
meals	Good pub/restaurant 0.5 mile.
closed	Rarely.
directions	From Mold A494 for Ruthin. Past Rainbow Inn & left for Maeshafn. There, past phone box, left fork (yellow sign) through woods; follow to end. House on right through gates & courtyard.

rooms	2: 1 double, 1 twin, both with shower.
price	From £54. Singles from £27.
meals	Dinner £15. Packed lunch £3. Good pub 3 miles.
closed	Rarely.
directions	From Chester, A55, B5122 left for Caerwys. 1st right into High St. Right at end. 0.75 miles to x-roads & left, then straight for 1 mile. House on left, signed.

Charmian & Ted Spencer
Pentre Cerrig Mawr,
Maeshafn,
Mold,
Flintshire CH7 5LU

tel	01352 810607
fax	01352 810607
e-mail	pentre.cerrig@virgin.net
web	www.pentrecerrigmawr.com

Mrs Nest Price
Plas Penucha,
Peny Cefn Road,
Caerwys, Mold,
Flintshire CH7 5BH

tel	01352 720210
fax	01352 720881
e-mail	nest@plaspenucha.freeserve.co.uk
web	www.plaspenucha.co.uk

Map 7 Entry 650

Map 7 Entry 651

Flintshire

Golden Grove

Pure Elizabethan, magical and intriguing – Golden Grove was built by Sir Edward Morgan in 1580. The Queen Anne dog-leg staircase, oak panelling and furniture are set off beautifully by the rich jewel colour schemes (the breakfast room red, the dining room a subtle aquamarine). The two Anns are wonderful hosts, serving breakfast from kitchens at each end of the morning room. The family foursome tend the formal garden, organic vegetable garden and nuttery and run a sheep farm as well as their relaxed B&B. People return again and again to this exceptional place.

Gwynedd

The Old Rectory

An immaculate drive leads to the rectory opposite the church; it's Georgian and grand but, thanks to Gabrielle, not intimidatingly so. Orchids in the gardens, horses in the paddock; Gabrielle rides and Roger sails. You get comfortable beds, ample pillows, delicious towels, fresh flowers, scrambled eggs with smoked salmon if desired; come and go as you please. Seagrass and Persian rugs, big mirrors and family antiques, log fires on cool evenings, a smart guest drawing room – and beaches and mountains to explore without the traffic and crowds. People book for one night and stay for more.

rooms	3: 1 double with bath; 1 twin, 1 double, both with separate bath & wc.
price	£90. Singles £55.
meals	Dinner £28.
closed	Mid-November–mid-February
directions	Turn off A55 onto A5151 for Prestatyn. At Texaco before Trelawnyd, right. Branch left immed. over 1st x-roads & right at T-junc. Gates 170 yds on left.

rooms	4: 2 twins/doubles, 1 double, all with bath; 1 double with shower.
price	£85. Singles £50-£60.
meals	Dinner, 2-3 courses, £20-£25 (Oct-March). Packed lunch £6.50. Pub/restaurant 1.5 miles.
closed	Christmas.
directions	From Pwllheli, A499 to r'bout. Right onto A497 Nefyn & Boduan road for 3 miles; left opp. church; house set back, on right.

Ann & Mervyn and Ann & Nigel
Steele-Mortimer
Golden Grove,
Llanasa,
Holywell,
Flintshire CH8 9NA
tel   01745 854452
fax   01745 854547
e-mail golden.grove@lineone.net

Gabrielle & Roger Pollard
The Old Rectory,
Boduan,
Pwllheli,
Gwynedd LL53 6DT
tel   01758 721519
fax   01758 721519
e-mail thepollards@theoldrectory.net
web   www.theoldrectory.net

Map 7 Entry 652

Map 6 Entry 653

Gwynedd

Plas Tan-yr-allt

Who shot Shelley in the drawing room? The poet fled in 1813, the mystery unsolved. The Grade II-listed house has a colourful history, irresistible to the new owners. They have just finished a glorious restoration: roll-top baths, deep luscious colours, underfloor heating, handsome furniture. *The Guardian* described it as "a spanking new Soho club with a view". Indeed, there is a touch of swagger – and impeccable taste. The views from the terrace and gardens stretch over the bay and estuary. There are 47 acres of wooded hillside and a mountain backdrop. Great food and company, too.

rooms	6: 3 doubles, 2 four-posters, all with bath/shower; 1 twin with bath & shower.
price	£95–£120. Singles £70–£95.
meals	Pubs/restaurants 10-minute walk.
closed	Rarely.
directions	From Tremadog, right onto A498 towards Beddgelert. After 0.5 miles, sign on left for drive. House at top of hill.

Michael Bewick & Nick Golding
Plas Tan-yr-allt,
Tremadog,
Porthmadog,
Gwynedd LL49 9RG
tel   01766 514545
e-mail   info@tanyrallt.co.uk
web   www.tanyrallt.co.uk

Map 6 Entry 654

Erw

Edwardian Erw is a delightful warm home whose one-acre organic garden frames glorious sea views. Bedrooms are havens of comfort: top quality beds and linens, good lighting, pictures, books and well-fitted bathrooms with huge towels on heated rails. Downstairs: a split-level drawing room and deep turquoise dining room furnished with hand-made furniture and contemporary art and pots. Trudie, larger than life and full of fun, has a deep knowledge of Snowdonia to help you plan lazy days around the coast – or active days on mountain tops! Breakfasts are mostly organic and irresistible.

rooms	2: 1 twin/double with bath & shower; 1 double with shower.
price	£85–£120. Singles £60–£75.
meals	Dinner £28.
closed	Rarely.
directions	On A496 in Llanfair; entrance directly opp. signed 'Slate Caverns'.

Trudie Hunt
Erw,
Llanfair,
Harlech,
Gwynedd LL46 2SA
tel   01766 780780
fax   01766 781010
e-mail   erwharlech@waitrose.com
web   www.erwharlech.co.uk

Map 6 Entry 655

Gwynedd

Tan-y-Coed Isaf

In a dramatic valley descending from the steep mountains of Cader Idris to the sea, this is the sort of retreat that has city dwellers vowing to leave for the country. Cottagey, informal bedrooms are fresh in blues and whites, with flowers in each and exceptional mattresses. The pretty terraced garden tumbles down from the house and merges with the scenery beyond. The cosy sitting room, beamed and warmed by the fire in the inglenook, is entirely for guests. Dining will be an experience as Jane is a professional Cordon Bleu chef and uses seasonal vegetables from the garden.

Abercelyn Country House

The 1729 rectory comes with rhododendron-rich grounds, an immaculate kitchen garden and a mountain stream. The stream has its own history: its waters poisoned Cromwell's horses in the Civil War, enabling the opposition to skedaddle. Today Abercelyn is a less battle-scarred retreat. Shutters gleam, logs glow and bedrooms have space, light, smart bathrooms and luscious views. The drawing room overflows with outdoor guides, Ray orchestrates adventure trips to Snowdonia National Park and Lindsay cooks and looks after you beautifully. All this and Bala Lake a 10-minute stroll.

rooms	2: 1 double, 1 twin/double, both with bath. Single available, let to same party only.
price	£50-£60. Singles by arrangement.
meals	Dinner, 2 courses, from £18.50; 3 courses, from £25. BYO. Good pub/restaurant 1 mile.
closed	Rarely.
directions	A487 from Machynlleth for Dolgellau. Left onto B4405, through Abergynolwyn. 2nd farmhouse on right after 1 mile.

rooms	3: 2 doubles, 1 twin/double, all with bath/shower.
price	£56-£70. Singles. £40.
meals	Dinner, 2-3 courses, £15-£18. Good pub 10-minute drive.
closed	Rarely.
directions	On A494 Bala-Dolgellau road, 1 mile from the centre of Bala, opposite Llanycil Church.

	Mrs J Howkins
	Tan-y-Coed Isaf,
	Bryncrug,
	Tywyn,
	Gwynedd LL36 9UP
tel	01654 782639
fax	01654 782639
e-mail	tanhow@supanet.com
web	www.tanycoedisaf.co.uk

	Ray & Lindsay Hind
	Abercelyn Country House,
	Llanycil,
	Bala,
	Gwynedd LL23 7YF
tel	01678 521109
fax	01678 520848
e-mail	info@abercelyn.co.uk
web	www.abercelyn.co.uk

Map 7 Entry 656

Map 7 Entry 657

Gwynedd

Dolgadfa

Gasp at the jaw-dropping beauty of the road to Dolgadfa, every bend revealing yet another camera shot of soft southern Snowdonia – the gentle prelude to the ragged peaks. The youthful Robertsons' slice of this bliss is unexpectedly luxurious, and the deep, limpid river winds past the newly-converted guest barn. The rooms – one with stone steps straight onto the riverside garden – are fresh yellow, with wall-to-wall beige carpet, hunting prints and all the trimmings. A bright living room with roaring fire, sofas and stripped floor is yours. Louise does a fine breakfast. *Fishing & shooting available.*

rooms	2: 1 double/twin with bath; 1 double/ twin with separate bath.
price	£80-£90. Singles £45.
meals	Excellent pub and restaurant in village.
closed	Christmas.
directions	From B4401 after Llandrillo take 2nd right. Single track road; over bridge. At T-junc. left, follow road for approx. 1.5 miles; 2nd grey stone farmhouse on left. White gate.

	Louise Robertson
	Dolgadfa,
	Llandderfel,
	Bala,
	Gwynedd LL23 7RE
tel	01678 530469
e-mail	dolgadfa@btinternet.com
web	www.dolgadfa.co.uk

Map 7 Entry 658

Monmouthshire

Castle Acre

Between castle and church, the house lies hidden in a walled garden. A low stone and brick building full of light, cleverly converted from stabling and a coach house. Breakfast in the salmon-pink dining room with its glossy antiques, books and garden views. Choose between the terracotta bedroom, overlooking the castle ruins, or the primrose room with adjoining attic – perfect for children – overlooking the church. Bathrooms have tongue and groove panelling; all is cool, pretty and relaxing. Walk Offa's Dyke or the Black Mountains, browse Hay's bookshops, doze in the garden. Sue is warmly efficient.

rooms	2: 1 twin/double, 1 double, both with bath.
price	£80. Singles £40.
meals	Good pubs 1-4 miles.
closed	Never.
directions	M4 junc. 24, onto A449. 12 miles; exit Abergavenny. A40 for 9 miles, A465 for Hereford; 6 miles on, right marked Grosmont to T-junc., right to village, right to castle. Drive on right.

	Sue Gill
	Castle Acre,
	Grosmont,
	Monmouthshire NP7 8LW
tel	01981 241078
fax	01981 240874
e-mail	greatcampston@aol.com
web	www.castleacregrosmont.co.uk

Map 7 Entry 659

Monmouthshire

Little Mill Farm

Ann and Michael, an architect, ran from London 15 years ago and here they found peace. They are welcoming and helpful, yet never intrusive. Encircled by trees, three miles from Offa's Dyke Path, their organic homestead is a reflection of their values. The sitting room is yours: good rugs on planked floors, chunky beams and white walls, an oak corner stair dating from 1575. Bedrooms share a beautiful simplicity and have delicious touches – snowdrops, sheepskin rugs, Indian throws. Meals are organic; each mouthful of the saddleback sausage reminds you of the delights of real food.

Penpergwm Lodge

A large Edwardian house in the lovely Usk valley. The Boyles have been here for 28 years and pour most of their energy into the garden: big and beautiful, with a folly and summer house you may use. Catriona sells plants and runs a garden school. The house is pretty and rambling; breakfast round the mahogany table, relax in the comfortably old-fashioned sitting room. Bedrooms have fine bedcovers and garden views; small bathrooms share a corridor. Great walking all around in the nearby Brecon Beacons National Park, swimming in the summer pool. Good, solid B&B.

rooms	3: 1 double with shower; 1 double, 1 twin sharing bath (let to same party).
price	£42-£54. Singles from £25.
meals	Dinner, 3 courses, £15 (weekends only). Pubs/restaurants 5-10 miles.
closed	Rarely.
directions	Monmouth B4233 for Rockfield; B4347 to Newcastle. In village, left into hidden lane immed. Past phone box; 1 mile; at staggered x-roads, right then left (church on right); at end after 1km.

rooms	2 twins, both with separate bath.
price	£60-£70. Singles £40.
meals	Good pub within walking distance.
closed	Rarely.
directions	A40 to Abergavenny; at big r'bout on SE edge of town, B4598 to Usk for 2.5 miles. Left at King of Prussia pub, up small lane; house 200 yds on left.

Ann Eggleton
Little Mill Farm,
Llanfaenor,
Newcastle,
Monmouth,
Monmouthshire NP25 5NF
tel   01600 780449
e-mail   anneggleton@waitrose.com

Catriona Boyle
Penpergwm Lodge,
Abergavenny,
Monmouthshire NP7 9AS
tel   01873 840208
fax   01873 840208
e-mail   boyle@penpergwm.co.uk
web   www.penplants.com

Map 7 Entry 660

Map 7 Entry 661

Pembrokeshire

Bowett Farm

An ancient bluebell wood pulsates with colour in the spring and wild flowers of all kinds bloom in profusion. If you're lucky, you might see a badger lumbering into the garden. This is a friendly, gracious house, filled with gorgeous Welsh antiques, candles and crystal. One of the bedrooms has a fine, restored half-tester bed and a giant private bathroom with Victorian washstand and fluffy bathrobes to envelop you. To fuel yourself for a day's walking, breakfast on local produce, homemade jams and marmalades, fresh fruit salad and yogurt... the Pembrokeshire coastal path runs through the farm.

rooms	3: 1 double with separate bath; 1 twin with separate shower; 1 single (let to same party only).
price	£60. Singles £30.
meals	Packed lunch £5. Pub/restaurant 0.5 miles.
closed	Mid-October-Easter.
directions	B4320 from Pembroke for Hundleton. After woods, house 1st on right. Approx. 1 mile from Pembroke centre.

Ann & Bill Morris
Bowett Farm,
Hundleton,
Pembroke,
Pembrokeshire SA71 5QS
tel 01646 683473
fax 01646 683473
e-mail bowett@pembrokeshire.com
web www.bowettfarmhouse.co.uk

Map 6 Entry 662

Cresswell House

'Make yourself at home' is Philip's style: easy to do in the old quay master's house with its laid-back atmosphere and estuary views. The Wights have decorated boldly but with respect for the Georgian interior, and the bedrooms are carpeted and cosy, particularly the one with the wrought-iron four-poster. Warm breads from a coal-fired oven and suppers delicious and wholesome: perhaps their own wild smoked salmon and home-grown veg. Picnic at the end of the garden amid kingfishers, herons and curlews. It's fun and easy, the setting is wonderful and there's a great little pub two minutes away.

rooms	3: 1 double with shower; 1 twin with separate bath/shower; 1 four-poster with bath.
price	£65. Singles £45.
meals	Supper £10-£15. Packed lunch £7.50.
closed	Occasionally.
directions	From A477, right onto A4075. Left at brown sign for Cresswell House; on left after 1.4 miles, just before bridge.

Philip Wight
Cresswell House,
Cresswell Quay,
Pembroke,
Pembrokeshire SA68 0TE
tel 01646 651435
e-mail phil@cresswellhouse.co.uk
web www.cresswellhouse.co.uk

Map 6 Entry 663

Pembrokeshire

Knowles Farm

The Cleddau Estuary winds its way around the boundary of this 1,000-acre organic arable and dairy farm; the lush grass feeds the cows that produce milk for the renowned 'Rachel's' yogurts. It's quite a collection of quirky farm buildings, best seen from the back lawns where you can picnic, barbecue and explore the woods. Ginny is a helpful and unobtrusive host, and rustles up delicious organic dinners that are served in a dining room rich with dark wood antiques. Bedrooms are simple yet comfortable; there are floral curtains and bedspreads, comfy beds and fresh woodland flowers.

Haroldston Hall

The sandy beaches and clifftop walks of the Pembrokeshire coast are a mile from the pretty, medieval, country house. It is secluded and surrounded by rolling farmland, with horses, peacocks and a croquet lawn. Inside are antiques, open fires and a large orangery that opens onto the walled garden. Ben, a lively host and retired cabinet-maker, has made some of the attractive furniture. The bedrooms are simple: some beds are ornate, some firmer than others, fabrics are floral, Ben's fathers oil paintings hang on the walls. Drink in the stunning sunsets over St Bride's Bay. *Minimum stay two nights.*

	Knowles Farm		Haroldston Hall
rooms	3: 1 double with bath; 1 double with shower; 1 twin with separate bath.	rooms	3: 2 doubles, both with bath; 1 twin/double with separate bath.
price	£52-£60. Singles £25-£32.	price	£50-£70. Singles from £40.
meals	Dinner, 4 courses, £22. Supper from £12. Packed lunch £6. Pub 1.5 miles.	meals	Packed lunch £7. Good pubs/restaurants 2-3 miles.
closed	Rarely.	closed	Rarely.
directions	A4075 to Cresselly; turn right. Follow signs for Lawrenny to first x-roads; straight over; next x-roads right; 100 yds on left.	directions	B4341 to Broad Haven thro' Portfield Gate. After 2 miles, turn for Timber Hill Holiday Lodges; keep following lodge signs. On right, 0.5 miles before lodges.

	Knowles Farm		Haroldston Hall
	Ms Virginia Lort Phillips Knowles Farm, Lawrenny, Pembrokeshire SA68 0PX		Ben & Judith Stewart-Thomas Haroldston Hall, Haroldston West, Broad Haven, Pembrokeshire SA62 3LZ
tel	01834 891221		
fax	01834 891221	tel	01437 781549
e-mail	ginilp@lawrenny.org.uk	e-mail	benjamin@stewart-thomas.fsnet.co.uk
web	www.lawrenny.org.uk	web	www.haroldstonhall.co.uk

Map 6 Entry 664

Map 6 Entry 665

Pembrokeshire

Trevaccoon

Port and flowers in your room, logs in the grate, breakfast from the farmers' market: it doesn't get much better than this. The Georgian house borders the National Park with its coastal path and each restful bedroom has a sea view. Caroline's Swedish-style décor echoes the west coast light – white floorboards, pale antiques, original shutters – and the drawing room welcomes you with a vast sofa. Hire bikes and spin off with a picnic (homemade, delicious) in search of unspoilt beaches, dolphins and seals – or stay put: there's a secret walled garden and a pottery studio for classes.

rooms	5: 3 doubles, 2 twins, all with bath/shower.
price	£75-£110. Singles £50-£70.
meals	Packed lunch from £4. Good pub & restaurant 1.5 miles.
closed	Rarely.
directions	From Fishguard A487. Right at Croesgoch x-roads, 6 miles from St David's. After 1 mile, left at Llanrhian x-roads. House on left, 0.5 miles on.

Caroline Flynn
Trevaccoon,
Llanrhian, St David's,
Haverfordwest,
Pembrokeshire SA62 6DP
tel   01348 831438
mobile   07870 929461
e-mail   flynn@trevaccoon.co.uk
web   www.trevaccoon.co.uk

Map 6 Entry 666

Pentower

What an entrance! The hallway has deep raspberry and pistachio walls with Arts & Crafts lamps and a medieval-style chandelier. Mary and Tony are easy-going and fun and have spent several years restoring it all. Sir Evan Jones built Pentower to have the best views of the harbour, for which he was the civil engineer. Pretty bedrooms are modern, light and airy with sheer curtains and huge showers. You breakfast in the formal, quarry-tiled dining room or on the terrace; curl up in the evening with a cat on rattan chairs; from French windows watch the comings and goings in the harbour below.

rooms	3: 2 doubles, 1 twin, all with shower.
price	£60-£65. Singles £40.
meals	Packed lunch £5. Pubs/restaurants 5-minute walk.
closed	Rarely.
directions	A40 to Fishguard town; at r'bout, 2nd exit onto Main Street. Before sharp left bend, right fork onto Tower Hill; 200 yds on, through house gates.

Tony Jacobs
& Mary Geraldine Casey
Pentower,
Tower Hill,
Fishguard,
Pembrokeshire SA65 9LA
tel   01348 874462
e-mail   pentowerpembs@aol.com
web   www.pentower.co.uk

Map 6 Entry 667

Powys

Glangrwyney Court

It's all here: croquet and boules, a piano that you are welcome to play, a jacuzzi for one of the bedrooms, log fires in the sitting rooms, a cosy honesty bar – and acres of gardens to roam. The Brecon Beacons National Park is close by, and in these glorious four acres there are two huge magnolias and other ancient trees to sit and dream under. Inside, all is solid and traditional rather than informal, and almost luxurious: fitted carpets, antiques and modern furniture, big pelmeted floral curtains and perfect comfort – everything reliable, nothing out of place. It is impressive, and terrific value.

Tyr Chanter

Warmth, colour, children and activity: this house is fun. Tiggy welcomes you like family; help collect eggs, feed Gertie the pig, drop your shoes by the fire. The farmhouse and barn are stylishly relaxed; deep sofas, tartan throws, heaps of books, views to the Brecon Beacons and Black Mountains. Bedrooms are soft, simple sanctuaries with Jo Malone bathroom treats. Children's rooms zing with murals; toys, kids' sitting room, sandpit – child heaven. Walk, fish, canoe, book-browse in Hay or stroll the estate. Homemade cakes, whisky to help yourself to: fine hospitality.

rooms	5: 1 family, 1 twin, both with shower; 1 suite, 1 West Wing double, both with bath/shower; 1 twin with jacuzzi.	
price	£55-£80. Singles £45-£70.	
meals	Packed lunch £7. Good restaurants 500 yds.	
closed	Rarely.	
directions	From Abergavenny, A40 for Brecon & Crickhowell; 2 miles, pass car sales garage on right; 200 yds, county sign. Next drive on right with lodge at gate.	

rooms	4: 1 double with separate bath/shower; 1 double with bath & separate wc; 2 children's rooms.
price	£80. Singles £60.
meals	Packed lunches £7. Good pub 1 mile.
closed	Christmas.
directions	From Crickhowell, A40 towards Brecon. 2 miles left at Gliffaes Hotel sign. 2 miles, past hotel, house is 600yds on right.

Mrs Christina Jackson
Glangrwyney Court,
Crickhowell,
Powys NP8 1ES
tel   01873 811288
fax   01873 810317
e-mail   info@glancourt.co.uk
web   www.glancourt.co.uk

Tiggy Pettifer
Tyr Chanter,
Glanusk,
Crickhowell,
Powys NP8 1RL
tel   01874 731144
fax   01874 731155
e-mail   tiggy@tyrchanter.com

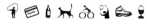

Map 7 Entry 668

Map 7 Entry 669

Powys

The Old Post Office

Gleaming oak floors and staircases are proud features of the little guest house that began life as an inn. Bedrooms are large, simple and fresh, beds comfortable, colours earthy. There's a restful sitting room in which exhausted hikers and their dogs can collapse after a recce in the Black Mountains, while bookworms can seek out the second-hand bookshops of Hay-on-Wye. Whatever you do, you'll be captivated by the region. Linda serves sumptuous vegetarian breakfasts in a cosy, cottagey dining room; she and Ed tend to keep to their own part of the house and you come and go as you please.

Hafod Y Garreg

The oldest house in Wales — a medieval 1402 cruck-built hall house on a hillside overlooking the Wye Valley. Annie and John have imbued this restoration of the former bishop's summer house with their distinctive and delightful personalities — and a fascinating mix of Venetian mirrors, Indian rugs, pewter plates, gorgeous fabrics and Welsh oak furniture. Both bedrooms have antique patchwork quilts; one has a dramatic half-tester. You reach the Grade II*-listed house by a bumpy cobbled track across gated fields; chickens, cats, goats, birds... a special, secluded place.

rooms	3: 1 double, 1 double with extra bed, 1 twin/double, all with shower.
price	£60. Singles £35.
meals	Good pub 2 miles. Pubs/restaurants in Hay-on-Wye.
closed	Rarely.
directions	Hay-on-Wye to Brecon; 0.5 miles, left, signed Llanigon; on for 1 mile,left before school. On right opp. church.

rooms	2 doubles, both with bath.
price	£50. Family room £65. Singles from £40.
meals	Dinner, 3 courses, £15. BYO. Pubs/restaurants 2.5 miles.
closed	Christmas.
directions	From Hay-on-Wye, A479 then A470 to B. Wells. Through Llyswen, past forest on left, down hill. Next left for Trericket Mill, then immed. right & up hill. Straight through gate across track to house.

	Linda Webb & Ed Moore
	The Old Post Office,
	Llanigon,
	Hay-on-Wye,
	Powys HR3 5QA
tel	01497 820008
web	www.oldpost-office.co.uk

	Annie & John McKay
	Hafod Y Garreg,
	Erwood,
	Builth Wells,
	Powys LD2 3TQ
tel	01982 560400
e-mail	john-annie@hafod-y.wanadoo.co.uk
web	www.hafodygarreg.co.uk

Map 7 Entry 670

Map 7 Entry 671

Trericket Mill Vegetarian Guesthouse

Erwood, Builth Wells, Powys LD2 3TQ

Part guest house, part bunk house, part youth hostel – all Grade II*-listed. The dining room has been created amid a jumble of corn-milling machinery: B&B guests, campers and bunkers pile in together to fill hungry bellies with Nicky and Alistair's delicious and plentiful veggie food from a chalkboard menu. Stoves throw out the heat in the flagstoned living rooms with their comfy chairs; the bedrooms are simple pine affairs. Set out to explore from here on foot, horseback, bicycle or canoe; lovers of the outdoors looking for good value and a planet-friendly bias will be in heaven.

Energy consumption has been reduced by installing efficient lighting systems inside and dusk-to-dawn switches out; there are thermostats on the hot-water systems and loft insulation keeps the heat in. Recycling bins are available for guests and as much waste as possible is composted. Delicious vegetarian dinners include fair-trade, wholefood and free-range produce. The house is set on an SSSI and the garden goes down to the river – the biodiversity of flora, fauna and wildlife here is a joy.

rooms	3: 1 twin, 1 double, both with continental bath/shower; 1 double with shower.
price	£50–£60. Singles from £35.
meals	Dinner, 3 courses, £15.50. Simple supper £6. Good pub/restaurant 2 miles.
closed	Rarely.
directions	12 miles north of Brecon on A470. Mill set slightly back from road, on left, between Llyswen & Erwood.

SPECIAL GREEN ENTRY
see page 12

Alistair & Nicky Legge

tel	01982 560312
email	mail@trericket.co.uk
web	www.trericket.co.uk

Map 7 Entry 672

Powys

The Old Vicarage

For devotees of Victoriana, the house, designed by Sir George Gilbert Scott, is a delight both inside and out. Behind the French gothic façade lies the evidence of a lifetime's collecting by Paul: splendid brass beds, cast-iron radiators, period light fittings, original porcelain loos. Sumptuous bedspreads and fabrics add to the exotic mood. Dine by gaslight (the food is superb), ring the servants' bell for early morning tea. You are on the English side of Offa's Dyke: look north to the heavenly Radnorshire hills, south to all of Herefordshire. Paul is cultured, charming and fun.

Cwmllechwedd Fawr

Wild Wales at its best — drive across the moor where the ponies run free, or arrive via the Route 25 cycle track. This was the first brick house built in the area (1815) and it's now a working farm. There's a big organic vegetable plot (you should sample the results), a landscaped garden and a large sheltered terrace with wooden loungers and long, lush views. Inside, your hosts have gone for a pleasingly simple style: bedrooms have plain wooden furniture and colourful throws and rugs. Curl up by the woodburner, or relax in the dining room with its flagstones, rugs, painted murals and piles of books.

rooms	3: 1 double with bath/shower; 1 double with bath; 1 twin with shower.
price	£85. Singles £50.
meals	Dinner, 4 courses, £28. Good restaurant 10-minute drive.
closed	Rarely.
directions	B4355, between Presteigne & Knighton; in village of Norton, immed. north of church.

rooms	2: 1 double, 1 twin/double, both with bath/shower.
price	£50. Singles £30.
meals	Dinner, 3 courses, £15. BYO.
closed	Rarely.
directions	From A483 to Llanbister on B4356. Follow for 2 miles past chapel on right; across common. Immed. sharp left to Llanbadarn Fynydd; follow hedge on right for 0.3 miles to gate.

	Paul Gerrard
	The Old Vicarage,
	Norton,
	Presteigne,
	Radnorshire,
	Powys LD8 2EN
tel	01544 260038
e-mail	oldvicarage@nortonrads.fsnet.co.uk
web	www.oldvicarage-nortonrads.co.uk

	John Rath & John Underwood
	Cwmllechwedd Fawr,
	Llanbister,
	Llandrindod Wells,
	Powys LD1 6UH
tel	01597 840267
fax	01597 840267
e-mail	postmaster@cwmllechwedd.u-net.com
web	www.cwmllechwedd.u-net.com

Map 7 Entry 673

Map 7 Entry 674

Wrexham

Worthenbury Manor

Homemade bread and Hepplewhite!
This is a real home, if a grand one.
You sleep in a Georgian or Jacobean
four-poster in a chandeliered bedroom
(books, games and flowers adding a cosy
touch) and breakfast on local bacon and
sausages – even, perhaps, blueberry
muffins. Elizabeth is an IT consultant;
Ian retrained as a chef after retiring from
lecturing and worked at the Bryn Howel
Hotel in Llangollen. Dinner with them is
quite an occasion. The listed house is
close to Chester yet in a quiet, rural
setting; the original building was
enlarged in the 1890s in the William and
Mary revival style.

rooms	2: 1 four-poster with bath; 1 four-poster with separate bath.
price	£60-£80. Singles £38-£49.
meals	Dinner, 3 courses, £20. Lunch £12.
closed	December-February.
directions	Between A525 Whitchurch-Wrexham & A41 Whitchurch-Chester, on B5069 between Bangor-on-Dee (also called Bangor-is-y-coed) and Malpas. Manor on right before bridge.

Elizabeth & Ian Taylor
Worthenbury Manor,
Worthenbury,
Wrexham LL13 0AW

tel	01948 770342
e-mail	enquiries@worthenburymanor.co.uk
web	www.worthenburymanor.co.uk

Map 7   Entry 675

Fine breakfast Scheme

We are now in the second year of our Fine Breakfast Scheme in this guide and it is proving a great success. We have had positive feedback from the press and from readers – some buying the guide specifically because of the scheme. Owners, many of whom have been providing local and organic breakfasts for years, feel the scheme is a great way to encourage people to eat more healthily. The scheme is also working well for those in our Ireland and Garden Bed & Breakfast book.

'B&Bs across the land, from medieval Scottish castles to Kent country cottages, are turning to organic produce to woo their increasingly eco-conscious guests. Over half the 700 B&Bs in Alastair Sawday's Special Places To Stay guidebook have agreed to include organic, home-grown or locally sourced food on their breakfast menus.'
The Guardian – 5 February 2005

'Who could resist staying in a beautiful private home with engaging hosts and home-cooked meals? One of the latest additions to Alastair Sawday's Special Places to Stay series is the ninth edition of British B&B. It includes B&Bs that range from chic and contemporary to traditional and rustic and there is an emphasis on owners who use organic or locally-sourced ingredients in the preparation of their breakfasts.'
Country Living, January 2005

Photo previous page Chris Banks

'A wonderful initiative.
We love the cards as they make a great talking point at breakfast'.
Pam & Nick Broadhurst,
Cote Bank Farm

'An excellent idea, appreciated by guests.'
Mary Dixon,
Broome

'Guests place high importance on quality of food at breakfast.
It is rewarding when you receive compliments about the food you have cooked'.
Amanda Fearon,
Ballaminers House

The importance of good food has a high profile just now.
The Soil Association, Jamie Oliver and others have stimulated positive changes to school dinners.
In 2005 the government approved a higher budget per child for lunches to allow for the use of non-processed, nutritious food, and there are moves afoot to introduce healthier food into hospitals.
Consumer influence means more supermarkets are supporting organic and local food, farmers' markets are springing up all over the country and people are enjoying a personal contact with local suppliers.

By accepting their pledge, we are relying on owners' integrity and honesty to keep to the points listed below. It's not a perfect scheme but the message is right – that it is important to choose food carefully and support local economies. Over 500 owners have signed the pledge. Please understand that those who have not signed the pledge have done so for a variety of reasons and this does not mean they do not provide delicious breakfasts, too.

Fine Breakfast Scheme – Pledge

1. I promise always to serve breakfasts of only the best available ingredients – whether organic or locally sourced.

2. Any certified organic ingredients will be named as such. (Note that the word 'organic' is a legal term. Any uncertified 'organic' ingredients cannot be described as organic.) Where there is a choice of organic certifier I will prefer the Soil Association if possible, recognising that their standards are generally the most demanding.

3. All other ingredients will be, whenever reasonably possible, sourced locally from people and institutions that I know personally and have good reason to believe provide food of the best quality.

4. Where I have grown food myself, I will say so.

5. I will do my best to avoid shopping in supermarkets if good alternatives exist within a reasonable distance.

6. I will display the Fine Breakfast cards in the breakfast room or, if I prefer, in the bedrooms. (We accept that some of you may not want to use the cards.)

7. I know that the scheme is an imperfect instrument but accept its principles.

Leave the car at home

There's a wonderful feeling of freedom and adventure to be gained from leaving the car at home and going away with all you need, transported on your back or in a wheelie-case – and knowing that you are lessening your impact on the environment and helping to reduce pollution.

Cycling to/from your B&B

You can travel by public transport but take your bike, too. Many trains have special compartments for bikes, and tickets can be arranged for a small fee. Or, hire a bike from the owners listed (pp 399), leave the busy roads behind and enjoy exploring the area in peace.

National Cycle Network – planning your route (pp 400-401)

We have teamed up with Sustrans again; their flagship project, The National Cycle Network, has over 8,000 miles of safe and attractive cycling and walking routes around the UK. The map shows the routes in red; cross-refer to our maps at the front of the book to plan your trip. We have listed the B&Bs within two miles of the Network so you could plan an entire trip cycling your way between our special places.

Sustrans is a charity working on practical projects to encourage people to walk, cycle and use public transport, in order to reduce motor traffic and its adverse effects. In 2003, the Network carried 126 million trips by cyclists, walkers and other users including people with wheelchairs or pushchairs.

Contacts

For more information on the National Cycle Network and Sustrans and a copy of their free information pack, call 0845 113 0065 or fax 0117 915 0124. Their user-friendly web site www.sustrans.org.uk allows you to search by town or postcode to find the nearest route to your B&B. They can also help you choose where to visit and plan your journey by train, ferry or bike. Email the Sustrans team at info@sustrans.org.uk

Travel by train/bus (pp 402-402)

The owners listed in this section can tell you about the nearest train or bus station to their B&B and arrange collection, either driving into town to pick you up or organising a taxi in advance. Leave the motor at home, sit back, relax and head for the countryside. For travel times and prices contact www.thetrainline.co.uk Or call 08457 484950.

Travel by horse to your B&B (pp 403)

If travelling on horseback suits you, choose a B&B closer to home and ride there on your own horse. Or take a trailer; the owners listed here will be able to provide a stable or field for your steed, too. Obviously, details need to be discussed before booking.

Photo Russell Wilkinson

You can either borrow or hire bikes here.

The National Cycle Network

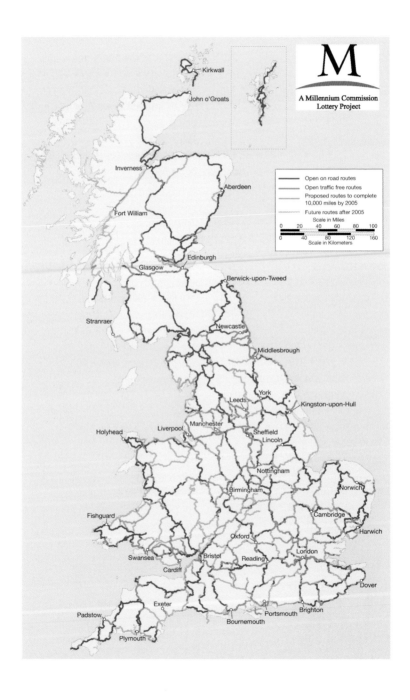

Kirkwall

John o'Groats

M

A Millennium Commission
Lottery Project

Inverness

Aberdeen

Fort William

— Open on road routes
— Open traffic free routes
— Proposed routes to complete
   10,000 miles by 2005
⋯ Future routes after 2005

Scale in Miles
0   20   40   60   80   100

0   40   80   120   160
Scale in Kilometers

Edinburgh
Glasgow

Berwick-upon-Tweed

Stranraer

Newcastle

Middlesbrough

York

Leeds

Kingston-upon-Hull

Holyhead   Liverpool   Manchester

Sheffield
Lincoln

Nottingham

Birmingham

Norwich

Fishguard

Cambridge

Harwich

Oxford

Swansea   Bristol   Reading

London

Cardiff

Dover

Padstow

Exeter

Portsmouth   Brighton

Plymouth

Bournemouth

These Special Places are within two
miles of the National Cycle Network.

Travel by train, bus or horse?

Owners at these Special Places are within 10 miles of a coach/train station and can arrange collection.

England
Bath & N.E. Somerset 4 • 11
Berkshire 15 • 16
Cambridgeshire 21 • 23
Cheshire 24 • 25 • 27
Cornwall 30 • 32 • 35 • 36 • 39 • 40 • 42 • 49 • 50 • 53 • 55 • 68 • 69 • 70 • 74
Cumbria 82 • 86 • 87 • 88
Derbyshire 94 • 98
Devon 100 • 102 • 103 • 107 • 108 • 111 • 112 • 113 • 115 • 118 • 121 • 122 • 126 • 127 • 129 • 130 • 138 • 140 • 141 • 142
Dorset 145 • 148 • 150 • 156 • 157 • 158 • 159 • 162 • 163 • 164 • 168 • 169 • 171
Essex 179 • 180
Gloucestershire 182 • 183 • 184 • 186 • 187 • 191 • 192 • 193 • 194 • 201 • 204 • 205 • 206 • 207
Hampshire 208 • 210 • 212 • 213 • 215 • 216 • 218 • 220 • 221 • 222
Herefordshire 223 • 224 • 225 • 227 • 228 • 231 • 237 • 238 • 240 • 241
Hertfordshire 242
Kent 247 • 249 • 254 • 256 • 258 • 259 • 260 • 262 • 263 • 264 • 265 • 268
Lancashire 270 • 271 • 273
Leicestershire 276
Lincolnshire 280 • 283 • 285
London 297
Norfolk 304 • 305 • 308 • 309 • 310 • 312 • 314 • 315
Northamptonshire 329 • 330
Northumberland 332 • 333 • 336 • 337 • 343 • 344 • 345
Nottinghamshire 347 • 348
Oxfordshire 349 • 351 • 358 • 361 • 362
Rutland 363
Shropshire 364
Shropshire 365 • 367 • 369 • 370 • 373 • 374 • 375 • 376
Somerset 379 • 380 • 383 • 384 • 387 • 388 • 391 • 395 • 396 • 399 • 401 • 402 • 404 • 405 • 406 • 409
Staffordshire 412 • 413
Suffolk 416 • 417 • 418 • 419 • 421 • 422 • 423 • 424 • 426 • 430 • 431 • 432 • 433 • 434 • 437 • 440 • 441
Surrey 442 • 443 • 445 • 446 • 447
Sussex 450 • 451 • 452 • 453 • 456 • 458 • 460 • 462 • 463 • 464 • 465 • 466 • 467 • 468 • 473 • 474 • 475 • 476 • 477
Warwickshire 478 • 481 • 482 • 483 • 486
Wiltshire 493 • 498 • 499 • 502 • 503 • 506 • 507 • 509 • 511 • 513 • 514 • 517
Worcestershire 518
Yorkshire 520 • 521 • 527 • 529 • 530 • 531 • 532 • 535 • 540 • 543 • 544 • 545 • 547 • 548 • 549 • 550 • 551 • 552

Scotland
Angus 559
Argyll & Bute 561 • 563

Want to travel with your trusty steed? Stabling available here.

ALASTAIR SAWDAY'S
SPECIAL PLACES

PUBS & INNS
OF ENGLAND & WALES

BAR

The latest pub guide, with the immitable Sawday touch: opinionated, colourful, trustworthy and beautiful.

EDITED BY DAVID HANCOCK

Gloucestershire

The Victoria
Eastleach Turville

The golden-stoned Victoria pulls in the locals – whatever their age, whatever the weather. Propping up the bar, welly-clad with dogs or indulging in great home-cooked grub by the inglenook, the locals and their laughter suggest a whale of a time is had by all. If frolic you must, this is the place to do it: summer brings river tug-o-war and the village's Frolic Day. (The highlight of which involves a large oak tree, children in sacks and a loaf of treacle-coated bread.) Refreshments are available for all from proprietors Stephen and Susan Richardson who, in spite of opening up the rooms, have kept much of the character and cosiness of the low-ceilinged pub. Who could fail to enjoy warm smoked chicken, steak and mushroom pie, lamb shank on minty mash, real ale hand-pulled by Arkell's on handpump or a New World wine? Several wines are served by the glass, and there are picnic tables out front, from where you can look down onto the pretty stone cottages and the churches of the village below.

directions   Off A361 between Burford &
             Lechlade.
meals   12pm-2pm; 7pm-9.30pm
             (9pm Sundays).
             Main courses £6.50-£14.50.

Stephen & Susan Richardson
The Victoria,
Eastleach Turville,
Fairford,
Gloucestershire GL7 3NQ
tel   01367 850277

map: 9 entry: 183

Hampshire

The Yew Tree Inn
Highclere

The staff, smartly turned out in long white aprons, may look dauntingly posh; rest assured, they're courteous and friendly. A contemporary and sympathetic makeover stitches the elegant dining room into the old fabric and character of this building, with its inglenooks, timbers and light uncluttered walls. A spent magnum of Bollinger may stand alongside bowls of crisps and nuts on the bar, but there's ale on tap, scrubbed tables softened by lamplight and an informal feel. Still, the Yew Tree is more restaurant than pub, the dining room's crisp white napery contrasts stylishly with its backdrop of exposed brick and timber, and chef Neil Thornley's menu, the best of modern British – fillet of beef, lili root vegetables and madeira jus, salmon and mussel pie with saffron cream – is overseen by Marco Pierre White. Bedrooms are being stylishly revamped.

directions   Exit M4 junc. 13 onto A34 for
             Newbury. A343 Andover road for
             Highclere. Just after village.
meals   12pm-3pm (4pm Sundays);
             6pm-10pm; 7pm-9pm Sundays.
             Main courses £12.50-£19.50.
             Lunch £16.50 (2 courses).
rooms   6: 4 doubles, 2 twins, £60.

Gareth McAinsh
The Yew Tree Inn,
Hollington Cross, Andover Road,
Highclere, Hampshire RG20 9SE
tel   01635 253360
web   www.theyewtree.net

map: 4 entry: 184

'The church is near and the way is icy. The tavern is far, but I will walk carefully'
Ukranian proverb

We've chosen and inspected over 550 special pubs and inns throughout England and Wales. Fresh, accurate and lively write-ups paint an honest picture, together with colour photos – so you choose. The range is wide, from little-changed authentic locals to stylish gastropubs. Never be stuck in a grim, swirly-carpeted, juke box-rattled corner again. Clear symbols and indices show, for example, where children and pets are welcome, where there's a wide choice of beers, wines, locally-sourced food, good gardens, great walks or open fires.

'Brilliant new pub guide.'
Observer Food Monthly

'Sorts out the barnstorming boozers from the woeful watering holes of England and Wales.'
Food and Travel

The B&Bs below also appear in our Bed & Breakfast for Garden Lovers guide (£14.99).

England
Bath & N.E. Somerset 7 • 11
Cheshire 25
Cornwall 46 • 48 • 56
Derbyshire 96
Devon 113 • 137
Dorset 150
Gloucestershire 181 • 183 • 187 • 198 • 201 • 203
Hampshire 217 • 220
Herefordshire 225 • 228 • 229 • 235 • 236 •
Isle of Wight 244

Kent 250 • 252 • 253 • 266 • 268
Norfolk 305 • 308 • 326
Oxfordshire 349 • 355 • 356
Shropshire 369 • 374
Somerset 380 • 401
Suffolk 427
Sussex 449 • 462 • 475
Warwickshire 481 • 483 • 486 • 487 • 492
Wiltshire 508 • 511
Yorkshire 524 • 538 • 540 • 546

Scotland
Ayrshire 569

Wales
Ceredigion 646

ALASTAIR SAWDAY'S
SPECIAL ESCAPES

Home • Search • Hotlist • Owners • Links

Shutters on the Harbour, St Ives

Cornwall, England

You'd never guess that this 1875 former fishermans' cottage in the belly of the old-town is the lap of modern luxury inside. Georgie and Janin have cleverly renovated this tiny dwelling into a funky palace with lots of surprising touches. Originally pilchards were pressed in the old lounge and shipped to Tuscany – now the only remaining sign is the wooden grooves in the stone walls. From the neutral stone-floored lounge with sheep-skin rugs on the rattan chairs, scamper into the shower/washing room to wash off the sand – perfect for surfers. Up to a suspended floor with the kitchen with round table, built-in benches and all mod-cons and a second chill-out space – from both look down to the lounge. A spiral stair leads up to the bedrooms. Here Janin's furniture-design skills were brought in to create wacky bedside tables using driftwood and stylistic shapes. There are painted wooden floors, funky light sculptures, neutral colours and portholes leading to the bathroom - separated by a vibrant sari curtain. It has a beach-house style with a modern home-spun element; they have carefully made the most of the limited space – it can be tight in some corners but somehow that adds to the fun. An ideal spot to make the most of St Ives.

'Shutters on the harbour' Bethesda Hill

Owner's Notice Board

BEAUTIFUL ST IVES

2 weeks still available in September - 17th and 24th - arguably the best time of year.. when the kids go back to school! STUNNING CONVERSION OF FISHERMAN'S COTTAGE IN HEART OF ST IVES

Note: This information has been provided by the owner or management of Shutters on the Harbour and is not verified or endorsed by ASP.

Bedroom 1

Details for Shutters on the Harbour

Contact Georgina Lenain

tel: +44(0)7770 431558

fax: +44(0)20 8877 0700

@ Send E-mail Enquiry

sleeps:

rooms: 2 doubles with shower; shower room.

price: £550.00 – £960.00. In winter short breaks negotiated

closed: Never.

changeover: Saturday - negotiable.

? Details Explanation

Currency Converter

? Symbol Explanations

Sitting room with winter rugs

Views on Porthminster Beach

A whole week in a rented cottage with your friends or family is precious, and you dare not get it wrong. So to whom do you turn for advice and who on earth to trust when the web is awash with advice from strangers. We launced Special Escapes to satisfy an obvious need for impartial and trustworthy help

– and that is what it provides. The criteria for inclusion are the same as for our books: we have to like the place and the owners. It has, quite simply, to be 'special'. The site, our first online-only publicaton, is featured in www.thegoodwebguide.com and is growing fast.

www.specialescapes.co.uk

who, what, where, when and why organic?

for all the answers and tempting offers go to
www.whyorganic.org

- Mouthwatering offers on organic produce
- Seasonal recipes
- Expert advice on your food and health
- Soil Association food club – join for just £1 a month

Plus the organic directory:

- Where to find veg boxes, farmers; markets and cafes

Something to read if your car, or better still your bike, breaks down

Next time you book into a B&B, spare a thought for the owners; not only have they been swooping around cleaning and polishing, bed-making and breakfast shopping, not to mention stirring a preserving pan of homemade strawberry jam for those warm scones you're going to tuck into on arrrival... they may have been turning the house upside down looking for a set of false teeth left behind by a guest the night before (they found them). Here are a few more snippets from some of our owners on the highs and occasional lows of running a B&B:

• A Canadian couple who had never come across the concept of 'B&B' before, tipped up for breakfast in their scanty pyjamas.

• A couple from Hong Kong who arrived at sheep-shearing time and pitched in much to everyone's delight and amusement.

• Guests arrived as owner was knee-deep in sewage while attempting to unblock a drain. Guests stood around and cheered when the blockage was cleared.

• B&B completely flooded and guests rolled up trousers, waded in and helped pump out.

• Owner recalls spraying a party of naked guests blue in the barn before they were let loose on Ledbury High Street in aid of charity.

• Owner who went up to guests' bedroom to put a hot water bottle in their bed. Threw off the covers, slung in the hottie to find the guests back from dinner and in bed.

And the award for the most popular nationality as guests goes to...
The Dutch - yes, it seems that they top the list (closely followed by Brits, Australians, Americans and oh, lots of others). Reasons given are that they are smiley, appreciative, polite, clean and tidy, willing to explore, interesting, fun and they LOVE English gardens. They must have some bad points but none were expressed. (what about the wear and tear to door lintels?).

Our owners' dream guest:
Michael Palin as he's easy-going, not too bothered about high-end luxury(!), is a wit and a great raconteur. Prince Charles was not far behind and was imagined to be a model guest as he would be a mine of gardening tips and might encourage rampant growth in the veg patch if he had a word with the brassicas.

Least favoured celebrity guest and nationality:
Oh dear, we've run out of room...

Sarah Bolton, Press Officer

Quick reference indices

Wheelchair-accessible
These places have full and approved wheelchair facilities.

Limited mobility
Need a ground-floor bedroom and bathroom? Try these.

Photo Jo Boissevain

Quick reference indices

On a budget?
These places have a double room for
£60 or under:

Singles
These houses either have a single room or charge no single supplement.

Tennis
A tennis court in the grounds which
you may use, by arrangement.

Photo Laura Kinch

Pool
Houses with a pool which you may use, by arrangement.

Photo John Coe

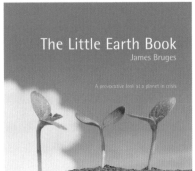

The Little Earth Book
Edition 4, £6.99
By James Bruges

A little book that has proved
hugely popular – and provocative.
This new edition has chapters on
Islam, Climate Change and The
Tyranny of Corporations.

The Little Food Book
Edition 1, £6.99
By Craig Sams, Chairman
of the Soil Association

An explosive account of the food we
eat today. Never have we been at such
risk – from our food. This book will
help understand what's at stake.

The Little Money Book
Edition 1, £6.99
By David Boyle, an associate
of the New Economics Foundation

This pithy, wry little guide will tell
you where money comes from,
what it means, what it's doing
to the planet and what we might
be able to do about it.

Six Days

Celebrating the triumph of creativity over adversity.

An inspiring and heart-rending story of the making of the stained glass 'Creation' window at Chester Cathedral by a woman battling with debilitating Parkinson's disease.

"Within a few seconds, the tears were running down my cheeks. The window was one of the most beautiful things I had ever seen. It is a tour-de force, playing with light like no other window ..."
Anthropologist Hugh Brody

In 1983, Ros Grimshaw, a distinguished designer, artist and creator of stained glass windows, was diagnosed with Parkinson's disease. Refusing to allow her illness to prevent her from working, Ros became even more adept at her craft, and in 2000 won the commission to design and make the 'Creation' Stained Glass Window for Chester Cathedral.

Six Days traces the evolution of the window from the first sketches to its final, glorious completion as a rare and wonderful tribute to Life itself: for each of the six 'days' of Creation recounted in Genesis, there is a scene below that is relevant to the world of today and tomorrow.

Heart-rending extracts from Ros's diary capture the personal struggle involved. Superb photography captures the luminescence of the stunning stained glass, while the story weaves together essays, poems, and moving contributions from Ros's partner, Patrick Costeloe.

Available from Alastair Sawday Publishing £12.99

Order Form

All these books are available in major bookshops or you may order them direct.
Post and packaging are FREE within the UK.

British Hotels, Inns & Other Places	£13.99
Bed & Breakfast for Garden Lovers	£14.99
Pubs & Inns of England & Wales	£13.99
London	£9.99
British Bed & Breakfast	£14.99
French Bed & Breakfast	£15.99
French Hotels, Châteaux & Other Places	£14.99
French Holiday Homes	£12.99
Paris Hotels	£9.99
Ireland	£12.99
Italy	£12.99
Mountains of Europe	£9.99
Spain	£14.99
Portugal	£10.99
Turkey	£11.99
India	£10.99
Morocco	£10.99
The Little Earth Book	£6.99
The Little Food Book	£6.99
The Little Money Book	£6.99
Six Days	£12.99

Please make cheques payable to Alastair Sawday Publishing   Total _____

Please send cheques to: Alastair Sawday Publishing, The Home Farm Stables,
Barrow Gurney, Bristol BS48 3RW. For credit card orders call 01275 464891 or
order directly from our web site www.specialplacestostay.com

Title _____ First name _____ Surname _____

Address _____

_____

Postcode _____ Tel _____

BBB10

If you do not wish to receive mail from other like-minded companies, please tick here ☐
If you would prefer not to receive information about special offers on our books, please tick here ☐

Report Form

If you have any comments on entries in this guide, please let us have them. If you have a favourite house, hotel, inn or other new discovery, please let us know about it. You can e-mail info@sawdays.co.uk, too.

Existing entry:

Book title: _____

Entry no: _____ Edition no: _____

New recommendation:

Country: _____

Property name: _____

Address: _____

_____

_____

_____

Tel: _____

Comments: Report:

_____

_____

_____

_____

_____

_____

_____

_____

Your name: _____

Address: _____

_____

_____

Tel: _____

Please send completed form to ASP, The Home Farm Stables, Barrow Gurney, Bristol BS48 3RW or go to www.specialplacestostay.com and click on 'contact'. Thank you.

Index by surname

Index by surname

Index by place name

Wiltshire

Puckshipton House

An intriguing name, Puckshipton: it means Goblin's Barn. The house is deep in the lush countryside of the Vale of Pewsey, reached by a long tree-lined drive. You stay in the Georgian end, with a private entrance that leads to a Regency-blue hall. Rooms are stylish and uncluttered, an attractive mix of old and new. One bedroom has a splendid four-poster, the other has oak beds made by James, forester and fine furniture-maker. He and Juliette are a charming young couple with four small children. The dining room has a woodburner and the sitting room an open fire: a relaxed and lovely place to stay.

rooms	2: 1 twin/double with separate bath/shower; 1 four-poster with bath & shower.
price	£70–£75. Singles £50.
meals	Good pubs & restaurant 5-minute drive.
closed	Christmas.
directions	Devizes A342 towards Rushall; left to Chirton, right to Marden & through village. On for 0.25 miles; right into private drive.

Juliette & James Noble
Puckshipton House,
Beechingstoke, Pewsey,
Wiltshire SN9 6HG
tel   01672 851336
e-mail   noble.jj@gmail.com
web   www.puckshipton.co.uk

🍴 ✗ ♿ 🐾 🍷
Map 3 Entry 500

Wiltshire

St Cross

Everything is small-scale, pretty and very English. Serena's 17th-century thatched cottage is at the end of a russet-brick terrace on a tranquil country road. Guests have their own sunny sitting room (and log fire if it's chilly) overlooking a garden full of wisteria and lavender. The bedrooms are sloping-ceilinged and cosy: the double is chintzy and bright, with a bay window, the twin dramatically criss-crossed with beams. Serena is an artist and you'll enjoy her company. She has a nice sense of humour and knows masses about the area, crop circles included – 'croppies' from many nations meet at an inn nearby.

rooms	2: 1 double, 1 twin sharing bath.
price	£55–£60. Singles £40–£45.
meals	Dinner £15–£25, by arrangement. Good pub 0.5 mile.
closed	Rarely.
directions	From Marlborough A345 to Pewsey. After station right to Woodborough. Follow road through village. Manor House on right. St Cross next door, up lane on left.

Mrs Serena Gore
St Cross,
Woodborough, Pewsey,
Wiltshire SN9 5PL
tel   01672 851346
fax   01672 851346

✗ 🐕 🐄 ♿ 🐾
Map 3 Entry 501

Explanation

---

❶ write up

Write up written by us, after inspection.

---

❷ rooms

We do not use the words 'en suite' but instead, 'with' bath or 'with' shower.
If a room is not 'en suite' we say 'with separate bathroom' or 'with shared bath':
the former you will have to yourself, the latter may be shared with other guests or
family members; both will have a wc, basin and either a bath or a shower.

---

❸ price

The price shown is the one-night price for two sharing a room with breakfast.
A price range incorporates room/seasonal differences. We also give single occupancy
rates – the amount payable by one person staying in a room for two.

---

❹ meals

Prices are per person. All meals must be booked in advance. Most often you may bring
your own wine.

---

❺ closed

When given in months, this means for the whole of the named months and the
time in between.

---

❻ directions

Use as a guide; the owner can give more details.

---

❼ symbols

See the last page for a fuller explanation:

 wheelchair facilities

 easily accessible bedrooms

 all children welcome

 no smoking

 credit cards accepted

 good vegetarian dinner
options

 licensed premises

 guests' pets can sleep in
room

 owners' pets live here

 farm

 pool

 bikes on premises

 tennis on the premises

 walking info provided

 fine breakfast scheme –
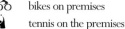 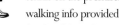 locally-sourced/organic

---

❽ map & entry numbers

Where on the web?

The World Wide Web is big - very big. So big, in fact, that it can be a fruitless place to search if you don't know where to find reliable, trustworthy, up-to-date information about fantastic places to stay in Europe, India, Morocco and beyond...

Fortunately, there's **www.specialplacestostay.com**, where you can dip into all of our guides, find special offers from owners, catch up on news about the series and tell us about the special places you've been to.

WWW.SPECIALPLACESTOSTAY.COM